The Terrorist-Criminal Nexus

An Alliance of International Drug Cartels,
Organized Crime, and Terror Groups

The Terrorist-Criminal Nexus

An Alliance of International Drug Cartels, Organized Crime, and Terror Groups

Jennifer L. Hesterman

CRC Press
Taylor & Francis Group
Boca Raton   London   New York

CRC Press is an imprint of the
Taylor & Francis Group, an **informa** business

CRC Press
Taylor & Francis Group
6000 Broken Sound Parkway NW, Suite 300
Boca Raton, FL 33487-2742

Printed on acid-free paper
Version Date: 20130220

International Standard Book Number-13: 978-1-4665-5761-1 (Hardback)

Library of Congress Cataloging-in-Publication Data

Hesterman, Jennifer L.
   The terrorist-criminal nexus : an alliance of international drug cartels, organized crime, and terror groups / author, Jennifer L. Hesterman.
      pages cm
   Summary: "We are currently faced with a new national security challenge that is both vexing and complex. The once clear lines between the international drug trade, terrorism, organized crime, domestic terror, and Mexican drug cartels are blurring as groups increasingly join forces to further individual interests and goals. The synergistic potential of the alliance between nonstate actors and terrorists is alarming. Factor in a rise in domestic terror and cartel activity spilling over U.S. borders and the resulting impact to America is grave. This text highlights the often disregarded, misunderstood, or obscured criminal/terrorist nexus threat to the U.S. Destroying the myth that such liaisons don't exist due to differing ideologies, the book provides a thought-provoking and new look at the complexity and phenomena of the criminal/terrorist nexus."-- Provided by publisher.
   Includes bibliographical references and index.
   ISBN 978-1-4665-5761-1 (hardback)
   1. Drug control--International cooperation. 2. Organized crime. 3. Terrorism. I. Title.

HV5825.H443 2013
364.1--dc23   2012050913

Visit the Taylor & Francis Web site at
http://www.taylorandfrancis.com

and the CRC Press Web site at
http://www.crcpress.com

Contents

            Financing Methods: Adapting for Success   165

            Funding Terror   166

            Earning, Moving, Storing   167

                Tactics   167

                    Earn   168

                    Move   168

                    Store   168

            Earning   169

                Charities   169

                Designation   169

                Zakat   172

                Commodities Smuggling and Organized Retail Crime   173

                Intellectual Property Crime (IPC)   175

                Identity Theft   179

                Other Fund-Raising Methods   183

                Mortgage Fraud: Emergent Earning Method   184

            Moving   186

                A Paper Chase in a Paperless World:
                Informal Value Transfer Systems   186

                Hawala   188

            Storing, Earning, and Moving   189

                Precious Metals and Diamonds   189

                Money Laundering   192

                Fronts, Shells, and Offshores   194

                Bulk Cash Smuggling   196

                E-gambling and E-gaming: Emergent
                Money-Laundering Concerns   197

                    E-gambling   197

                    E-gaming   198

            The Way Forward   200

            References   200

Preface

September 11, 2001 began as all others, with a morning office meeting to discuss the daily schedule and downing a few cups of coffee to fuel the way ahead. I was an Air Force lieutenant colonel, stationed at Seymour-Johnson Air Force Base, North Carolina, an Air Combat Command base with several squadrons of F-15E fighter aircraft and thousands of military personnel and their families. We were gathered around the office television to watch live video of the "aircraft accident" in New York City and the increasingly thick smoke pouring out of the North Tower of the World Trade Center. At 9:03 A.M., a collective gasp filled the room as we witnessed the second aircraft impacting the South Tower. The mood immediately shifted from concern to horror as we realized our country was under attack. And I instantly knew from years of research and study: the attacker was unmistakably al Qaeda.

Suddenly, I was in the unexpected position of trying to secure a major military installation and its panicked residents from an enemy with unknown intentions and capabilities. In the command center, my stunned colleagues and I watched the Defense Readiness Condition change to DEFCON 3, the highest level since the Cuban Missile Crisis in 1962. The Pentagon, which I had just left three months earlier, was attacked and burning. I had to suppress thoughts and concerns about my E-ring office and my many colleagues in danger or possibly dying. With more hijacked aircraft airborne, our jets were immediately loaded with weapons and crews put on alert. My husband, then a colonel, commanded the fleet of fighter aircraft and crew members; he had to make sure his pilots were prepared to shoot down a civilian airliner on command, something they had never trained for or considered a remote possibility prior to this fateful morning. We soon received the order to launch, and I could hear the aircraft thundering into the skies to fly Combat Air Patrol sorties over major east coast cities to guard from further attacks.

My job at the helm of the Emergency Operations Center was chaotic for the next thirty-six hours. As the installation gates were locked down, we had children (including our young daughter) outside the fence in community schools and worried parents who were trying to get to them. Landlines and cellular phone networks crashed, and our most reliable way to communicate was through handheld radios, known as "bricks" for their cumbersome bulk. I ordered the communications squadron to break into deployment kits and access every other storage area on base to harvest bricks, batteries, and charging stations for commanders and first responders. Upon wise counsel from a staff member, I immediately executed a long standing contingency contract to withdraw bottled water from the base commissary for safekeeping in case the installation became a self-sustaining island. Sure enough, within hours, the grocery store was inundated with base employees and family members who understandably stripped the shelves of basic essentials. My security forces defenders established Force Protection Delta posture, emptying the base armory of battle gear, M-16s and service revolvers. Snipers and counter snipers took positions around the base to protect us from attack. As I watched the surreal situation unfold, I remember thinking that the hundreds of mundane exercises endured during our careers were paying off: we were a calm, precise, well-oiled machine during the most intense stress of our young lives.

As I executed seven binders of emergency checklists, my team was faced with several unanticipated threats, starting with the escape of an inmate from a minimum security federal prison on base. A convict with an "interesting" background had taken advantage of the 9/11 morning confusion to jump the base fence; a quick check of records revealed he routinely participated in work details all over the base, in unclassified facilities and along the flight line, mowing grass, picking up trash and likely interacting with base personnel. The standard operating procedure was to put up search helos, however the state police were denied flight clearance due to the national emergency. Instead, we implemented a coordinated ground search with local sheriffs, but without further intelligence about the 9/11 attackers, we were flying blind: the prisoner's intimate knowledge of our base and possible intentions were of extreme concern. A few hours later, an FBI agent from a local office requested a secure phone call with our military federal agents residing in the base Air Force Office of Special Investigations (AFOSI). We listened with surprise as his staff described ongoing surveillance operations and suspicious activities within the state and at nearby facilities, some frequented by military personnel. The most worrisome call came later in the day, from a local military retiree whose daughter was in an arranged marriage with a Middle Eastern citizen, both residing near the base. His son-in-law, who had visited our base on many occasions including during airshows, had unexpectedly left the U.S for a "country of interest" in the days prior to 9/11. We later learned the man had remote connections to the 9/11 attack planners; however, our contacts at the embassy overseas were unable to lay eyes on him. In light of these potential external dangers, the base was suddenly not the "island" it had always seemed. I also learned to operate within a new realm, that of ambiguity and the "inescapable unknowables."

Thankfully, no threats to the installation materialized in the coming days, and eventually our attention shifted from protecting the homeland to taking the battle to the enemy. Sworn to protect our country from enemies foreign and domestic, we were anxious to leverage years of combat training and enter the fight of our lives to eradicate the threat. Indeed, in the intervening time since 9/11, our country has taken the fight to terrorists around the globe. Yet, after 11 years, trillions of dollars, and most importantly, the thousands of young, promising lives lost in battle, the terrorist threat remains.

Despite our efforts, the radical Islamic ideology has spread like wildfire, ignited by globalization and technological advances in the information, financing, and social networking realms. Al Qaeda is the most feared organization, but other international terrorist groups are poised to endanger our country, whether through direct engagement or circuitously through trafficking or financial corruption. Many of our challenges at home are also fed by modernized transnational crime, which, despite our countering efforts, is on the rise. Anarchy resulting from the end of the Cold War led to a boom in transnational crimes and groups involved operate with a level of sophistication previously only found in multinational corporations, exacerbating the problem. Hezbollah, Hamas, FARC, drug cartels, and increasingly violent gangs and domestic groups such as the Sovereign Citizens are threatening us in new, provocative ways and now joining forces despite differing ideologies.

I have spent more than two decades leading organizations. Some were the high performing, well-oiled machine I worked with on 9/11. Others were dysfunctional and dying. The size, type, and business of an organization are virtually irrelevant as to whether it fails or succeeds. All organizations share the basics: structure, culture, and environment. They all have customers, stakeholders, and products. Activities are the same—recruiting, retention, planning, and execution. Organizations are populated by human beings, all of whom are driven by the same basic instincts and needs. In fact, the rise of modern terrorist and criminal groups can be predicted when viewed through the lens of foundational organizational and sociological theories. Furthermore, viewing the lifecycles of the groups and how they start, thrive, and terminate is extraordinarily helpful when discussing mitigation and engagement. It may be quite possible to inject game changers at the micro level that force groups to alter course and even implode from the inside – without ever firing a shot in anger or losing a life.

Perhaps the most powerful statement in the 9/11 Commission report comes from Chapter 11 and is entitled "Foresight–And Hindsight," as the committee cites a lack of *imagination* as a root cause of the two worst attacks in our country, Pearl Harbor and 9/11. Certainly, any study of the terror-criminal nexus requires a fusion of imagination, "dot connecting" intuition, and corroborated, foundational evidence. As such, this book synthesizes more than 350 sources, including congressional testimony, subpoenas, scholarly studies, and historical documents. My objective was to academically frame the nexus issue, providing policy makers, strategists, operators, and students both new evidence and a different perspective for their planning and research efforts.

In the following chapters, we will explore current and future threats from international and domestic groups, and identify specific instances in which they are working together or in parallel to achieve goals. The money trail is increasingly the "lifeblood" of modern organizations, and this work examines how nefarious groups are leveraging both traditional funding methods and e-commerce to raise, store, move, and launder money. An exploration of the social networking phenomenon will reveal how it is the perfect clandestine platform for spying, communicating, recruiting, and spreading propaganda. Finally, this work investigates emergent tactics such as the use of human shields, and the targeting of first responders, schools, hospitals, and churches; the enemy doesn't play by our rules, creating a dangerous blindspot that must be addressed.

I would like to thank the many colleagues, friends and family members who supported my efforts to produce this book. Numerous federal agents, state, and local law enforcement officers, intelligence analysts, and military personnel spoke with me off record, not to provide specific information, but to lend validation and context to the nexus challenges. They truly added a "voice" to this work and I appreciate their intense dedication to keeping us safe, despite being under resourced and overtasked. I would like to convey special thanks to a former student, Mark Manshack, a veteran law enforcement officer in Texas and member of my "brain trust" who gave great insight into the expanding presence of cartels in his state. Sadly, as I put the finishing touches on the manuscript, Mark called with distressing news: his best friend, Deputy Brandon Nielsen, and his partner were killed in an ambush in La Place, Louisiana by a group of heavily armed Sovereign Citizens. Between them, the deputies leave behind six children and a grieving community. The La Place case is explored in Chapter 4, and serves as a reminder of both the importance of information sharing between agencies and the need for enhanced emergent threats training for our frontline defenders. Our new reality is that Americans will kill fellow citizens in the name of many things, be it faith, guns, drugs, money, or ideology. Loyalty to faction now transcends loyalty to nation; undeniably this is a hard concept to grasp, but we must prepare and be resilient.

On the work front, a special thank you to Alex Anyse and Tae Kim at the MASY Group and to Chris Graham, the editor of the *Counter Terrorist* magazine, for your friendship and ongoing support of my myriad endeavors. Also, I would like to thank my doctoral cohort colleagues and friends, Lisa Greenhill, John DiGennaro, and Aaron Clevenger for their encouragement and good humor. You wouldn't let me abandon my studies during the juggling of this book project with school, and for that, I am forever grateful. Also, I owe a large debt of gratitude to my patient and extraordinary editors at Taylor and Francis, Mark Listewnik, Prudy Taylor Board, and Stephanie Morkert.

I would like to give special appreciation to my family for their love and support. My parents, Lloyd and Barbara Whitnack, bestowed both a great work ethic and the belief that anything is possible. Thank you to my brother, Matt Whitnack, for a lifetime of friendship. Much appreciation and love to my wonderful family, husband, John and daughter, Sarah for always supporting my dreams. Finally, thanks to my office companion and good-natured Lab, Hunter, for somehow always knowing when I needed to take a walk in the park for fresh air and perspective.

You all inspire me to be a better person and to live each day richly and without regret.

About the Author

Colonel (Ret.) Jennifer L. Hesterman was commissioned in 1986 as a graduate of Air Force ROTC at Penn State University. During her twenty-one-year career, she served three Pentagon tours and commanded multiple units in the field. Her last assignment was Vice Commander, 316th Wing at Andrews Air Force Base, Maryland, the home of Air Force One. She was responsible for installation security, force support, and the 1st Helicopter Squadron, and regularly greeted the President and other heads of state on the ramp. Her decorations include the Legion of Merit and the Meritorious Service Medal with five oak leaf clusters.

Colonel Hesterman is a doctoral candidate at Benedictine University where she is completing her dissertation regarding espionage on our college campuses. She also holds master's degrees from Johns Hopkins University and Air University. In 2003, she was a National Defense Fellow at the Center for Strategic and International Studies in Washington, DC, where she immersed herself in a year-long study of the nexus between organized crime and international terrorism. Her resulting book won the 2004 Air Force research prize and was published by AU Press. Colonel Hesterman is also a 2006 alumnus of the Harvard Senior Executive Fellows program. Since her retirement in 2007, Jenni has worked as a cleared professional for The MASY Group, a global intelligence firm, and was a full-time instructor and then director of the national and homeland security programs at American Military University. She is a contributing editor for *The Counter Terrorist* magazine and a guest lecturer for federal and state law enforcement agencies.

CHAPTER 1

A Poisonous Brew

While organized crime is not a new phenomenon today, some governments find their authority besieged at home and their foreign policy interests imperiled abroad. Drug trafficking, links between drug traffickers and terrorists, smuggling of illegal aliens, massive financial and bank fraud, arms smuggling, potential involvement in the theft and sale of nuclear material, political intimidation, and corruption all constitute a poisonous brew— a mixture potentially as deadly as what we faced during the Cold War.

—R. James Woolsey
Former director, CIA[1]

Al Qaeda works with the Mafia. The Mafia works with outlaw motorcycle gangs. Biker gangs work with white supremacists. Surprised?

Ten years ago, when I wrote my first book on this subject, the number of experts who would acknowledge that a nexus may exist between terrorists and criminals could be counted on one hand. In fact, Mr. Woolsey's chapter-opening statement was made in 1994, long before most people heard of al Qaeda, human trafficking, and loose nukes. Unfortunately, the "poisonous brew" is becoming more toxic with time. Transnational organized crime is escalating, the cartels are global and undeterred, and the list of State Department Foreign Terrorist Organizations continues to grow.

Transnational crime is a growing U.S. national security concern, and it threatens us in new, provoking ways. For example, Americans formerly viewed drug use as a law enforcement or health issue. Only very recently has drug trafficking been established as a global crime with a corresponding national security threat. A lesser known and understood example of a growing transnational threat reaching our borders is human trafficking. When a boat filled with women and children leaves the shores of a distant country, delivering them to a life of enslavement and unimaginable abuse, we obviously feel compelled to engage out of moral obligation and belief that human dignity must be upheld and protected.

Consider that 18,000 to 20,000 of these human beings are delivered annually by criminals to the United States and forced into labor or prostitution; trafficking becomes an obvious and direct threat to the fabric of our society. Unbeknownst to many, our National Security Strategy contains a goal entitled "Champion Aspirations for Human Dignity," which ties human trafficking to our nation's safety and prosperity. Factor terrorists and their use of established drug- and human-trafficking routes in and around our country into the equation, and these issues take on new and pressing significance.

Despite economic woes at home, our government continues to spend billions of dollars to help other countries identify and battle their transnational crimes issues, all of which impact our national security. Globally, drug-trafficking routes are robust and plenty; the ghastly business of human trafficking is flourishing; and money is laundered in amounts and ways never before imagined. Many resource-constrained countries struggle to deal with their role in this epidemic and are attempting to contain it. Others are corrupt and choose to look the other way, or worse, benefit from illicit activity. Bad actors are smart; they prey on nations in turmoil where the rule of law is weak and leadership lacking. Many nation-states are on the brink of thriving or failing, and their fate depends either on us ... or on the help of organized crime and terrorists. Therefore we must engage. History also reveals that failing countries are like dominoes; they lead to failing regions, an even greater threat to our national security.

In the last decade, after eradicating al Qaeda's base in Afghanistan we watched the group franchise and scatter throughout the Middle East and Africa. Bound by ideology, and despite the death of leader Osama bin Laden and others, radical Islamists continue undaunted on their mission of establishing the caliphate under Sharia law. They envision the Islamist flag flying over world capitals, including ours. Besides radical ideology, what fuels these terrorist groups? How can they continue to operate with such abandon despite our efforts and those of our allies to fight a global war on terror? One answer is the corresponding rise in transnational crime. Another is the ability to leverage unexpected and emergent funding methods such as mortgage fraud and the e-gaming industry. Additionally, exploitation of the unpatrolled, uncontrolled Internet has allowed terrorist groups unrestrained recruitment, morale-boosting, and propaganda campaigns.

As this book reveals, the nexus exists. The executive branch of our government is so troubled about the partnering of terrorists and criminals that they issued a strongly worded document in July 2011 entitled *Strategy to Combat Transnational Organized Crime: Addressing Converging Threats to National Security*. The White House, acknowledging the nexus, stated, "Terrorists and insurgents increasingly are turning to criminal networks to generate funding and acquire logistical support."[2]

Groups with dissimilar ideologies are working together to further their goals. They are also copying successful tactics, learning from each other's mistakes, and at the very least operating in the same physical or virtual "space." To fully grasp the complex issue of the nexus, we must first investigate root causes and the environment contributing to its rise and persistence.

Transnational criminal groups now have sophisticated business models that parallel legitimate corporations. Feeding on globalization and advances in communications and logistics technology, modern transnational crime is more expansive, far deadlier, and extremely difficult to eradicate. Adding further context to the issue is an overview of international agencies involved, methods used, and lessons learned in the fight against transnational crime, all of which should be simultaneously applied to the global war on terror.

The discussion of the rise of postmodern terrorist groups is deeply rooted in the soft sciences; a fusion of psychology, sociology, and organizational development and behavioral theory allows insight into many of the vexing "whys" about the terrorism phenomenon. Viewing the life cycle of terrorist groups yields a new solution set for engagement and an intuitive understanding as to why and when they liaise with actors espousing dissimilar ideologies. The "Big Three" international terrorist groups that most threaten the homeland, al Qaeda, Hezbollah, and FARC, are morphing in structure and changing strategy and tactics. Understanding their new goals and methodology is important for policy makers, strategic planners, and operators alike.

Domestic terrorism from right-wing, left-wing, and single-issue groups remains a great concern for our law enforcement agencies. The growing propensity of these organizations and their members to "act out" and to step up and engage law enforcement is alarming. The radicalization of Americans continues, with several successful attacks and more than fifty thwarted in our country since 9/11. Lacking a rehabilitation program, we have no way of ensuring that jihadists who serve their prison sentence and return to society will not go back to their old ways ... with a vengeance. The threat of the lone wolf, already embedded in society and acting alone with unyielding determination, is extremely worrisome. Factor in an unprecedented increase in hate groups and gangs in our country, and the domestic terrorism picture is quite grim with resource-constrained law enforcement agencies struggling to juggle myriad challenges.

Drug-trafficking organizations are flourishing south (and north) of our border with Mexico. Now operating in the United States, cartels are using gangs to move product and are attempting to corrupt border patrol officers to open lanes for moving people, drugs, and potentially worse into our nation. The Los Zetas cartel provides the most vexing threat, as a paramilitary organization with the tactical knowledge and equipment of a small army. Two questions are posed for the reader's consideration: Are the Mexican cartels a U.S national security risk, or have we overblown the threat? Is their activity in the United States terroristic or merely criminal in nature?

The lifeblood of any nefarious group is money. For criminal organizations and cartels, money is the motivation, with a side goal of corruption and influencing the political process in their favor to keep profits flowing. However, for terrorist groups, the driver is the religious ideology, extreme and even apocalyptic. Financing operations off of law enforcement's radar is critical, and the cost to move and train people, as well as procure material, is rising. For all groups, earning, moving, storing, and laundering are critical, whether "dirty" money that must be cleaned or "clean" money that will become dirty when funding a terror operation. Many traditional avenues of financing that funded the 9/11 attacks have been under intense scrutiny, such as charitable giving; therefore, terror groups are increasingly turning to intellectual property crime, counterfeit goods, and physical precious metals as ways to deal with money issues. The e-commerce boom has presented other opportunities such as e-gambling, digital precious metals, e-gaming, anonymous fronts and offshores, and the use of gift cards and e-banks to move money outside the regulated banking sector.

Money is a precious resource to terror groups, but if ideology is their center of gravity, then people are perhaps an even greater commodity. The rise of social networking as a "Black Swan" is explored, and viewing the mind as the battlefield provides a framework for discussion regarding exploitation of Facebook, Twitter, YouTube, and virtual worlds such as Second Life. The use of steganography, combined with networking sites, provides a unique opportunity for clandestine communication between groups and their followers. A provocative discussion regarding patriot hackers and cyber vigilantes gives insight into citizens as combatants and their rights to engage the enemy.

Finally, investigation of the sharing and copying of tactics between groups, and emergent threats to first responders rounds out the discussion regarding the nexus of groups, their surprising commonalities, and how they will and do work together to further their goals. The modern terrorist threat is asymmetric, and as such, countering it requires an asymmetric approach.

Material regarding nexus activities is typically buried in court documents, obscure government press releases, and articles printed in the foreign press that often do not appear domestically. Through the synthesis of hundreds of sources, this body of work attempts to pull together a compendium of information regarding the nexus, answering the questions who, why, and how for the reader. The material will appeal to policy makers, strategic planners, operators, as well as citizens with an interest in our national security and emergent challenges who want to be force multipliers in this fight.

The overarching goal is less armchair speculation and a more practical, informed view of the persistence of transnational criminals, cartels, and terrorists and their impact on our future.

REFERENCES

1. Cilluffo, Frank J., and Linnea R. Raine. *Global Organized Crime: The New Empire of Evil*. Washington, DC: Center for Strategic & International Studies, 1994.
2. The White House. *Strategy to Combat Transnational Organized Crime: Addressing Converging Threats to National Security*. http://www.whitehouse.gov/sites/default/files/Strategy_to_Combat_Transnational_Organized_Crime_July_2011.pdf.

CHAPTER 2

Transnational Organized Crime
The Dark Side of Globalization

Transnational crime will be a defining issue of the 21st century for policymakers—as defining as the Cold War was for the 20th century and colonialism was for the 19th. Terrorists and transnational crime groups will proliferate because these crime groups are major beneficiaries of globalization. They take advantage of increased travel, trade, rapid money movements, telecommunications and computer links, and are well positioned for growth.

—Louise I. Shelley[1]

The concept of transnational crime is not new. Drugs, money, and in-demand commodities have always been smuggled across borders and oceans, as criminals circumvent laws to enhance their illicit activity. For example, during the prohibition period in the United States, alcohol was illegally brought into the country from Mexico, Canada, and the Caribbean. Criminals and Mafia syndicates soon discovered that "boot-legging" was a far more profitable activity than extortion, prostitution, and gambling.

Early transnational crime was confined to regions, was not overly violent in nature, and consisted of small groups with a very orga-nized leadership structure. However, modern transnational crime is more expansive, far deadlier, and extremely difficult to eradicate due to a sophisticated, layered organizational structure, and "franchis-ing." The vast threat posed by modern transnational organized crime to the political, economic, and social fabric of societies appeared in the mid-1990s. Contributing factors to its rise include globalization of business networks, lowered trade barriers, communication and techno-logical advances, and turmoil caused by the collapse of communism. A new class of actors emerged during this period, operating outside the traditional nation-state system, subsequently hindering our ability to apply diplomatic and economic pressure to compel nations to address their organized crime issues.

The situation is increasingly complex, and transnational organized crime (TOC) is penetrating our society in new and dangerous ways. According to the National Security Council's *Strategy to Combat Transnational Organized Crime*, TOC is a growing threat to national and international security.[2] Grant D. Ashley, former assistant director of the Criminal Investigative Division at the Federal Bureau of Investigation (FBI), testified, "It is our belief that the international growth of these very dangerous, criminally diverse and organized groups and their emergence in the United States has caused a significant expansion of our crime problem."[3] Former attorney general Michael B. Mukasey further stated, "Organized crime threatens the economy, national security, and other interests of the United States."[4] Naturally, expansion of any type of criminal activity is of interest to law enforcement. However, these vast global enterprises are increasingly used as a vehicle by terrorists to move resources, recruit, raise capital, or simply spread their sphere of influence, raising the stakes. The liaison of criminals and terrorists makes the proliferation of TOC a pressing national security concern; however, as with all modern threats and groups, engagement is not easy and success is elusive.

MULTINATIONAL CORPORATE SOPHISTICATION

While studying the nexus as senior defense fellow at the Center for Strategic and International Studies, a think tank in Washington, DC, I published my first book on the nexus topic. *Transnational Crime and the Criminal-Terrorist Nexus: Synergies and Corporate Trends* (AU Press, 1995) provides a detailed look at the sophistication of groups and serves as the basis for the following discussion. Although routinely underestimated, TOC syndicates are very sophisticated, act as networks, and pursue the same types of joint ventures and strategic alliances as legitimate multinational corporations. A multinational corporation (MNC) is defined as one operating on a worldwide scale, without ties to any specific nation or region. The global business environment is unique and multifaceted, requiring extra considerations. Due to the complexity of international operations, the right people (e.g., lawyers, accountants, and subject-area experts) must be on the payroll. Analysis of the international customer base, product demand, and proper positioning of the product is necessary to maximize profit. The company must assess the cost of doing business and streamline staff and operational activities, thus cutting overhead as much as possible. Any business must have good supply-chain management, from procurement to storage to product delivery; this process requires extra planning and an enhanced level of sophistication when applied to a global market. For example, understanding international commerce laws and issues related to the operation of offshore businesses is a necessity. The company must acquire cultural knowledge of the countries involved in the transactions, including languages, currencies, and business practices. Also, the corporate strategy must be in sync with these cultural nuances for success. Savvy business ventures are low risk and high return, and most are able to extract profits throughout the process. Finally, an MNC is able to leverage rapidly changing communication and transportation technology to stay viable.

The preceding could easily be a description of the Sinaloa drug cartel. Successful international criminal enterprises follow the same business plan and often work in parallel with unsuspecting legitimate corporations by using their business practices as a model. They maximize profits and shift strategies as technology evolves, or when detected by law enforcement. The organizations are well resourced; most own and operate a variety of aircraft and boats, with skilled and highly paid operators at the helm. Sophisticated satellite phones and use of Global Positioning System equipment keeps criminals on the run and investigators in the dark. Unfortunately for governments battling this issue, not only are transnational criminal networks harder to detect and infiltrate than ever, but despite their best efforts, business is booming.

TRANSNATIONAL ORGANIZED CRIME ON THE RISE

As opposed to terrorism, which is motivated by ideology, organized crime is motivated by money. Tracking the increased sophistication and scope of organized crime, the FBI's definition of the activity has morphed and expanded in the last ten years. In 2003, it was defined as "a continuing criminal conspiracy having a firm organizational structure, and a conspiracy fed by fear and corruption."[5] The 2012 definition is longer and more specific. The FBI now defines organized crime as "any group having some manner of a formalized structure and whose primary objective is to obtain money through illegal activities. Such groups maintain their position through the use of actual or threatened violence, corrupt public officials, graft, or extortion, and generally have a significant impact on the people in their locales, region, or the country as a whole."[6] The terms "organized crime" and "continuing criminal enterprise" (CCE) are often used interchangeably, although the laws vary slightly regarding the definition of criminal activity falling within the CCE realm. The FBI defines a criminal enterprise as "a group of individuals with an identified hierarchy, or comparable structure, engaged in significant criminal activity. These organizations often engage in multiple criminal activities and have extensive supporting networks."[7] Although organized crime is typically associated with the Mafia or drug trafficking, it extends to any CCE such as money laundering, human trafficking, or white-collar crimes like insurance, mortgage, and prescription fraud.

There are other categories of crime. For instance, *reactive crimes* are violent or nonviolent crimes perpetrated by an individual or a small group, such as hate crimes or protests that turn violent. There are also *crimes of opportunity*, such as pickpocketing or a lone carjacking, in which the criminal targets the easiest mark or acts because of the target's carelessness. Although any of the aforementioned methods could generate resources, transnational criminal and global terrorist organizations are more likely to affiliate with a CCE with a proven track record of success, established and protected logistics lines, and the help of government officials who have been bribed, threatened, or corrupted.

Several factors contribute to the existence and proliferation of TOC originating, traversing, or committed in a country. One major consideration is available resources, including a desperate populace upon which to prey and a weak economy that will welcome profit from illegal activity. Geographical and geological features often play a significant role, for instance the availability of fresh water and crops, or the presence of precious minerals. Border security and strength of the rule of law are critical, and will either repel or attract transnational criminal activity. A weak government invites penetration by organized crime, and the resulting corruption further delegitimizes the country's government. The presence of terrorist groups in the region exacerbates crime problems across the spectrum, adding to existing instability.

The extent and global impact of transnational crime problem fully emerged in 2003 when State Department and FBI officials were called by Congress to testify regarding its alarming increase and mitigation efforts. Their prescient testimony, along with statements of other experts in the past ten years, provides unique insight into hotbeds of existing and emerging transnational crime.

SCOPING THE TOC CHALLENGE

When I began studying transnational crime ten years ago, the evolution from regionally contained networks to those with global reach was only beginning. Leaps in information, communication, and logistics technology contributed to the rise of syndicates with global reach, sophisticated operating methods, and fluid structures. TOCs can now "surveil the surveillers," quickly closing business and moving elsewhere when detected by law enforcement. Remaining anonymous is now possible through the use of virtual offshores, legitimate business fronts, and other e-commerce technology discussed in Chapter 7. Every nation's culture and citizenry is now affected by this new brand of organized crime and must increasingly devote precious resources to combat its spread.

Eurasian Transnational Crime: Size, Wealth, Reach

According to the FBI, Eurasian organized crime (EOC) poses some of the greatest threats because of its size, wealth, and global reach.[8] EOC is associated with Russia, Eastern and Central European countries, and the independent states formed after the fall of the Soviet Union. Although a victory for democracy, the demise of communism and the resulting leadership void caused great economic and social chaos allowing for the rise of many organized crime groups. Civil wars are still unresolved, and corruption is widespread. Massive criminal activity is destabilizing an area where nuclear weapons remain deployed, with rumors of "loose nukes" and a viable black market for nuclear material emerging from political upheaval in the region. Understandably, the national security implications of destabilization in this region are worrisome.

The U.S. government is concerned about the unique blend of circumstances in Eurasia. Terrorism, international organized crime, trafficking in persons and drugs, ethnic separatism, religious extremism, and corruption are present and thriving. Corruption of government officials in Eurasian countries is a main concern and contributes to the proliferation of transnational crime in this region. Steven Pifer, former deputy assistant secretary of state in the Bureau of European and Eurasian Affairs, is an expert on how a vacuum in institutions and privatization led to corruption in the region. According to his assessment, after the fall of the Soviet Union, absent state resources or statutory structure, valuable state assets were privatized in "insider transactions." Since property rights were uncertain and no court of law was available to settle disputes, savvy insiders and organized crime took advantage of the chaos to seize major companies, paying far less than their actual value. As small businesses began to form under *Perestroika*, criminals also took advantage of the lawless environment and moved in. Small-businesses owners often turned to gangsters to provide a *krysha* (roof) of protection, eventually compelled to turn over control and capital to their benefactors. Accumulated capital was then used by criminal elements to take over large companies in the privatization process, giving them public status and ascension to political office.[9] Within just a few years, the corruption problem was rampant in the region, with 4,000 organized crime groups in Russia alone. In February 1993, Boris Yeltsin, the first elected president of the Federation of Russian States, said: "Organized crime has become the No. 1 threat to Russia's strategic interests and to national security. Corrupted structures on the highest level have no interest in reform."[10]

According to the FBI, the Russian interior ministry estimates that more than one-half of the Russian economy, including significant portions of its vast energy and metallurgical sectors, is now controlled by organized crime. Experts believe that the wide range of criminal activity engaged in by Russian organized crime groups exceeds in scale and economic impact the Cali Cartel at the height of its power.[11] Powerful groups such as the Russian Mafia have defrauded newly formed governments of billions of dollars and take large profits through tax-evasion schemes and using corrupt officials to embezzle government funds. Well connected and embedded in society, criminal groups in Russia effortlessly use the country's banks to illegally transfer billions out of the country annually. Finally, the proximity of one of the two major narcotics-trafficking routes, the golden crescent of Pakistan, Afghanistan, and Iran, puts Tajikistan, Uzbekistan, Kazakhstan, Turkmenistan, and Kyrgyzstan at the crossroads of the opiate trade to Europe and Russia.

In addition to a thriving drug trade, Eurasian countries are rife with human-trafficking violations. Men, women, and children are procured from the region, transported, and sold for forced labor and sexual exploitation. Populations vulnerable to human trafficking are the poor and uneducated, and for criminals in the region, it is not only a high-profit venture but very low risk. Many Eurasian countries are lagging in instituting and enforcing laws to punish perpetrators of trafficking. In fact, of the Tier 2 watch list and Tier 3 noncompliant/no effort nations indicated in the 2011 report and covered later in this chapter, Eurasian countries are the leading offenders.[12]

Eurasian organized crime spread to the United States in the 1970s and 1980s with the arrival of more than 100,000 Soviet émigrés, known as "Refuseniks." Mixed in with law-abiding people was a very small group of criminals known as Vory V Zakone or "thieves-in-law," career criminals becoming the base of U.S. domestic Eurasian organized crime.[13] The dissolution of the Soviet Union in 1991 brought thousands more émigrés fleeing social strife and dismal economic conditions. The exodus added to the existing Eurasian criminal enterprise in the United States.

Fraud is prevalent with these groups, which will latch on to any crisis and turn it into profit. Recent activities in the United States include mortgage fraud, money laundering, extortion, drug trafficking, auto theft, hostage taking, extortion of celebrities and sport figures, insurance (staged auto accidents), medical fraud, counterfeiting, credit card forgery, and murder. Eurasian crime in the United States is big business; in October, 2011, law enforcement officials arrested fifty-two individuals from an Armenian-American syndicate for health care fraud defrauding companies and their customers of more than 163 million U.S. dollars. For the first time in fifteen years, a "thief-in-law" was arrested on a federal charge. However, Ukrainian Semion Mogilevich, one of the top ten fugitives wanted by the FBI, remains at large. Mogilevich's organization, using a front operation outside of Philadelphia, bilked investors of nearly 150 million U.S. dollars. Mogilevich is also wanted on arms trafficking, prostitution, extortion, and murder-for-hire charges. Although once in custody in Russia, he was released by government officials, and he and members of his group have simply disappeared.

As illustrated, no crime is off limits to EOC groups, and the breadth and depth of their criminal activity is astounding. Understanding the roots and rise of Eurasian crime is important for international and national security purposes, and this historical example should be incorporated in postconflict reconstruction and democratization planning. Rapidly establishing and enforcing the rule of law following governmental upheaval is essential to prevent a void that soon becomes a haven for criminals and terrorists. Unfortunately, this scenario is now playing out in other countries and regions where ruling governments have been overthrown or challenged by the Arab Spring movement.

Italian Transnational Crime: Not Your Grandfather's Mafia

The Italian criminal societies known collectively as the Mafia have existed since the 1800s and are now firmly entrenched in the political, social, and economic realms in Italy and around the world. Historically, the Mafia arose from four centuries of invasions in Italy and the people's response was to become clans, relying on family ties instead of the ruling government for protection and justice. The clans morphed into a secret society of resistance, meant to protect allied families from invaders. The protectors, known as "men of honor," were highly respected and revered in the community. Soon the clans fought each other for control and sought to expand their influence and power, becoming Mafias, or bodies of criminals. During the late 1800s and early 1900s, thousands of Sicilian Mafiosi entered the United States illegally, establishing the domestic Mafias persisting today. Surprisingly, New Orleans was the site of the first major Mafia incident in this country on October 15, 1890, when Police Superintendent David Hennessey was murdered execution-style. Law enforcement detained hundreds of Sicilians, and nineteen were indicted for the murder. However, a jury later acquitted the group, causing an outrage among the citizens of New Orleans; an organized lynch mob found and killed eleven of the nineteen defendants. Two were hanged, nine were shot, and the remaining eight escaped.[14]

Through the years, various gang factions of the Mafia have ascended and attempted to take control, such as Al Capone's syndicate in Chicago in the 1920s. Italian organized crime (IOC) groups currently active in the United States include La Cosa Nostra (LCN); the Camorra or Neapolitan Mafia; the 'Ndrangheta or Calabrian Mafia; and the Sacra Corona Unita or United Sacred Crown. The FBI estimates that the four groups have approximately 25,000 core members and 250,000 affiliates worldwide, and experts estimate the Mafia's worldwide criminal activity at more than $100 billion annually.[15]

In the United States, there are more than three thousand Mafia members and affiliates, with the largest presence centered in New York, southern New Jersey, and Philadelphia. Criminal activities are international, including collaboration with other international organized crime groups from all over the world, especially those involved in drug trafficking. The Mafia in Italy is extremely violent and has assassinated public officials and targeted law enforcement with car bombs and other incendiary devices. The Mafia in the United States is not as brazen, yet has plenty of blood on its hands and continues to wield influence with political figures and corporate leaders.

La Cosa Nostra (translated to "this thing of ours") is the most persistent Mafia threat in our country. In 1946, LCN leader "Lucky" Luciano was convicted for running a prostitution ring in the United States and was deported. However, his return to Italy delivered a transnational capability to the LCN, as he became the liaison between the two countries. LCN grew in power through the years; major threats now posed are drug trafficking and money laundering, but naturally the group is engaged in a broad spectrum of illegal activities including murder, extortion, corruption, gambling, labor racketeering, prostitution, and financial fraud. In January 2011, the largest coordinated arrest in FBI history netted 127 members of La Cosa Nostra in New York, New Jersey, and New England. More than thirty were "made" members of LCN, serving as underbosses, street bosses, and *consiglieres*, or close family advisors.[16] Although a major blow to the U.S. arm of the organization, the LCN operates with multinational corporate sophistication and will persist.

The Camorra or Neapolitan Mafia is based in Naples. The Camorra is the largest of the Italian organized crime groups, emerging from the 1970s "Camorra War," which resulted in the deaths of 400 members of the Sicilian Mafia. Great opportunists, the Camorra made their primary fortune in reconstruction after an Italian earthquake in the region in 1980. They are also expert cigarette smugglers and participants in the gamut of other illegal activities. There are nearly 200 Camorra affiliates residing in the United States, many of whom arrived during the Camorra Wars.

The 'Ndrangheta or Calabrian Mafia is based in Calabria, Italy. The word *Ndrangheta* comes from the Greek meaning "loyalty." The 'Ndrangheta formed in the 1860s when a group of Sicilians was banished from their island by the Italian government and settled in Calabria, Italy, forming small criminal groups. There are currently at least 160 'Ndrangheta cells worldwide, with 6,000 members. The group specializes in kidnapping and political corruption, but also engages in drug trafficking, murder, bombings, counterfeiting, gambling, frauds, thefts, labor racketeering, loan-sharking, and alien smuggling. Cells are loosely connected family groups based on blood relationships and marriages. In the United States, there are an estimated 100 to 200 members and associates, primarily located in New York and Florida.

The Sacra Corona Unita, or United Sacred Crown, is based in the Puglia region of Italy, after emerging in the late 1980s from its roots as a prison gang. The Sacra Corona Unita consists of fifty clans with approximately 2,000 members worldwide and specializes in smuggling cigarettes, drugs, arms, and people. The organization also collects payoffs from other criminal groups for landing rights on the southeast coast of Italy, a natural gateway for smuggling to and from post-Communist countries like Croatia, Yugoslavia, and Albania. The Mafia group works with Balkan organized criminal groups, which engage in arms and cigarette smuggling and human trafficking.[17] Very few Sacra Corona Unita members have been identified in the United States, although some individuals in Illinois, Florida, and New York have links to the organization.

IOC provides a perfect example of shifting ideology. Early Mafia godfathers stated they would never get into the drug-trafficking business or work with people of color. However, the organizations changed their philosophy in the name of making money and spreading power and influence. By leveraging new "business opportunities" through the years, the Mafia not only persists but remains an extremely powerful force at their base in Italy and many other countries. Similar to their activities to bring alcohol to thirsty patrons during the prohibition, they now supply drugs and sex slaves with no moral restraint. During the global financial crisis, any prior successes with diminishing their strength were lost, as IOC gained stronger footing in their host country. IOC expert Antonio Roccuzzo states, "The mafia has enormous liquidity. It may be the only Italian 'company' without any cash problem." Banks and at least 180,000 business owners in Italy turned to various IOC groups for loans during the financial crisis, with interest rates upwards of 120 percent. The full ramifications of these loans, made in desperation, have not yet been felt.[18]

IN FOCUS: THE IMPACT OF LABOR RACKETEERING

Labor racketeering is the domination, manipulation, and control of a labor movement in order to affect related businesses and industries. The resulting denial of workers' rights is not only illegal but an affront to their constitutional rights. Economic loss due to increased labor costs is vast and undermines the fabric of free enterprise.

Why do criminal elements such as the Mafia target labor unions? The primary reason is their vast pension, welfare, and health funds. Consider that in the United States, there are approximately 75,000 union locals with 14 million members. In the mid-1980s, the Teamsters Union controlled more than 1,000 funds with total assets of more than $9 billion. Racketeers infiltrate unions by offering "sweetheart" contracts, offering to broker peaceful labor relations with management, or worse, by rigging union elections.

Labor racketeering has become one of La Cosa Nostra's fundamental sources of profit, national power, and influence. The rise of LCN's involvement from small factories to our largest unions in our country was swift and stunning.

- In the late 1950s, a major U.S. Senate investigation found systemic racketeering in both the International Brotherhood of Teamsters and the Hotel Employees and Restaurant Employees International Union.
- In the early 1980s, former Gambino Family boss Paul Castellano was overheard saying, "Our job is to run the unions."
- In 1986, the President's Council on Organized Crime reported that five major unions, including the Teamsters and the Laborers International Union of North America, were dominated by organized crime.

New York, Buffalo, Chicago, Cleveland, Detroit, and Philadelphia are the primary hubs for unions, attracting racketeers and other criminal elements.

The FBI leverages the Racketeer Influenced and Corrupt Organization (RICO) Statute to infiltrate, gather evidence, and bring racketeers to justice. RICO allows law enforcement to engage the entire operation instead of individuals, who can be easily replaced in a vast organization such as the Mafia. For at least twenty years, the Teamsters union has been substantially controlled by LCN, with four of the last eight presidents indicted on criminal charges.

Source: FBI, http://www.fbi.gov/about-us/investigate/organizedcrime/italian_ mafia/

Baltic Transnational Crime: Emergent and Deadly

Balkan organized crime (BOC) describes activity originating from, or operating in, Albania, Bosnia-Herzegovina, Croatia, Kosovo, Macedonia, Serbia, Montenegro, Bulgaria, Greece, and Romania. Similar to Italian organized crime, BOC began as a familial or clan activity as a source of safety and protection during occupation of the Balkans by other countries in the fourteenth century and later. Communist rule led to contained, regional black-market activities in the Balkans; however, the collapse of communism allowed rapid worldwide expansion. Organized crime elements grew in scope, corrupting new rulers and allowing institutions to expand power and profit. Leadership of BOC groups is decentralized and, similar to the Mafia, along family lines. European nations now recognize BOC as one of the greatest criminal threats they face; the enterprise controls upwards of 70 percent of the heroin market in some of the larger European nations, and they are rapidly taking over human smuggling, prostitution, and car-theft rings.

According to the State Department, terrorists and Islamic extremist groups have already exploited inadequate border security and institutional weaknesses in the Balkans. Middle Eastern charities identified as supporting terrorist activities are currently providing assistance to Islamic extremist groups in the region. Terrorists also exploit the region's liberal asylum laws, open land borders, and weaknesses in their investigative, prosecutorial, and procedural processes while using these countries as operational staging areas for international terrorist attacks.[19] Albania and Kosovo lie at the heart of the Balkan route traversing the narcotics golden crescent. The Balkan route starts with the shipment of Afghan opiates through Pakistan and Iran, and into Turkey. The drugs are then shipped onward through the Balkans and into Western Europe, where they are distributed and consumed. This route is worth an estimated $400 billion a year and handles 80 percent of heroin destined for Europe. In 2010, an estimated seventy-five to eighty metric tons of heroin were trafficked to Western and Central Europe. The bulk of this drug, some sixty metric tons, was trafficked via the Balkan route.[20]

BOC activity has been detected in the United States since the mid-1980s, at first in petty crimes like theft and burglary. Then, ethnic Albanians began partnering with LCN families in New York; however, as their communities and presence became more established, the groups expanded to lead and control their own organizations. At one point, after establishing presence and growing in power, the FBI believes that the Albanians challenged the LCN for control of some traditional criminal activities in New York City. Balkan organized crime is an emerging threat in the United States, and although they don't share the criminal sophistication of Eurasian or LCN groups, they have proven themselves

capable of adapting to expanding and becoming involved in new activities, such as mortgage fraud.[21] Albanian organized crime groups in the
United States have been involved in murders, bank and automated teller
machine burglaries, passport and visa fraud, illegal gambling, weapons
and narcotics trafficking, extortion, and mortgage fraud. Hallmarks of
BOC activity are acts of extreme violence.[22]

Asian Transnational Crime: Sophisticated and Multicultural

In the early 1900s, signs of Asian criminal enterprises emerged in the
United States with the onset of criminally influenced Chinese groups,
which thrived and expanded. Asian criminal enterprises have now been
identified in more than fifty metropolitan areas and many other smaller
communities. Groups are predominantly from East and Southeast Asia,
including members of Chinese, Korean, Japanese, Thai, Filipino, and
Cambodian, Laotian, and Vietnamese descent. However, other Asian
criminal enterprises are now emerging as domestic and international
threats, including groups from the South Pacific Island nations as well as
organizations from Southwest Asia such as Pakistan, India, Afghanistan,
Nepal, and Iran. These groups are described as very fluid and extremely
mobile, easily adapting to changes and thus able to evade law enforcement. They are multilingual, can be highly sophisticated in their criminal operations, and are well financed. Some groups have commercialized
and commingled their criminal activities into business firms of various
sizes, from small family-run operations to large corporations. The FBI
also believes that the criminal conduct engaged in by Asian criminal
enterprises includes not only traditional organized crime activities but
human smuggling, technology theft, and intellectual property crime as
well. A unique characteristic of Asian organized crime groups is their
ability to elicit cooperation of other groups that cross ethnic and racial
heritage lines. Maturing groups are now structuring their groups hierar-
chically like corporations to be more competitive.[23]

An emergent area of concern in the region is the Malaysian straits,
an area of considerable established and uncontrolled organized crime.
The Indonesian archipelago is a series of 17,000 islands, a vast amount
of territory to govern, to patrol, and in which to enforce the rule of law.
Human trafficking is rampant in Indonesia, largely because of the tens
of millions of people mired in poverty, corrupt governments, and little to
no law enforcement capability. The region is subjected to sporadic violence created by a handful of separatists grouping with gangsters engaged
in weapons smuggling, money laundering, and drug trafficking. These
criminal activities are fueling international terrorist activity. Previously,
most terrorist activity in East Asia was related to domestic political

IN FOCUS: MACAU

The former Portuguese colony of Macau is worthy of close scrutiny. Macau, consisting of two islands and a peninsula connected to mainland China, is one of two "special administrative regions" governed by the Chinese, the other being Hong Kong. The area is an offshore financial hub, with a free port, tax protection, and no foreign control of their financial schemes. Throw in a booming gambling market, with thirty-three casinos with annual profits of 52 billion U.S. dollars (as opposed to 1 to 2 billion U.S. dollars in Las Vegas), and Macau is a haven for shadowy groups seeking to make, store, and launder money. Gambling and gaming for profit is illegal in China; therefore, the Chinese people turn to one of two hundred "junket" companies to arrange their transportation to Macau and handle their gambling outlay and debt. These companies are heavily infiltrated by Chinese organized crime syndicates, who use kidnapping, extortion, and heavier-handed tactics on tourists to recover their money, often with a large commission attached. The Las Vegas Sands and Wynn Resort are heavily vested in Macau, with casinos earning far more than their austere counterparts in Las Vegas. The website at http://www.casinoleaks-macau.com/ is hosted by the International Union of Operating Engineers (IUOE,) consisting of thousands of casino workers in Las Vegas who are concerned about what is happening in Macau and how the nefarious activity could undermine the credibility and stability of the U.S. gaming system. A repository of court documents and other material on the site provides a unique look into the criminal elements penetrating the Macau market.

disputes, but now the area is home to several lethal international terrorist groups. Organizations with direct links to al Qaeda were discovered in 2001 in Malaysia and Singapore, and their activities, movements, and connections now traverse the entire region. The al Qaeda offshoot Jemaah Islamiyah (JI) is responsible for many large hotel and embassy bombings in the last decade, impacting the tourist market and affecting the region's economy. The Abu Sayyaf Group (ASG) is an Islamic extremist organization in the Philippines allied with al Qaeda through Ramzi Yousef, the mastermind of the first World Trade Center bombing in 1993. Yousef is the nephew of Khalid Sheikh Mohammed, who was one of the principal architects of the 9/11 attacks. An ASG subsidiary, the Abu Haf al-Masri Brigades, emerged as a lethal new group, initiating hotel bombings in Malaysia and possibly executing the train bombings in Madrid. Although many of JI's and ASG's leaders have been arrested, the groups remain on the Foreign Terrorist Organization designation list as worthy of watching. A final concern in the region is Islamic extremists operating in and around western China, the Uighur Muslims. ETIM is a militant Uighur organization advocating creation of the independent Islamic state of East Turkestan in the Xinjiang region. The group has received training, equipment, and inspiration from al Qaeda, the Taliban, and others in Afghanistan. ETIM threatened the 2008 Summer Olympics in Beijing, yet there were no incidents.[24]

African Criminal Enterprises: Internet Savvy and Vast

African organized crime has been on the rise exponentially in the last ten years, fed by globalization and political and social unrest in the region. Economic conditions with failing or failed states have opened the door to corruption, and the leveraging of stable African countries has led to global expansion of formerly contained, regional crime.

The FBI reports that Nigerian criminal enterprises are the most considerable transnational threat, operating in more than eighty other countries. Drug trafficking provides the most profit, as the country is a transit point for heroin between Southeast and Southwest Asia into Europe and the United States and cocaine from South America into Europe and South Africa. Ethnic Nigerians in India, Pakistan, and Thailand have access to 90 percent of the world's heroin production and serve as operational conduits, and money laundering from these activities is accomplished worldwide. Nigerian groups are skilled at financial frauds and schemes, which costs the United States alone an estimated 1 to 2 billion U.S. dollars each year. Leveraging the Internet, they are the masters of "419" schemes, e-mail correspondence indicating winning from lottery winnings or estates. A new sector of 419 activities includes virtual kidnapping fraud, where the recipient is notified of the abduction of a family member and asked to send their bank wire information to help secure their release. African criminal enterprises in the United States are also heavily engaged in identity theft and are most prevalent in Atlanta, Baltimore, Chicago, Dallas, Houston, Milwaukee, Newark, New York, and Washington, DC.[25]

A new concern in Africa concerns the mass killing of elephants to harvest ivory. In 2011, at least 25,000 elephants were slaughtered in Central Africa, with violence escalating between poachers and anti-poachers resulting in the death of hundreds. China, Thailand, and the Philippines are the countries with the greatest demand for ivory based on religious beliefs, among them many Catholics and Buddhists, that ivory honors God.[26] The countries are paying exorbitant rates for the tusks, causing an elephant-killing frenzy on the continent. Ivory is moved

IN FOCUS: THE LATIN AMERICA DRUG
WAR EXPANDS TO WESTERN AFRICA

In 2009, the Department of Defense (DOD) took on a new role: countering the expanding drug trade in Western Africa. The FY 2009 defense authorization bill, House Resolution (H.R.) 5658, Section 1024, provided funding for counterdrug equipment in the republics of Ghana, Guinea-Bissau, and Senegal. The Senate Armed Services Committee voiced concern about the rapid growth of illegal drug trade in the region and directed the State Department and DOD to jointly prepare a region-wide, counterdrug plan for Africa, with a special emphasis on West Africa and the Maghreb.

Since 2003, 99 percent of all drugs seized in Africa have been found in the west. The volume seized has increased fivefold in the last few years. Agencies involved in counterdrug operations acknowledge that the situation in several West African countries is rapidly deteriorating. For instance, Ghana has become a significant transshipment point for illegal drugs, particularly cocaine from South America, and DOD has identified it as the "anchor country" for emerging counternarcotics efforts through AFRICOM. Perhaps the greatest threat lies in Guinea-Bissau, which the UN has dubbed Africa's first "narco-state." With a landmass equal to the state of Maryland, Guinea-Bissau is one of the poorest countries in the world, with two-thirds of its 1.5 million population living below the poverty line. The country is attractive to traffickers due to its unpatrolled coastline, numerous hidden bays, and close proximity to several other declining countries and their weak rule of law. In a country lacking a main source of electricity, the police force has no cars, no radios, and few weapons. The military is thought to be complicit in the drug trade; in 2008, two military personnel were detained along with a civilian in a vehicle carrying 635 kilos of cocaine. The army secured the soldiers' release from prison and they were not charged.

Trafficking and unrest is not new to Guinea-Bissau; it was first known as the "Slave Coast" when African rulers prospered from the slave trade. After centuries of Portuguese rule, a paramilitary group emerged and, aided by arms and supplies from Cuba, Russia, and China, fought a protracted war to eventually win the country's independence in 1974. Years of unrest ensued; thousands of citizens who had fought alongside the Portuguese against the rebels were slaughtered and buried in unmarked graves. The country has subsequently faced bloody uprisings, conflicts, and even a complete economic collapse. The United States' and Britain's official diplomatic presence pulled out of the country in 1998 during a civil war, moving to nearby Senegal. In just a few years since the first cocaine was brought to its shores, Guinea-Bissau has become a major hub for drug trafficking, bringing with it new prosperity. In a country where the average income is $1 a day, Colombians are regularly seen driving expensive SUVs and sports cars, and living in new Spanish-style villas with swimming pools and armed guards in the countryside. UN investigators say that up to 2,200 pounds of cocaine are now flown into Guinea-Bissau every night, along with an unknown amount arriving by sea.

Europe, primarily Spain and Portugal, is the main recipient of cocaine from West Africa. According to the UN Office on Drugs and Crime (UNODC), a quarter of all cocaine consumed in Western Europe is trafficked through West Africa. Responding to the situation, the executive director of UNODC, Antonio Maria Costa, stated: "In the 19th century, Europe's hunger for slaves devastated West Africa. Two hundred years later, its growing appetite for cocaine could do the same." At least fifty tons of cocaine now passes through West Africa every year.

The impact of the booming narco-trafficking trade in West Africa is now reaching our shores; DEA and UNODC report that Guinea-Bissau and other West African countries are being targeted by Asian and African cartels trafficking heroin to the United States. In 2007, the DEA and police in Chicago tracked nine West Africans who had moved heroin originating in Southeast Asia through various West African countries, markedly Guinea-Bissau, to the central United States.

Primary Source: http://www.unodc.org/unodc/en/frontpage/assisting-guinea-bissau.html

through Sudan, Chad, and Nigeria, with warlords and possibly terrorist groups taking their fee along the route.

Emerging Area of Concern: North Korea

North Korea and its littoral region is the newest front in transnational organized crime. Unlike other cases discussed where organized crime attempts to infiltrate a country and its government, the government of North Korea is infiltrating organized crime. As the economy continues to decline, the government of North Korea is increasingly turning to drug trafficking (methamphetamines, opium, heroin, and sexual enhancement drugs) to raise revenue. Japan, Australia, and China have all received drug shipments from North Korea. However, the providers are now also becoming users; reports indicate that government officials and senior military officers as users and addicts are now prevalent, a scary prospect considering the country's nuclear arsenal.[27] According to experts, members of the armed forces, the diplomatic corps, and the intelligence service are engaging in narcotics trafficking.[28]

Human trafficking is another lucrative venture for the country, which is now a Tier 3 offender, per the State Department's 2011 report. Further, there is evidence of printing plants being used to produce high-quality counterfeit U.S. currency, especially $100 bills. As stated in the report *North Korean Crime-for-Profit Activities*, North Korean criminal activity generates as much as $500 million in profit per year, with some estimates reaching the $1 billion level. North Korean crime is posed to expand beyond the nation's borders, thus becoming a transnational threat in the region. The Treasury Department took action against the Banco Delta Asia bank in Macau, China, for laundering money for North Korea, which merely moved its accounts to Switzerland. Finally, the DPRK knock-off cigarette production capacity is possibly the largest in the world, at more than 2 billion packs a year. North Korean counterfeit cigarettes have been found in Taiwan, the Philippines, Vietnam, Belize, and several major U.S. cities.[29]

Drugs, humans, and cigarettes aren't the only ways North Korea is raising funds transnationally. On June 30, 2009, the U.S. Department of Treasury designated Hong Kong Electronics, a North Korean company, as an integral part of the country's nuclear weapons proliferation and ballistic missiles and weapons program. Hong Kong Electronics was based on Kish Island, Iran, and had been transferring millions of dollars from Iran to North Korea.[30] Naturally, any liaison between these two countries is extremely worrisome.

FIGHTING TRANSNATIONAL CRIME OVERSEAS … AND WITHIN OUR BORDERS

Transnational organized crime has been likened to a cancer, spreading across the world. It can undermine democracy, disrupt free markets, drain national assets, and inhibit the development of stable societies. In doing so, national and international criminal groups threaten the security of all nations.

—U.S. State Department[31]

As discussed, TOC may be based in various world regions but its tentacles extend directly into our communities. Transnational crime impacts us in ways not previously imagined. Not only does it bring drugs and illicit activity into our country, but there is a direct financial cost with subsidies added to everyday necessities including food, clothes, insurance, and health care to cover industry losses due to fraud, theft, and counterfeit goods. In terms of the overarching national security threat, the potential strategic-level impact of corruption on our businesses, the institution of law, and leadership is a far more pressing concern.

Other than arresting and prosecuting local criminal elements in the United States, how do we harness our myriad state powers and engage at the source of transnational crime?

Palermo Convention: First Strike on TOC

The United Nations Convention against Transnational Organized Crime, also known as the Palermo Convention, was created to "promote cooperation to prevent and combat transnational organised crime more effectively."[32] At the signing conference on December 12, 2000, UN Secretary-General Kofi Annan stated:

> If crime crosses all borders, so must law enforcement. If the rule of law is undermined not only in one country, but also in many, then those who defend it cannot limit themselves to purely national means. If the enemies of progress and human rights seek to exploit the openness and opportunities of globalization for their purposes, then we must exploit those very same factors to defend human rights, and defeat the forces of crime, corruption, and trafficking in human beings.[33]

Palermo was significant for many reasons. The convention validated the TOC issue as urgent, and encouraged international cooperation to address its complex challenges. Countries ratifying Palermo committed their resources and, at the very least, agreed to be part of the solution, not the problem. Of the 148 nations present at the conference, 120 signed the primary UN Convention, later joined by another 27 who signed but noted specific disagreements with the Convention. Interestingly, the original document was signed by China, the Russian Federation, Iran, and many other countries hosting the bulk of transnational crime activities. The Convention also covered three specific areas of interest, in which countries could add further support: the Protocol to Prevent, Suppress and Punish Trafficking in Persons, especially Women and Children; the Protocol against the Smuggling of Migrants by Land, Sea; and the Protocol against the Illicit Manufacturing and Trafficking in Firearms, Their Parts and Components and Ammunition. Not all countries signed these protocols for a variety of reasons, possibly shedding light on their capacity or willingness to address problems within their own borders. The original signatories and documents can be found on the UN website, in the Treaty Collection repository.[34]

Palermo provided the first global, legally binding instrument to address TOC and produced agreed upon definitions on contentious terms such as "trafficking," "confiscation," and "organized crime." With a nod toward the importance of protecting sovereignty, Palermo certainly opened the door for countries to engage at the source of the crime when it affects their own national security and interests. In light of the agreement, law enforcement and other government agencies may directly coordinate with host countries to battle TOC, and provide technical assistance, manpower, or funds as needed. Technological advances such as the ability to intercept satellite phone calls, interact on the Internet, and use drones to collect information and/or target bad actors has blurred the once precise parameters set by Palermo, although the Convention still provides the foundation for our present-day activities to engage TOC at its source.

NATIONAL STRATEGY TO COMBAT TRANSNATIONAL ORGANIZED CRIME

Our government moved forward quickly to combat TOC after the signing of the Palermo Convention, and even more expeditiously after the 9/11 attacks when it was found that terrorists were operating in the same "space" as criminals. Certainly, any efforts to combat TOC will directly impact the human capital, wealth, logistics routes, and operational capability of terrorist groups traversing many nations, some allies and others not. Therefore the president and his executive cabinet, namely the National Security Staff, direct our country's overarching counter-TOC strategy.

In January 2010, our government completed a comprehensive review of international organized crime, the first since 1995. On July 25, 2011, in response to the dramatic growth in size, scope, influence, and threat of TOC and the nexus with terrorist groups, the National Security Staff released the *Strategy to Combat Transnational Organized Crime: Addressing Converging Threats to National Security*.[35] The following is a summary of the six main strategic priorities along with relevant highlights:

1. Start at home: take shared responsibility for transnational organized crime.
   Actions: Drug use fuels the industry; we must lessen demand. Weapons trafficking from the United States is aggravating criminal activity abroad, particularly in Mexico. The illicit cross-border flow of people and currency must stop.

2. Enhance intelligence and information sharing.

   Actions: We must enhance SIGINT and HUMINT collection on TOC threats. Employing the Open Source Center to draw upon "grey" literature, smaller press outlets covering crime in foreign countries, and social media will enhance development of profiles of individuals, companies, and institutions linked to TOC networks. We must continue to build better relationships between U.S. intelligence, law enforcement, and military agencies.

3. Protect the financial system and strategic markets against TOC.

   Actions: Prevent or disrupt criminal involvement in emerging and strategic markets. Increase awareness and provide incentives and alternatives for the private sector to reduce facilitation of TOC. Develop a mechanism that would make unclassified data on TOC available to private sector partners. Enhance capabilities to combat transnational cyber crime. Identify foreign kleptocrats who have corrupt relationships with TOC networks and target their assets for freezing, forfeiture, and repatriation to victimized governments. (Note: a *kleptocrat* is a government official who steals funds earmarked for public amenities, such as schools, hospitals, or roads.)

4. Strengthen interdiction, investigations, and prosecutions.

   Actions: Enhance U.S. authority's ability to identify, investigate, interdict, and prosecute top transnational criminal networks. Develop a strategy denying TOC networks and individuals in the United States access to their infrastructure and their enabling means. Strengthen efforts to interdict illicit trafficking in the air and maritime domains.

5. Disrupt drug trafficking and its facilitation of other transnational threats.

   Actions: Develop a comprehensive approach to dismantle drug trafficking organizations (DTOs) with connections to terrorist organizations. Work with international partners to reduce the global supply of and demand for illegal drugs and thereby deny funding to TOC networks. Sever the links between the international illicit drug and arms trades.

6. Build international capacity, cooperation, and partnerships.

   Actions: Raise international awareness of TOC and build multilateral cooperation against it. Build partnerships and leverage assets to enhance foreign capabilities, including counterterrorism capacity building, foreign law enforcement cooperation, military cooperation, and the strengthening of justice and interior ministries.

IN FOCUS: THE ATTORNEY GENERAL'S ORGANIZED CRIME COUNCIL (AGOCC)

The AGOCC convened for the first time in 1970 as an outgrowth of an executive order, issued by President Lyndon B. Johnson in 1968, placing the attorney general in charge of coordinating all federal law enforcement activity against organized crime. At the time, and for many years to follow, the AGOCC efforts were primarily focused on La Cosa Nostra Italian organized crime and met regularly until 1993. The AGOCC was reintroduced in 2008 as part of the Law Enforcement Strategy to Combat International Organized Crime. The strategy notes that "in recent years, international organized crime has expanded considerably in presence, sophistication and significance." Further it states that "in short, international organized crime is a national security problem that demands a strategic, targeted and concerted U.S. Government response." In addition to the standard illegal activities committed by organized crime groups such as drug trafficking and money laundering, the AGOCC noted new strategic goals, indicating that groups may attempt to:

- Penetrate the energy and other strategic sectors of the economy.
- Provide logistical and other support to terrorists, foreign intelligence services, and governments.
- Smuggle/traffic people and contraband goods into the United States.
- Exploit the U.S. and international financial systems to move illicit funds.
- Use cyberspace to target U.S. victims and infrastructure.
- Manipulate securities exchanges and perpetrate sophisticated frauds.
- Corrupt or seek to corrupt public officials in the United States and abroad.
- Use violence or the threat of violence as a basis for power.

As the MNC sophistication of TOCs grew, their goals became loftier and deadlier. The response from our government to this complex growing threat was to broaden the scope of agencies combating organized crime beyond the traditional law enforcement sector, adding the following agencies and representatives to the revitalized AGOCC: the deputy attorney general (chair);

the assistant attorney general, Criminal Division; the chair of the Attorney General's Advisory Committee; and the heads of the following nine participating law enforcement agencies: FBI; Drug Enforcement Administration; Bureau of Alcohol, Tobacco, Firearms and Explosives; ICE; U.S. Secret Service; Internal Revenue Service, Criminal Investigation; United States Postal Inspection Service; U.S. Department of State, Bureau of Diplomatic Security; and the U.S. Department of Labor, Office of the Inspector General.

The Council provides a unified approach to combating international organized crime. Their new Top International Criminal Organizations Target List (TICOT) product assists investigators and prosecutors with concentrating their limited resources on those TOCs posing the greatest threat to the United States.[36]

AGENCIES AND METHODS

Although not the "sexy" work of black-world operators, strengthening the rule of law, building anticrime programs, and conducting law enforcement training will reap the greatest gains in countering international crime. According to Steven Schrage, "targeted intelligence and operations may remove specific terrorist, drug trafficking, or organized crime groups, but unless we address the environments allowing them to thrive, we will have at best created a void that can be filled by others."[37] To understand how our government is battling transnational crime and shaping the global environment to best meet our needs, it is imperative to review agencies, methods, progress, and lessons learned.

INL

Due to the sensitive nature of working criminal and terrorist issues with foreign countries, the State Department is heavily involved in associated operations. State Department's Bureau of International Narcotics and Law Enforcement Affairs (INL) is a large part of the multifaceted U.S. response to international crime. INL's mission is to strengthen criminal justice systems, counter the flow of illegal narcotics, and minimize transnational crime. INL programs support two of the State Department's strategic goals: to reduce the entry of illegal drugs into the United States and to minimize the impact of international crime on its citizens. INL's annual budget has increased in the years since the 9/11 attacks and hovers around 1 billion U.S. dollars to fund policies and programs to combat transnational criminal threats and strengthen the rule of law and relevant institutions in "at-risk" countries or emerging democracies.

Each government agency involved in counter-TOC activities possesses different statutory responsibilities, specialized skill sets, and unique "culture." The State Department is in the diplomacy and relationship-building business; thus INL is involved in myriad training, negotiating, and coordinating activities. Areas of focus include counternarcotics, demand reduction, money laundering, financial crime, terrorist financing, smuggling of goods, illegal migration, trafficking in persons, domestic violence, border controls, document security, corruption, cyber crime, intellectual property rights, law enforcement, police academy development, and assistance to judiciaries and prosecutors. Their work crosses into the jurisdiction of many other government agencies and is accomplished with the help of investigators (FBI), prosecutors (Department of Justice), money experts (Department of Treasury), intelligence gatherers (Central Intelligence Agency), military trainers (Department of Defense), and myriad other U.S. agencies.

The G8 Roma-Lyon Group (RLG), chaired by INL and formed in 1996, is an effective tool in coordinating efforts to fight international crime. RLG was originally known as the Lyon Group, named for the city in France hosting the 1996 G8 conference. However, following the attacks of 9/11, the Lyon Group merged with counterterrorism experts in Rome in October 2001 and expanded work to include all aspects of organized crime and terrorism. RLG consists of senior security experts from the G8 countries and meets several times a year to discuss current and emergent challenges, such as increasing cyber threats. The body made great progress in setting international standards and in enhancing law enforcement cooperation against transnational crime and terrorism, including identifying and removing obstacles to cooperation and facilitating information sharing. The *G8 Recommendations on Transnational Crime* consists of forty recommendations made by the RLG, as well as twenty measures to specifically address international terrorist threats.[38]

DOJ

Under the umbrella of INL's program, DOJ works extensively to develop foreign law enforcement institutions, build the rule of law, and provide resident legal advisors to countries to give them on-the-ground advice on how to best confront transnational threats. This work is primarily accomplished through the International Law Enforcement Academies (ILEA).[39] The ILEA program has an annual budget of 30 million U.S. dollars and is an interagency effort with all major U.S. law enforcement agencies participating. Serving as a global model for advancing the common fight against international crime and promoting the rule of law, the ILEA program builds relationships between law enforcement officials, supports democracy in policing operations, and raises the professionalism of officers involved in the fight against crime. The focus of instruction is not just technical in nature but, more importantly, includes the development of leadership and management skills to deal with the modern challenges facing law enforcement. Although the target countries may change based on world events, ILEAs are organized to serve four general regions: Europe, Africa, South America, and Asia. Current ILEAs are located in Budapest, Hungary; Gaborone, Botswana; San Salvador, El Salvador; Bangkok, Thailand; and Roswell, New Mexico.

DOJ's Office of Overseas Prosecutorial Development, Assistance and Training (OPDAT) is the arm specifically addressing transnational organized crime issues. OPDAT gives prosecutors and investigators specialized tools and familiarization with unique aspects of pursuing organized crime. The office provides a money-laundering seminar designed to familiarize law enforcement personnel, policy makers, and legislators with international standards. Attendees are trained on developing and using legislation, investigative techniques, and prosecutorial tools in fighting money laundering, bank fraud, terrorist financing, and other complex financial crimes. In 2012, OPDAT fielded fifty-four resident legal advisors in thirty-two countries and directed 817 programs involving eighty-nine countries.[40] The OPDAT program is primarily funded through the State Department, but they also receive funding from USAID and the Millennium Challenge Corporation.

Another tool, mutual legal assistance treaties (MLATs), leverages our ability to fight transnational crime. The MLAT allows U.S. authorities to obtain evidence and other types of law enforcement assistance from other countries, and foreign governments may use the treaty to request assistance from the United States. This tool greatly helps when pursuing and extraditing international criminals and is effective in the pursuit of terrorists and their supporters. The first MLAT was signed with Switzerland in 1975 to assist U.S. law enforcement with their investigation of financial crimes related to Mafia operations. Since then, the United States has signed MLATs with sixty countries, including Russia.

FBI

Since 9/11, the FBI has morphed from a primarily domestic-focused federal law enforcement agency to a national security-focused, intelligence-driven, global organization.

More than ever, the FBI is "forward deployed" with an extensive on-the-ground capability, not only through the ILEA and OPDAT efforts

IN FOCUS: FBI COMBATING TOC

AFRICAN CRIMINAL ENTERPRISES

The FBI participates in two initiatives to bolster efforts to combat African criminal enterprises:

- The DOJ Nigerian Crime Initiative coordinates the federal investigations of Nigerian criminal enterprises by using joint task forces in six major U.S. cities.
- The Interpol West African Fraud annual conference brings together law enforcement agents from around the world to discuss and share information about the financial frauds perpetrated by Nigerian criminal enterprises.

EURASIAN ORGANIZED CRIME

The FBI belongs to several international working groups to combat the influence and reach of Eurasian organized crime and limit its impacts on all countries.

- Eurasian Organized Crime Working Group: Acting under the auspices of the G8, this working group evolved from a group established in 1994. The organization meets to discuss and jointly address the transnational aspects of Eurasian organized crime impacting member countries and the international community in general. Member countries are Canada, Great Britain, Germany, France, Italy, Japan, the United States, and Russia.
- Central European Working Group: This group is part of a project bringing together the FBI and Central European law enforcement agencies to discuss cooperative investigative matters covering the broad spectrum of Eurasian organized crime. A principal concern is the growing presence of Russian and other Eurasian organized criminals in Central Europe and the United States. The group includes law enforcement agencies and representatives from Romania, the Ukraine, Russia, Israel, Great Britain, and Belgium.
- Southeast European Cooperative Initiative: The Initiative is an international organization to coordinate police and customs regional actions for preventing and combating

transborder crime. Headquartered in Bucharest, Romania, the group has twelve fully participating member countries and is a clearing house for rapid information and intelligence sharing. The group also supports specialized task forces for countering transborder crime such as the trafficking of people, drugs, and cars; smuggling; financial crimes; and terrorism.

Source: Adapted from the FBI.gov website.

but also manning over sixty legal attaché (Legat) offices overseas. Legats bring together agents, analysts, and their foreign counterparts to share information and accomplish casework.

With a renewed focus on cross-agency partnering and the ability to flex capability to meet urgent or emergent threat needs, the FBI created threat focus cells (TFCs), which are diverse teams consisting of FBI and other agency subject-matter experts. For example, two TFCs focus primarily on Eurasian organized crime; the first concentrates on the Semion Mogilevich Organization, and the second on the Brother's Circle criminal enterprise. TFCs harness capabilities from many disciplines within the FBI such as cyber, criminal, and counterintelligence.

Global partnering is necessary to address global problems. Proactive engagement by the State Department, Department of Justice, Treasury, and other government agencies builds trust, creates an atmosphere of information sharing, and facilitates a greater ability to work transnational criminal cases as they arise.

MAJOR AREAS OF CONCERN, PROGRESS, AND LESSONS LEARNED

The State Department highlights four areas of major concern in the battle against transnational crime: counternarcotics, trafficking in persons, money laundering, and corruption. Any progress made in one of these areas will make a significant impact on curtailing transnational crime and thwarting terrorist acts.

Counternarcotics

The U.S. government continues to expend resources fighting the global drug cultivation and trafficking epidemic on many fronts, including work with UNODC, a global leader in the fight against illicit drugs and international crime. Established in 1997 through a merger between the United Nations Drug Control Programme and the Centre for International Crime Prevention, UNODC operates in all regions of the world through an extensive network of field offices. UNODC relies on voluntary contributions for 90 percent of its budget, mainly from governments. UNODC's report is based on reporting from the ground, typically from law enforcement sources engaged in seizures at transportation hubs and in major cities. Unfortunately, the UNODC *World Drug Report 2012* paints a grim picture.[41] Despite global efforts to combat the use of drugs and drug trafficking, there has been no significant change in the global status quo regarding the use, production, and health consequences of illicit drugs. This stagnant state has persisted for five years.

Globally, the two most widely used illicit drugs remain cannabis and amphetamine-type stimulants (ATSs), including ecstasy, methamphetamine, and amphetamine. Cannabis is the world's most widely used illicit substance, with between 119 and 224 million users worldwide. Consumption is stable, but propagation appears to be on the rise, particularly on a smaller scale, possibly to evade law enforcement's detection. There is also a rise in indoor cultivation of cannabis, which yields a more potent resin and impacts the likelihood of addiction. ATS is the second class of most widely used drug in the world. The U.S and European demand for ecstasy is climbing, although methamphetamine is still in higher demand in both regions. There is also growing evidence to suggest criminal organizations involved in smuggling ATSs, particularly methamphetamine, are exploiting West Africa, as are other drug traffickers.

Along the largest heroin trail, the Balkan route, which leads from Afghanistan to Western and Central Europe via southeastern Europe, there was a decline in seizures. The report notes the return to high levels of opium production in Afghanistan in 2011 after a poppy plant disease caused crop failure in 2010. Due to a decrease in eradication efforts in the last few years by coalition forces due to the drawdown, Afghanistan is once again the world leader in poppy production, and surprisingly, the country is also now the most vast and worrisome source of cannabis resin. Many farmers turned to the cannabis crop when their poppy fields were eradicated.

Bolivia and Peru are quickly becoming leaders among cocaine-producing nations in the world with major markets in North America, Europe, Australia, and New Zealand. A decline in cocaine use in the United States was noted, from 3 percent (2006) to 2 percent (2010) among adults aged fifteen to sixty-four. However, the appetite for cocaine in Europe has not declined and is steadily rising in Australia. The main route for cocaine into Europe is now via the west coast of Africa, with product arriving daily from Latin America. Most of the cocaine arriving in the United States still comes from Colombia but is

IN FOCUS: CHEMICALLY ENGINEERED DRUGS

Chemically engineered psychotropic substances are an emergent illicit-drug concern. They are manufactured specifically to avoid detection, confiscation, and international control, a testament to the adaptability and technological savvy of illicit-drug producers and traffickers. The most notable of these substances are MDPV, mephedrone, and methylone, chemical "cousins" containing synthetic cathinones, and lab created to mimic the parent compound, which is found naturally in the plant khat and chewed for its mild stimulant effects in many Middle Eastern countries. Mephedrone and MDPV are thought to be produced in China and smuggled into the United States, where they are often sold as "bath salts" or "plant food" and used as substitutes for cocaine or ecstasy. Also known on the streets as "meow meow," the substances were first detected in the United States in 2008 and available for sale in tobacco shops and adult bookstores until a law was passed in 2012 making the products illegal. However, they are still widely available in Europe in tourist shops, and a quick look on the Internet under "Ivory Wave," "Vanilla Sky," and "Bliss" reveals European dealers who will mail the substances to the United States.

The American Association of Poison Control Centers received 6,100 calls about mephedrone in 2011, up from just 304 the year before, and more than 1,700 calls in the first half of 2012. Distributors of mephedrone products are trying to keep one step ahead of law enforcements, and are now selling the drug as "insect repellant," "jewelry cleaner," "iPOD cleaner," or "pump-it-up powder."

Another concern is synthetic cannabinoids called "spice" or K2. These chemical substances mimic the hallucinogenic effects of marijuana but may not stay in the body as long. The key chemical components of the last generation of spice were banned at the same time as mephedrone, but new versions are already in the works using slightly different compounds that are still legal. These synthetic chemicals pose new challenges for the law enforcement community and will likely add to standard drug-related crimes such as burglary, gun crime, extortion, and even murder. The medical community is also concerned since the long-term effects of synthetic drugs on the body are unknown, and the products may contain dangerous additives.

The DEA's website (http://www.justice.gov/dea/druginfo/factsheets.shtml) contains thorough and current information concerning the emergent synthetic drug threat.

being pushed through the Caribbean Islands due to our increased law enforcement activities in Mexico and at the border.

Illicit-drug use is now concentrated among youth, especially young males living in urban environments, and the demand is moving more toward psychoactive substances. Many factors feed the shifting use, such as preference, buying ease, and demographic data. For instance, disposable income plays a large role in the drug of choice for users. Also, a change in value system in society will impact use, as will prevalent trends among the younger generations.

The major takeaway from the UNODC 2012 report is an ongoing shift away from developed to developing countries in terms of production and supply routes. This is a dangerous trend due to the lack of strong government and rule of law in these nations and regions. This void will certainly attract criminal and terrorist elements, and this is already is happening on the west coast of Africa in Guinea-Bissau and Mali with the presence of FARC, Hezbollah, al Qaeda, and Mexican DTOs.

Human Trafficking

A $32 billion industry, human trafficking is now the second most lucrative criminal activity, outpaced only by drugs. The State Department's 2012 report is very grim, estimating that there are now 27 million men, women, and children being held against their will in forced labor, in prostitution, or for sale as sex slaves.[42] The figure is up dramatically from the 2005 report, which put the number around 12 million. Somewhere between 1 and 2 million humans are trafficked each year, up from 800,000 in 2005. The crime is escalating and heinous, violating basic human rights, introducing serious public health risks, and, unfortunately, fueling organized crime and terrorism.

The State Department regularly issues the Trafficking in Persons Report (TIPR) with vignettes of survivors, an assessment of the problem, and a tiered ranking of countries and their individual challenges. The tiered system is as follows:

> Tier 1: Countries whose governments fully comply with the Trafficking Victims Protection Act's (TVPA) minimum standards.
> Tier 2: Countries whose governments do not fully comply with the TVPA's minimum standards, but are making significant efforts to bring themselves into compliance with those standards.
> Tier 2 Watch List: Countries whose governments do not fully comply with the TVPA's minimum standards, but are making significant efforts to bring themselves into compliance with those standards and:

a. The absolute number of victims of severe forms of trafficking is very significant or is significantly increasing;
b. There is a failure to provide evidence of increasing efforts to combat severe forms of trafficking in persons from the previous year; or
c. The determination that a country is making significant efforts to bring itself into compliance with minimum standards was based on commitments by the country to take additional future steps over the next year.

Tier 3: Countries whose governments do not fully comply with the minimum standards and are not making significant efforts to do so.

The global distribution of this report has certainly pressured governments to comply, although many Tier 3 countries are not making significant efforts to stop the crime.

Tier 3 countries in the 2012 report include:

1. Algeria
2. Congo
3. Cuba
4. Eritrea
5. Iran
6. North Korea
7. Kuwait
8. Libya
9. Madagascar
10. Papua New Guinea
11. Saudi Arabia
12. Sudan
13. Syria
14. Yemen
15. Zimbabwe

Human trafficking is happening worldwide, but viewing the issue by regions is most helpful in understanding where the crime is most prolific (see Figure 2.1).

There are two approaches to the human-trafficking issue: law enforcement and victim care. The Palermo Convention's Human Trafficking Protocol's "3P" paradigm of prevention, prosecution, and protection reflects a comprehensive victim-centered approach incorporating criminal justice activities with ensuring that the human rights of individuals are guaranteed. Although the United States is a Tier 1 nation, thousands of victims cross the nation's borders annually to work in a variety of industries, and in 2010, 2,515 human-trafficking cases

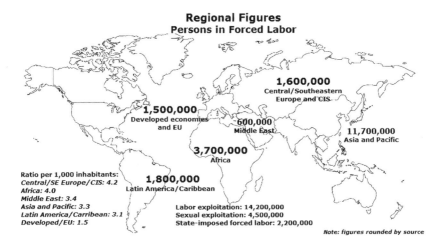

FIGURE 2.1 (*Source:* U.S. Department of State 2012 Trafficking in Persons Report.)

were under investigation by the Justice Department. The 3P approach in the United States consists of the National Human Trafficking Resource Center hotline, which receives 1,000 calls a month about suspected trafficking victims. Also, the Trafficking Victims Protection Act enforces the rule of law and allows global pursuit of traffickers. Encouragingly, twenty-seven states now have their own human-trafficking laws.

Money Laundering

Money laundering is an activity working hand in hand with most profit-generating criminal activities. The individual or group has "dirty money" and must find an opaque way to hide, move, or transform it to protect operations. Identifying methods of money laundering can help eliminate criminal activity, and tracing the money often reveals other criminal operations.

The Financial Action Task Force on Money Laundering (FATF) is an intergovernmental body of thirty-six member countries. FATF's purpose is to develop and promote policies at national and international levels and to combat money laundering and terrorist financing (ML/TF). Through participation in the FATF, INL plays an important role in formulating global anti-money-laundering training, programs, and policies. INL also funds and participates in the Council of Europe's anti-money-laundering organization, MoneyVal, which is comprised of twenty-four member states. MoneyVal is a forum to discuss the implementation of international money-laundering standards and to evaluate effectiveness in implementation.

In their February 2012 report,[43] the FATF money laundering "black-list" of Non-Cooperative Countries or Territories (NCCT) included:

Countermeasures apply to these countries—high-risk and noncooperative:

1. Iran
2. Democratic People's Republic of Korea

Countries Not Committed to an Action Plan—high-risk and noncooperative:

1. Cuba
2. Bolivia
3. Ethiopia
4. Ghana
5. Indonesia
6. Kenya
7. Myanmar
8. Nigeria
9. Pakistan
10. São Tomé and Príncipe
11. Sri Lanka
12. Syria
13. Tanzania
14. Thailand
15. Turkey

The previous NCCT list, published in June 2009, had only five not-committed countries, and the escalation is likely due to a global increase in money-laundering activities leveraging technology such as hosting virtual offshores, fronts, and shells. Many of these countries were criticized for being party to terrorist financing as well as for money-laundering activities. Typically, if another TOC activity is prolific such as human trafficking or drug trafficking, ML/TF activities are prevalent as profiteers need to find ways to store and move massive amounts of money.

Corruption

A corrupt government is one that is susceptible to organized crime and potentially to terrorists. INL plays a major role in efforts to assist countries in combating corruption. In response to growing corruption in the region, the Council of Europe's Group of States against Corruption

EMERGENT THREAT: TRANSNATIONAL CYBER CRIME

The FBI is a leading agency in investigating cyber crimes committed both inside and outside our national borders against U.S. persons, businesses, and critical infrastructures by cyber criminals whose physical presence and operations are often located in multiple countries. Cyber criminal groups have evolved into international enterprises with professional management business models, complex technical communications networks, and highly sophisticated cyber tools suggesting that cyber crime, as an industry, has a future of expansion and sustainable growth. The FBI's legal attaché program, which consists of more than seventy offices overseas, is on the forefront of our nation's efforts to combat transnational organized cyber crime groups.

(GRECO) was established in 1999. Members include thirty-seven European countries and the United States. GRECO provides a forum to discuss and evaluate anticorruption efforts of member states. Recent hot topics include the lack of transparency in political funding (especially in Italy), city administration activities, and strengthening antibribery laws within participating countries. GRECO published an interesting report in 2012 with a look back at their progress and challenges since establishment.[44] Along with helping countries establish and enforce the rule of law, the formation of regional groups such as GRECO is another type of capacity building that will fortify nations and help repel corruption.

LESSONS LEARNED

After almost twenty years of engaging in the transnational organized crime realm, the State Department has four major learning points that serve to inform policy makers and implementers, as well as operators on the ground who are fighting crime and terror.[45]

1. Fighting transnational organized crime takes regional and international cooperation. Promoting the rule of law and fostering international law enforcement cooperation is a preeminent objective of U.S. foreign policy and of the international community of nations. The rule of law and effective law enforcement form a foundation on which commerce and investment, economic development, and respect for human rights can be built. This nation-building activity will also prevent corruption, which fuels organized crime.

2. Interagency coordination is important. The United States provides an excellent model to the world by drawing from the strengths of our various government agencies to fight crime at home. The State Department asserts that the most progress is seen in countries when the various strengths of different agencies can be brought to bear as part of a unified strategy, with a strong recognition and respect for the great expertise shared by U.S. law enforcement officials.

3. A project-based approach to programs focused on integrated country strategies is critical. INL moves aggressively to institute a project-based approach to programs, signing letters of agreement with host governments detailing not only the various projects and funding levels in assistance programs but also the obligations of the host government. This activity reinforces that fighting transnational crime is a shared fight, using shared resources and having shared responsibility.

4. Linking country strategies to crosscutting international strategies is essential. In confronting transnational threats, efforts in different bilateral programs are coordinated so they are focused on areas having the greatest impact in promoting U.S. objectives. For instance, methods of engagement may depend on the type of actor, such as a former enemy, a rogue state, or an unwilling participant. In this sense, country or regional strategies to battle transnational crime must be coordinated with U.S. overarching goals and objectives.

Despite the resources expended by the United States and countries around the world, transnational crime persists, is adaptable, and appears to be growing in scope and scale. The same holds true for international terrorist groups, which have either entrenched and become part of the political process in the host nation, or franchised and scattered to keep their ideology alive.

With crime feeding terror and terror feeding crime, breaking the cycle will take continued international cooperation and an eye on emergent trends and regions.

REFERENCES

1. Louise I. Shelley, "Methods and Motives: Exploring Links between Transnational Organized Crime & International Terrorism," (U.S. Department of Justice, 2005).

2. The White House, *Strategy to Combat Transnational Organized Crime: Addressing Converging Threats to National Security*, July 25, 2011, http://www.whitehouse.gov/sites/default/files/Strategy_to_Combat_Transnational_Organized_Crime_July_2011.pdf.

3. U.S. Senate Committee on Foreign Relations, Subcommittee on European Affairs, *Transnational Organized Crime*, 2003.
4. Michael B. Mukasey, "International Organized Crime" (Center for Strategic and International Studies, 2008).
5. *Transnational Organized Crime*.
6. Federal Bureau of Investigation, "Organized Crime Glossary of Terms," http://www.fbi.gov/about-us/investigate/organizedcrime/glossary
7. Ibid.
8. FBI, "Organized Crime: Eurasian Criminal Enterprises," http://www.fbi.gov/about-us/investigate/organizedcrime/eurasian
9. U.S. Senate Committeee on Foreign Relations, *Combating Transnational Crime and Corruption in Europe*, October 30, 2003.
10. "Yeltsin Assails Underworld for Hurting Reform," Associated Press, 1993.
11. U.S. Senate Committee on Foreign Relations, *Combating Transnational Crime and Corruption in Europe*.
12. U.S. State Department, Trafficking in Persons Report," http://www.state.gov/j/tip/rls/tiprpt/2012/index.htm.
13. FBI, "Organized Crime: Eurasian Criminal Enterprises."
14. FBI, "Organized Crime: Italian Criminal Enterprises," http://www.fbi.gov/about-us/investigate/organizedcrime/italian_mafia
15. Ibid.
16. FBI, "Mafia Takedown: Largest Coordinated Arrest in FBI History," http://www.fbi.gov/news/stories/2011/january/mafia_012011
17. *Combating Transnational Crime and Corruption in Europe*.
18. Mary Jordan, "As Italy's Banks Tighten Lending, Desperate Firms Call on the Mafia," 2009.
19. U.S. General Accounting Office, "Combating Terrorism: Interagency Framework and Agency Program to Address the Overseas Threat," May 2003.
20. United Nations Office on Drugs and Crime, *World Drug Report 2011*, 2011.
21. FBI, "Organized Crime: Balkan Criminal Enterprises," http://www.fbi.gov/about-us/investigate/organizedcrime/balkan
22. *Transnational Organized Crime*.
23. "Organized Crime: Asian Criminal Enterprises," http://www.fbi.gov/about-us/investigate/organizedcrime/asian
24. Jennifer L. Hesterman, "The People's Republic of China vs. Islam," *The Counter Terrorist Magazine*, August/September 2009.
25. FBI, "Organized Crime: African Criminal Enterprises," http://www.fbi.gov/about-us/investigate/organizedcrime/african
26. Louisa Lombard, "Dying for Ivory," *New York Times*, September 21, 2012, http://www.nytimes.com/2012/09/21/opinion/elephants-dying-for-ivory.html?_r=0

27. Raphael Perl and Dick K. Nanto, "North Korean Crime-for-Profit," Congressional Research Service, 2007.
28. Frank Cilluffo, "*The Threat Posed from the Convergence of Organized Crime, Drug Trafficking, and Terrorism*," U.S. House Committee on the Judiciary, December 13, 2000.
29. Perl and Nanto, "North Korean Crime-for-Profit."
30. "Iranian Entity: Hong Kong Electronics," http://www.iranwatch.org/suspect/records/hong-kong-electronics.html
31. U.S. Department of State, *Arresting Transnational Crime* 6, no. 2 (2001).
32. United Nations, *United Nations Convention against Transnational Organized Crime*, http://www.unodc.org/documents/treaties/UNTOC/Publications/TOC%20Convention/TOCebook-e.pdf.
33. Kofi Annan, December 12, 2000.
34. United Nations, "Treaty Collection," http://treaties.un.org/
35. The White House, *Strategy to Combat Transnational Organized Crime*.
36. U.S. Department of Justice, "Attorney General Announces Center to Fight International Organized Crime," May 29, 2009, http://www.justice.gov/opa/pr/2009/May/09-ag-525.html
37. *Combating Transnational Crime and Corruption in Europe*.
38. Council of Foreign Relations, *Experts Group on Transnational Organized Crime (Lyon Group): 40 Recommendations*, http://www.cfr.org/international-crime/experts-group-transnational-organized-crime-lyon-group-40-recommendations/p28086
39. FBI, "International Training," http://www.fbi.gov/about-us/training/ilea
40. OPDAT, Office of Overseas Prosecutorial Development, Assistance and Training, http://www.justice.gov/criminal/opdat/
41. United Nations Office on Drugs and Crime, *World Drug Report 2012*, http://www.unodc.org/documents/data-and-analysis/WDR2012/WDR_2012_web_small.pdf.
42. U.S. Department of State, *Trafficking in Persons Report*, 2012, http://www.state.gov/j/tip/rls/tiprpt/2012/index.htm
43. Financial Action Task Force, "High-Risk and Non-cooperative Jurisdictions," February 16, 2012, http://www.fatf-gafi.org/documents/repository/fatfpublicstatement-16february2012.html
44. GRECO, *Lessons Learnt from the Three Evaluation Rounds (2000–2011)*, http://www.coe.int/t/dghl/monitoring/greco/general/Compendium_Thematic_Articles_EN.pdf.
45. *Combating Transnational Crime and Corruption in Europe*.

CHAPTER 3

Postmodern
Terrorist Groups

Future war will not be waged by armies but by groups whom today we call terrorists, guerillas, bandits, and robbers, but who will undoubtedly hit upon more formal titles to describe them themselves.[1]

—**Martin van Creveld (1991)**

Martin van Creveld's future is here, and the shadowy groups he so astutely predicted are terrorizing and destabilizing the world. Nation-states have found themselves pulled into long, draining conflicts with these actors, unable to eliminate or even diminish the threat.

This chapter will reframe and shift your perspective of modern terrorists and their organizations. What follows is not the standard "Terrorism 101" discussion but a fresh look at the rise and persistence of the threat through a fusion of psychology, sociology, and organization development and human behavior theory. Unlike criminals who are driven by money and greed, terrorists are driven by ideology, which is more difficult to understand and counter. The modern terrorist threat is asymmetric, and as such, countering it requires an asymmetric approach. Traditional means of addressing national security threats, through a combination of diplomatic, economic, or military means, will likely not work against this enemy, which is global and operates without permission of a host nation-state.

Similarly, viewing the threat through one lens will not yield the best assessment. For instance, the various government agencies engaged in this issue have different perspectives, operating techniques, and goals. These differences, if acknowledged and leveraged, will lead to a more powerful solution set. The creation of cross-agency organizations post-9/11 was an attempt to solve this bureaucratic problem by facilitating an environment of trust and information sharing. The success of this organizational redesign is debatable but certainly a step in the right direction.

However, countering this threat will take not just an interagency approach but also interdisciplinary methodology. For instance, we now acknowledge that understanding the mind of a terrorist, his or her unique psychological and sociological framework, is a helpful tool when profiling or identifying possible triggers leading to the terrorist lifestyle. Those studying demographics and migration patterns are learning that poverty, hunger, and a disheartened populace create an environment ripe for planting the radical Islamist ideology, which offers redemption. We shouldn't overlook the importance of "soft-power" engagement with failing states before they turn into a fertile breeding ground for terrorists and criminals who will certainly seize the opportunity to move in unopposed and take control.

A scientific approach to the phenomenon of terrorism is perhaps the purest way of viewing the topic. The very root of the word "terrorism," "terror," naturally provokes an emotional and personal response. Many Americans lost loved ones in acts of extreme violence perpetrated on 9/11 and in the two major combat engagements that were fought in its aftermath. We also remember the horrific scenes broadcast live on the then-new CNN network of Marines being pulled out of the embassy rubble in Lebanon in 1983, and in 1985 when navy diver Robert Stethem's lifeless body was thrown from his plane onto the tarmac of the Beirut airport by Hezbollah hijackers. The bombing of the World Trade Center in 1993 and the Oklahoma City bombing in 1995 again brought the horror of terrorism, foreign and domestic, into our homes, minds, and hearts.

There are many persistent disagreements regarding the rise of modern terrorism, such as those revolving around democracy, capitalism, and Christianity, all of which may make the United States a target … or hegemon and invader. The specific characterization of terrorism is also very difficult to define: criminal act, holy obligation, reaction to oppression, or freedom fighting? Each government agency has its own definition and interpretation, but we intuitively know that, whatever the reason or definition, one thing is clear: terrorism is a threat to our national security. Investigating the terrorism phenomenon through a scientific lens eliminates both individual and institutional bias and removes emotion such as fear and anger. This approach also helps organizations move beyond sunk cost, groupthink, and other unproductive and dangerous decision-making behaviors.

Although underlying issues aggravating the challenges presented by modern terrorism are topics for consideration in the classroom and workplace, this book will simply view terrorism as something present in our society that we want to address, weaken, and ultimately eradicate. Before discussing the major terrorist groups posing the greatest threat, organizational theory will provide the framework for understanding how they are similar and why they would work together and with outside groups to further their goals.

POSTMODERN ORGANIZATIONAL THEORY: THE RISE OF MODERN TERRORISM AND GROUPS

Perhaps organizations are really socially constructed realities that rest as much in the heads and minds of the members as they do in concrete sets of rules and relations.

—Gareth Morgan[2]

I read this comment in Gareth Morgan's original book, *Images of Organization*, in 1995 while in a master's degree program at Johns Hopkins University, studying applied behavioral science and organizational development. I find it a very accurate statement when applied to modern terrorist groups such as al Qaeda, which is less about organizational structure and more about shared ideology. Leveraging the Internet, these socially constructed realities may be virtual, but they are very much "alive."

There seems to be a sense of helplessness around the terrorism topic, with many unanswered "whys." Much time is spent analyzing and dissecting the operational activities of groups, yet very little on the people themselves and why they engage. In order to understand how the postmodern terrorist group forms, evolves, persists, and eventually dies, it is important to peel back the underlying factors and environment. This information will help when the intelligence, law enforcement, and military communities formulate strategic, operational, and tactical plans, so energy and effort is directed at the correct center of gravity.

The following information on postmodern theory builds upon unpublished research accomplished at American Military University in 2009.[3]

Genesis of Postmodern Groups and Thinking

A few decades ago, our world became far more complex with the arrival of the postindustrial era. The industrial age was organized around issues of labor and the production of goods; however, the postindustrial society is organized around the creation of knowledge and the use of information.[4] According to organization theory experts, this new postmodern era is defined in several ways distinguishing it from the last:

Environment:
- Global
- Decentralization of capital with respect to a nation-state
- Fragmentation of markets
- Rise of social movements, diversity

Social structure:
- New organization forms: networks, strategic alliances, and virtual organizations
- Flatter hierarchies

- Influences such as culture
- Loose boundaries between units and functions

Culture:

- Embraces uncertainty and paradox

Physical Structure:

- Reduction in transportation time encourages globalization
- Compression of temporal dimension leading to simultaneity

All organizations are affected by these external environmental factors, no matter the size or purpose for existence. We can certainly see these group distinctions present in the major terrorist groups; for example, al Qaeda, Hezbollah, and FARC all reflect the postmodern organizational structure, culture, and ethos.

Before delving into the specifics of postmodern organizational theory, it is necessary to grasp the fundamentals of the associated thinking process. If you are reading this book, you are a critical thinker who approaches complex problems with an open and inquisitive mind and a balanced, unbiased approach. This mind-set is particularly useful when current solution sets are failing and a fresh perspective is warranted, such as with vexing problems in our world like terrorism. Several types of thinking constitute the postmodern approach and will set the stage for a later discussion of the terrorist groups that most threaten our country.

Upstream Thinking

One type of postmodern reasoning is called "upstream thinking," which is the polar opposite of the more common approach of "downstream thinking." Downstream thinking is the conventional path, or going with the flow—it is, quite simply, a closed, stagnant process. Traces of past patterns of thought constrain originality, and the past serves as a formative influence during the creation of knowledge and "new" realities.[5] Facts are deemed irrefutable, and there are universal truths espoused and accepted. Denial and blind spots develop as the thinker arrives at what is not considered just the right answer but the *only* answer. Quite often, the solutions developed as a result of downstream thinking do not fully address the problem, nor result in its resolution.

Upstream (postmodern) thinking is quite the opposite. Jean-Francois Lyotard (1924–98), a French philosopher and one of the great articulators on this subject, calls postmodern thinking the "collapse of grand narratives." One of his classic statements requires some thought but certainly applies in this world of many unknowns and unknowables: "What I say is true because I prove that it is—but what proof is there my proof is true?"[6] Indeed, before we spend billions of dollars and put lives on the line to mitigate or engage a threat, we need to make sure we have proof that our proof is accurate—in other words, corroboration.

The enemy merely saying they have a capability could easily be a ploy to drag us into a resource-depleting situation in support of their goals. More than ever, intelligence and security analysts must have a sense of what they can presume to know or predict for policy makers to make informed decisions. When a threat is found to be a false flag or a non-issue, better to just store the intelligence gathered and move on before fatal organizational enemies like "sunk cost" and "groupthink" materialize. Naturally, failure is not an option in the WMD (weapons of mass destruction) arena; so if a source states that a dangerous threat exists, we have no choice but to defend ourselves and it is understandable that we would take preemptive measures.

Lyotard was known for his opposition to universal truths and generalities, particularly as applied to organizations. Instead, he focused on micro political alliances and small groups as the most significant changers of society: temporary, loose coalitions of people organized over single issues. Lyotard's ideas are certainly powerful when addressing phenomena such as the rise of radical and terrorist organizations in the late twentieth century. Hezbollah's organizational development will not be the same as FARC's, which will not be the same as al Qaeda's. Accordingly, our tactics to counter modern terrorist groups may be more powerful at the micro level, with the use of psyops, cell by cell, or even person by person.

Epistemology

To understand postmodern organizational theory, it is also critical to embrace the concept of epistemology. Epistemology is a branch of philosophy regarding "how we see" the world combined with ontology, which is "what is known" to exist.[7] A far cry from the industrial era's data-driven outlook of the world, this new view requires the user to have a good understanding of his or her own biases, to be open to the use of symbolism and metaphor when defining and exploring an organization, and most importantly, to tear apart long-held beliefs and assumptions through a process called "deconstruction."

Deconstruction

Postmodernism is all about deconstruction. Deconstruction of theories is the best approach when challenging central assumptions and the aforementioned "grand narratives." By moving against the current, deconstruction allows for challenging paradigms such as groupthink and sunk cost, which typically result in the continued downward spiral of failing nation-state policies and operations. Through deconstruction, we are able to tear apart mainstream theories and open our minds to new ways of approaching the same problem and driving more effectively to the desired end state.

Jacques Derrida (1930–2004), a French philosopher born in Algeria, is known as the father of deconstruction theory. Although his initial deconstruction efforts centered on literature, eventually he applied it to the broader continuum, including the social sciences. In the 1990s, he engaged in deconstruction of political systems, theorizing about a "democracy to come" and thinking about the limitations of existing democracies in the emergent new world order. He developed what he called the "10 Plagues" of postmodernism, some of which were quite prescient: the increase of interethnic wars; "phantom-states" within the world of organized crime; and the spread of weapons of mass destruction to smaller groups, not just nation-states. Similar to other postmodern thinkers, he also believed a structure could not be fully understood without thinking about its genesis, and he was a proponent of the use of metaphor to explore organizations.[8]

Deconstruction's Danger

Modern change is both exciting and terrifying. For instance, the Cold War was "fought" with the intention of expediting the self-destruction and collapse of Communist Russia. Our efforts were realized; walls fell and there were exciting developments such as democratic elections and new religious and speech-related freedoms for the Russian people. Also, there were opportunities for new markets and capital investment from the West. However, this new world also delivered undesirable outcomes in the form of genocide and war. There are ongoing questions about Russia's missing and unsecured nuclear material, corruption is widespread, and the rule of law is weak. We are still dealing with breakaway republics that strain our relations with Russia on the diplomatic and, potentially, the military fronts. The Russian economy was initially decimated, and alcoholism wracked the population, lowering the life expectancy for men by as much as twenty years. The region is still unstable and the future a wild card.

A deconstructed ideology, whether political or religious, must be replaced with something else, and herein lies the dilemma. Much thought must be given to the "new world" that will emerge as a result of our activities, and these realities must be worked into the planning process.

Postmodern Organizational Theory

Postmodern organizational theory is meant to reveal paradoxes, instabilities, and simulacra. It is for the dialectic thinker who is open to seeing new realties and challenging long-held assumptions. The theorists who ushered in the postmodern era certainly fell into this category, and their assertions were not popular nor were they embraced. However, in the dawn of the twenty-first century as we face unprecedented challenges in the world, it is possible to see that these philosophers were really futurists and that many of their dire predictions have come true.

Neo-Marxist Organizational Theory

Karl Heinrich Marx (1818–83) was a German philosopher and revolutionary whose ideas were the foundation for many Communist societies that arose in the twentieth century. Marx argued that the capitalist system of production dissociates laborers from their own fruits of labor. As a result, workers feel alienated, and this alienation gives birth to political actions ("class struggle") against the capitalist sociopolitical and economic superstructure. Practicing Marxists throughout the world based their revolutionary activities on the theory of class struggle.[9] Marxist thought also speaks to the dominant ideology of capitalism and the rights of the worker class to overthrow the "bourgeois."

Although the fall of the Soviet Union challenged some of Marx's beliefs, they still stand as a way of viewing the world and its challenges. Certainly, the radical Islamic ideology rejects the Western world, namely capitalism. We are seeing the rise of terrorist groups from a part of society that is undereducated and underfed and has no dreams for a bright future. The Western culture stands in stark contrast to their world, and this hopelessness and resentment allows susceptibility to the powerful call of jihad, either as a way to be heard or as salvation. An Afghani acquaintance who came to the United States for graduate school and returned to work in the government explained why young men willingly become suicide bombers in his country. He stated, "They would rather die for a cause, than as an 'old' man on a cot." The life expectancy in Afghanistan is forty-eight years for men, so considering a despondent populace with a war-torn past and little sense of hope for a better future, it is somewhat easier to understand their actions. Another factor at play in our modern world is we expect instantaneous results; yet consider that it takes several generations for cultural change to embed into a society.

Neo-Marxist thought builds upon and extends Marx's theories by incorporating other viewpoints such as critical criminology, which attempts to explain modern criminal behavior and also addresses anarchism. The Mexican drug cartels, which we will explore in depth in Chapter 5, are pushing many areas of their country into anarchy as they stake their claim to major cities and trafficking routes. There is no moral, political, or judicial restraint, and murders are heinous in nature, with law enforcement and government leaders brazenly ambushed and executed. There is no fear of the rule of law or potential punishment for actions. Those in power are seduced and corrupted by the vast amount of money promised if they help the traffickers. Understanding this new type of criminal, as well as the growing anarchism in society, is paramount to addressing these potential threats to our country.

Two main theories that emanated from neo-Marxist thought, those of hegemony and ideology, are absolutely present in the growing instability in our world and the pressing threat of modern terrorism.

Hegemony "Hegemony" is derived from the Greek word *hēgemōn*, meaning leader. However, the concept of hegemony has evolved through the years into one of domination and is now widely accepted to explain the dominance of one social group over another. It is important to note that the hegemon acquires some degree of consent from the subordinate, as opposed to dominance purely by force.[10] This is facilitated through *false consciousness*, as labeled by Marx. False consciousness occurs in a social structure when the oppressed actually create oppression by treating the oppressors with deference. They legitimize the oppressor's activity by serving their interests; thus the hegemon assumes greater authority and power over the people.

The terms "first world" and "third world" quickly categorize groups into the dominant and the submissive, the "haves" and "have-nots." We are now just starting to understand that by addressing cultural problems such as poverty, hunger, and education, we might win the hearts and minds of those who would otherwise rebel against the hegemony through violent acts. As we watch the disappearance of the middle class during the current global financial crisis, it would seem the world is divided into those who are successful and those who are struggling, with no group in between that is stagnant, meaning content. The strugglers certainly have animosity towards the "haves," and this resentment can easily be preyed upon by terrorist groups searching for new recruits.

To be fair, Marxist theory doesn't explain the struggles found in the Western world in the 1960s and 1970s from "first world" middle- and upper-class citizens. For example, there were extensive and often violent demonstrations in Western Europe by students and workers. Of course we had our own issues at home with citizens protesting the Vietnam War, a grassroots campaign turning into an extensive antigovernment movement resulting in the end of the war. Social scientists postulate that when expectation outstrips achievement—regardless of the economic status of the discouraged group—it generates frustration. This collective frustration turns to anger and, finally, to violence.[11] Therefore we should expect not only the "third world" people to become terrorists but middle- and upper-class citizens as well.

Ideology Marx believed hegemony is also achieved through cultural domination by a powerful and formidable tool: ideology. As previously discussed, hegemony is fueled by ideology. Ideology is visionary theorizing;

a systematic body of concepts especially about human life or culture; the manner or the content of thinking characteristic of an individual, group, or culture; and the integrated assertions, theories, and aims that constitute a sociopolitical program.[12] But most importantly, an ideology is a powerful tool that can induce a tide of change quickly in society.

Marx's idea of ideology can be summed up in a quote to describe his followers: "They do not know it, but they are doing it."[13] This gives ideology almost a mystical quality, as if it is more as an illusion than reality, something we witness with modern terrorist groups with radical religious or revolutionary political ideologies. An ideology is closely tied to the culture of an organization and can be the glue holding a loosely organized or morphing organization together. Once espoused and adhered to by the group, it is difficult to dislodge an ideology; the believer will simply not accept contrary arguments, even if presented with irrefutable facts. An ideology of this nature has been described as "in you more than yourself."[14] The unique power of radical religious ideology cannot be underestimated, as it drives sane people to strap on a suicide vest or young American boys with bright futures to leave their middle-class homes to take up the cause of al Qaeda thousands of miles away.

Diagnostic Tools of Postmodernism

Along with postmodern theory and thinking comes a unique set of tools we may cross-apply to view, diagnose, and change any organization, including a terrorist group.

Systems Theory

Systems thinking and theory is a postmodern approach to problem solving in organizations. This approach views "problems" as part of an overall system. Often, we react only to outcomes or events—a reaction that potentially contributes to further development of the undesired issue or problem.[15] A modern example could be a displaced populace striking back at those who displaced them. The basic needs of the group's members are not being met—using Maslow's hierarchy, say food, shelter, and/or safety. Out of a sense of helplessness, with no way to legitimately voice their concerns and in the ultimate cry for help, the displaced group mounts an attack on the displacer. The more powerful group retaliates with disproportionate force, in the hopes of silencing the displaced group. The displaced group suffers death and injuries, loss of housing and food, exacerbating their inability to meet basic needs and pushing them back down the needs hierarchy. Eventually, this causes them to lash out again, and the cycle is repeated. Several decades-old conflicts in the world are stuck in this endless, unproductive cycle.

Using systems theory, by including the root problem of lack of basic human needs as a situation that is part of the system and a reason for the lashing out, the displacer might instead address those issues with the refugees or displaced persons, in turn preventing violence. Naturally, there is resistance to this approach; as a group and its members move up the hierarchy of needs, the situation becomes more complex as self-actualization is sought. There is fear the displaced group will grow in power, so it is far easier to simply keep them at the bottom of the pyramid, blaming them for the situation. This is a dangerous dance in the modern world; desperate times call for desperate actions, and access to WMD or the ability to lash out with large weapons and sophisticated bombs is not beyond the reach of separatist and terrorist groups in many regions. Liaising with other groups could exponentially further the agenda.

Another way to use the systems view is to question how change in a seemingly unrelated subsystem can impact the targeted group. For instance, how could a fundamental change in Western media's reporting of events impact the power of a terrorist group? Greatly, if you consider terrorism as a major marketing campaign, with fear being the product. Consider social psychologist Kurt Lewin's Force Field Analysis, a system for predicting the motivated behavior of an individual in his or her "life space." He defined the life space as an individual's perceived reality based on the many factors at play. In terms of the threat of terrorism, it is important to emphasize the word "perceived" for this analysis. For instance, if a man believes he is being followed down a dark alley, this is his *perceived reality* and whether a pursuer actually exists is irrelevant. The man will suffer physiological changes associated with fear and panic, and his "fight-or-flight" instinct will involuntarily take over. Factors feed our perceived reality of the threat of terrorism such as press coverage, panic induced by quick spread of false information through social media, and if the terrorists are savvy enough, a psyops campaign to make us believe something that isn't true. In systems theory, recognizing that the system is living and that changes on one side of the equation can produce wanted (or unwanted) changes to the other is critical. Entities on either side of the equation have control.

Environmental Theory

With relation to groups, postmodern theory holds that it is not valuable to view them as individual entities, without giving credence to the way their interaction with the environment has allowed them to form, grow, and prosper. In this theory, interaction with the environment, or what lies outside of the organization, is critical to the success and survival of an organization.

The dominant perspective in postmodern organizational analysis, the contingency approach, asserts that understanding the environment is the key. Why? Organizations will change and morph based on the environment. In the words of Gareth Morgan, "organizations are open systems that need careful management to satisfy and balance internal needs and to adapt to environmental circumstances."[16] The organization cannot be separated from its environment, since it makes up the environment, along with all other groups. An organization cannot be viewed as an island but as part of a constellation of factors having distinct impact on its viability.

Symbolic Theory

Finally, postmodern thinkers embrace the use of symbolism to analyze organizations, particularly through the use of metaphor. In Morgan's book entitled *Images of Organization*, he uses metaphor to describe organizations, for instance likening them to organisms, brain, and machines. He asserts that metaphor is a very helpful tool when viewing one element through the lens of another, yielding fresh thoughts about the organization's structure and challenges and solution sets.

According to Morgan, many organizational problems rest in our ways of thinking. In line with postmodern thinking, this allows the viewer to take ownership and realize that perhaps his or her way of viewing the situation has contributed to the formation of the problem at hand. Imagine the solution set that might come from a critical analysis of our country's actions in the last thirty years and how they may have contributed to the rise of modern terrorism. A fascinating college class might be entitled "Failures in National Security," to encourage critical and dialectic thinking. The use of metaphor is "critical thinking that encourages us to understand and grasp the multiple meanings of situations and manage contradiction and paradox, rather than to pretend they don't exist."[17]

Postmodern Theory and the Rise of Modern Terrorism

Now, we can clearly see how the early organizational theorists had a substantial impact on the way we view organizations and their members. Postmodern theories and the associated thinking process build on this foundation and provide a remarkable means for understanding and diagnosing the rise of revolutionary and terrorist organizations in the latter twentieth century. This original model encapsulates the theories and perspectives studied thus far and how they relate to the rise and persistence of modern terrorist organizations (see Figure 3.1).

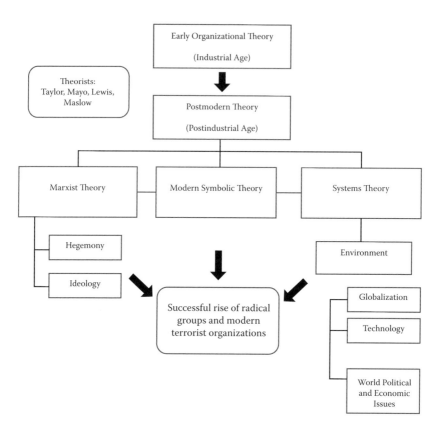

FIGURE 3.1   Organizational Theories and the Rise of Modern Terrorist Organizations (Hesterman 2012).

Final Thoughts on Postmodernism

Why are we using postmodern theory to address the phenomenon of terrorism? In this protracted fight against terror, it may be useful to deconstruct theories proving inadequate against this uncommon and asymmetric enemy. Perhaps accepting ambiguity as part of the equation is helpful; although many are uncomfortable with the unknown, it is the world in which we live and the realm in which we must operate. We likely won't know everything or have a perfect data set with which to make critical decisions, but we have to move forward operationally. The successful raid on the bin Laden compound is the perfect example of balancing what is known with what isn't known but can be surmised based on history, culture, and prior behaviors. Sometimes, to look forward we must look back.

Ultimately, we are responsible for the realities we create and inherit. Perhaps this is the greatest lesson taught by the postmodern theorists. By exploring our role in the formation, growth, and persistence of terror organizations, we can more effectively engage and potentially enable the eradication of the current threat. Most importantly, through continued introspection, we may protect our country and citizens from the rise of new nation-state and asymmetric threats.

MODERN TERRORISM'S ROOTS

The era of modern terrorism began on July 22, 1968, with the hijacking of an airliner traveling from Rome to Tel Aviv by the Popular Front for the Liberation of Palestine, or the PFLP, whose goal is the establishment of a Palestinian state. For five weeks, twenty-one passengers and eleven crew members were held hostage in Algiers as the world watched and learned about the PFLP cause. Eventually, the terrorists released the hostages in exchange for sixteen Arab prisoners held in Israeli jails. This was not the first hijacking of an airliner; however, the PFLP's brazen use of the tactic to draw attention to its political cause, and concessions given to the hijackers, ignited the phenomenon of modern terrorism as we know it today.[18] The State Department has designated fifty-one groups as foreign terrorist organizations (FTOs) that are actively engaged in some type of terrorist activity threatening our national security; this list has steadily grown throughout the last decade. The PFLP remains on the list and is thriving, conducting attacks forty-five years after its brazen hijacking that shocked the world.

A quick scan of the FTO list (see the Appendix) illustrates the variety of worldwide terrorist threats, from dormant groups such as Aum Shinryko/Aleph in Japan to the resurgent Irish Republican Army. Also included are separatist groups operating in only one country, such as ETA in Spain, to vast organizations such as al Qaeda and its numerous affiliates around the world. Missing from the list but providing an equally vexing and emerging national security threat are global organized crime syndicates and Mexican cartel groups, which exhibit brutal tactics and are equipped like small armies.

What Is Terrorism?

Terrorism is different from other crimes. Through acts of extreme violence, terrorists seek to advance an agenda, be it political change or religious domination. Terrorism is a crime but does not lend itself to the same disincentives other crimes do. The threat of prison or even death does not deter. We also must be careful in our approach due to a paradox when dealing with modern terrorists; the more brutal and oppressive we are, the more we make them martyrs to be emulated by others.[19] For drug-trafficking groups like FARC, money is the ideology and they will eliminate anything and everyone getting in the way. However, FARC also seeks political change and gain, liaising with leaders of other countries and infiltrating the political system of multiple countries, which is why the group is on the FTO list and included in this chapter.

Terrorism is a complex phenomenon. There is no one root cause fueling terrorist activity; if there were, we could simply fix the issue by addressing the aggravators and dissuading other groups from forming. Although the "hearts and minds" strategy is important to pursue, focusing solely on factors such as poverty and illiteracy fails to explain why groups with far greater grievances do not resort to terrorism.[20] Of course we should continue to address these root causes while addressing how to eliminate terrorist groups and understand the propensity for their formation, but we must continue to study the ambiguity of these groups and myriad factors involved in their formation.

Terrorism's Target

Everything that makes democracies great makes them vulnerable to this enemy. Terrorism is much more effective against democracies than closed societies such as North Korea and China. For instance, consider the free press. Terrorism is an elaborate marketing campaign, and publicity adds to the legitimacy of the group and furthers its goals of creating fear. Democracies believe in freedom of information, providing the perfect tool both for group member motivation and recruitment and to garner sympathy. Technology plays a role, since unfiltered news is often generated and distributed within seconds of an event taking place through Twitter, Facebook, and other social media outlets, in addition to traditional news channels. A closed society wouldn't provide the terrorist organization this type of advantage.

Also, closed societies would not exercise restraint when retaliating against terrorist groups and their members, taking swift, brutal countermeasures to suppress activity. In a democracy, we believe one is innocent until proven guilty in a court of law. We provide due process and legal representation to even the most heinous bad actors in society and give them a chance to present their case to a jury of their peers for decision. For conviction, the law requires proof beyond reasonable doubt, something difficult to come by when it comes to the arrest of sleeper cell members and would-be terrorists; if they haven't pulled the trigger on an operation, they may receive light sentences and return to society quickly and without mandated rehabilitation. Again, this aspect of the judicial system in Western culture is attractive to terrorist groups.

When a terrorist is identified and detained in our country, innocent family members are not a target for retaliation; however, in other societies their homes may be razed and they are punished and sometimes killed. Finally, the ease of moving about in a democracy undetected is attractive to terrorists. Our country lacks internal checkpoints and is heterogeneous, with a broad demographical base. This allows terrorists to more easily move across our borders and then just disappear into society. In short, our democracy is fertile ground for terrorists.

Alan Dershowitz, who wrote the book *Why Terrorism Works* (Yale University Press, 2002), proposes that amoral societies would engage in several (arguably successful) ways to stop the terrorist threat. For example, they would completely control the media's reporting on terror incidents and simultaneously use the media for disinformation operations; monitor all citizen communications; criminalize "advocacy" of the terrorist group through inciting speech; restrict movement within the country with layered identification checkpoints and even segregation of certain demographics within the country; carry out collective punishment on family members and even entire villages to dissuade future activities; and initiate preemptive attacks against the group. Naturally, this does not sound like a course of action likely taken by the United States, due to our protections under the Constitution and innate sense of justice our country. However, consider the impact any of these activities, taken alone or in total, would have in our fight against terror. Is there a gray area? The events of 9/11 led to enhanced law enforcement activity, such as more extensive surveillance and wiretapping powers under the USA PATRIOT Act. The resulting skepticism was warranted, as we certainly must safeguard our constitutional protections and closely monitor any erosion of our civil liberties since this is a slippery slope. However, in the asymmetric fight against an unpredictable, dangerous, and adaptable enemy, we may not be able to have it both ways when dealing with modern terrorist groups. We clearly need a corresponding modern and flexible solution set. To summarize, the very ideals constituting a democracy are leveraged and exploited by terrorist groups ... and are a primary reason we are struggling to contain the threat.

The New Anatomy of a Terrorist Group

A contemporary definition of a *terrorist group* is "a collection of individuals belonging to a nonstate entity that uses terrorism to achieve its objectives."[21] State-sponsored terror is a dying concept, as groups form around ideology and leverage Internet technology and communication to form, train, fund, and execute operations. Similarly, the structure of terrorist groups is no longer hierarchical. Groups used to have a distinct leader, chain of command, directors of training, logistics, and operations, and a financial arm. The emergent terror group or supercell can be flat, fluid, or rigid as needed for the situation. The military tenet of decimation no longer works; taking out the leader and the top 10 percent of the organization will not lead to the demise of the group. We can no longer see the group in terms of organizational charts; think of the modern terrorist organization as a shared reality.

Terrorist groups differ in goals. Some international groups are driven by religious ideology, such as al Qaeda and Aum Shinryko/Aleph. History bears out that religious groups have longer staying power than others[22] and are also more violent, even apocalyptic in nature. Other groups have political ideology, such as Basque Fatherland and Liberty (ETA) in Spain and the Continuity Irish Army (CIRA) in Northern Ireland, both of which seek government changes within the nation-state. Some terrorist groups were initially driven by political goals, and the ideology shifted to money, pushing behavior more toward criminal acts. This is true with the major narco-trafficking group from Colombia, Revolutionary Armed Forces of Colombia (FARC), which will be discussed later in the chapter. Domestic terror groups can be left-wing with a revolutionary socialist agenda and the self-proclaimed protectors of the populace against capitalism and "U.S. imperialism." Other domestic groups are considered right-wing, such as white racial supremacists or extreme Christian groups. Also on the table are extreme groups seeking animal rights or hoping to protect the environment; however, instead of voicing their concerns in a lawful manner, they resort to violent activities resulting in destruction of property and even murder. Groups also vary in lethality, size, and scope. Some are very structured with one leader and a leadership hierarchy, such as ETA. Others have franchised and are basically leaderless, such as al Qaeda.

A 2008 RAND study entitled *How Terrorist Groups End* found that there is no statistical correlation between the duration of a terrorist group and ideological motivation, economic conditions, regime type, or the breadth of terrorist goals.[23] Then what are the commonalities? How can we force their demise? All terrorist groups have some type of organizational structure. They have goals and a distinct culture; they must communicate; they plan and they execute. Terrorist groups all consist of human beings who exhibit certain behaviors, are motivated to join/stay/perform, and act as members of a group. Collectivism is at play, where the group gives the members their sense of identity and demands loyalty for the sense of implied security. Therefore it is possible to view each group through same lens—the organizational-science lens.

Life Cycle Study

Organizations have historically been studied through the lens of organizational life cycles (OLCs). The theory is that all postmodern organizations move through the same continuums, making their life cycle somewhat predictive in nature. The study of terrorist group life cycles is certainly of interest to those interested in disruption activities and the point where groups will mature and start working together to further individual goals. A landmark article was published in the 1972 *Harvard Business Review* by Larry Greiner, a professor of organizational behavior at the Harvard Business School.[24] He used five organizational growth phases to describe modern organizations: growth through creativity; growth through direction; growth through delegation; growth through coordination; and growth through collaboration. Each growth stage encompassed two phases:

1. The term "evolution" is used to describe prolonged periods of growth where no major upheaval occurs in organization practices.
2. The term "revolution" is used to describe those periods of substantial turmoil in the organization's life.

He updated the work in 1999, resulting in the *evolution and revolution* model. His study was ahead of his time and viewed as dialectical and deconstructive in nature; therefore, his work embodies postmodern thinking and fits this discussion. There are various stages Greiner believes every organization will experience with a period of evolution and revolution. Notably, as the group ages, after experiencing turmoil in leadership, finding direction, and maintaining control, it will have a crisis of internal growth, forcing it to collaborate with other groups. Later, in the final stage, the organization will form alliances from these collaborations but after a period of calm will suffer a crisis of identity. Viewing the modern terrorist group through the lens of Greiner's model allows for a unique solution set and areas to actively engage and disrupt, as well as understanding that groups will eventually work together, despite dissimilar ideologies.

Another perspective comes from Dipak Gupta in his book *Understanding Terrorism and Political Violence* (Routledge, 2008), where he tackled the subject of terrorist groups and corresponding life cycles. By using a using unique combination of economics and social science, Gupta studies al Qaeda, Hamas, the IRA, and the Naxalites in India and analyzes the groups through the stages of birth, growth, transformation, and demise. Illustrating "upstream thinking," the author also examines the role of the authorities in promoting, maintaining, and suppressing violent dissent.

Much more research in this area is warranted. Is it possible, through extensive study of the life cycle of terrorist groups and analysis of their behaviors, barriers to growth, and reasons for escalation, splintering, or decline, to create a risk management model providing analysts a way to predict possible courses of action? Can we then create a tool for intelligence analysts to better assess and frame the problem, and for operators to better understand when and how to infiltrate a group in order to destroy it? It might also be possible to create a value system addressing risk tolerance for different phases of the operational life cycle. This product would be of use to both policy makers and those at the operational level.

Terrorist Group Members

After covering the structure and life cycle of the modern terrorist group itself, let's examine the individuals who make up these groups. After intense study of modern terrorist activity and having taught a psychology of terrorism course at the university level for four years to first responders and intelligence analysts, I have come to the conclusion that terrorist group members are very rational actors. There is no conclusive evidence that terrorists are abnormal or psychotic or have personality disorders. Consider that in the last few years, foiled terror plots included rational actors who were educated, middle- or upper-class, and dedicated to their jobs and families. Statements from those closest to the terrorist suspect are usually very telling and typically indicate no suspicion that the person they knew and loved for years would load a jeep with explosives and park it in Times Square, or fly to an unfamiliar country and detonate their suicide vest. Therefore, for purposes of this chapter, assume that individual (and thus group) behavior is similar among all organizations, including terror groups.

Behavior

Individuals are drawn to certain groups, feeling a unique connection at some level. Perhaps there is a demographic similarity among the membership such as religious belief or shared collective experience. Or the group's goals may be the individual's goals as well, thus making it a vehicle for success. Individual behavior and traits also imprint on the entire group, so with the admission of a new member, the group changes in subtle but perhaps important ways. Viewing a terrorist group through a construct made popular by organizational behavior experts Szilagyi and Wallace is extremely valuable.[25] Group members bring their biographic background (including any "baggage"), abilities, intelligence, expectations, and personality into the organization. In terms of structure and culture, the group has norms, roles for members, and a level of cohesion. Size plays a role in a group's behavior as well as its composition. In terms of performance, there are several possible outcomes; members are either satisfied or there could be turnover and even desertion.

Note that every variable and dynamic in a terrorist group could be specifically targeted in order to change the group's overall behavior and course. Adapting standard organizational behavior theory as it pertains in the workplace to terrorist behavior yields a new set of truths:

1. Behavior in terrorist groups is caused.
2. Behavior in terrorist groups is purposive and goal directed.
3. Behavior of the terrorist group is learned.
4. Individuals differ, but a terrorist group will have a shared set of values and characteristics.

Understanding group dynamics could yield new solution sets.

Motivation

What motivates an individual to join a terrorist group? Jessica Stern, a noted Harvard professor and terrorism expert, has interviewed numerous members of terrorist organizations all over the world. When discussing al Qaeda, Stern notes: "Over time, however, militants have told me, terrorism can become a career as much as a passion. Leaders harness humiliation and anomie and turn them into weapons. Jihad becomes addictive, militants report, and with some individuals or groups—the 'professional' terrorists—grievances can evolve into greed: for money, political power, status, or attention."[26]

The area of terrorist motivation is ripe for further exploration. Before taking up the cause, the terrorist group member was influenced. What trigger flipped the switch from "off" to "on" and turned a father, son, student, or professor into a jihadist? By exploring this central question, we may develop a type of preemptive deprogramming operation preventing the spread of the radical Islamist ideology or supplanting a counternarrative, pushing the continuum toward our goals.

There are three general schools of thought on what motivates an individual toward group membership, regardless of the type of organization:

1. Instinct theory: the behavior is a function of a person's instinct rather than activities that are conscious, purposeful, and rational.
2. Reinforcement theory: a person's current behavior is strongly affected by knowledge of consequences or rewards for past behaviors—this is learned behavior.
3. Cognitive theory: behavior is not as much a function of consequences as it is a person's future belief and expectations.

Looking at mature groups/corporations such as Hezbollah in total can be overwhelming when it comes to engagement and disruption. However, excavating the group down to the individual members and their motivation could be significant. In postmodern society, micro-level changes are proving to be much more powerful than those taken at the macro level.

Culture

Contrary to what many assume, a terrorist group is a not a unique culture. Similar to religious cults or college alumni associations, there is a force at play that is described as "collectivism." When the group gives the member his or her sense of identity and demands (or subtly elicits) loyalty for the sense of security imparted, collectivism emerges. Organizational culture is the personality of the group, comprising the assumptions, values, norms, and tangible signs or artifacts of organization members and their behaviors.[27] Terrorist groups may each have a unique culture; however, they share identifying attributes, all of which can be targeted by disruptive activities. Culture can also be "managed" and driven by external forces. By altering norms and values, the culture and behavior of an organization will change.

These are the four focus areas when addressing the culture of a terrorist group:

1. Assumptions. What are the assumptions of the particular group? How do we trump those by injecting something unexpected, something that will change the culture and inject doubt? What cognitive biases are shared by the group in terms of distortion in perception, faulty logic, and the way members perceive reality? How can these be exploited to unravel the group from the inside?
2. Values. What is the value system of the group? Is it an open system or closed? How can we change what they value?
3. Norms. Norms are the acceptable behavior in a group. Elton Mayo, noted Australian organization theorist, found that group norms are strong enough to override individual behavior or externally imposed norms. What are the terrorist group norms? Are there discouraged behaviors that could lead to an uprising or fracturing within of the group?
4. Artifacts. Culture develops as an ethos created and sustained by social processes, images, symbols, and ritual. To study artifacts we must contextualize or try to understand them from inside the group. How does the group identify itself? What are important places, buildings, and dates? Are there certain tattoos, symbols, or colors representing the group?

Subcultures in a group can be a powerful force. It may be possible to build coalitions and countercultures within the overarching group, subcultures that divide loyalties. Further, postmodern theory encourages the *fragmentation perspective* to deconstruct the view that a group's culture is naturally harmonious and everyone subscribes. Fractures are present in all groups, and in terrorist groups they can be exploited to start the internal unraveling process. Therefore, when viewing a terrorist group culture, we should look for ways organizations are inconsistent, ambiguous, multiplicitous, and in a constant state of flux.[28]

Environment

As previously discussed, postmodern theory holds the environmental relationship as key to the forming and operational "health" of an organization. When it comes to terrorist groups, we should ask several significant questions such as "who and what controls the environment?" and "how and where can we engage to alter or control factors and change outcomes?" Figure 3.2 shows one way to view the environment surrounding a terrorist organization.

At the center, we have the terrorist organization itself as the primary actor. The network, in this case, would be partners, competitors, and suppliers, possibly including other terrorist and criminal groups. Terrorist groups are increasingly network organizations; no longer standing alone, this type of organization replaces vertical communications and control relationships with lateral relationships.[29] A networking structure emerges when operations are fragmented, when time is compressed, and as the operational base is penetrated or destroyed, with funding and logistics trails cut off. This forces the group to change course, and work with another for survival. Therefore the nexus of groups may provide opportunity for engagement where none existed before.

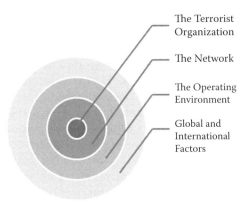

The Terrorist Organization

The Network

The Operating Environment

Global and International Factors

FIGURE 3.2 Concentric circles of a terrorist organization (Hesterman 2009).

The operating environment could be anything from the town or village the group operates within, to nation-state sponsorship, to the Internet. Finally, the outermost ring indicates the strategic-level environment consisting of global and international factors, which both fuel and frustrate the organization. Applying postmodern thinking, the larger environment includes us. With introspection, we must analyze what impact our presence and activities have on the group.

Still focused on the outer ring, it is obvious that globalization has fueled the modern terrorist group, which operates internationally. The ease of transportation and communication has allowed formerly small, local groups to expand into multinational corporations. Technological advances have fueled nefarious groups as they make, move, and store money through nonbanks and prepaid cards. Terrorist groups have websites to communicate their ideology and recruit new members from around the globe. Any changes in this part of the model will likely influence the group itself, thus an important factor to consider when addressing how the environment writ large has fueled the rise and sustainability of these groups and could conversely do more to *control* their growth and viability. Consider the potential impact of international laws on every subsequent ring leading up to the group itself, perhaps regarding e-commerce or exploitation of the Internet. There is much opportunity in this outer ring for powerful multinational organizations such as NATO, the European Union (EU), and the United Nations (UN) to have great impact on the environment serving as the lifeblood of a terrorist organization.

How Terrorist Groups End

After discussing the rise of modern terror group and how they thrive and persist, it is interesting and important to consider their demise. The 2008 RAND study by Seth Jones and Martin Libicki entitled *How Terrorist Groups End* analyzes 648 former terrorist groups from the period 1968 to 2006 and how they terminated. The purpose of the study was to assess implications for countering terrorist groups, specifically al Qaeda. The RAND research is also of interest to those engaging in small, incremental disruptive tactics that can have powerful overarching effect.

Of the 648 groups active at some point between 1968 and 2006, a total of 268 completely ended during the period. Another 136 groups splintered, and 244 remain active today. The study found that there are four major ways in which terrorist groups end: policing, politicization, military force, or victory. Figure 3.3 summarizes the results.

The research found that military force was effective in destroying only 7 percent of the groups. Victory was achieved in 10 percent of the

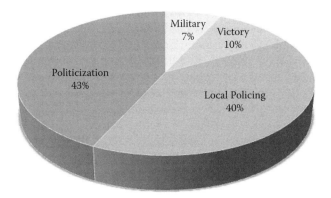

Data represents 268 groups, excluding from the original 648 groups those still
active (244 groups) and those ending by splintering, since members still actively
use terrorism (136 groups) Source: Rand, 2008

FIGURE 3.3   Data taken from RAND Study: *How Terrorist Groups
End.*

groups, and transition to a political group ended 43 percent of the organizations, due to narrowing of goals and restriction of operating area
to a nation-state. In terms of controllable factors, local policing is likely
to be the most effective strategy and resulted in 40 percent of groups
ending. The study found that indigenous police and intelligence services
have better training and information to penetrate and disrupt terrorist
organizations than the military or other federal government agencies.
They are the primary arm of the government focused on internal security
matters, have "boots on the ground," have a better understanding of the
threat environment, and are in a position to leverage human intelligence.
The State Department activities mentioned in Chapter 2 regarding building police forces and rule of law in unstable countries impacts not only
transnational organized crime but terrorist organizations as well.

The study also found that religiously motivated terrorist groups took
longer to eliminate than other groups but rarely achieved their objectives;
no religiously motivated group achieved victory during the period studied. Also, size significantly determined a group's fate. Groups exceeding 10,000 members were victorious more than 25 percent of the time,
while victory was rare for groups below 1,000 members.[30] Although this
appears to bode well for the failure of al Qaeda, adding together all of
the terrorist groups in the world sharing the radical Islamist ideology,
the number far exceeds 10,000.

To conclude before moving on to a study of the three groups posing the
greatest threat to our world, we are not helpless. There is much we know

and can explore regarding terrorists and their groups, beyond dissecting their operations and logistics activities. However, successfully fighting terrorism will take much more than military force. We must also harness the power of the soft sciences to understand the terrorist group life cycle from birth to growth, persistence, and death. By bringing a myriad of competencies and experts to the table, we can possibly predict the course and future actions of these complex and ideology-driven organizations.

INTERNATIONAL TERRORIST GROUPS: THE "BIG 3"

The fifty-one FTOs on the State Department's list of organizations threatening U.S. national security are listed in the Appendix. Although the groups share many characteristics, as explored earlier in the chapter they do not all pack the same punch. For example, the Shining Path in Peru does not threaten the homeland but are a threat to visiting U.S. citizens and also are engaged in transnational crime impacting the country—narco-trafficking. Other FTOs have already struck on our soil and have caused massive destruction of our facilities and death of our citizens abroad. For purposes of nexus studies, al Qaeda and its splinter groups, Hezbollah, and FARC, are the three international groups that alone, or working together, present the greatest threat to our national security.

AL QAEDA AND AFFILIATES

"We remain at war with al Qaeda."

—NCTC director Matthew Olson
July 27, 2012[31]

Perhaps the most vexing and persistent threat to our national security is al Qaeda, which has morphed from a centralized operation to a high-performing, decentralized, leaderless organization. Although AQ leader Osama bin Laden was killed in 2011, his death did not result in the dissolution of al Qaeda: the radical ideology serves as the glue holding this organization and its myriad affiliates together. After we destroyed much of their home base in Afghanistan, AQ has splintered and franchised with global cells, which train, equip, and fund-raise independently. These cells also do not require the "permission" of a leader to carry out a mission; the battle cry has been issued, the original fatwas remain in force, and the target is the Western world. An expert on modern terror networks, Marc Sageman, calls this a "bunch of guys" hypothesis; members reinforce their group identities through the adherence to an ideological orientation and a strong bond of mutual commitment.[32]

Like many emergent postmodern organizations, al Qaeda and its offshoots are leaderless yet high performing. In the book *The Starfish and the Spider: The Unstoppable Power of Leaderless Organizations*, the authors assert that the reason al Qaeda originally grew in power and persists is because bin Laden never assumed a traditional leadership role of the organization.[33] The book uses a very applicable illustration, discussing how the Apache Indians managed to hold off the Spanish Army for over 200 years. They had no chief with positional power; they consistently chose and followed a *Nant'an*, a spiritual and cultural leader who led by example and had no coercive power: the Apaches followed him because they *wanted* to, not because they had to. If a *Nant'an* died, another would fill the void. Geronimo was a *Nant'an*, and although he was never in an official leadership position, he had power and many wanted to take up arms and fight with him and on his behalf after his death. The Spanish Army also failed to defeat the Apaches due to their organizational structure; power and operations were both decentralized. Raids on Spanish settlements could be planned, organized, and executed in three different places simultaneously. Attacks by the Spanish over time made the Apaches even stronger; they learned, adapted, and became even more dispersed and decentralized to frustrate their enemy. Interestingly, the operation to kill bin Laden was dubbed "Geronimo," perhaps a nod to his mystique. The Apaches prevailed after the death of Geronimo, and al Qaeda lives on post-bin Laden.

The Ideology

Much has been written and discussed about the operational tactics of al Qaeda. However, as the group morphs and persists, a lesser studied and potential more valuable topic is their glue and fuel, the radical ideology. We start with Sayyid Qutb, who was born in Egypt and came to the United States for college in the late 1940s and early 1950s. His experiences as a college student in Colorado led to a hatred of the Western way of life; he believed that the society was amoral, and women were promiscuous and too independent and outspoken. Upon graduation and return to Egypt, he joined the Muslim Brotherhood and quickly became a respected leader. In 1952, Egypt's pro-Western government was overthrown by a group called the Free Officers Movement led by Gamal Abdel Nasser. Nasser initially appeared to court Qutb and the Brotherhood, yet was secretly plotting its demise. Once Qutb realized Nasser's intentions, he became an outspoken, forceful, and violent opponent of the ruling government, inciting the Muslim Brotherhood to action. The Nasser government cracked down on the dissidents, and Qutb was arrested in 1954, jailed, and routinely tortured. Eventually, he was left alone in prison and allowed some freedoms, including the ability to write. A prolific and powerful writer who masterfully used imagery and poetry to make his point, Qutb's two most important works were created during this period: *Fi Zilal al-Qur'an (In the Shade of the Qur'an)* and a manifesto of his view of Islam, *Ma'alim fi-l-Tariq (Milestones)*. Both of these works are still widely read and revered in the Islamist community and are recommended reading for all who want to understand the seeds of radicalism. The Egyptian government released Qutb from prison in 1964 by request of the Iraqi government; he immediately reconnected with the Muslim Brotherhood to plan the assassination of the Egyptian prime minister and overthrow of the ruling government. He was rearrested and executed in August 1966.

However, the damage was done: Qutb's timeless writings were his legacy, inspiring a school of thought called "Qutbism." Following Qutb's death, his brother, Muhammad, conducted lectures at King Abdulaziz University in Jeddah, Saudi Arabia, events regularly attended by Osama bin Laden. Qutb mentored Ayman al-Zawahiri, who went on to become a member of the Egyptian Islamic Jihad, mentor to bin Laden, and de facto leader of al Qaeda after bin Laden's death. Qutb's writings inspired the latest generation of radical Islamists; while imprisoned in Yemen, Anwar al-Awlaki would read hundreds of pages a day of Qutb's works, stating he was "so immersed with the author I would feel Sayyid was with me in my cell speaking to me directly."[34] Later, al-Awlaki himself would inspire domestic terror attacks in the United States such as the Ft. Hood shooting and the Christmas Day "underwear bomber," Umar Farouk Abdulmutallab.

Rise of bin Laden and al Qaeda

As a student of this subject, you have likely already studied the history of al Qaeda. To fully grasp how bin Laden and his group emerged as arguably the most dangerous and successful terrorist group in history, I strongly recommend the award-winning books *Age of Sacred Terror* by Daniel Benjamin and Steven Simon (2002, Floris Books) and the *Looming Tower* by Lawrence Wright (2007, Knopf). Both are extremely well written and should provide the basis of all academic discussions regarding the group.

In the 1980s, inspired by his mentors, bin Laden left a lucrative engineering career and a young family to volunteer in Afghanistan and assist the mujahedin-led and U.S.-supported fight against the Soviet Union's infiltration of what was considered holy and sacred Muslim land. As the Soviets withdrew in late 1980s, Abdullah al Azzam, the architect of the successful war, and his protégé, bin Laden, were left with a network of at least 10,000 Islamists. Azzam and bin Laden formulated a plan to use these forces to form a new group called *al Qaeda*, meaning "the base," and take their cause to other countries, not specifically to the West. However, any goodwill toward the West for their help in Afghanistan evaporated in 1990 when the United States postured for Operation Desert Storm, in support of Iraqi-invaded Kuwait. Bin Laden, who returned to Saudi Arabia in early 1990 as a hero for his efforts in Afghanistan, met with King Fahd and pleaded with him not to accept Western help with repelling Iraq from Kuwait and protecting the kingdom. He was rebuffed and went underground, plotting his revenge against the West while military operations were under way in the region. His first attack was the simultaneous bombing of two hotels in Aden, Yemen, on December 29, 1992, where U.S. troops were thought to be residing. A few months later, on February 26, 1993, the first attack on the World Trade Center was executed with Ramzi Yousef, nephew of Khalid Sheikh Mohammed, at the helm of operational planning. Yousef and KSM then planned the 1994 "Bojinka" plot to destroy U.S.-flagged airliners in the Pacific, but their plan unraveled when a practice bombing by Yousef himself failed to bring down the plane and a subsequent investigation uncovered the plot. The 1998 simultaneous embassy bombings in Africa and the 2000 bombing of the USS *Cole* further raised al Qaeda's profile and strength. But the catastrophic attacks on 9/11 would be bin Laden's greatest accomplishment, just nine years after his first attack against the West.

Emergent al Qaeda

Al Qaeda made its first appearance on the State Department's Foreign Terrorist Organization (FTO) list in 1999, in light of the embassy bombings the previous year.[35] In 1999, the FTO list consisted of twenty-eight groups; the 2012 list contained fifty-one groups, including a long list of radical Islamist al Qaeda offshoots or affiliates (see the Appendix). Twenty-six of the original list remain, with the addition of narco-terror groups such as FARC and ELN.

AQAP or Ansar al-Sharia

After the 9/11 attacks and our subsequent military operations to destroy its base in Afghanistan, al Qaeda scattered to safe havens in the Middle East, including Yemen, the ancestral homeland of the bin Laden family. Al Qaeda in the Arabian Peninsula (AQAP) quickly formed and grew in strength. The group was founded by Said Ali Al Shihri and Ibrahim Suleiman Al Rubaysh, both former Guantanamo Bay detainees whom the United States released to the Saudi de-radicalization program. Unfortunately, both these terrorists left the Saudi program, made their way to Yemen, and joined two other terrorists, Nasir Al Wuhayshi and Qassim Al Raimi, who escaped Yemen prisons. Together, these four terrorists built AQAP into a formidable, transnational enterprise. Al Shihri was killed by a drone attack in Yemen on September 10, 2012.

AQAP attracted supporters such as Anwar al-Awlaki, a U.S. citizen and radical Islamist. Awlaki was born in the United States and obtained a BS (in civil engineering) from Colorado State University, an MA (in education leadership) from San Diego State University, and worked toward a PhD at George Washington University. Inspired by the writing of Qutb, Awlaki met with and encouraged the 9/11 hijackers at the Dar al-Hijrah mosque in Northern Virginia and persuaded and supported Nidal Hassan's plan to kill soldiers at Ft. Hood through eighteen e-mails sent from abroad. He met Christmas Day airline terrorist Umar Farouk Abdulmutallab at an al Qaeda training camp in Yemen and inspired and encouraged Faisal Shahzad to bomb Times Square. In a somewhat controversial move, the U.S. government targeted and killed al-Awlaki in a drone attack in Yemen. Also in the vehicle was the editor of *Inspire*, al Qaeda's online magazine used for recruitment and rhetoric and to educate followers on bomb building and terrorist tactics. The killing of Awlaki rekindled a long-standing debate about the definition of "terrorist," since he was not a trigger puller but the inspiration behind attacks. The United States was sending a clear and unequivocal message: if you provide logistical support, or in this case, the ideological fuel fanning the flames of radicalism, you are a terrorist and you are a legitimate target.

By utilizing Internet archive services, it is possible to read Awlaki's writings and interaction with his followers.[36] Through his words, it is possible to understand his psychological and sociological construction, how he radicalized, and his initially quiet ascendance to power as a spiritual leader of a religious terrorist group. The comments of hundreds of followers posted on his blog give great insight to hatred against the West, and there are repeated calls for our destruction. With regard to Awlaki, we may ask what mechanisms were in place permitting his ascent; which laws and controls were absent on the Internet, with his tracked international travels unhindered and his very public, seditious lectures?

Other al Qaeda Splinter Groups

In the years following the 9/11 attack, al Qaeda affiliates grew worldwide in at least fifteen countries.

Al Qaeda in Iraq (AQI)   Operations in Iraq led to the rise of Islamic State of Iraq, or AQI, which has been responsible for horrific attacks in Iraq against coalition forces, mosques, and the country's new leadership following the ouster and death of Saddam Hussein. Withdrawal of the coalition has emboldened their efforts to establish a foothold in the country and infiltrate the newly established government.

Tehrik-e-Taliban Pakistan (TTP)   TTP is an alliance of militant groups in Pakistan and the force behind the failed Times Square bombing attempt. TTP provided training and logistics to American Faisal Shahzad, subsequently landing on the State Department's FTO list within days of the event.

Harakat al-Shabaab Mujahideen (al-Shabaab)   Al Shabaab's operations in Somalia exploited the country's continued descent into lawlessness, possibly exacting proceeds from pirating operations in the Gulf. An American commander in al-Shabaab, Abu Mansur al-Amriki grew up in Alabama as Omar Shafik Hammami, radicalized, and fled to Somalia in 2006 to join the effort. The group mostly consists of foreigners and, leveraging social media, has successfully recruited American-Somali men from Milwaukee and New Jersey to join the fight abroad. Several recruits successfully traveled to Somalia and died in suicide bombings; others were arrested in the United States as they prepared to leave the country. In 2012, U.S. Army veteran and intelligence specialist Craig Baxam was arrested in Kenya, boarding a bus to Somalia with the intent to join al Shabaab. Al Shabaab controls the southern part of Somalia and has started recruiting heavily from neighboring Kenya. In the ongoing Operation Linda Nchi, Kenya Defence Forces are targeting Al Shabaab's training camps with aerial bombing campaigns. Although it declared its loyalty to al Qaeda in 2008, this relationship was formally cemented in 2012 with a proclamation from Ayman al-Zawahiri welcoming the group and its members to al Qaeda.

Al-Qa`ida in the Islamic Maghreb (AQIM)   AQIM is centered in Algeria, where it has launched an insurgent campaign to turn the country into an Islamist state. AQIM arose from Salafist Group for Preaching and Combat, GSPC, and the group mainly engages in hostage taking and ambushes against government leaders and law enforcement.

Al-Nusra Front for the Protection of the People of the Levant (Jabhat al-Nusram)   Jabhat al-Nusram is a jihadist al-Qaeda affiliate emerging from the civil war in Syria. The group is possibly fed by Muslim Brotherhood members who simply walked into Syria from Egypt during chaotic 2011 Arab Spring uprisings in the region, which left key borders unguarded. Within months of formation, the group orchestrated a simultaneous car bombing of the main intelligence complex in Damascus, using 1,000 kilograms of explosives and killing at least fifty-five people and injuring four hundred others. Leveraging the Internet, the group communicates regularly with the populace to organize riots within the country. The radicalization of the Syrian revolt is of great concern as the bloodshed on both sides of the conflict will likely escalate, and the emergence of new groups further complicates international response and diplomatic engagement.

Although the al Qaeda affiliates may struggle in the face of stepped-up U.S. and regional engagement, they remain a formidable and flexible force, moving to and operating in areas of conflict and lawlessness and preying on their vulnerable populace.

Bin Laden Speaks

On May 2, 2011, a U.S.-led military team entered a compound in Abbottabad, Pakistan, and killed Osama bin Laden. A large amount of sensitive site exploitation (SSE) material was removed from the compound for analysis, with seventeen documents released to the public. The 2012 study "Letters from Abbottabad" (Combating Terrorism Center, West Point) analyzes the seventeen declassified documents gathered during the SSE operation at the compound, providing outstanding insight into and analysis of both bin Laden's unyielding role in shaping al Qaeda and the affiliates and his activities assisting other terrorist groups.[37] Bin Laden opined about conducting a mass attack on communications systems, targeting railroad systems, and striking smaller U.S. cities. He also pondered ways to use the media in his favor and induce political dissent in our system. Despite being in exile from the group, the documents revealed he had a hand in nearly all of the major terrorist attacks since 9/11, including the siege in Mumbai. Interestingly, bin Laden was not enamored with the affiliates; his personal journals and correspondence revealed thoughts of their incompetence, inability to engage in the political process and conduct media campaigns, and poorly planned operations resulting in the deaths of thousands of innocent Muslims. The TTP in particular were unpopular with bin Laden and his closest advisors while in exile, `Atiyyatullah and Abu Yahya al-Libi. The two wrote to TTP leader Hakimullah Mahsud expressing displeasure with the group's "ideology, methods and behavior." They also threatened to take public measures "unless we see from you serious and immediate practical and clear steps towards reforming [your ways] and dissociating yourself from these vile mistakes [that violate Islamic Law]."[38] Al-Libi was killed in a U.S. drone strike in North Waziristan on June 5, 2012.

Finally, bin Laden declined from formally recognizing al-Shabaab, despite their pledge of allegiance to al Qaeda. He seemed more interested in the turning Somalia around than destroying the country and voiced concern about turmoil and resulting decline in foreign aid to the country.

Al Qaeda's New Goals and Tactics

According to terrorism expert Bruce Hoffman, al Qaeda's goals are changing.[39] His key points are:

1. Al-Qaeda is increasingly focused on overwhelming, distracting and exhausting us.
2. In the wake of the global financial crisis, al-Qaeda has stepped up a strategy of economic warfare.
3. Al-Qaeda is still trying to create divisions within the global alliance arrayed against it by targeting key coalition partners.
4. Al-Qaeda is aggressively seeking out, destabilizing and exploiting failed states and other areas of lawlessness.
5. Al-Qaeda is covetously seeking recruits from non-Muslim countries who can be easily deployed for attacks in the West.

Often called the "death by a thousand cuts" strategy, those who want to turn the United States into an Islamic Republic hope to exhaust and overwhelm our government and people. The FBI often reminds us that in a 2004 video, bin Laden stated he "bled Russia for 10 years until it went bankrupt and was forced to withdraw in defeat. … We are continuing in the same policy to make America bleed profusely to the point of bankruptcy."[40] Of course the low cost to execute the 9/11 attacks and the resulting devastation to our economy from the airline industry, the many corporations suffering losses in the twin towers, and our extensive military engagement overseas has not gone unnoticed by groups wishing to do us harm. Dragging us into a "long slog" is not just a hope but an operational tactic.

Al Qaeda and Nexus

Although it usually doesn't make the headlines and some digging is necessary to unearth the evidence, al Qaeda is working with dissimilar groups to advance their goals. In his November 27, 2008, U.S. *News and World Report* article entitled "Paying for Terror: How Jihadist Groups Are Using Organized-Crime Tactics—and Profits—to Finance Attacks on Targets around the Globe," David E. Kaplan detailed numerous case of al Qaeda working with criminal groups and the mafia. His first startling piece of information is that Italian court records show contact between al Qaeda and the Mafia as early as 1998. He also reveals information that Italian authorities suspect that radical militants were running an extensive smuggling operation into Sicily, making over thirty landings and moving thousands of people across the Mediterranean for $4,000 apiece. Italian intelligence reports note that jihadists' human-smuggling

EMERGENT CONCERN: AL QAEDA'S NEW
FRONT IN WESTERN AFRICA

According to the State Department, terrorist attacks across Africa increased by 11.5 percent in 2011. Al Qaeda is taking advantage of declining states in the Western part of Africa and is operating in the same space as FARC, Mexican drug-trafficking organizations, and Hezbollah. With fifty tons of cocaine being moved through the region, the profit taking could be vast.

Guinea-Bissau: As discussed earlier in Chapter 2, Guinea-Bissau has become a hub of narco-trafficking activity. AQIM smugglers are now also operating in the area, using Tuareg tribesmen to move cocaine into Morocco and then on to Europe.

Mali: Following a military coup by government separatists in March 2012 and the resulting chaos and void in leadership and law, al Qaeda in the Islamic Maghreb (AQIM) quickly moved into Mali. In July 2012, al Qaeda's stunning destruction of ancient mosques in legendary Timbuktu was certainly meant to send a message to other countries in the region to comply with and accommodate their demands or face similar destruction. AQIM splinter the Movement for Unity and Jihad (MUJAO) now occupies northern Mali, splitting the country in half and threatening the southern region if it does not secede. In a few short months since its formation, MUJAO has kidnapped Algerian diplomats, used suicide bombers to attack Algerian military camps, and publicly executed Sharia law through stonings and limb severing.

Nigeria: The Boko Haram jihadist militia, with ties to AQIM, has attacked churches and government buildings in an attempt to establish Sharia law. The group carried out 130 attacks in Nigeria in 2011, killing thousands. Christians in Nigeria have been specifically targeted, with many fleeing the country in fear. However, not all Nigerians are against the presence of Boko Haram, with one stating, "If I was attacked by Boko Haram, it's like being attacked by God. It's God's wish and I have no problem with that."[45] Instability in Nigeria is also being exploited by Iran, which is creating a "Nigerian Hezbollah," known as Islamic Movement of Nigeria (IMN). The group's leader, Sheikh Ibrahim Zakzaky, draws inspiration from Hezbollah leader Nasrallah, whose picture is carried at IMN demonstrations. The nexus of al Qaeda and Hezbollah in Nigeria is worrisome and bears watching.

activity brings them into contact with criminal organizations. A former FBI agent stated: "I am aware of a high-level Mafia figure, who was cooperating with authorities, being asked if the Mafia would assist terrorists in smuggling people into Europe through Italy. He said, 'The Mafia will help whoever can pay.'"[41] Other sources point to al Qaeda interacting with the Neapolitan Camorra Mafia, which operates safe houses for illegal aliens.[42] The Camorra has provided sanctuary to al Qaeda, as well as helping them move operatives through Europe to safe houses in Paris, London, Berlin, and Madrid. According to DIGOS, Italy's political crime unit, the number of al Qaeda operatives passing through Naples may have exceeded a thousand.[43] The Camorra has also passed along their document forgery expertise to al Qaeda.

In 2006 during an undercover operation, FBI agents tracked a mafia member who was selling missiles to a person he thought was an al Qaeda member who turned out to be an FBI informant. The program manager for the FBI's Domestic and International Organized Crime Programs voiced his concerns, stating: "They [the Mafia] will deal with anybody, if they can make a buck. They will sell to a terrorist just as easily as they would sell to an order of Franciscan monks. It's a business relationship to them. If the mob has explosives and a terrorist wants them and they have the money, they could become instant friends."[44]

As al Qaeda's goals shift and morph with world events and logistical needs, our counterterrorism and counterintelligence tactics must change as well.

HEZBOLLAH

American terrorism is the source of every terrorism in the world.
—Hassan Nasrallah, Hezbollah leader

Prior to 9/11, Hezbollah was responsible for the deaths of more Americans than any other terrorist group. They had a hand in the 1983 bombing of the Marine barracks (241 U.S. military dead, 60 wounded); the kidnapping and murder of U.S. officials in Lebanon; and the 1996 Khobar Towers bombing in Saudi Arabia (19 U.S. military dead, 372 wounded). When tensions escalate between the United States and Iran or Syria, Hezbollah inevitably starts a campaign of saber rattling and threats of strikes against our country. Perhaps no group is better positioned to strike within our borders, since Hezbollah has a strong presence north and south of our border as well as internally with fund-raising cells and sympathizers. The potential for an undetected sleeper cell to lash out upon direction from one of their sponsors, Iran or Syria, cannot be overlooked.

Hezbollah has been in operation for thirty years and was designated as a Foreign Terrorist Organization by the State Department in 1995. The group is complex in nature with several "arms" including military, political, and community support. This complexity makes engagement extremely difficult. For example, due to the commingling of their activities, sanctioning one of its "charities" often means taking money away from militants as well as the needy. The group is now global with presence in Central and South America, Western Africa, and Europe, operating in the same "space" as other major terror groups such as FARC and al Qaeda. The liaison of Hezbollah with these groups, sharing tactics, trafficking routes, etc., is of great concern. As will be discussed in Chapter 6, the group vigorously raises funds in the United States through charities and intellectual property crime, especially through knock-off designer purses, DVDs, baby formula, and high-demand pharmaceuticals like Viagra.

Despite decades of overt and covert attempts to dismantle the group, it is still one of the world's most effective terrorist organizations. A review of Hezbollah reveals an organization that leverages unique sources of power and continues to wield influence not only in the Middle East but globally.

Unique Structure

Hezbollah's military philosophy revolves around the guerrilla-based concept of "Muslim Resistance" with an overarching strategy of soldiers having both military and civilian roles. Soldiers are integrated into the civilian populace during times of peace and form a well-trained, disciplined military force during war. The civilian populace supports this concept and is a catalyst for Hezbollah's endurance and success.

Following repeated defeats of Arab forces by the Israeli Defense Forces, Hezbollah adopted a new command structure encouraging initiative and leadership in junior ranks. A decentralized command structure allows for rapid response to any situation without consultation with group leadership. The military wing, however, answers directly to Hezbollah's central council of clerics for direction. A formidable paramilitary force in the region, the group continues to demonstrate it can blend unconventional warfare tactics with strategies typically employed by conventional forces.[46]

Methodology and Objectives

Hezbollah has a history of suicide bombing attacks; however, this tactic appears to have fallen out of favor in the past ten years. Kidnapping has been very effectively utilized as a way to engage in prisoner exchange, and Hezbollah also fields a unique weapon: the group is very adept at leveraging the global audience through press campaigns, political activity, and humanitarian engagement. Hezbollah has stated that one of its primary goals is to eliminate the state of Israel. Its other objectives include freeing Hezbollah prisoners in Israel; supporting the humanitarian and basic needs of Lebanon's Shi'ite civilian populace; maintaining a political presence in Lebanon's parliament; and fund-raising through both legitimate and illicit means.

Primary Area of Operations

Hezbollah operates in the formerly Syrian-controlled Bekaa Valley, the southern suburbs of Beirut, and southern Lebanon. The State Department's 2011 Country Reports on Terrorism gives a glimpse into their global reach, stating that Hezbollah has established cells in Europe, Africa, South America, North America, and Asia. The group's training bases are mostly in the Bekaa Valley, with headquarters and offices in southern Beirut. Hezbollah is now a "state within a state," similar to how the Palestinian Liberation Organization used to operate in Lebanon.

Tactical Depth and Breadth

According to the State Department and the FBI, Hezbollah remains the most technically capable terrorist group in the world. The group has spent decades posturing, preparing, and rebuilding its arsenal; Israeli officials claim Hezbollah has completely replenished its ranks, possessing more short- and medium-range rockets than it had before the 2006 war. The group has consolidated and moved arms back to southern Lebanon and is providing training to Hamas operatives from Gaza. Hezbollah's ability to move and posture large caches of arms was illustrated in June 2009, when they placed 40,000 rockets on the border of Lebanon and Israel in response to escalation. During the same year, an explosion at an ammunition bunker in a Lebanese village just twelve miles from the Israeli border gave further cause for concern. The weapons cache at this location, wrongly believed by the UN to be abandoned, consisted of AK-47s, artillery shells, mortars, and 122-millimeter rockets. A UN officer stated the facility was a violation of UN Resolution 1701, which imposed a cease-fire and arms ban after the war.

Hezbollah is undeterred by the presence of the UN Interim Force in Lebanon (UNIFIL), which fields 13,000 troops at an annual budget of

$546 million.[47] UNIFIL's mandate is to ensure compliance with resolutions, and it attempts to do so in a very unstable environment. Following the July cache explosion, UNIFIL attempted to examine a similar facility in the neighborhood, but the group was repelled by villagers throwing rocks, injuring dozens of inspectors.

Iran is supplementing Hezbollah's arsenal. According to the State Department, Iran's Qods Force continues to provide weapons, training, and funding to the group and has trained more than 3,000 fighters at camps in Iran. Finally, there are unconfirmed reports that Hezbollah is procuring Russian-made SA-8 and SA-18 surface-to-air missiles.[48]

Political Acumen

Hezbollah continues to improve its political position in Lebanon where the government and the majority of Arab nations recognize the group as a legitimate "resistance group" and political party, namely the Lebanese Islamist party. Since 1992, its political arm has fronted candidates in parliamentary elections. In 2005, Hezbollah secured an all-time high of 14 of the Lebanese Parliament's 128 seats. As part of the government, Hezbollah has participated in meetings with the EU and the International Monetary Fund.

After taking over West Beirut in 2008, the group's political power increased. As part of an Arab-brokered deal to end the fighting, Hezbollah was granted enough seats to have veto power over government decisions. Illustrating the synergy between its political and military efforts, Hezbollah's election campaign posters contained a mushroom cloud with the inscription "Oh Zionists, If You Want This Type of War Then So Be It!" This was likely a message from their Iranian sponsors, intended as a warning for Israel.

Leveraging the Community

Hezbollah's civilian wing provides a variety of social services for Lebanese Shi'ites, which comprise nearly one-third of the population of Lebanon. Providing protection and basic necessities to the populace has naturally increased the group's popularity among citizens. Hezbollah has mastered the art of communication and benevolence; the group publishes a newspaper and monthly magazine, operates radio and TV stations, and runs hospitals, schools, and orphanages. A substantial "Martyrs Fund" also provides support to families of dead, injured, or imprisoned Shi'ites.

Strong Leadership

Hassan Nasrallah, a former military leader and Shi'a religious expert, has led Hezbollah for more than twenty years. He is widely credited for driving Israel from Lebanon and for the successful prisoner exchange with Israel in 2004, freeing hundreds of Palestinians and Lebanese. Nasrallah demonstrated his animosity toward the United States in 2002 when he stated: "Let the entire world hear me. Our hostility to the Great Satan is absolute. Regardless of how the world has changed after 11 September, Death to America will remain our reverberating and powerful slogan: Death to America."[49]

Active and Deadly

The following is a timeline of major Hezbollah activity in the last seven years.

2012: In July 2012, a purported Hezbollah operative was arrested in Cyprus with photos of Israeli targets and plans to blow up a plane or tour bus.

2011: Hezbollah was reportedly behind a bombing in Istanbul in May 2011, wounding eight Turkish civilians in a possible assassination attempt on the Israeli consul to Turkey.

2009: When Israel engaged Hamas in Gaza, Hezbollah did not intervene militarily (possibly at the behest of Syria) but influenced the battlefield in a variety of ways. Prior to the conflict, Hezbollah's leadership invited Arab nations to join it in protesting Israel's embargo of goods entering Gaza. Their tactic contributed to the propaganda associated with the conflict and also demonstrated Hezbollah's ability to engage from afar via psychological operations.

2008: After three days of bloodshed, heavily armed Hezbollah fighters seized West Beirut. This was the first use of Hezbollah's military arsenal against their host nation to increase territory and span of control. The conflict was sparked when the government attempted to shut down Hezbollah's vast telecommunications network.

2006: Hezbollah militants kidnapped two Israeli soldiers in northern Israel, sparking the month-long "Lebanon War," which devastated the country's infrastructure. During the conflict, Israel bombed Lebanon and deployed troops and tanks, and Hezbollah fired 4,000 rockets across the border into Israel. In all, more than 1,000 Lebanese (mostly civilians) were killed, and 120 Israeli soldiers and 43 Israeli civilians lost their lives.

Global Operations

Hezbollah continues to methodically expand its sphere of influence around the world while receiving weapons and training support from Iran and Syria. The group now operates in the same space as other major terrorist organizations such as Revolutionary Armed Forces of Columbia and al Qaeda, and Hamas. Sharing resources, tactics, or established trafficking routes between the groups would have dire implications and is highly likely.

Latin America

Hezbollah has a stronghold in South America, especially in the tri-border area, where Paraguay, Brazil, and Argentina intersect. Approximately 25,000 immigrants from Lebanon came to the area in two waves, after the 1948 Arab-Israeli war and in 1985 after the civil war in Lebanon. Hezbollah has garnered support from these communities and is heavily engaged in charitable fund-raising, DVD piracy, tax evasion and money-laundering schemes, and other money-making ventures.

In 1992, Islamists attacked the Israeli Embassy in Buenos Aires, Argentina, with a car bomb, killing 29 people and injuring more than 250 others. The Islamic Jihad organization, directly linked to Hezbollah, claimed responsibility. In 1994, Hezbollah used a truck bomb to attack a Jewish community center in Buenos Aires, killing eighty-seven people and injuring hundreds. Investigators linked the plot directly back to Iran, which also executed copycat bombings, just eight days later, attacking the Israeli embassy and a Jewish community center in London. The tri-border region is not the only Hezbollah stronghold in the region. In 2009, the SOUTHCOM commander testified that Hezbollah presence was detected in Colombia and that the group is heavily involved in the drug trade.[50] Of course the profit reaped from trafficking is much greater than charitable giving and sale of bootlegged goods, so this emergent business venture is very worrisome. A final concern: Hezbollah's liaison with al Qaeda in Latin America was documented as far back as November of 2002. At this time, intelligence agencies reported that a "summit" meeting took place in Ciudad del Este between Hezbollah leaders and other radical Islamist terrorist groups, including al Qaeda.[51]

Nexus Concern: Venezuela

As the government in Colombia makes progress to stop drugs from moving through their country, the main route for product out of Latin America is now through Venezuela, where both Hezbollah and FARC have received logistical and training support. In May 2010, ten U.S. senators sent the secretary of state a letter of concern regarding Venezuela's president Hugo Chavez's increasing ties with FTOs and state sponsors of terrorism.[52] The letter details Chavez's ties to FARC, specifically asking about the type of surface-to-air missiles or man-portable air defense systems (MANPADs) Venezuela has provided to FARC or enabled FARC to obtain, and what threat the systems pose to Colombia and U.S. counterdrug efforts in the region. The letter also discusses the OFAC designation of two senior Chavez officials for material support of FARC.

Although Venezuela's ties to FARC are worrisome, perhaps their long-term, established liaison with Hezbollah is of greater concern. In 2006, following the end of hostilities in Lebanon with Israel, Hezbollah's leader, Hassan Nasrallah, called Hugo Chavez his "brother," and signs reading "Gracias, Chavez" were hung to publicly thank the Colombian president for his backing during the conflict. In response to the Israeli engagement in Gaza in 2009, President Chavez ejected the Israeli ambassador and staff from his country. Chavez has openly invited Hezbollah members to live in Venezuela, and his embassies in the Middle East have been used to launder Hezbollah money, per investigation by the U.S. Treasury Department. The government may also be providing arms to Hezbollah via countries sponsoring their efforts, Iran and Syria. In November 2009, the Israeli Navy intercepted a shipment of heavy arms from Venezuela to Hezbollah. The MV *Francop*, a German cargo ship flying the flag of Antigua, departed Guanta, Venezuela, and stopped briefly in Iran. The ship was preparing to dock in Syria when intercepted in international waters by Israel, based on intelligence that the ship contained arms. The *Francop* had thirty-six shipping containers with 500 tons of Katyusha rockets, mortars, and grenades and a half million rounds of ammunition.[53]

Chavez also has a close personal relationship with Iran's president Mahmoud Ahmedinejad, Hezbollah's primary benefactor. The two leaders and their staff regularly visit each other, and in 2007 they instituted biweekly flights between Tehran, Damascus, and Caracas, a trip dubbed by many as the "terror flight." Although national airlines were used for the flight, the passenger and cargo manifests were kept secret and outsiders were not able to procure a ticket. Due to government control of the mission, passports were not needed and there were no cargo restrictions. After intense diplomatic pressure from the United States, the flights ceased in 2010; however, the damage was likely done. Officials believe the aircraft transported not only weapons but possibly also radioactive material such as enriched uranium, per complaints filed by airline employees. U.S. intelligence officials are concerned about the manpower exchange as well; the flight brought Iranian Quds commanders to Venezuela and also transported Imad Mughniyeh, a most wanted Hezbollah leader, between Iran and Syria.[54] In January 2012, Ahmadinejad stopped in Venezuela while on a tour of Latin America,

VENEZUELA

FIGURE 3.4   Screen shot from a pro-Hezbollah website of a sign in Lebanon; the verse is from the Quran and means "In the name of God, most Gracious, most Compassionate."

posing for photographs outside of Chavez's presidential palace. Pointing to a nearby hill, Chavez said, "That hill will open up and a big atomic bomb will come out," and Ahmadinejad added that any bomb they would build together would be fueled by "love."[55] Figure 3.4 illustrates the emergent connection between the two groups.

A fascinating article by Michael Rowan and Douglas E. Schoen entitled "Terror at Hugo Chavez's Hand" discusses how an attack by Israel against Gaza could be fought asymmetrically by Hezbollah, with help from Venezuela and Chavez.[56] In light of the data regarding the strength of this relationship, we need to consider this type of tactical coordination not only possible but highly probable. Add in the resources and reach brought to the table by FARC, and the nexus of these two actors could be deadly for the United States.

West Coast of Africa

Similar to South America, Hezbollah depends on the 100,000 Lebanese descendants living on the Ivory Coast to support their operations in

Africa. Lebanese settlers moved to the area in the early 1900s and established a robust trade business, which continues today. Hezbollah is active in the region, reaping profits from booming narco-trafficking routes, "blood" diamond trade, and solicitation of funds from Muslims, either voluntarily or through an imposed "tax." In 2009, the United States designated two African supporters of Hezbollah, and others continue to funnel millions to the group from the region, some through contact with Hezbollah's commanders and others through front and shell companies.[57] Funds are illegally transferred from Africa to Lebanon and bulk cash smuggling is rampant. The liaison between Hezbollah and Africa is not new; in 2003 a charter flight en route to Beirut from Benin crashed on takeoff killing all onboard, including senior Hezbollah members who were carrying $2 million.[58]

Europe

According to the U.S. State Department, the EU as a whole remains reluctant to take steps to block the assets of charities associated with Hamas and Hezbollah. An EU official presented this view: "This is a difficult issue because Hizballah has military operations that we deplore, but Hizballah is also a political party in Lebanon. ... Can a political party elected by the Lebanese people be put on a terrorist list? Would that really help deal with terrorism?"[59] This clearly illustrates how Hezbollah's move to become a political force has strengthened their position as "legitimate" and allows them to avoid sanctions.

Iraq

In 2006, the Iraq Study Group, a ten-person panel appointed by Congress in 2006, revealed that Hezbollah trained thousands of soldiers of the Mahdi Army (an Iraqi Shi'ite militia) in Lebanon. Hezbollah operatives also traveled to Iraq to advise the Mahdi Army. The report revealed that Iran facilitated these activities and that Syria was also involved.[60]

Canada

Undeniably, Hezbollah has a very strong presence in Canada. In 2012, the United States uncovered a Hezbollah-related scheme to launder the proceeds of narcotics trafficking and other crimes through Lebanese financial institutions, with amounts totaling over $480 million. Proceeds were moved through West Africa, and the buying and selling of used cars was employed as a method of moving the dirty money. One bank of interest connected to the laundering was a Lebanese-Canadian institution, which forfeited $150 million of proceeds from the scheme. In a preview chapter from his upcoming book *Hezbollah: The Global Footprint of Lebanon's Party of God*, terrorism expert Matthew Levitt reveals that Hezbollah activated suspected "sleeper cells" in Canada to carry out an attack to avenge the death of Imad Mughniyeh, one of their top commanders who was targeted and killed in a car bomb.[61]

An interesting case of a possible Hezbollah sympathizer was of Khaled Nawaya, who was born in Saudi Arabia but is of Syrian descent. He moved to the United States at the age of seventeen and earned two degrees, in aeronautics and management. He was a flight instructor but lost his student visa status in the United States, filing and winning a lawsuit against Embry Riddle University for providing "bad immigration advice." He requested, and was approved for, residency in Canada. On October 6, 2009, Nawaya lied to Border Patrol when trying to cross into British Columbia during his move north. When repeatedly questioned about the amount of currency in his vehicle, he adamantly stated he had less than the $10,000 required by law. However, Nawaya actually had $800,000 in gold coins, another $70,000 in cash in the vehicle, and $10,000 in cash on his person. Contents of the vehicle included a ring bearing the insignia of the terrorist group Hezbollah, 9/11 conspiracy theory-themed DVDs, and a scarf adorned with the images of a former Israeli prime minister and a U.S. president depicted as monkeys.[62]

Mr. Nawaya had previously wired 1 million U.S. dollars to his brother overseas, who bought the Canadian gold coins on the Internet and had them shipped to Mr. Nawaya in the United States. Mr. Nawaya then loaded the coins into his car in the United States and attempted to drive them across the Canadian border. Canadian authorities labeled the case a "probable national-security nexus" and detained Mr. Nawaya for one month, eventually releasing him due to the inability to establish a case. However, he was charged with his failed declaration under the Proceeds of Crime (Money Laundering) and Terrorist Financing Act, and his money was confiscated. We may never know his full intentions or whether he was a Hezbollah sympathizer, but the case is worthy of consideration. In 2011, he petitioned to have his U.S. visa reinstated, but his request was declined.

United States

Within the United States, there were sixteen arrests of Hezbollah activists in 2010 based on Joint Terrorism Task Force investigations in Philadelphia, New York, and Detroit. The organization has attempted to obtain Stinger missiles, M-4 rifles, and night vision equipment in the United States.[63] As will be covered extensively in Chapter 6, Hezbollah is heavily engaged in intellectual property theft and other financial schemes in United States. They also have sympathizers willing to do some of their legwork; in 2010, seven Florida men who owned an export business in Miami were arrested for falsifying paperwork and invoices and illegally shipping electronics such as Sony PlayStations and digital cameras to a shopping center in Paraguay for resale. The men falsified wire transactions, moving and hiding money illegally.[64] The large shopping center, Galeria Page, is located in Ciudad del Este, Brazil, and serves as a Hezbollah fund-raising source in the tri-border area of Argentina, Brazil, and Paraguay. Since December 6, 2006, the Galeria Page has been a Specially Designated Global Terrorist entity, meaning anyone who does business with the businesses located in the mall is breaking not only U.S. but international laws. The managers of the mall give a certain percentage of their earnings to Hezbollah, estimated in the tens of millions of dollars annually.

U.S. Response

Groups like Hezbollah are not controlled by any one nation, so traditional means of applying pressure through diplomatic, economic, and military means are not effective, or even possible. International norms and laws are difficult to enforce upon such groups, particularly for organizations like the UN. The best way to counteract Hezbollah's growth and activities is to provide support to its home country for counterterrorism assistance. Perhaps indicative of growing concern, State Department support to Lebanon has increased significantly in recent years. For example, the Bureau of International Narcotics and Law Enforcement Affairs' efforts in Lebanon were funded at $9.8 million in FY 2009, jumping to the current level of $20 million annually. INL is actively training and equipping Lebanon's Internal Security Forces, which are reportedly countering Hezbollah and attempting to maintain stability in the country. In the last three years, the U.S. Department of Defense has also allocated tens of millions of dollars to Lebanon for counterterrorism assistance. Similar to its activities in Iraq, Hezbollah continues to get involved in emergent events, now engaging in Arab Spring uprisings. In August 2012, the State Department specially designated Hezbollah for its support of the Syrian regime. After decades of support from Syria, officials say Hezbollah is now "repaying its debt to Assad by providing training, advice, and extensive logistical support to the Government of Syria."[65]

FARC

Just to the south of the United States lies the "country" of *FARCLANDIA*. This term is widely used to define the area controlled by the Revolutionary Armed Forces of Colombia, or FARC. The group has successfully made the transition from a small Communist guerilla organization to major international terrorist group. FARC was established in 1966 as a Communist insurgency group with the goal of overthrowing the

Colombian government. As the revenue from the drug trade expanded, so has the power and influence of FARC, which now controls an estimated 40 percent of Colombia through a negotiated agreement with the government. This area includes FARC's "safe haven," which is used for the cultivation of narcotics and as training and staging grounds for assaults on the Colombian military. Figure 3.5 illustrates FARC's vast presence in Colombia, as indicated by the dark shaded areas. Experts estimate that FARC's illegal activities net $500 to $600 million annually, one-half from drug cultivation and trafficking, with the remainder coming from kidnapping, extortion, and other criminal activities. Fifty percent of the world's cocaine comes from Colombia.[66]

Colombia: A Sophisticated, Transnational Narco-State

FARC, by the nature of its business, is a regional transnational criminal organization. However, the government is concerned with FARC's global transnational activities, including increased cooperation with the Russian Mafia, a relationship cultivated over the last two decades. In the late 1990s, the Russians built an arms pipeline to Colombia, bringing in thousands of weapons and tons of other supplies to help FARC fight their war against the Colombian government. In return the planes were loaded with 40,000 kilograms of cocaine that the Russian Mafia then distributed for profit.[67] The liaison between these two entities is increasingly troublesome, as Russian organized crime flourishes and government corruption persists. FARC has also been linked to a Tijuana, Mexico, cartel; the State Department believes they supplied cocaine to the Tijuana cartel in return for cash and weapons.[68] In 2012, FARC was linked to the Beltran Leyva cartel, according to Colombian intelligence gleaned from an intercepted communiqué issued by a FARC leader.[69]

FARC is also known as "The People's Army," but not by the people of Colombia; this is the label put on FARC by their friend and conspirator, Hugo Chavez, president of Venezuela. As discussed in the Hezbollah section, FARC is now using Venezuela as a jumping-off point to push drugs into the United States and to the Western Coast of Africa, then into Europe. Venezuela has been closely linked to Hezbollah in recent years, and FARC's colocation in Africa, especially Guinea-Bissau, with groups such as Hezbollah and al Qaeda is extremely troublesome. FARC is a perfect example of a growing transnational threat evolving from being state sponsored, to sponsoring the state, to becoming its own entity.

Routinely underestimated in sophistication, FARC surprised many in the counterterrorism world when it began successfully employing remote-controlled submarines to ferry drugs. The subs, worth $2 million a copy, can carry up to five tons of cocaine and travel silently through the

FIGURE 3.5 Map with FARC presence in Colombia, National Counterterrorism Center (2012).

water to preprogrammed landing sites in Central America and Mexico. At least fifteen subs have been seized in the last few years by the U.S. and Colombian governments. As FARC's foothold in Colombia strengthens and they exact increasing profit from drug trade, we can expect them to employ modern tactics and leverage technology to stay at the helm of drug operations in the region.

FINAL THOUGHTS

The rise and persistence of international terrorist organizations is a postmodern phenomenon bringing even the most powerful nations to their knees. It seems diplomatic, economic, and military measures are not enough to dissuade their activity. Using the soft sciences, it is possible to explore how terrorist groups form and persist. By identifying their inherent vulnerabilities, we will find fractures that, if exploited, could lead to their demise. The rebuilding of human intelligence (HUMINT) capability in our military and intelligence communities will certainly help get to the root of the terrorism phenomenon: the people.

Leveraging technology, communications advances, and inevitable pockets of conflict in our world, these groups will continue to persist and thrive. As we now move to the study of the domestic terror threat, we will see the same forces, complexities, and challenges at play.

REFERENCES

1. Martin L. van Crevold, *The Transformation of War* (New York: Free Press, 1991).
2. Gareth Morgan, *Images of Organization* (Thousand Oaks, CA: Sage, 2006).
3. Hesterman, J., *Reverse Use of Organizational Development Theory: A Unique Methodology for Analyzing and Disrupting Terrorist Organizations.* American Military University, Charlestown, WV.
4. Daniel Bell, *The Coming of the Post-Industrial Society* (New York: Basic Books, 1973).
5. Mary Jo Hatch and Ann Cunliffe, *Organization Theory: Modern, Symbolic, and Postmodern Perspectives* (New York: Oxford University Press, 2006).
6. Robert Chia, *Organizational Analysis as Deconstructive Practice* (Berlin: Gruyter, 1996).
7. Ibid.
8. Hatch and Cunliffe, *Organization Theory*.
9. Jacques Derrida, *Specters of Marx: The State of the Debt, the Work of Mourning and the New International* (Hoboken, NJ: Taylor and Francis, 2006).
10. Dipak Gupta, "Toward An Integrated Behavioral Framework for Analyzing Terrorism: Individual Motivations to Group Dynamics," paper presented at the annual meeting of the International Studies Association, San Diego, CA, 2006.
11. Jonathan Joseph, *Hegemony: A Realist Analysis* (New York: Routledge, 2002).
12. Gupta, "Toward An Integrated Behavioral Framework."
13. Merriam Webster, http://www.merriam-webster.com/dictionary/ideology.
14. Slavoj Žižek, *The Sublime Object of Ideology* (London: Verso).
15. Ibid.

16. Joseph O'Connor and Ian McDermott, *The Art of Systems Thinking: Essential Skills for Creativity and Problem-Solving* (San Francisco: Thorsons, 1997), 11.

17. Morgan, *Images of Organization.*

18. Ibid.

19. Bruce Hoffman, *Inside Terrorism* (New York: Columbia University Press, 2006).

20. Alan M. Dershowitz, *Why Terrorism Works* (New Haven, CT: Yale University Press, 2002).

21. Ibid.

22. Seth Jones and Martin Libicki, *How Terrorist Groups End: Lessons for Countering al Qa'ida.* (Washington, DC: RAND, 2008).

23. Ibid.

24. Ibid.

25. Larry E. Greiner, "Evolution and Revolution as Organizations Grow," *Harvard Business Review* 50, no. 4 (1972): 37–46.

26. Andrew D. Szilagyi and Marc J. Wallace, *Organizational Behavior and Performance* (Glenview, IL: Scott, Foresman/Little, Brown Higher Education, 1990).

27. Jessica Stern, "The Protean Enemy," *Foreign Affairs* (July/August 2003).

28. Carter McNamara, "Organizational Culture," http://managementhelp.org/organizations/culture.htm.

29. Hatch, *Organization Theory.*

30. Ibid.

31. Ibid.

32. Matthew G. Olsen, "Understanding the Homeland Threat Landscape," http://homeland.house.gov/sites/homeland.house.gov/files/Testimony-Olsen.pdf.

33. Marc Sageman, *Understanding Terror Networks* (Philadephia: University of Pennsylvania Press, 2003).

34. Ori Brafman and Rod A. Beckstrom, *The Starfish and the Spider: The Unstoppable Power of Leaderless Organizations* (New York: Portfolio, 2006).

35. Seth G. Jones, *Hunting in the Shadows: The Pursuit of al Qa'ida since 9/11* (New York: Norton, 2012).

36. U.S. Department of State, *1999 Foreign Terrorist Organization Report*, http://www.state.gov/www/global/terrorism/fto_1999.html#fto.

37. "Archive of http://www.anwar-alawlaki.com/," http://wayback.archive.org/web/20110707150524*/http://www.anwar-alawlaki.com/.

38. "Letters from Abbottabad: Bin Ladin," U.S. Military Academy, 2012.

39. "Archive of http://www.anwar-alawlaki.com/."

40. Bruce Hoffman, "Al-Qaeda Has a New Strategy. Obama Needs One Too," *Washington Post*, January 10, 2010.

41. Federal Bureau of Investigation, "Agroterrorism," http://www. fbi.gov/stats-services/publications/law-enforcement-bulletin/ february-2012/agroterrorism/.
42. Frank S. Perri, Terrance G. Lichtenwald, and Paula M. MacKenzie, "Evil Twins: The Crime-Terror Nexus," *The Forensic Examiner* (Winter 2009): 16–29.
43. David E. Kaplan, "Paying for Terror: How Jihadist Groups Are Using Organized-Crime Tactics—and Profits—to Finance Attacks on Targets around the Globe," *U.S. News and World Report*, November 27, 2008, http://www.usnews.com/usnews/news/articles/051205/5terror_4. htm.
44. Ron Chepesiuk, "Dangerous Alliance: Terrorism and Organized Crime," *Global Politician*, September 11, 2007, http://www.global-politician.com/23435-crime.
45. Pat Milton, "FBI Worries about an Osama-Mobsters Link," *USA Today*, October 1, 2006, http://www.usatoday.com/news/washington/2006-10-01-terror-mob_x.htm.
46. Sudarsan Raghavan, "Niger Struggles against Islamist Militants," *Washington Post*, April 16, 2012.
47. Jennifer Hesterman, "Hezbollah: The Party of God, 2009," *The Counter Terrorist Magazine*, December 2009/January 2010.
48. "UNIFIL Facts and Figures," http://www.un.org/en/peacekeeping/ missions/unifil/facts.shtml.
49. Hesterman, "Hezbollah."
50. Ibid.
51. U.S. Senate Committeee on Armed Services, *Posture Statement, Commander, U.S. Southern Command*, March 17, 2009.
52. Mike Boettcher, "South America's 'Tri-border' Back on Terrorism Radar," CNN, http://articles.cnn.com/2002-11-07/world/terror. triborder_1_tri-border-israeli-targets-argentine-intelligence-docu-ments?_s=PM:WORLD.
53. U.S. Senate, "Letter to Secretary of State Regarding Venezuela's Support of Terrorist Organizations and Regimes," May 25, 2010, http:// venezuelafactual.net/wp-content/uploads/2012/05/US-SENATORS-DENOUNCE-CHAVEZS-TERRORISTS-LINKS.pdf.
54. Ibid.
55. Ed Barnes, "Mysterious Venezuelan Round-Trip 'Terror Flight' to Iran Canceled," *Homeland Security Newswire* (September 16, 2010).
56. José R. Cárdenas, "Iran in Latin America Is No Laughing Matter," *Foreign Policy, January 11*, 2012, http://shadow.foreignpolicy.com/ posts/2012/01/11/iran_in_latin_america_is_no_laughing_matter.
57. Michael Rowan and Douglas E. Schoen, "Terror at Hugo Chavez's Hand," *Forbes.com*, January 21, 2009.

58. Ely Karmon, "The Iran-Hezbollah Strategic and Terrorist Threat to Africa," *The Journal of Counter Terrorism* 18, no. 3 (2012): 18–25.
59. Douglas Farah, "Hezbollah's External Support Network in West Africa and Latin America." International Assessment and Strategy Center, August 4, 2006.
60. Steven R. Weisman, "Allies Resisting as U.S. Pushes Terror Label for Hezbollah," *New York Times*, February 17, 2005, http://www.nytimes.com/2005/02/17/international/middleeast/17diplo.html.
61. Michael R. Gordon and Dexter Filkins, "Hezbollah Said to Help Shiite Army in Iraq," *New York Times*, November 28, 2006.
62. Matthew Levitt, "Hizballah's Canadian Procurement Network," 2012, http://www.washingtoninstitute.org/uploads/Documents/opeds/Levitt20120813-2.pdf.
63. Jane Armstrong and Colin Freeze, "Hapless Immigrant or Terrorist Threat?," *Globe and Mail*, November 20, 2009.
64. U.S. Senate Committee on Homeland Security and Governmental Affairs, *"The Future of Homeland Security: Evolving and Emerging Threats,"* July 11, 2012.
65. Federal Bureau of Investigation, "Seven Charged with Illegal Export of Electronics to U.S.-Designated Terrorist Entity in Paraguay," 2010, http://miami.fbi.gov/dojpressrel/pressrel10/mm021910.htm.
66. Daniel Benjamin, "Briefing on the Designation of Hezbollah for Supporting the Syrian Regime," U.S. Department of State.
67. Stephanie Hanson, "FARC, ELN: Colombia's Left-Wing Guerillas," Council on Foreign Relations, http://www.cfr.org/colombia/farc-eln-colombias-left-wing-guerrillas/p9272.
68. Frank Cilluffo, *The Threat Posed from the Convergence of Organized Crime, Drug Trafficking, and Terrorism*, U.S. House Committee on the Judiciary, December 13, 2000.
69. Ibid.
70. Olle Ohlsen Pettersson, "Report Claims Links between FARC and Mexican Drug Cartel," *Columbia Reports*, July 5, 2012, http://colombiareports.com/colombia-news/news/24945-farc-mexican-drug-cartel-links-highlighted-report.html.

CHAPTER 4

Domestic Terrorism and the Homegrown Threat

Collateral damage.

~ Timothy McVeigh,
referring to the nineteen children killed in his attack

Perhaps nothing is as hard to comprehend and explain as domestic terrorism. What motivates individuals to kill fellow citizens and target the very institutions providing for their safety and prosperity? Many of the same drivers are in place as those found in international terrorism such as an extreme religious or political ideology and the ability to anonymously find inspiration, encouragement, tactical techniques, training, and resources through the Internet. With domestic terror, lone wolves are of particular concern, since they are already embedded in society and their clandestine activities are more difficult to predict and prevent. All of these factors make the detection and neutralization of the domestic threat extremely difficult for law enforcement agencies. Psychology is a factor as well; the inherent disbelief in the phenomenon of domestic terrorism may result in a blind spot for investigators and first responders, a vulnerability best mitigated through education and training.

As a nation, we seem more transfixed on the threat of international terrorist groups striking on our soil, yet the number of domestic terror attacks has historically far outpaced international attacks against our citizens. The FBI reports that from 1980 to 2001, there were 345 domestic acts of terrorism and 136 international acts of terrorism perpetrated against our citizens at home and abroad.[1] Certainly, the scope of violence differs, and international acts typically have higher death rates and property destruction, with the rare exception of the domestic Oklahoma City tragedy in 1995. Since 9/11, we have engaged in two major theater battles in the Middle East resulting in thousands of U.S. and coalition casualties, simultaneously invoking the wrath of terrorist groups around the globe to attack our embassies and military personnel. All the while, we continued to fight domestic extremism at home, interrupting at least forty-five radical terror plots on our soil. Clearly, securing our populace from the terror threat has evolved into an exhausting and complex situation for resource-constrained organizations, especially in light of ongoing fiscal stress. We can't merely prioritize and address threats accordingly; each is significant and could be catastrophic to our country and its citizens. Terror groups can prey on this situation by merely introducing a threat, and whether plausible or not, we will stop at nothing to defend our citizens.

The growing lack of trust in government institutions due to recent economic decline, along with relentless infiltration by a radical jihadist ideology have led to a persistent and growing domestic terrorism threat. The FBI defines domestic terrorism as:

> the unlawful use, or threatened use, of force or violence by a group or individual based and operating entirely within the United States or Puerto Rico without foreign direction committed against persons or property to intimidate or coerce a government, the civilian population, or any segment thereof in furtherance of political or social objectives.[2]

Section 802 of the USA PATRIOT Act amended the U.S. Code to state that a person engages in domestic terrorism if they undertake an act dangerous to human life and if the act appears to be intended to: intimidate or coerce a civilian population; influence the policy of a government by intimidation or coercion; or affect the conduct of a government by mass destruction, assassination, or kidnapping.[3] Some legal experts point to the broad nature of these definitions, which could lead to the monitoring of innocent civilians and the erosion of freedoms such as speech and protest. Certainly, the balance between constitutional rights and security is delicate and must be at the forefront of every discussion regarding the investigation and prosecution of all criminal activities. As the dangers and complexities associated with domestic terrorism continue to grow, so must our corresponding detection and mitigation activities to protect citizens from the rage of others.

HISTORY OF DOMESTIC TERRORISM
IN THE UNITED STATES

There is a long list of domestic terrorist attacks in the United States, which some believe date back to the Boston Tea Party. On December 16, 1773, a group of colonists called the "Sons of Liberty" disguised themselves as Native Americans, boarded British ships, and dumped cases of tea into the harbor as a sign of rebellion against the ruling government and their taxation laws. The attack prompted the passing of the Coercive Acts by the British, meant to contain and suppress rebellion among the colonists, yet they caused outrage and sparked the war for independence. Again, the definition of "terrorism" is the sticking point: was the Tea Party freedom fighting or an attack against the state? As Bruce Hoffman points out, terrorism is difficult to define since the meaning of the term has changed so frequently over the past 200 years.[4]

To support the discussion of the persistence and lethality of modern domestic terrorism, we will start in 1865 with the emergence of the Ku Klux Klan (KKK) at the end of the Civil War, marking the beginning of a new era of violence and unrest in our country. A secret vigilante group with extreme methods, the KKK violently murdered and intimidated African Americans and the white legislators who fought for their freedom from slavery and full integration into our society. The KKK's attempts to keep black Americans from exercising their constitutional rights such as voting led to the passing of the Civil Rights Act of 1871. The act banned the use of terror, force, or bribery by the KKK to prevent people from voting and made these and other terroristic activities federal offenses. The Klan continues to be an underlying current of hate in our country, with other white supremacists expanding the racist agenda to include anti-Semitism, such as the Christian Identity offshoot Aryan Nations, which formed in the 1970s. Expert Bruce Hoffman considers the Aryan Nations the first "truly nationwide terrorist network in the U.S."[5]

The United States has had the bloodiest and most violent labor history of any industrial nation in the world.[6] Union violence emerged at the turn of the century, when unions sought to increase their footing and power in the emergent industrial society, which was favoring union-free companies. The International Association of Bridge and Structural Iron Workers was the most violent of the groups, perpetrating 110 bombings between 1906 and 1911. The deadliest attack was committed on October 1, 1910, when two Irish-American brothers, James and John McNamara, bombed the *Los Angeles Times* building, killing twenty-one people and injuring one hundred. The paper was targeted because the editor had voiced strong opposition to the unions. The bomb consisted of sixteen sticks of dynamite, and the timer was meant to expire at 4:00 a.m. when the building was empty; however, the timer malfunctioned and the bomb exploded at 1:00 a.m. while workers were constructing the next day's paper. A gas line was hit during the initial explosion, leading to a massive fire and more destruction than the brothers intended, although they proudly took credit for the death and destruction. As covered in the transnational crime chapter, the mafia has allied with the unions, which still use heavy-handed, violent tactics to keep power and protest benefit changes in what they consider an ongoing "class war" against the working people of the country. Union extremism is founded in left-wing perspectives such as Marxism.

Violent anarchism has been present in the United States for almost one hundred years. In April 1919, an anarchist group, the Galleanists, mailed thirty-six dynamite bombs to high-ranking officials, including the attorney general of the United States. Intending their delivery on May 1st when Americans would celebrate the international labor movement, several bombs exploded early and their unique packaging led to the discovery and neutralization of the other devices. Not content with this operation, the group struck again on the evening of June 2, 1919, when large dynamite and metal slug bombs simultaneously exploded in eight U.S. cities. The group was targeting government officials and judges who endorsed antisedition laws and had sentenced anarchists to prison. On September 16, 1920, a horse-drawn wagon bomb exploded on Wall Street in front of the J. P. Morgan bank, killing thirty-eight people. The device consisted of one hundred pounds of dynamite and five hundred pounds of cast iron weights. Although investigated for many years, including by the fledgling FBI in 1944, no one person or group was ever officially charged with the crime. Continuing labor struggles and anticapitalist sentiment led by anarchist groups such as the violent Galleanists were likely at the root of this bombing. Anarchists are very active around the world, protesting and resorting to violent tactics as needed to spread their message. They are especially known for their blatant disregard for law and willful destruction of property.

Bath, Michigan, was the scene of a "lone wolf" antigovernment attack on May 18, 1927. Andrew Kehoe, upset with policies and tax law he believed led to his farm foreclosure, murdered his wife then detonated three dynamite bombs at the Bath Consolidated School where he worked as the treasurer. Kehoe spent months planting explosive material throughout the building in a premeditated act that stunned the country. When confronted at the scene by law enforcement, he detonated a vehicle bomb, killing himself and the school superintendent. Eighty-three years later, in a similar act of rage, software engineer Joseph Stack set his house on fire, then flew a small aircraft into the Internal Revenue Service building in Austin, Texas, which housed 300 workers. Stack was furious about his tax problems and angry with collection agencies. His February 18, 2010, suicide note stated:

> Violence not only is the answer, it is the only answer ... I saw it written once that the definition of insanity is repeating the same process over and over and expecting the outcome to suddenly be different. I am finally ready to stop this insanity. Well, Mr. Big Brother IRS man, let's

try something different; take my pound of flesh and sleep well. The communist creed: From each according to his ability, to each according to his need. The capitalist creed: From each according to his gullibility, to each according to his greed.[7]

Stack's attack killed an IRS manager, seriously injured fifteen other workers, and cost the IRS $38 million to replace the building and its operation.

The 1960s and 1970s saw the rise of far left violent antiestablishment groups such as the Weather Underground, which held Marxist views of the elite ruling the middle class and bombed both the Pentagon and the State Department. The Symbionese Liberation Army, which started as a black revolutionary group and grew into a violent guerilla-type organization, carried out robberies, bombings, and murders, once using hollow-point bullets packed with cyanide to kill a school superintendent and his deputy. The militant Black Panthers began with a socialist agenda but soon morphed into an antiestablishment group routinely targeting law enforcement. Spurred by religious ideology, the Jewish Defense League (JDL) launched twenty-seven attacks against organizations it perceived to be anti-Semitic. Black September, the Palestinian group responsible for the killing of eleven Israeli athletes at the 1972 Munich Olympics, were quite active in the United States, plotting to kill Prime Minister Golda Meir during a visit to New York City in 1973 with three prepositioned car bombs, which failed to detonate. Political ideology fueled the Puerto Rican paramilitary group, the Fuerzas Armadas de Liberación Nacional (FALN), which was particularly brutal in its tactics and executed 120 bombings in the United States between 1974 and 1983. The FALN was a Marxist-Leninist group wanting the United States out of Puerto Rico both militarily and otherwise.

Moving forward to 1978, the country was transfixed by attacks perpetrated by Theodore Kaczynski, a Harvard University graduate and former mathematics professor. Kaczynski was a self-professed "Neo-Luddite," or one opposing modern technology and destroys private property as a means of protest. He lived in a wood shack in the forest, forgoing water or electricity; Kaczynski became enraged when developers moved into the area, destroying trees and displacing animals. Over the course of next seventeen years, Kaczynski sent sixteen letter bombs to academics and others working in technological fields, killing three people and injuring twenty-three. Now labeled the University & Airline Bomber (UNABOM) by the FBI, his lengthy manifesto was published in 1996 in the *New York Times* and the *Washington Post*, under the threat of more attacks. Kaczynski's campaign of terror ended with capture when his brother recognized his work and called authorities.

On April 19, 1995, in the deadliest act of domestic terror in our country's history, Timothy McVeigh detonated a truck bomb in Oklahoma City, killing 168 people and injuring 680 others. McVeigh and coconspirator Terry Nichols met in the army, becoming antigovernment survivalists who supported the militia movement. McVeigh was likely aligned with the Christian Identity group, and Nichols the Sovereign Citizen movement. McVeigh was enraged with the government's handling of the 1992 Ruby Ridge, Idaho, standoff, as well as the 1993 Waco, Texas, standoff with the Branch Davidian religious sect. McVeigh visited Waco both during the siege and after its tragic ending, when the compound caught on fire, killing seventy-five occupants including children. McVeigh stated that the Oklahoma City bombing was retribution against the government for Waco. Prior to his death by lethal injection in 2001, McVeigh was housed in the Supermax wing known as "Bomber's Block," with Ted Kaczynski and Ramzi Yousef, al Qaeda mastermind.

Eric Robert Rudolph, formerly an explosives expert in the army, was responsible for a series of deadly bombings between 1996 and 1998, killing two people and injuring over one hundred. His targets included Centennial Park at the Olympic Games in Atlanta, two abortion clinics, and a gay bar. Rudolph was a member of the Christian Identity movement, a white nationalist sect that believes God's chosen people are white and all others are condemned to Hell. Although Rudolph claimed religious motivation and his antiabortion, antigay agenda for his attacks, he stated that his actions were not racially motivated. He was on the run until 2003, when he was caught in a small North Carolina mountain town, rummaging through a dumpster and looking for food. After pleading guilty and apologizing to family members of those he killed and injured, Rudolph avoided the death penalty and is serving a life sentence at the Supermax facility, just down the hall from Kaczynski and Yousef.

In 2009, an act of domestic terror occurred on a military installation at Fort Hood, Texas. Former Major/Dr. Nidal Malik Hasan, a man who took not only the oath to protect and defend our country but also the Hippocratic oath to prevent harm to humans, stunned our country when he ambushed and killed thirteen of his fellow soldiers at the deployment processing line. Inspired to carry out his plan by radical Islamist Anwar al-Awlaki through a series of e-mails, Hasan voiced his extremist views and opposition to his upcoming deployment to Afghanistan to his chain of command prior to the shooting but no action was taken. Federal law enforcement agencies were aware of the communication between Awlaki and Hasan, yet the information was not passed to the base. Hasan has been charged with thirteen counts of premeditated murder and thirty-two counts of attempted murder, facing the death penalty if convicted at his court martial.

THE TWENTY-FIRST CENTURY AND THE
RISING TIDE OF DOMESTIC EXTREMISM

The Department of Justice is the lead agency for tracking hate groups and radical organizations, as well as gathering evidence, making arrests, and prosecuting their criminal activities. Unfortunately, there is no open-source government repository for information regarding the number and scope of domestic terror groups in the United States. Other groups have stepped into the void, most notably the Southern Poverty Law Center (SPLC). The SPLC is a nonprofit civil rights organization "dedicated to fighting hate and bigotry, and to seeking justice for the most vulnerable members of society." Founded in 1971, the organization has successfully prosecuted cases against white supremacist groups and other extremist organizations on behalf of its clients. Part of their mission is to "track the activities of hate groups and domestic terrorists across America," and many federal agencies are the benefactors of their vast repository of information. The groups tracked by SPLC include antigovernment, radical religious, neo-Nazi, Ku Klux Klan, Aryan Nations, black separatist, antigay, anti-immigrant, and the newest category, anti-Muslim.

The number of hate groups in the United States has steadily climbed in the last decade. In 2006, the SPLC reported 844 domestic hate and extremist groups; this number jumped to 1,018 in 2012. Hate-fueled incidents during the period of escalation include the 2009 killing of a guard at the Holocaust Museum in Washington, DC, by a self-proclaimed neo-Nazi; the 2010 bombing of a mosque in Jacksonville, Florida; the 2011 attempt to bomb the Martin Luther King parade in Spokane, Washington; and the 2012 shooting at a Sikh temple in Oak Creek, Wisconsin, killing six worshippers.

Chemical, biological, and radiological weapons are on the table for use by domestic groups. A study conducted by Syracuse University's Maxwell School of Public Policy and the New America Foundation examined 114 cases of domestic terrorist acts and plots since 9/11, none involving al Qaeda or groups or individuals motivated by Islamist radicalism. The ideologies studied span the spectrum from neo-Nazism and militant Christian fundamentalism to anarchism and violent environmentalism.[8] Among the vast number of weapons, destruction of property, and conspiracy charges, the group found five cases of domestic terrorism involving chemical, biological, and radiological agents, which could have killed thousands of Americans if executed.[9] Add to this the Fort Hood shooting, the failed "underwear bomber" plot, the Times Square vehicle-borne improvised explosive device (VBIED), and others: the domestic terror picture is extraordinarily complex and dangerous.

Postmodern domestic terror is similar to international terror since groups are often loose coalitions and franchises, held together by ideology, not a strong and charismatic leader. According to radicalization expert Daveed Gartenstein-Ross, the most frequently cited work on the concept of "leaderless resistance" was published by white supremacist Louis Beam in his *Inter-Klan Newsletter & Survival Alert* in 1983 and again in his journal *The Seditionist* in 1992. Beam believed that the traditional hierarchical methods of organizing the white separatist group left it vulnerable to destruction by the government; therefore, at some point, white separatists would not have the option of belonging to a group. He proposed a "leaderless resistance" structure, modeled after "committees of correspondence that existed throughout the thirteen colonies during the American Revolution." Beam postulated that each committee received information from the government but was a secret cell, operating independently, and action was taken on a local level. He also proposed organization around "very small or even one man cells of resistance" and advocated staying away from pyramidal organizations that are "an easy kill" for the government in light of federal informants and intelligence-gathering capabilities. "The last thing Federal snoops" would want, according to Beam, are "a thousand different small phantom cells opposing them."[10] Leaderless resistance, or the "phantom cell," has moved from the white supremacist realm into all other areas of domestic terrorism. By leveraging the Internet, groups can give tactical direction, guidance, inspiration, and money to followers, who then conduct operations independently. The leaderless-resistance methodology also culls lone wolves from society and encourages and enables them to act.

Domestic terror groups and incidents are often categorized as right-wing, left-wing, "single-issue," and radical Islamist, or in this case, "homegrown." Although impossible to cover all groups in one mere chapter, several certainly exhibit the characteristics and reach, placing them as most vulnerable to liaising with international groups and other criminal elements.

Right-Wing Extremism

Right-wing groups often adhere to the principles of racial supremacy and embrace antigovernment, antiregulatory beliefs. Right-wing terrorism is typically associated with those espousing neo-Nazi and racist ideologies as well as opposition to foreigners and immigration. According to the FBI, in the late 1990s right-wing extremism overtook left-wing terrorism to become the most dangerous domestic terrorist threat to the country. The Ruby Ridge confrontation and the Waco siege cemented the right-wing faction and ideology in our country. Post-9/11, DHS believes that hot-button issues such as immigration, gun control, abortion, and anti-Muslim sentiment, along with the election of the first African American president, present "unique drivers for right-wing radicalization and recruitment" per their controversial 2009 report. *Rightwing Extremism: Current Economic and Political Climate Fueling Resurgence in Radicalization and Recruitment* was a study crossing administrations by being completed in one and released in the next. The material was withdrawn by DHS due to political backlash but was certainly a significant piece of open-source intelligence, rarely shared with the public. The authors also found that "lone wolves and small terrorist cells embracing violent rightwing extremist ideology are the most dangerous domestic terrorism threat in the United States." The report warned that groups might seek to recruit military personnel due to their access to bases, equipment, and tactical knowledge. "Returning veterans possess combat skills and experience that are attractive to rightwing extremists. DHS/I&A is concerned that rightwing extremists will attempt to recruit and radicalize returning veterans in order to boost their violent capabilities." Finally, the report controversially stated that returning veterans who were "disgruntled, disillusioned, or suffering from the psychological effects of war" would be vulnerable for recruitment.[11] This assessment was likely due to the involvement of several military veterans in previous attacks and proved to be quite prescient with the Fort Hood shooting and other violent incidents. A quick online search provides proof that extremist groups are actively recruiting military and law enforcement to join their ranks. A video entitled "2012 ALERT! An Open Message to Police and Military" (see Figure 4.1) is posted on several militia and antigovernment extremist websites.

From the video transcript:

> You may tell yourself that you will draw your line in the sand later, that there is a certain point where you will say no, but in reality, you crossed the line a long time ago. You are standing on the wrong side of history right now. You are already participating in the destruction of this country, in the trampling of our rights, of your children's rights, and grandchildren's rights. You are the enforcement arm of a criminal enterprise, you are a servant of a rapidly expanding police state, and you DO have a choice. I'm not telling you this to condemn you. I'm telling you this because we the people desperately need you to take a stand. We desperately need you to have the courage to face your commanding officers, and tell them no, I didn't sign up for this. No this isn't right. No, I will not obey these unlawful orders. You took an oath to defend the constitution against all enemies foreign and domestic. Time to start taking that oath seriously.

2012 ALERT! An Open Message to Police and Military

FIGURE 4.1   Screen shot from an online video posted by a U.S. militia group.

Data gathered by several watchdog groups and think tanks support the DHS report finding of the rise of right-wing extremism: 56 percent of domestic terrorist attacks and plots in the United States since 1995 have been perpetrated by right-wing extremists, as compared to 30 percent by ecoterrorists (left-wing) and 12 percent by Islamic extremists (homegrown). In fact, right-wing extremism has been responsible for the greatest number of terrorist incidents in the United States in thirteen of the seventeen years since the Oklahoma City bombing.[12]

Militias

By definition, a militia is a military force comprising ordinary citizens to provide defense and law enforcement without pay. The original militias were force multipliers during the Revolutionary War, protecting towns and citizens from the British Army. However, modern militias are right-wing groups with paramilitary training that stockpile weapons and explosives and have a conspiracy-oriented ideology. The modern militia movement arose after the Waco and Ruby Ridge events, as members disagreed with the government's actions. Timothy McVeigh was aligned with the Michigan militia, which has the most prolific member in the country, Lee Miracle, a postal worker who goes by the moniker "Weapon

M." Miracle has his own webpage, video repository, and MySpace page, and participated in an interview with a major news network showing his young daughter expertly handling a shotgun. Although Miracle is a moderate in the militia realm, advocating for his troops to stockpile and prepare for a homeland defense mission, most militia websites are replete with paranoid, antigovernment rhetoric, and warnings about a dark future filled with disasters, calamity, and FEMA "concentration camps," which are currently under construction. Videos on the Internet further spread their conspiracies about martial law and the upcoming crackdown by the "New World Order."

The overarching motto for militias is to protect the Constitution against all enemies, foreign and domestic; however, the definition of a "domestic enemy" is worrisome and can include government leaders they believe are sapping rights and freedoms. For instance, militias see health care reform and any type of gun control as unconstitutional. There is a long list of orders they refuse to follow, many of which could bring them weapon-to-weapon with law enforcement and our military during states of emergency. The Oath Keepers, a group formed in 2009, has been linked to the militia movement. A prominent Oath Keeper stated openly, "The greatest threat we face today is not terrorists; it is our federal government,"[13]—a declaration that became a mantra for members of all right-wing extremist groups.

Sovereign Citizens

The sovereign citizens domestic terror group is unusual in its tactics, ranging from white-collar crime to impersonating and killing law enforcement officers. Experts believe that the group comprises 100,000 members and has been operating in the United States for at least twenty years. A spinoff of the defunct, violent Posse Comitatus, a white-supremacist, anti-Semitic group from the 1980s, the group's most famous member is Terry Nichols, who coconspired with Timothy McVeigh to destroy the Murrah Building. The sovereign's ideology has changed through the years, first believing "God gave America to the white man" and espousing conspiracy theories regarding Jewish control of the government. The group has moved away from this ideology to believing they can operate outside of any government authority and therefore do not adhere to laws or pay taxes. They also believe in the "Redemption Theory"—that the U.S. government went bankrupt when it abandoned the gold standard basis for currency in 1933 and began using citizens as collateral in trade agreements with foreign governments. This theory fuels the sovereign's belief that the government does not act in the best interests of its citizens and gives permission to steal from the U.S. Treasury to rightfully secure money with the people. The group creates and sells fraudulent documents such as driver's licenses, diplomatic and law enforcement credentials,

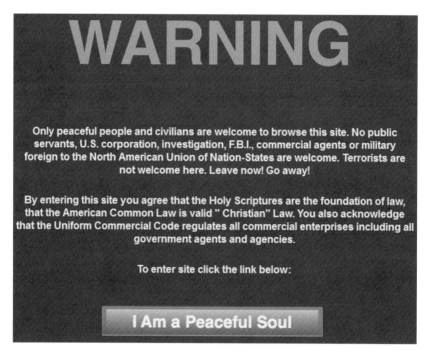

FIGURE 4.2 Password-protected entry to the main sovereign citizen website.

and concealed-firearms permits. The sovereign citizen Declaration of Independence states:

> We the People inhabiting the North American continent, free men and women convened under God, having been granted by the Creator domin-ion over all the earth, to restore the blessings of liberty for ourselves and the posterity, do hereby invoke our sacred right to alter or abolish destructive government as memorialized in The unanimous Declaration of the thirteen united States of America, c. 1776 by declaring herewith this solemn declaration to the people of the earth and all governments and nations derived there from. (Grammatical errors included)

What lies beyond the password-protected gate shown in Figure 4.2 is anything but peaceful. For example, any confrontation with law enforce-ment is likely to end in violence. Since 2000, group members have killed eight law enforcement officers, wounding several others. In 2010, two Arkansas police officers stopped sovereign citizen extremists Jerry Kane and his sixteen-year-old son, Joseph, during a routine traffic stop on Interstate 40. Joseph Kane immediately jumped out of the vehicle and opened fire with an AK-47 assault rifle, instantly killing both officers. In 2011, sovereign citizen James Michael Tesi shot a police officer in Texas on a traffic stop; the officer survived. In 2012, sheriff's deputies Brandon Nielsen and Jeremy Triche were ambushed and killed at a trailer park in La Place, Louisiana, when investigating an earlier shooting in which two deputies were shot and wounded working a traffic detail. A SWAT team entered the trailer park and apprehended the group, four men and three women, some with ties to the sovereign citizens and others with criminal records. The group had been under surveillance in Tennessee and then De Soto Parish, Louisiana, after brushes with the law including weapons charges, high-speed chases, and having sovereign citizen's paraphernalia. Unfortunately, the group left law enforcement radar just a few weeks prior to the shooting, moving to La Place.[14]

Sovereigns have also engaged in elaborate planning to kill law enforcement and government officials. For example, in 2011 five people, including popular activist Schaeffer Cox, were arrested in Fairbanks, Alaska, for conspiring to kill multiple Alaska state troopers and a federal judge, his children, and grandchildren in what is labeled the "241" murder conspiracy case. The group had stockpiled grenades and weapons with silencers and conducted surveillance on the homes of their targets. Arrests were made by the Alaska state troopers' Special Emergency Reaction Team, along with Fairbanks troopers, the FBI, the U.S. Marshal's Service, and the Fairbanks Police Department. The five faced several state charges, including conspiracy to commit murder, conspiracy to commit kidnapping, conspiracy to commit arson, and tampering with evidence, according to troopers. All pled guilty and were convicted, facing a possible life sentence in prison.[15]

Cox, who unsuccessfully ran for Congress in 2008, was on law enforcement's radar since 2009 as the leader of the Alaska Peacemakers Militia and the Second Amendment Task Force. He organized multiple gun-rights and personal-freedoms rallies and was a member of a "Liberty Bell network," which sends out mass notifications to assemble a crowd of witnesses when a member believes his or her rights are being violated by the police. Cox's video repository can still be viewed online and serves as a great education tool about the mind-set of a sovereign citizen, the conspiratorial nature of their ideology, and the willingness to use violence to "kill in the name of liberty."[16]

Sovereigns may be identified through the following behaviors:[17]

- Using the terminology "freeing money from the strawman," a reference to the redemption theory and the U.S. Treasury
- Names spelled in all capital letters or with colons (e.g., JOHN SMITH or Smith: John)

- Signatures followed by the words "under duress," "Sovereign Living Soul" (SLS), or a copyright symbol (©)
- Signing in red crayon on personal seals, stamps, or thumb prints in red ink
- The words "accepted for value"
- Presenting false identification, especially driver's licenses

Sovereigns not only have an inherent distrust of law enforcement; they step up and engage, then videotape, analyze, and share the officers' response. Sovereign Cop Watch, which has a branch specializing in "undercover and reverse sting police conduct investigations," has a strong presence on the Internet. Although their home website moves, the Facebook page is static, with over 1,100 connections, and directs users to the new location.[18]

Sovereign citizens present a complex and dangerous challenge for law enforcement and society. Training and recognition of the group's culture and tactics, as well as information sharing between agencies and states, are critical to engaging and mitigating the threat.

Left-Wing

Left-wing groups typically possess a revolutionary Socialist doctrine, viewing themselves as the protectors of the people from capitalism and imperialism. Left-wing activism in the United Stated was spurred by anti-Vietnam sentiment, the perception that law enforcement was spying on citizens, and events such as the shooting of students at Kent State by National Guard personnel in the 1970. These events caused government distrust, which led to protest and violent clashes. Leftist extremists were responsible for a preponderance of the domestic violence in the 1960s and 1970s and three-fourths of the officially designated acts of terrorism in America in the 1980s. The United States wasn't the only country facing a strong threat from the left; internationally, of the 13,858 people who died between 1988 and 1998 in attacks, 74 percent were killed by leftist organizations. The threat from the left in the United States diminished in the 1980s and 1990s, as a result of the arrest of many group leaders and the loss of support from nations formerly affiliated with, or part of, the Soviet Union. However, the threat from the left remains formidable, especially from anarchist and single-issue activists.

Anarchists

Anarchism is a political philosophy that considers the state undesirable, unnecessary, and harmful and instead promotes a stateless society, or anarchy. An anarchist is an individual who furthers his or her political and/or social goals through force or violence and violation of law. Anarchists may typically espouse anticapitalist, antiglobalization, Communist, Marxist, and Socialist philosophies. There are branches of the movement with specific agendas like Left, Green, Freemarket, and People of Color.

Anarchists are now present at nearly every international gathering and they escalate fear among attendees, residents, and business owners, driving up security costs. For instance, Canada spent $900 million to secure Toronto for the G-20 summit in 2010, but it wasn't enough to keep anarchists from wreaking havoc on the streets, burning police cars, smashing storefronts, and terrorizing citizens. Those arrested weren't just Canadians; anarchists from the United States and European countries traveled to the summit location to participate in the violence. Anarchist groups continue to use the black bloc technique, which originated in German riots in the 1970s, where protestors wear black hoods, balaclavas, and helmets as a show of solidarity and as disguise. After the violent acts are perpetrated, the clothing can be stripped off so the anarchist will blend in with other citizens and escape.

Anarchists are now moving beyond protests at events to actively planning attacks. In 2011, an anarchist group was arrested by the FBI for a plot to blow up a bridge in Cleveland, Ohio, using C-4 explosive. The attack was meant to bring down financial institution signage on the bridge, not necessarily the bridge. This event served as a good reminder about target selection not always being what it appears; had the bridge fallen due to the attack, the investigatory process may have leaned toward a homegrown terror theory and away from the true perpetrators and their rationale.

In Chapter 8, we will cover the anarchists' use of Twitter to give real-time directions about where to rally, what to wear, and how to engage law enforcement. The anarchists also extensively use websites and chat rooms to communicate, educate, and coordinate protests. When Los Angeles transit police officer Johannes Mehserle shot and killed Oscar Grant early New Year's Day, 2009, the anarchist community vigorously protested. Their activity escalated on July 8, 2010, when Mehserle's court case came to an end with a verdict and sentence. When monitoring anarchist websites and Twitter, I captured the following communiqué:

> To everyone coming out to 14th and Broadway on Verdict Day: Some of us will be with you at 14th and Broadway on the day of the verdict. We know that the pigs will be looking to cause trouble, but we're not going to give them an excuse. We want everyone in Oakland to come out to 14th and Broadway. We'll leave it to the will of the people assembled to decide what goes down there. Also, we just heard that Alameda County dropped at least $675,000 on an LRAD 300X sonic weapon system, so bring earplugs.

The communiqué indicates the very essence of leaderless resistance and the ability of the group to gather inside information and adapt operations based on law enforcement's posture.

The establishment of the Center for a Stateless Society (CSS), an anarchist think tank, has brought a group of academic elites to the table. CSS has a staff and advisory panel of experts, including professors from large universities, and also collects donations for their cause. The website includes a 106-question quiz to identify social and political "philosophy," and there is a large repository of well-written articles on anarchy.[19] The lesson CSS teaches is that we should not envision anarchists as mere thugs, storefront smashers, and "occupiers." Some of our academic elites believe in a stateless society and are in a position to compel others.

After 9/11, some American anarchists joined the ranks of the "truthers" who developed conspiracy theories about the attacks, including that the World Trade Center contained bombs, the Pentagon was hit with a missile, Israel was behind the attacks, or the event was an inside job done by the CIA. However, most anarchists give little or no thought to 9/11, actively attempting to devalue the event and its impact on our country and world. The only significance they see is how follow-on laws such as the Patriot Act impacted their cause. For instance, consider the following quotes from a recent document entitled *Ten Years after 9/11: An Anarchist Evaluation*:[20]

- "Anarchists, I argue, were among the few radicals whose analysis of history and power was not transformed, directly or indirectly, by the events of 9/11."
- "A host of obvious questions accompany an attempt to encapsulate an event such as 9/11 and the ten years that followed, foremost among them: Why situate 9/11 as a date of exceptional importance? Does a reflection of this kind merely contribute to, for example, neoconservative attempts to enshrine 9/11 as a propagandistic tool? The response of the US government (and capitalist states worldwide) to 9/11 diminished the capacity of anarchist social movements through a barrage of draconian laws, militarization of police forces, and repressive new forms of technological surveillance."
- In a discussion about the "We Will Never Forget" slogan, the counterproposal is "The Forgetful Memory of 9/11."[21]

While accomplishing research for an article on anarchism, I participated in an online chat anonymously with self-professed anarchists. We were discussing terrorist threats from al Qaeda and other groups, and most participants did not perceive any kind of danger at all, believing the government has overblown the situation to justify military activities abroad and added policing activities in the United States. I mentioned the overarching goal of extremists who want to turn the United States into an Islamic republic under Sharia law. One of the participants stated he would "rather see the flag of any group or country flying over our Capitol than the flag of the US," and several others piled on with their concurrence. I found this discussion extremely shocking and worrisome, not because these opinions are provocative or different from the mainstream. The concern arose from the perspective of anarchists being hyperfocused on an ideology to the point where they don't perceive outside threats and exclude the possibility they may exist, or that they, as Americans, are in the crosshairs. Further, in terms of liaising with international or domestic terror groups, although not a goal of anarchists, the groups do all share a common enemy: the government, *any* government.

Anarchism and the Military   The increasing number of ex-military members posting on anarchist blogs is also something of interest; they typically receive a warm welcome and of course bring a host of expertise to the table for the movement. Figure 4.3 is a screenshot of a military veteran's posting in an anarchist forum.

The case of U.S. Army PFC Michael Burnett and his three accomplices allows insight into a case of dissension within the active military ranks. On August 27, 2012, Burnett testified about his role in a plot to overthrow the government, as part of an anarchist/militia group called FEAR, Forever Enduring Always Ready. Burnett, along with three other soldiers, killed a fellow soldier who had recently left the military and his girlfriend because they were "loose ends" to eliminate so the plot would not be revealed. FEAR spent almost $100,000 on equipment and firearms, money taken from the life insurance policy of the deceased pregnant wife of one of the group's members; her death is now under investigation as a possible murder. FEAR plotted to take over their home station, Fort Stewart, Georgia, and then bomb targets in Savannah, Georgia, including the Forsyth Park fountain. They also wanted to destroy a dam in Washington State and poison the apple supply. Group members had matching tattoos resembling an anarchy symbol. The ultimate goal of FEAR was to assassinate President Obama and "give the government back to the people."[22]

anon - Mon, 2012-08-27 15:15

Look at this   troll.

Signed, a US army combat veteran, who does support the overthrow of the state, but also knows what anarchy is.

FIGURE 4.3   Post from a popular Anarchist forum.

Single-Issue or Special-Interest Terrorism

Single issue or special-interest terrorism is a different brand of extremism than right- and left-wing terrorism, as groups try to influence specific issues, not effect political change. Actors are on the extreme fringes of animal rights, environmental protection, pro-life, and antinuclear movements, attempting to sway public opinion in their favor. A difficult extremism to comprehend, group members often believe it is justifiable to kill a human being in the name of saving an animal, a tree, or an unborn child. Groups typically operate underground, with no hierarchy. They are basically leaderless with small cells around the world and the ideology (and the Internet) serving as the glue for the cause. Thousands of acts of violence and property damage in the last ten years have been attributed to special-interest terrorism.

The Earth Liberation Front (ELF)

Per their press office, ELF uses "economic sabotage and guerrilla warfare to stop the exploitation and destruction of the environment." This activity is also known as "ecotage." Originating in the United Kingdom in 1992, ELF's first activity in the United States occurred in 1996, when the group spray-painted buildings and used glue to damage locks on McDonald's restaurants in Oregon. The FBI classified ELF as the top domestic threat in March 2001, due to a string of arsons destroying a ranger station, large houses, and a Land Rover dealership, as well as the firebombing of a lab at Michigan State University. The group was active throughout the next decade, destroying a 206-unit condominium complex in San Diego in 2003 and four multimillion-dollar homes on Seattle's "Street of Dreams" in 2008. Oddly enough, the Street of Dreams homes were "green," and the emissions from the ELF fire did far more environmental damage than the homes would have in one hundred years.

The British eco group "10:10 org," which was originally a campaign to get individuals, companies, and institutions to reduce their carbon footprints by 10 percent during 2010, issued a series of violent videos showing children being blown up by their teacher for not espousing "green" philosophies.[23] Meant as an attention-getting mechanism, the videos enraged citizens who were concerned that the message that "there will be blood" shed for eco issues would be taken literally by groups already harboring violent tendencies.

Animal Liberation Front (ALF)

Members of ALF see themselves as the liberators and rescuers of animals. Also, a primary goal is to inflict economic damage on those who profit from the misery and exploitation of animals. ALF's roots are in the United Kingdom, dating as far back as 1976, appearing in the United

IN FOCUS: AGROTERRORISM

The agroterror threat is not given as much weight as other dangers, for instance WMD. However, as terror groups increasingly realize that striking the economic structure is a powerful means to get attention and concessions, the possibility of an asymmetric attack to the food supply is escalating. Also, as other avenues of attack are closed down or increasingly are difficult to navigate, agroterrorism may seem increasingly attractive alternative.

The quarantine of stock, the economic loss to farmers, and the international impact of sudden withdrawal from the food market would likely cause the fear and economic loss sought by terror groups. Also, this type of attack is relatively inexpensive compared to other operations, making it all the more attractive. Experts believe foot-and-mouth disease (FMD) is the most likely and pressing threat. Although eradicated from our country, FMD can still be found on other continents and is extremely contagious, with humans able to carry the virus for up to forty-eight hours. The virus can travel fifty miles to affect other herds, and persists for weeks on cloth and in straw. Our "mega farms" with 10,000 head of cattle are especially vulnerable targets to FMD. The impact of FMD on the economy was experienced in Great Britain in 2001, when 9,000 farms were infected, leading to the slaughter of over 4 million animals. Naturally, this type of mandatory process would also anger animal activists and likely lead to their uprising.

Another type of attack, with bacteria such as botulism, *E. coli*, and salmonella, could be launched against packing plants. The 2008 case of salmonella contamination at the Peanut Corporation of America (PCA) sheds light on the vulnerability of the packing industry. PCA peanut butter and peanut meal were used in 3,919 products manufactured by 361 companies, and the recall related to the contamination was the largest in U.S. history. The sale of all peanut butter dropped 25 percent as scared consumers avoided the product completely. At least 9 people died and over 714 were sick as a result of salmonella. The fruit and vegetable supply chain is possibly the most vulnerable, with the least amount of bioterrorism protection measures in place and little to no processing with bacteria killers such as heat.

A major problem with investigating these types of issues is that state and local law enforcement have jurisdiction. Establishing the adequate quarantine upon detection, consisting of hundreds of square miles and possibly crossing state lines, would be difficult to enact without federal oversight. The same holds true for stopping trucks and trains with contaminated cattle or food in transit throughout the country. Resource-constrained departments would be stretched to the limit responding to such a disaster. The FBI emphasizes that the theft of vaccines, medicines, and livestock-related equipment must be reported and is of concern from a national security perspective. Certainly, local and state inspectors and law enforcement must take care to gather evidence and assume that a mass outbreak or contamination could be the work of terrorists.

Finally, the PCA case also shed a light on the seasonal workers employed at packing plants, typically an unscreened, transitional populace. Lack of preparedness is a weakness the enemy seeks to exploit; therefore, our training and vigilance are paramount to protecting our agriculture industry from an agroterror attack.

Primary source: FBI's Law Enforcement Bulletin, Agroterrorism: Threats to America's Economy and Food Supply by Dean Olson, February 2012.

States in 1982. Early ALF activities identified illegal animal research and resulted in legal action against the perpetrators of the crimes; however, ALF abroad became violent in the 1980s, sending letter bombs to government leaders. The group then began to engage in elaborate hoaxes, claiming to have poisoned food products and cosmetics and costing companies millions of dollars in recalls, product destruction, and lost customers. Fur companies were firebombed and devices planted on executives' vehicles and at their doorsteps. This brand of violence moved to the United States in the 1990s and grew in intensity, with a string of incidents leading to injuries to innocent bystanders and millions of dollars in property damage.

On January 20, 2006, as part of Operation Backfire, the U.S. Department of Justice announced charges against nine Americans and two Canadian activists calling themselves the "The Family." At least nine of the eleven pleaded guilty to conspiracy and arson for their role in a string of twenty arsons from 1996 through 2001, damage totaling $40 million dollars. The Department of Justice called their activity "domestic terrorism," with incidents including arson attacks against meat-processing plants, lumber companies, a high-tension power line, and a ski center in Vail.[24] Environmental and animal rights activists have referred to the legal action by the government as the "Green

Scare," and the roundup doesn't seem to have deterred the groups. ELF has been somewhat quiet in 2012, but ALF has stepped up their efforts, breaking into farms and liberating exotic animals; hacking websites, sabotaging race tracks, and burning meat trucks. Their press office website, which has a section with pictures of federal agents who investigate the group, as well as "snitches and informants," instructs followers: "Talking to law enforcement will always hurt you and others. The Feds or the local police are not your friends no matter how much they ensure you that they are trying to help you. Law enforcement will always resort to fear and intimidation and we must resist such divisional tactics."[25]

In terms of future operations, ALF and ELF's ideology could certainly be in line with attacks against the food supply in our country or companies producing meat products. Many experts believe they would easily liaise with other terror groups to further their goals and bring attention to the cause.

HOMEGROWN TERROR

Our long-held belief that homegrown terrorism couldn't happen here has created a situation where we are today, stumbling blindly through the legal, operational, and organizational minefield of countering terrorist radicalization and recruitment occurring in the U.S.

—Bipartisan Policy Center (2010)

At least fifty domestic terror plots have been identified, been mitigated, or failed since the tragic events of 9/11. Some are more memorable than others: Richard Reid, the shoe bomber; Jose Padilla, the dirty bomber; the Lackawanna Six; the Fort Dix plot; the LA Airport "Doomsday" plot; the Raleigh Jihad Group; Najibullah Zazi's backpack plot against the New York City subway; Shahzad, the Times Square bomber; and Abdulmutallab, the underwear bomber. Other homegrown plots since 9/11 include the planned or attempted bombing of buildings, bridges, and landmarks and the targeting of malls, railroads, and subways. The Heritage Foundation has compiled a thorough list of disrupted domestic attacks since 9/11 and it is worthy of review as a reminder of the breadth, depth, imagination, and scope of our homegrown terrorists.[26]

Many times I have unknowingly stood in the very spot in East Potomac Park where Rezwan Ferdaus, a U.S. citizen from Ashland, Massachusetts, with a degree in physics, planned to launch a remote-controlled aircraft packed with twenty-five pounds of C-4 plastic explosives to attack the Pentagon in 2011. Following the initial strike, Ferdaus planned to use six people armed with AK-47s to shoot into the panicked crowd in the aftermath. He acquired one of the aircraft through a PayPal account under a false name, a six-foot-long drone, capable of flying up to one hundred miles per hour. While planning this attack, Ferdaus also rigged IED detonators and gave them to FBI agents he believed were al Qaeda operatives who would deliver them downrange. He was pleased to learn from agents that his first detonator "killed" American soldiers. Scientists tore the plot apart, detailing for the press exactly why it wouldn't have worked based on radio frequencies and the weight of the C-4 load, feeding the correct data to future plotters, no doubt. So much rhetoric surrounded the improbability of such an attack that the very essence was lost: it was creative, asymmetric, and plotted by a fellow citizen who will gladly kill us in the name of his ideology. Ferdaus was determined to kill Americans and attack what he called the "great Satan"—his own country of birth.

The number of disrupted plots is on the rise, meaning there are potentially many other undetected would-be terrorists or terrorist cells operating in our country. Radicalized Americans are typically educated, like Ferdaus. Leveraging the Internet, they move quickly along the continuum from contemplation, to planning, to execution. They are creative and highly adaptable, learning from failed operations. For example, when the Times Square bomber Faisal Shahzad left his vehicle with a smoking dud for a bomb, failing to stay and work on the device until it exploded, internal al Qaeda correspondence indicated that this doomed scenario would never happen again. The enemy is watching and learning; there is no such thing as a failure, only a stumbling block on the path to perfection. Unfortunately, our culture is to hyperfocus on the last attempt and not look forward, yet terrorists continue to progress in methodology and target selection. They go on surveillance missions and measure the number of people and cars passing by and the distance from weapon to target. They probe and accomplish dry runs, perfecting the plot. Our very public "celebration" over a disrupted plot should be tempered by the thought the next bomber is American and in his or her home tonight, watching the same newscast, creating new and improved ways to kill us and destroy our way of life.

Not much time is spent contemplating what happens after the domestic terrorist is arrested. Few, if any, receive the life sentences given to Reid, Padilla, and Zazi. Many sentences are between three and twenty years, with the long periods of time spent in jail awaiting the court case awarded as time served and deducted from the length of the sentence. As a result, several convicted domestic terrorists and conspirators have already served their prison sentence and were quietly released back to society, including members of the Lackawanna Six and Portland Seven terror groups who traveled to Afghanistan for training with the Taliban. Many other Americans convicted on terrorism charges are set to come out of prison in the next five to ten years, yet we have no plan for their rehabilitation and reintegration into our neighborhoods. Reradicalization is likely and perhaps with a renewed fervor due to anger projected toward the government. With the spread of al Qaeda affiliates around the world, and an increasingly disenfranchised population, the radicalized homegrown threat will at the very least remain constant, but is likely to rise.

Rehabilitation and the Domestic Terrorist

> A terrorist is only temporarily neutralized by imprisonment.
>
> —Dennis Pluchinsky[27]

A few years ago, I was approached by the editors of *The Counter Terrorist Magazine* to write an article on jihadist recidivism, those who leave prison and return to a life of terror, for the April/May 2010 issue.[28] I found an extraordinarily small body of research on the topic, despite the pressing nature of the problem. The list of former Guantanamo Bay detainees who are assuming leadership positions in al Qaeda offshoots continues to grow, as discussed in the previous chapter. Jihadist recidivism is a persistent and growing feeder of manpower to the international and domestic terror groups and operations. Also, recidivism provides a valuable resource to terrorist groups: experienced jihadists who have gained firsthand insight into enemy counter terrorism practices and agents through their arrest, sentencing, and detainment.

Capturing a terrorist is a resource-intensive event, and taking an enemy combatant off of the battlefield and out of our neighborhoods is clearly a victory. However, the process must not end with the arrest, or even conviction; the apprehension is merely the tip of the iceberg. Perhaps an even greater investment must be made on activities occurring during a prisoner's incarceration, rehabilitation, and release to ensure the jihadist remains permanently out of the fight. Unfortunately, our homegrown terrorists, many of whom have already returned to our communities having served their sentence or been acquitted on technicalities, are not rehabilitated. They merely walk out the door, and the onus is back on resource-constrained law enforcement agencies to ensure they remain law-abiding citizens. And while in prison, they have a chance to recruit and radicalize others and to cross paths with terrorists and criminals. By studying the international lessons learned regarding jihadist recidivism, we can effectively cross-apply those tactics, techniques, and observations to our domestic challenges.

Jihadist Defined

According to terrorism expert Dennis Pluchinsky, a global jihadist can be defined as a Muslim who believes Islam is under attack by the West with the objective of destroying Islam, perceives that the United States is the primary enemy of Islam, believes it is Islam's manifest destiny to the rule the world, and believes the only proper response to this threat to Islam and the Muslim Ummah (members of the Islamic community) is militant jihad.[29]

Jihadists differ from terrorists who are not religiously motivated. The call to jihad (which means "struggle" in Arabic) is powerful and typically comes in response to a fatwa, or binding religious decree. Jihadists are also revered as martyrs for the cause, which means carefully selecting operational tactics so as not to amplify their deaths. Former secretary of defense Donald Rumsfeld once remarked that for every jihadist we kill, we recruit three more.[30] Islamic scholar and journalist M. J. Akbar provides great insight into jihad, describing it thus: "The power of jihad pervades the mind and soul of Islam. The mind is where the current battle will be fought, and this is why it will be a long war."[31]

Recidivism

A recidivist is defined as one who, after release from custody for commission of a crime, is not rehabilitated.[32] Although the term is now applied in the counterterror realm, recidivism is closely tracked in the U.S. prison system and the statistics are startling; according to the Department of Justice, of the 300,000 prisoners released in fifteen states in 1994, two-thirds were rearrested within three years. Recidivism substantially increased from the previous decade, in spite of extensive education and job-training efforts and life skills and readjustment counseling provided to convicts during incarceration. Data from a follow-up study of prisoners released in 2005 is due from the Bureau of Prisons in late 2012. Recidivism by convicted criminals clearly illustrates that arrest, confinement, and rehabilitation alone does not preclude further nefarious activities. The same is true for jihadists, for whom the stakes are much higher.

Terrorist Recidivism

Of the 779 original detainees at the Guantanamo Bay detention center, at least 603 have been released and 168 remain. The released detainees have been transferred to forty-four countries, including Ireland, Bermuda, Palau, and the United States. Of greatest interest are those transferred to Afghanistan (199), Saudi Arabia (120), Pakistan (63), and Yemen (22), all hotbeds for radical recruitment and activity.[33] According to the Office of the Director of National Intelligence (ODNI) in 2012, the recidivism rate of former Guantanamo detainees who were either confirmed or suspected of reengaging in militant activity stands at 27.9 percent.[34] The number has steadily increased in the last five years as more prisoners were released, accounting of their whereabouts improved, and of those, more turned back to their old ways.

Counterradicalization Efforts

Jihad is a powerful call, and dislodging (or neutralizing) the radical ideology is not an easy task, not even for lifelong Muslims. Many countries have established jihadist rehabilitation and engagement programs, including Algeria, Egypt, Jordan, Singapore, Indonesia, and Malaysia. Notably, Yemen's program is now defunct, and there is no curriculum or facility in place today to process returning Yemeni nationals from Guantanamo.

When releasing detainees from the Guantanamo facility, the U.S. government has heavily relied on the "Saudi Program." The program was established after the 2003 bombings in Riyadh and is a "soft" counter-terrorism program, meant to combat violent extremism and mitigate the ideological and intellectual justifications of jihad. The program is not punitive, but a benevolent, second-chance program with a large social welfare component. Although the exact numbers are questionable, the Saudis claim an overall 80 to 90 percent success rate for the program. They have processed approximately 3,000 individuals and 1,400 have reportedly renounced their former ways and been released. Of the group, there are thirty-five acknowledged recidivists. The rest of the extremists will remain in the program until deemed ready for release. Of 120 Saudi citizens sent to the rehabilitation program from the Guantanamo facility, 10 remain in the program and 6 have been rearrested by officials. Of the 110 released, many reradicalized and became "most wanted" men in Saudi Arabia.[35] In December of 2009, a most-wanted recidivist turned himself in to Saudi authorities, and another was killed after crossing the Yemeni border with an explosive vest. Eleven more of the released are on Saudi Arabia's most-wanted list.[36]

Inside the Saudi Program

Christopher Boucek is a Middle East specialist who has studied the Saudi approach to recidivism since its inception. His 2008 paper entitled "Saudi Arabia's 'Soft' Counterterrorism Strategy: Prevention, Rehabilitation, and Aftercare" gives an inside look at this secretive program.[37]

The Saudi Program relies on several primary tenets:

- Violent radical Islamic extremism cannot be defeated by traditional security means alone.
- Violent ideology is based on corrupted and deviant interpretations of Islam.

- Obedience and loyalty to the state and its leadership are key.
- Extremists lack the authority and understanding of religious doctrine.

These principles are enforced through a program of co-optation and persuasion by a system called PRAC, which consists of three interconnected phases:

- Prevention: The phase fosters cooperation between the state and the public, highlights the damage done by terrorism and extremism, and ends public support and tolerance for extremist beliefs. Hundreds of programs are aimed at youth in and out of school; there are also massive public information campaigns, and highway billboards decrying terrorism as part of this phase.
- Rehabilitation: The focal point of this phase is counseling by clerics and academics to reeducate and rehabilitate jihadists. It begins with the assumption these individuals were misled by extremists who follow a corrupted form of Islam and misinterpret the Koran.
- Post Release Care: Most Guantanamo returnees entered the program at this point, since they were not tried and convicted of crimes in Saudi Arabia. During this phase, residents live in a "halfway house," the Care Rehabilitation Center. The Center has guards and fences, but the prisoners are not confined or restrained in any way. The post release phase focuses on reintegration into Saudi society; the Guantanamo returnees receive additional psychological counseling and participate in activities designed to help them adjust to freedom.

Once an individual has satisfactorily renounced his or her extremist beliefs, job placement services are provided along with other benefits, including a government stipend, a car, and an apartment. The added social support is intended to deter the rehabilitated terrorist from returning to his or her former lifestyle.[38] The Saudi Program has been the source of scrutiny; after several former Guantanamo detainees returned to al Qaeda, DHS sent a team of FBI officials and terrorism specialists to the center for a firsthand look. Although a formal report to the public was not released, one of the team members spoke to the press about his experience. Dr. John Horgan, director of the International Center for the Study of Terrorism at Pennsylvania State University, stated, "When I asked Saudi officers how they knew these people were safe to release, all they could say was they got a feeling." He also opined that the prisoners are not being de-radicalized and their fundamental views have not changed. Another criticism was the lack of any reliable risk assessment to decide whether an individual should be allowed back into society.

"Sex offenders have to meet all sorts of criteria before they are released," Mr. Horgan said. "Why shouldn't it be the same for terrorists?"[38]

Mr. Pluchinsky estimates there are 5,000 global jihadists imprisoned worldwide, and only 15 percent of captured jihadists are given life sentences or executed, meaning the rest are in prisons, either being rehabilitated or planning reengagement with their original group once released. Prisons are a hotbed of radicalization; as discussed in the previous chapter, notable recidivists Sayyid Qutb and Ayman al-Zawahiri were prisoners and responsible for the formation of al-Qaeda. Aggravating the recidivism challenge, lacking international protocol, laws, or oversight, the country of imprisonment dictates the rules of engagement. For example, sentence reductions are available for good behavior, prisoners may be released for religious holidays, and prisoner exchanges could take place. Keeping track of jihadists is a daunting task, and related information is very difficult to corroborate.

Possible Solutions in the Homeland

In addition to using portions of "PRAC" domestically, a potential model for a domestic rehabilitation program comes from the U.S. military, which successfully delved into the rehabilitation realm in Iraq through the decommissioned Task Force 134 and its "House of Wisdom" program. Through this operation, vetted Iraqi clerics encouraged debate with detainees for the purpose of refuting and mitigating extremist arguments.[39] Also, scientific study shows that disengagement of radical ideology is best done through support of an individual's social network[40]; therefore, including the American public in the dialogue is a necessity. Avoiding the issue and simply sending the terrorist back to society without a support structure is unwise. Finally, the government previously announced intentions to acquire the Thomson Correctional Center, a large, vacant state prison in northwestern Illinois, to house detainees transferred from the Guantanamo facility. Since this plan never came to fruition, perhaps the facility could be used to rehabilitate American jihadists before returning them to society.

There must be more comprehensive research conducted and published on the issue of recidivism. When contacted for comment regarding my 2010 magazine article, Mr. Pluchinsky offered his current view of the situation: "Jihadist recidivism remains a problem that has not been properly mapped. We have no idea how many released global jihadists turned into recidivists. We still do not know the level and scope of the problem. Most of the evidence, including my 2008 article on the issue in Studies in Conflict and Terrorism is anecdotal. For that matter, terrorist recidivism in general has not been properly and adequately researched." Very little has been published on the subject in the intervening years, yet global and domestic jihadist activity continues to grow in scope and intensity.

Counterterrorism and homeland security experts are perhaps not the best researchers for this complex issue. Similar to the analysis of the other terrorism-related issues, the answer may instead lie in the "soft" sciences—psychology, sociology, organizational theory, and theology—disciplines that provide a multifaceted understanding and approach to the problem. Professionals in these fields could best answer the following questions:

- Do religious terrorists have a higher recidivism rate than terrorists without the radical religious ideology? If so, why?
- Can any parallels to be drawn between terrorist rehabilitation and cult deprogramming or the successful neo-Nazi and leftist guerilla rehabilitation programs?
- How can we better use psyops and the Internet to introduce a deliberate theological counterideology to jihad and prevent reradicalization?
- Are there any aspects of the Saudi Program that can be applied to would-be domestic terrorists in the United States if they eventually return from detention to our communities?

Recidivism is just one source of manpower for al-Qaeda and other radical Islamic groups seeking to harm the United States and its allies. Understanding how the switch is flipped from "off" to "on" is critical for prevention, and knowing how to turn it "off" again is fundamental to the domestic de-radicalization process. Recidivism is undesirable and likely unavoidable. There's no such thing as a perfect criminal justice system: the question must be in which direction we want to deflect the likelihood of error.

THE LONE WOLF

According to the FBI, a lone wolf draws ideological inspiration from formal terrorist organizations but operates on the fringe. Despite their ad hoc nature and generally limited resources, they can mount high-profile, extremely destructive attacks, and their operational planning is often difficult to detect.[41] The FBI considers the lone wolf the most significant domestic terrorism threat, especially since detection and mitigation are hampered by relative anonymity. A lone wolf doesn't necessarily mean one person working alone; McVeigh's bombing of the Murrah Federal Building in Oklahoma City is a good example. McVeigh and his accomplice were influenced by the ideology of a group, yet worked clandestinely on the fringe to develop an undetectable plan for mass destruction. Other notable lone wolves include Ted Kaczynski, Eric Robert Rudolph,

IN FOCUS: HUMINT AND DOMESTIC TERROR

Recent domestic cases involving terrorists were foiled not with high-tech equipment but with human sources. Officials in Israel have spoken openly about recent success hindering suicide bombings previously causing their country incalculable psychological and economic damage. Although the United States has been spared this particularly brutal means of terrorizing the populace, law enforcement must be ever vigilant of the threat of suicide bombing in public areas such as shopping malls, amusement parks, sports venues, restaurants, and hotels. Lessons learned by Israel and other countries combating suicide bombings are certainly applicable and worthy of analysis by all engaged in the war on terror.

Israel places a high value on human intelligence and weaves HUMINT into all aspects of their law enforcement activities. A prevalent saying in their intelligence community guides their efforts: "The small brings in the big." Israeli law enforcement and intelligence collection agents build long-term, lasting relationships on the ground with all types of businesspeople. For instance waitresses, bartenders, taxi drivers and barbers can provide a wealth of information. Emergency room employees, gas station workers, and grocery or drugstore employees are all good collection sources. Around a specific target, street vendors are worthy of engagement since they frequent the same area and have a perfect viewpoint for noticing out-of-the-ordinary activity. If protecting a church is the objective, the clergy and worshipers are valuable informants. The key is to cultivate the relationship; visit the sources regularly, build their trust, instruct them on what to look for, and make sure they have a way of contacting you at any time if they notice something suspicious.

Sources are force multipliers and critical to gleaning the information needed to identify, monitor, and then disrupt terrorist activities. As the recent domestic cases illustrate, source cultivation is time well spent by law enforcement. Recent "See something, say something" campaigns will be effective only if we also educate the community on the threat so they are looking for the right indicators and reporting the most effective details.

the perpetrator of the Tylenol poisoning event in 1981, the perpetrator of the anthrax letters just after 9/11, and Joseph Stack, who flew his aircraft into the IRS building. Many of the domestic terror attacks and plots since 9/11 were planned by a lone individual.

Other countries have also experienced horrific lone-wolf events. Anders Behring Breivik, thirty-two, was a Norwegian lone wolf who planned his operation for nine years and committed two stunning attacks on July 22, 2011. First, Breivik detonated a VBIED in Oslo outside of the prime minister's office, killing eight people. The device was constructed with fertilizer and explosive primer. Breivik then traveled to Utøya Island by boat, infiltrating a Norwegian Labour Party camp for children. Dressed as a police officer to garner unimpeded access and trust from children, he opened fire, killing sixty-nine children and counselors before law enforcement arrived. Breivik surrendered without a fight. With a right-wing extremist ideology and racist, anti-Muslim viewpoints, Breivik believed that killing the children was justified. In his estimation, he eliminated the next generation of Marxists who were going to turn Europe into what he calls "Eurabia." Convicted in August 2012, Breivik received the maximum sentence given in Norway to convicted killers, twenty-one years; then, his release will be considered by the courts. Breivik published his manifesto on the Internet just prior to executing the attacks, a long missive entitled "2083: A European Declaration of Independence,"[42] and also posted a video urging conservatives to "embrace martyrdom" and showing himself dressed in a uniform and pointing a Ruger Mini-14.[43] A self-professed Freemason and Knight Templar officer, Breivik continues to espouse his right-wing ideology and has started the "Conservative Revolutionary Movement" of activists across Europe from his prison cell. Profiling Breivik would be helpful toward understanding the motivation and activities of lone wolves.

As these cases amply illustrate, the human behavior and motivations of a lone wolf are broad, complex, and somewhat unpredictable; in this case, the criminal may not be completely motivated by ideology, and many psychological factors such as anger and paranoia can be at play. Certainly, the radicalized homegrown lone wolf is the most dangerous, fueled by religious ideology and a duty to answer a divine call. Cyber attacks will likely be perpetrated by lone wolves, or possibly a loose coalition of criminal hackers who have never met but are a part of a community flourishing in the anonymity of the Internet.

GANGS: EVOLVING AND COLLABORATING

Although not officially labeled as domestic terrorist groups, gangs are clearly a threat to the fabric of society as they blatantly disregard the law, are liaising with other criminal enterprises, and are expanding operations from urban areas into small towns and neighborhoods. The FBI estimates that there are now 33,000 street, prison, and outlaw motorcycle gangs (OMGs) in the United States with 1.4 million active members, and they are responsible for 48 percent of violent crime in the country. According to their 2011 National Gang Threat Assessment report, the FBI is concerned about the gangs moving into nontraditional realms such as human trafficking, identity theft, and financial fraud schemes. Also, other notable trends include the overall increase in gang membership and collaboration with rival gangs and other criminal organizations.[44]

Similar to other organizations, as gangs mature their modus operandi shifts to a more sophisticated model. In terms of this generational and predictive analysis, John Sullivan, from the LA County sheriff's office, has authored significant research concerning the evolution of gangs.[45] By viewing gangs through the lens of generational growth, it might be possible to foresee their future activity and apply resources accordingly.

- *First-Generation Gangs* (1G2) are traditional street gangs with a turf orientation. When they engage in criminal enterprise, it is largely opportunistic and local in scope. 1G2 are limited in political scope and sophistication.
- *Second-Generation Gangs* (2G2) are engaged in business. They are entrepreneurial and drug centered. They protect their markets and use violence to control their competition. Their operations sometimes involve multistate and even international areas.
- *Third-Generation Gangs* (3G2) have evolved political aims. They operate or aspire to operate at the global end of the spectrum, using their sophistication to garner power, aid financial acquisition ,and engage in mercenary-type activities.

Additionally, according to Sullivan's model, when politicization, internationalization, and sophistication are low the gang is 1G2. However, as these three factors mature, the group progresses through the various stages leading to 3G2. A 3G2 gang may also acquire and hold territory, for instance, establishing a narco-state.

MS-13—Moving toward 3G2

Mara Salvatrucha 13, or MS-13, is the deadliest, fastest-growing gang in the United States, with many experts calling it the second-deadliest threat in the country behind al Qaeda. Found in just two states in the late 1980s, MS-13 has now has expanded to at least forty-two states, with upwards of 10,000 members nationwide.[46] Although smaller than other domestic gangs, its quick evolution and lethality of recruiting and operational tactics put MS-13 directly in the crosshairs of the U.S. government with FBI director Robert Mueller declaring the group the highest priority in his criminal enterprise branch.

History

Following a bloody twelve-year civil war in El Salvador, taking more than 100,000 lives, many citizens fled to the United States for sanctuary. Along with law-abiding citizens came those with criminal intentions, having been exposed to extreme violence in their homeland. Some were members of government-trained death squads, with extensive knowledge in explosives, military tactics, and firearms. Others served as guerrillas with the Farabundo Marti National Liberation Front, known as "Salvatruchas." Some were members of a street gang known as "La Maras." The convergence of these groups in immigrant communities led to what is now known as the MS-13 gang.

Structure

MS-13 has a pyramid-shaped operation. Loosely affiliated groups labeled "cliques" operate at the local level. There is now some regional connectivity with leadership meetings, and an emerging national command structure is possible.

Operational Activities

Most major criminal activities are present such as gun running, drugs, kidnapping, human trafficking, rape, and extortion. Known for their brutal murderers, victims including pregnant women and children, and deaths often are perpetrated with machetes or knives. MS-13 has vicious initiation rites, starting as early as grade school. Membership is a lifelong contract; many members have tried to leave the gang, only to be killed.

Adaptable and Morphing

MS-13 recently began to changing its outward image to the public. Leadership is encouraging members to hide their highly recognizable, prolific tattoos. Members are also making significant clothing changes, for instance, not wearing the gang's blue-and-white colors or wearing mainstream clothing so as to avoid law enforcement interest.

Sophistication

MS-13 members and leadership have been known to leverage technology to recruit, spread their ideology, and communicate through chat rooms, texting, and websites.

Internationalization

MS-13 in the United States has direct ties with members in other countries. According to the FBI, gang members in a prison in El Salvador have been able to reach out and kill gang members in Los Angeles. As we deport these gang members, they return to their countries with newfound knowledge and maintain their connections in the States. MS-13 has also spread to Europe. It is important to note that MS-13 is considered a terrorist group in El Salvador and Honduras, with a population of over 70,000 members combined.

Rival Gang

Mara 18 (M18), or the 18th Street Gang, is the adversary group to MS-13. With an estimated 50,000 members, M18 is larger than M-13 and has rapidly expanded into thirty-two states. With international connections, organizational structure, and sophistication, law enforcement is concerned the M-13/M18 rivalry may push gang warfare into a new realm.

It is unknown whether MS-13 has ties to international terrorist groups; however, they are now working in the same "space," for instance, trafficking drugs and humans through Central America and Mexico and across our border as well as involvement in financial schemes and fraud in the United States. In 2004, officials neither confirmed nor denied widespread reporting that Adnan El Shukrijumah, a U.S. citizen and FBI most-wanted al Qaeda terrorist, was observed in a Honduras meeting with leaders of El Salvador's MS-13 organization.[47] Al Shukrijumah is an elusive and highly wanted man; the U.S. government has posted a $5 million reward for his capture. Also known as "Jafer the Pilot," Al Shukrijumah completed commercial flight school in the United States and an associate's degree in computer engineering from Broward Community College, Florida, through the Internet. Khalid Sheik Mohammed fingered him as an associate and possibly also an accomplice in planning the attacks of 9/11. Al Shukrijumah later attempted to obtain material in Canada to build a dirty bomb and was complicit in assisting with planning of the thwarted attack on fuel tanks and pipelines at JFK Airport in New York City. The prospect of a liaison between al Qaeda and MS-13 should not be marginalized and must be factored into the analysis of intelligence gathered on each group—particularly since there are MS-13 groups located at and around the U.S. border with Mexico, possibly engaged in human-, gun-, and drug-smuggling operations side by side with terrorists.

Additionally in 2004, U.S. intelligence authorities indicated that al Qaeda operatives may have been in Tegucigalpa, Honduras, planning attacks against British, Spanish, and U.S. embassies. Speculation abounded that al Qaeda was interested in the plaza maintained by MS-13 and Mexican cartels in Matamoros, used to move illegal aliens across the border into the United States. According to the FBI's 2011 Gang Threat Assessment, the MS-13 connection to Mexican drug-trafficking organizations within the United States is irrefutable; DHS reports that Los Angeles-based Sinaloa cartel members regularly use local gang members to assist in or commit kidnappings, acquire or sell drugs, and collect drug proceeds. Other street gangs such as the Latin Kings maintain working relationships with DTOs, and the Sureños gang in California and South Carolina maintain an association with the Los Zetas Cartel.[48]

Outlaw Motorcycle Gangs (OMGs)

OMGs such as the Hells Angels (HA), Mongols, Pagans, and Bandidas are growing in membership and sophistication. The violent groups raise most of their capital through narcotics trafficking, mainly heroin and methamphetamine, but also participate in theft, protection rackets, prostitution, and the sale of illegal firearms. Major cases in the last few years included a two-year, ninety-one-count RICO investigation resulting in the arrest of nineteen members of the HA in North and South Carolina. The Hells Angels have expanded into Canada, where they are working with Mexican drug organizations to bring drugs into the country, especially the Manitoba region. Thomas Gibsy, a Canadian who ran a large international criminal empire, had direct ties to HA and was killed in a cartel hit in Mexico.

Surprisingly, connections between the Hells Angels and the Italian mafia go back to the 1980s, when the bikers started out as "heavies" or enforcers to assist with extortion schemes. The two dissimilar groups then became business partners. In Rhode Island, La Cosa Nostra would allow bikers to continue their illegal trafficking activities on their turf without interfering, and the Hells Angels would pay a percentage in return to the mob. In 2008, Patriarca New England crime family leader David Achille was caught on a police wiretap discussing using a Hell's Angels member for a classic mob shakedown. According to the FBI, the relationship between the biker gang and the Mafia continues today.[49]

The latest OMG trend is a blending of hate groups with motorcycle gangs. In 2012, a seven-year investigation dubbed "Operation Primitive Affliction" came to a close with the arrest of six members of white supremacist motorcycle gang 1st SS Kavallerie Brigade. The 1st SS was part of the popular Outlaws OMG and was considered the "motorcycle division" of the neo-Nazi Aryan Nations. According to undercover officers embedded with the biker gang, members were preparing for a race war, constructing homemade devices, and planning violent hate crimes against minorities in the state.[50]

Prison Gangs

The FBI estimates that there are 230,000 gang members in prisons across the United States.[51] Most belong to the original "traditional prison gangs": the Aryan Brotherhood, Black Guerilla Family, La Nuestra Familia, Mexican Mafia, Texas Syndicate, and Ñeta Association. Known for their extreme violence, prison gangs formed in the 1960s and 1970s in the California corrections system by inmates as a means to protect themselves from other groups and inmate predators. Using contraband phones, family, friends, and corrupt guards, prison gangs communicate with the outside to exert control over street gangs and routinely liaise with them on operational matters such as coordinating hits on rivals. According to the Gang Threat Assessment, the FBI believes that gang members are extremely vulnerable to radicalization and recruitment for involvement in international or domestic terrorism organizations as a disenfranchised and resentful population. Incarcerated gang members in some jurisdictions are adopting radical religious views in prison, and those who were previously dedicated to political or social issues are often more susceptible to influence by extremist ideologies, adopting their symbolism and ideology. Prison and street gang members are also susceptible on an individual basis to radicalization, and prison officials are tracking data for emergent trends.

Special Concern: Gangs and the Military

Members of nearly every major street gang, as well as some prison gangs and OMGs, have been reported on both domestic and international military installations. As of April 2011, the National Gang Intelligence Center has identified members of at least fifty-three gangs whose members have served in or are affiliated with the U.S. military. Furthermore, law enforcement officials in at least one hundred jurisdictions have come into contact with, detained, or arrested an active-duty or former military gang member within the past three years.[52] The issue is twofold: gang members are attempting to join the military, and gangs are actively recruiting former and active-duty military and even their dependents. Gang access to military installations is worrisome, as are the combat training and weapons and bomb-related knowledge that can be shared between military members and their gangs. These activities may pose a national security and public safety threat.

THE WAY AHEAD

Domestic terrorism is not a new concept, but its modern version is increasingly violent. Members now step up and confront law enforcement, bringing heavy arms to the fight. They anonymously use the

Internet for training, operational material, and camaraderie. Extremists at both ends of the spectrum are becoming bolder and more violent. Groups are working together to further their objectives, despite differing ideologies and goals. Between battling the international threat and keeping domestic groups constrained, it seems the challenges are almost beyond the reach of our current capabilities.

The cartel activity spilling over our border from Mexico only adds to the crime and terror threats in the United States, as the next chapter will explore.

REFERENCES

1. FBI, "Terrorism in the United States: 2001," 2002.
2. FBI, "Terrorism 2002/2005," (2006).
3. Uniting and Strengthening America by Providing Appropriate Tools Required to Intercept and Obstruct Terrorism (USA PATRIOT ACT) Act of 2001, H.R. 3162, 107th Congress, October 26, 2001.
4. Bruce Hoffman, *Inside Terrorism* (New York: Columbia University Press, 2006).
5. Bruce Hoffman, "Sources of Concern and Future Prospects," in *Recent Trends and Future Prospects of Terrorism in the United States* (Washington, DC: RAND, 1988).
6. Philip Taft and Philip Ross, "American Labor Violence: Its Causes, Character, and Outcome," in *The History of Violence in America: A Report to the National Commission on the Causes and Prevention of Violence*, eds. Hugh Davis Graham and Ted Robert Gurr (New York: Bantam, 1969), 281.
7. "Man Angry at IRS Crashes Plane into Office," February 19, 2010, http://www.cbsnews.com/2100-201_162-6219986.html.
8. New America Foundation, "Right- and Left-Wing Terrorism Since 9/11," The Homegrown Threat, 2012, http://homegrown.newamerica.net/overview_nonjihadists.
9. New American Foundation, "Non-Jihadist Cases, 2001–2011," The Homegrown Threat, 2012, http://homegrown.newamerica.net/nonjihadist.
10. Daveed Gartenstein-Ross and Madeleine Gruen, "Leadership vs. Leaderless Resistance: The Militant White Separatist Movement's Operating Model," Foundation for Defense of Democracies, February 18, 2010, http://www.defenddemocracy.org/media-hit/leadership-vs-leaderless-resistance-the-militant-white-separatist-movement/.
11. U.S. Department of Homeland Security, "Rightwing Extremism," (April 7, 2009).

12. Ken Sofer and Molly Bernstein, "17 Years after Oklahoma City Bombing, Right-Wing Extremism Is Significant Domestic Terror Threat," Think Progress, April 19, 2012, http://thinkprogress.org/security/2012/04/19/467384/chart-right-wing-extremism-terror-threat-oklahoma-city/?mobile=nc.

13. Oath Keepers, Lincoln County Watch, http://www.lincolncounty-watch.org/links.html.

14. Claire Galofaro, "7 Suspects in St. John Deputy Shootings Are Tied to Violent Anti-government Group," Nola.com *Times-Picayune*, August 17, 2012, http://www.nola.com/crime/index.ssf/2012/08/7_suspects_in_st_john_deputy_s.html.

15. Jill Burke, "Guide to Alaska Sovereign Citizens Trial: Patriots, Militias and Going to Extremes," *Alaska Dispatch*, May 20, 2012, http://www.alaskadispatch.com/content/guide-alaska-sovereign-citizens-trial-patriots-militias-and-going-extremes.

16. "The Solution, Schaeffer Cox Speaks on the Future of the Liberty Movement," 2012.

17. FBI, "Sovereign Citizens: A Growing Domestic Threat to Law Enforcement," Counterterrorism Analysis Section, http://www.fbi.gov/stats-services/publications/law-enforcement-bulletin/september-2011/sovereign-citizens.

18. "Sovereign Copwatch," http://www.facebook.com/sovereign.copwatch.

19. "C4ss: Center for a Stateless Society," http://c4ss.org.

20. "Ten Years after 9/11: An Anarchist Evaluation," *Anarchist Developments* 1 (2011), http://www.anarchist-developments.org/index.php/adcs/issue/view/5/showToc.

21. Ibid.

22. Russ Bynum, "Prosecutor: Army Soldiers Planned Terror Plot," *Northwest Herald*, August 27, 2012, http://www.nwherald.com/2012/08/27/prosecutor-army-soldiers-planned-terror-plot/a9cmznn/.

23. 10:10.org, "No Pressure," http://www.youtube.com/watch?v=5-Mw5_EBk0g.

24. U.S. Department of Justice, "Eleven Defendants Indicted on Domestic Terrorism Charges," January 20, 2006.

25. North American Animal Liberation Press Office (NAALPO), http://animalliberationpressoffice.org/NAALPO/.

26. James Jay Carafano, Steve Bucci, and Jessica Zuckerman, *Fifty Terror Plots Foiled since 9/11: The Homegrown Threat and the Long War on Terrorism*, vol. 2682, *The Backgrounder* (Washington, DC: Heritage Foundation, 2012).

27. Dennis A. Pluchinsky, "Global Jihadist Recidivism: A Red Flag," *Studies in Conflict & Terrorism* 31, no. 3 (2008): 182–200.

28. Jennifer Hesterman, "Catch and Release: Jihadist Recidivism," *The Counter Terrorist Magazine*, April/May 2010.

29. Pluchinsky, "Global Jihadist Recidivism."

30. Ibid.

31. M. J. Akbar, *The Shade of Swords: Jihad and the Conflict between Islam and Christianity* (London: Routledge, 2002).

32. Pluchinsky, "Global Jihadist Recidivism."

33. "The Guantanamo Docket," *New York Times*, http://projects.nytimes.com/guantanamo.

34. Office of the Director of National Intelligence, *Summary of the Reengagement of Detainees Formerly Held at Guantanamo Bay, Cuba*, 2012.

35. Evan F. Kohlmann, "'The Eleven": Saudi Guantanamo Veterans Returning to the Fight," http://www.nefafoundation.org/miscellaneous/FeaturedDocs/nefagitmoreturnees0209-1.pdf.

36. Hesterman, "Catch and Release."

37. Christopher Boucek, "Saudi Arabia's 'Soft' Counterterrorism Strategy: Prevention, Rehabilitation, and Aftercare," Carnegie Endowment for International Peace, Carnegie Papers, September 2008).

38. Christina Lamb, "Guantanamo Closure Delayed Amid Rehab Failures," *The Australian News*, January 11, 2010, http://www.theaustralian.com.au/news/world/guantanamo-closure-delayed-amid-rehab-failures/story-e6frg6so-1225817851821.

39. Jeffrey Azarva, "Is U.S. Detention Policy in Iraq Working?," *Middle East Quarterly* (Winter 2009): 5–14.

40. Christopher Boucek, "Clearing a Path for Guantanamo Returnees: Rehabilitation and Risk-Assessment," Carnegie Endowment for International Peace, January 28, 2009, http://www.carnegieendowment.org/2009/01/28/clearing-path-for-guantanamo-returnees-rehabilitation-and-risk-assessment/34l.

41. FBI, "FBI Strategic Plan 2004–2009," 2004.

42. Andrew Berwick (Anders Behring Breivik), "2083: A European Declaration of Independence," 2011.

43. Anders Behring Breivik, "2083—a European Declaration of Independence," http://www.youtube.com/watch?v=KjCy90NVLQM.

44. FBI, "2011 National Gang Threat Assessment," 2012.

45. http://www.d-n-i.net/fcs/pdf/wilson_sullivan_gangs_terrorism.pdf.

46. http://www.fbi.gov/page2/jan08/ms13_011408.html.

47. "Al Qaeda Seeks Tie to Local Gangs," *Washington Times*, September 28, 2004, http://www.washingtontimes.com/news/2004/sep/28/20040928-123346-3928r/.

48. FBI, "2011 National Gang Threat Assessment."

49. WPRI, Newport, RI, "Unusual Mob Partnership: Inside the Mafia Reveals Relationship with Gangs," February 5, 2008, http://www.wpri.com/dpp/target_12/inside_mafia/Target_12_Investigators_Unusual_Partnership_263259.
50. Heidi Beirich and Laurie Wood, "Robert Killian's Years of Posing as a Neo-Nazi Biker Cost Him Dearly," in *SPLC Intelligence Report* (2012).
51. FBI, "2011 National Gang Threat Assessment."
52. Ibid.

CHAPTER 5

Drug-Trafficking Organizations Go Global

This is the most alarming situation I've seen in Mexico in 15 years. Our own interests are at stake. We must stand with these people; they're literally fighting for their lives.

—Former U.S. drug czar General Barry McCaffrey[1]

This statement by General McCaffrey set off a firestorm of debate inside Washington, DC, policy-making circles. Are the Mexican cartels a U.S national security risk, or have we overblown the threat? Is their activity in the United States terroristic, or merely criminal in nature? The answers to these pressing, complex questions will certainly determine our course of action as a nation. The challenges posed by Mexican drug-trafficking organizations (DTOs) are escalating in Mexico, as well as in the United States and other countries. Further, the dangerous liaisons between DTOs, international terrorist groups, and transnational gangs such as MS-13 are worrisome to law enforcement not only at the border but in our country.

THE BATTLE IN MEXICO

Just south of our border, Mexican forces are fighting an insurgency against multiple DTOs, which threaten their country's economy and security. This conflict is a perfect example of what some call fifth-generation warfare: shadowy organizations using asymmetric tactics against the state. What many find inexplicable, the inability of large governments to easily put down rising and persistent threats such as DTOs and small terrorist groups, is perfectly explainable and quite predictable when viewed through the fifth-gen lens, which will be covered in Chapter 9 while discussing tactic sharing and replicating by dissimilar groups.

In 2009, the previous director of the CIA, General Michael Hayden, surprised many when he stated, "Escalating violence along the U.S.-Mexico border will pose the second greatest threat to U.S. security this year, second only to al Qaeda."[2] Furthermore, according to the Justice Department, Mexican DTOs represent the greatest organized crime threat to the United States.[3] Our government has responded in part by placing thousands of National Guard troops on the border as part of "Operation Jump Start," assisting U.S. Customs and Border Protection. Also, hundreds of federal agents have been pulled from other duties and sent to robust DEA, ATF, and FBI offices in major cities in border states. And despite economic woes, the United States is aiding Mexico's fight against the DTOs under the provisions of the Merida Initiative, a multiyear $1.5 billion antinarcotics package increasing law enforcement cooperation and intelligence sharing between our countries as well as supplies, training, and equipment to the fight. Finally, the $6 billion "virtual fence" project, SBInet, and deployment of expensive aerial drones to monitor the border certainly indicate the government's concern regarding border issues.

Mexican authorities are attempting to contain DTO (cartel) activity to certain geographical regions and keep it from spilling over into their major cities, lucrative vacation areas, and our shared border. Mexico's military is heavily engaged, with 45,000 soldiers augmenting more than 5,000 federal police, and this combined force is engaging in small-scale combat with the cartels. This is particularly true with the paramilitary Los Zetas, who have the exact same weapons, training, and tactics as the government force and therefore are able to meet the confrontation head-on.

Several leaders of the major Mexican DTOs have been indicted on charges within the United States and are fugitives with a $5 million reward offered for their capture, the same amount offered for the apprehension of "most wanted" terrorists, indicating the serious nature of the threat against our citizens and communities. The players, tactics, alliances, and leaders of the DTOs morph, but the threat to our country persists ... and is growing.

Ideology: Money

It is important to understand that prior to U.S. engagement in the so-called drug war beginning in the 1980s, the primary drug-trafficking route into the United States was from Colombia, through the Caribbean and into Florida. As we closed off these avenues and failed to lower user demand in our country, Mexico became the primary conduit for the drug pipeline. As criminal elements exacted their "fee" for moving the product through the country, we witnessed the rise of alliances, or cartels. In addition to moving Colombian drugs, cartels now oversee the cultivation of marijuana and large labs producing methamphetamines. The money at stake is exorbitant; a Justice Department report estimates that Mexican and Colombian DTOs generate, remove, and launder between $18 and $39 billion in wholesale drug proceeds annually.

Consider this important fact, which serves to frame the discussion of drugs and the existing or potential nexus with other nefarious groups: dealers and users in the United States do not care who supplies their drugs. It could be a cartel or al Qaeda; all that matters is the product and getting it into the hands of the 35 million users in our country, most of whom will give their last dollar or possession to get high. Cocaine is the leading drug threat in the United States, followed by methamphetamine, marijuana, heroin, pharmaceutical drugs, and MDMA (ecstasy). The DTOs have responded to the demand, and with crackdowns at the border, they have moved inside the United States and now oversee the planting of marijuana fields in U.S. national parks—although surprisingly, the National Park Service (NPS) reports that marijuana has been grown on our public lands for over twenty-five years. Furthermore, in 2010 and 2011, their internal reports documented the vast amount of marijuana eradicated on NPS land during the period. Between standing plants, or plants harvested and packaged for distribution at the time of interdiction, they estimated a total street value of over $405 million. Nearly all these cases of marijuana grown in national parks were identified as transnational organized crime-related operations.[4]

Tactic: Brutal Violence

Protecting this vast drug enterprise is critical for the DTOs. In Mexico, the areas of operation for the cartels are called *plazas*. Pipelines are the supply corridors into, through, and out of Mexico, safely passing through the *plazas* in which the cartels have the upper hand by bribing or intimidating officials and citizens. Some of these formerly vibrant areas have turned into ghost towns due to the persistent, escalating violence unleashed by the DTOs to maintain control of the *plazas*.

DTO violence is like no other. The perpetrators have no respect for the rule of law and employ no moral restraint, willfully (and exuberantly) killing innocent people every day. Kidnapping, rape, human trafficking, extortion, larceny, arson, and weapons offenses: nothing is off the table for DTOs in the name of making money, widening their sphere of influence, and controlling *plazas* and pipelines. DTOs are transnational organizations; the U.S. National Drug Intelligence Center reports

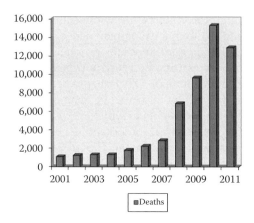

FIGURE 5.1 Deaths related to TOC Violence in Mexico. (*Source:* Viridiana Rios Cory Molzahn, David A. Shirk, "Drug Violence in Mexico: Data and Analysis Through 2011," [University of San Diego, Joan B. Kroc School of Peace Studies, 2011]).

that not only are they operating in the United States and nineteen Latin American countries, but they are also present in unexpected regions, such as Australia. This indicates their global reach and ability to transport their products worldwide.

Prior to December 2006, DTO violence was sporadic and contained by the government. During the election that year, Mexican president Felipe de Jesús Calderón Hinojosa stated that his primary goals were to grow his country's economy by creating jobs and to reduce poverty. However, once in office in late 2006, President Calderón opened a strategic front against the DTOs, declaring "war" against the cartels. Interestingly, this action was not unilaterally supported by the citizens of the country, whose small towns benefit financially from the movement of drugs through the area. Also, as they feared, innocent civilians inadvertently ended up on the front lines of the battle. Mexican authorities reported 47,515 people killed in the violence between the start of President Calderón's offensive and December 2011, or one every hour (see Figure 5.1).

According to Mexico's National Human Rights Commission, these numbers do not include the 5,000 kidnapped and missing citizens, suspected to have suffered brutal deaths at the hands of the cartels, with their bodies unceremoniously dumped in the desert.

The battle between cartels for control has led to the preponderance of these deaths, as Figure 5.2 illustrates. Bombs regularly explode in front of police stations and at city halls. Shootouts in the street happen daily, as thousands of videos taken by civilians and posted on the

Drug War Killings by Group
(December 2006 to December 2010)

Groups in conflict	Killings	% of Total
Sinaloa vs. Juárez	8,236	23.8%
Sinaloa vs. Betran Leyva	5,864	16.9%
Sinaloa vs. Gulf-Zetas	3,199	9.2%
Sinaloa vs. Tijuana	1,798	5.2%
La Familia vs. Zetas	1,744	5.0%
Gulf vs. Zetas	1,328	3.8%
Other	12,442	35.9%
Total DTO Conflict Killings	34,611	100%

FIGURE 5.2   DTO Conflict Killings. (*Source:* Cory Molzahn, "Drug Violence in Mexico: Data and Analysis Through 2011.")

Internet attest. Innocent men, women, and children caught in the cross-fire are seen by DTOs as collateral damage and are now the very targets of the rampant violence by groups sending "messages" to towns and each other. Many murders are premeditated and gruesome, such as beheadings, death by gasoline-induced fire, dismemberment, and acid baths. Politicians and police officers are often hung in effigy from bridges in major cities with signs threatening those who are battling the cartels to back off. In January 2010, thirty-six-year-old Hugo Hernandez was kidnapped in the state of Sonora by Sinaloa cartel members who carved his body into seven pieces, dropping them at separate locations. Finally, his face was sliced off and stitched to a football, which was then delivered with a warning to the Juárez Cartel to Los Mochis city hall in Sinaloa.[5] Cartel violence often begets violence; a few days later, masked gunmen attacked teenagers in the border city of Ciudad Juárez, children who were enjoying a combination birthday and high school soccer victory party: sixteen dead, fourteen wounded. The very same evening in Torreón, in the border state of Coahuila, gunmen ambushed students in a college bar: ten dead, eleven wounded. In the case of the children and college student massacres, the shootings were simply meant to send a message to rival cartels, law enforcement, and government leadership, with a by-product of terrorizing the public.[6]

Many of these activities are carried out by the "enforcement arms" of the cartels, which are paramilitary groups possessing the training knowledge and sophisticated equipment of small armies. Street gang spinoffs of the main organization will also accomplish some of this dirty work, so if they are apprehended by authorities, the main leadership of the cartel and its business activity remain unaffected.

There is great debate about the actual scale of violence in Mexico as related to their population of 113 million and the vast area of the country. Comparisons are regularly drawn to the U.S. murder rate, with pundits saying it is not as bad in Mexico as depicted by the press. However, this "rates per thousand" discussion is irrelevant considering the unique factors at play such as the large and powerful groups involved; the gruesome nature of the violence; the deliberate targeting of public officials; the undaunted confrontations with Mexican forces; the strong, deep leadership structure in the DTOs and their operational planning to achieve goals; and the persistence and willingness to escalate the bloodshed as required. There is no group or groups in the United States engaged in this type of activity against the state and fellow citizens. Comparisons between violence south and north of the border distract from the issue at hand and marginalize the danger to our country. If the murder statistics and the fact the Mexican Army is engaged in conflict with its own citizens isn't shocking enough, consider that 53 percent of Mexicans believe the drug cartels are winning the ongoing battle.

Goals: Money, Power, Control

The primary goal of cartels is to gain power, territory, and control so they can move drugs, money, guns, and human cargo unopposed. They seek to create a void in leadership and rule of law in cities so they can step in and take control. Corruption of police, military, and government leadership is a tool used to create instability, ruin the government's reputation with citizens, and cause them to turn to others for protection. Instilling fear in the populace is a primary goal, compelling citizens to assist the DTOs, or at the very least, not resist their land grabs and activity in the community. Anything and anyone standing in the way of their progress is seen as a threat that must be eliminated. Conversely, anything and anyone helping attain their goals is an ally.

MAJOR DTOS IMPACTING THE UNITED STATES

Nuevo Cartel de Juárez

The Juárez Cartel was renamed in late 2011 to Nuevo Cartel de Juárez, or the New Juárez Cartel. It is also referred to as the Carillo Fuentes Organization, named after former leader Amado Carillo Fuentes. At its height in the late 1990s, located at one of the more influential border areas of Chihuahua and pushing 50 percent of the cocaine coming into the United States, the Juárez Cartel was considered the most powerful in the world, exacting a $200 million profit per week. The Juárez Cartel has an ongoing war with its former partner, the Sinaloa Cartel, for control of Juárez and is currently fighting with the Los Zetas for control of the Nuevo Laredo area. On July 15, 2010, the New Juárez Cartel employed a game-changing tactic: they used vehicle-borne incendiary explosive devices (VBIEDs) to target federal police officers. The cartel has weakened in the last few years but is still powerful, having joined alliances with the Gulf Cartel. La Linea, the enforcement arm of the Juárez Cartel, has used gangs to orchestrate brutal killings including the premeditated murder of a U.S. consulate employee, her husband, and their unborn child in 2011 at the Laredo border crossing. The group's leader, Jose Antonio Acosta Hernandez, a former police officer, was sentenced to seven consecutive life sentences in the United States for his role in those murders.

Gulf Cartel/New Federation

The Gulf Cartel is the oldest DTO in the world. The self-proclaimed "godfather" of the Gulf Cartel, Juan Nepomuceno Guerra, started the Matamoros criminal syndicate that smuggled alcohol into the United States during the prohibition in 1933. The group later ran cross-border prostitution and gambling rings, and participated in tobacco smuggling. In the 1970s, Guerra and his nephew entered the cocaine-trafficking business as the Gulf Cartel, and worked with the Cali Cartel to secure routes out of Colombia. The 2003 arrest and life imprisonment of the Gulf Cartel leader, Osiel Cárdenas, weakened the organization, and the 2010 split with the Los Zetas, formerly their "enforcers," made them far less powerful. However, they recently formed an alliance with the Sinaloa Cartel and are now battling the Zetas and Tijuana Cartel for northeast Mexico.

Sinaloa Cartel

The Sinaloas, also known as the Federation, began to contest the Gulf Cartel's domination of the coveted southwest Texas corridor after Cárdenas's arrest. Their ultimate rise to power and domination of critical routes into the United States resulted in the U.S. intelligence community labeling them "the most powerful drug trafficking organization in the world." Joaquín Guzmán Loera, aka "El Chapo," is the leader of the Sinaloa Cartel, and the DEA believes his wealth and power exceeds Pablo Escobar's at the height of the Cali Cartel. Sinaloa dominates the "Golden Triangle," consisting of the states of Sinaloa, Durango, and Chihuahua and the Laredo, Texas, area, which constitutes 40 percent of all cross-border traffic between Mexico and the United States. The Golden Triangle is also a major producer of Mexican opium and marijuana. The Sinaloas are now challenging the Tijuana Cartel in Baja to take over their cross-border operations into San Diego and are using the new Jalisco New Generation Cartel, or CJNG, as their armed enforcement wing. The CJNG is directly engaging the Zetas; both groups escalated the violence and rhetoric in May 2012 with retaliatory massacres occurring within hours and the hanging of the murdered civilians from bridges along the border. The CJNG is tactically clever; it is believed they are killing innocent civilians, leaving behind Zetas markings and banners, in the attempt to deflect government efforts away from them and toward eliminating the rival Zetas. They made significant inroads to uprooting the Zetas in 2012, particularly in the Veracruz region.

Beltran Leyva Organization (BLO)

The Beltran Leyva brothers, extravagant and powerful dealers of poppy products, broke away from the Sinaloa Cartel in 2008 to form their own syndicate, BLO. An extremely violent organization, BLO immediately claimed the Sonora region; however, they began battling their former partners, the Sinaloas, who either killed their leadership or gave information to the Mexican government, leading to their deaths. The remaining brother attempted to reinvent the BLO by renaming it the Pacific Cartel, but they eventually lost all ground in the region. The BLO is very weak and recently formed an unstable liaison with the Zetas in an attempt to stay viable. The BLO is present in the United States, and the alliance gave the Zetas a larger footprint.

Tijuana/Arellano Felix Organization (AFO)

The Tijuana Cartel, founded in 1989 by the Arellano Félix brothers, was at one time the largest and most violent DTO. The group still operates in fifteen Mexican states in addition to dominating the Baja area, although it has been greatly weakened. AFO is likely in some sort of truce with the Sinaloas due to the relative peace in the Baja region where they have strong political and business ties, which would make their uprooting extremely difficult for rival factions.

La Familia Michoacana (LFM)

LFM started in 1980s as a group of vigilantes working to protect the poor and counteract kidnappers and drug lords. Their daring escapades in the region imparted a reputation of mythical proportions. In the early 1990s, this increasingly violent group was brought in by the Gulf Cartel to become their armed paramilitary wing to fight rival DTOs. In 1999, the Gulf Cartel's leadership sought additional protection and recruited Army Special Forces troops, who later became the Zetas. The LFM faction trained with the Zetas on special tactics and weaponry. In 2006, the group split from the Gulf Cartel to pursue its own trafficking opportunities, spouting a bizarre combination of Christian values and narco-violence. LFM's leader, Moreno González, proclaimed the group's "divine rights" to kill enemies and declared religious justification for beheadings and other gruesome killings.

LFM operated in the Michoacan area, injecting itself into the political process by financing campaigns of supporting politicians and threatening to kill the opposition. Banners espousing religious and family values are prevalent in LFM territory, and they regularly loan money to schools and farmers. To bolster their ranks, LFM started a unique campaign to rehabilitate drug addicts, then recruit them into the cartel; however, refusal to join meant death. LFM's violent gang affiliate, the Knights Templar, acts as the killing enforcement arm of the group. The death of their leader, González, in November 2011 as well as an extensive federal law enforcement investigation in the United States called "Project Delirium" closed LFM's operations north and south of the border, potentially ending the group. However their cultlike, semireligious ideology and violent nature calls to mind similar terrorist groups such as Aum Shinryko, which merely change names and go underground. The Knights Templar group is still active in the region and was suspected of dismembering innocent civilians as a threat to politicians prior to elections in June 2012.

SPECIAL CONCERN: LOS ZETAS

Imagine, for a moment, that one of America's elite special operations units goes "rogue" and starts using its specialized skills, equipment, and training *against* the U.S. government. The members of the unit participate in illegal activities such as drug trafficking, gun running, and human smuggling. They also serve as hit squads, willing to murder innocent victims in return for cash. The unit does not fear, hide, or run from law enforcement; rather, it engages.

Meet the Los Zetas organization. The fastest-growing DTO in Mexico, this is the first to use the Internet, the first to savagely behead innocent civilians to send "warnings," and the first to air-drop propaganda leaflets from aircraft. With an estimated membership of 2,000, the core of the Zetas is composed of former members of the Grupo Aeromóvil de Fuerzas Especiales, or the GAFE. The GAFE is the special forces arm of the Mexican Army; its members receive specialized training in jungle, amphibious, urban, and high-mountain operations from the best counterterrorism and counterinsurgency units in the world. They are also trained to deploy forward into hostile foreign territory and to blend in and operate undetected. In recent years, the GAFE's primary mission morphed from providing protection to key officials and buildings to one of assisting the country in dismantling drug cartels.

During their 1999 expansion, Gulf cartel leadership recruited at least thirty GAFE troops, including Heriberto Lazcano, known as "El Lazca," forming the Los Zetas. Therefore, as former GAFEs, Zeta leaders have an intuitive understanding of the inner workings of cartels and the government's plans to counter their activities. Along with their counterintelligence, disguise, and insurgency training, the Zetas are a complex and lethal force. Under the umbrella of the Gulf Cartel, the Zetas acted as hit squads to eliminate the "enemy," which typically consists of members of law enforcement and the Mexican government. Although other paramilitary or "enforcement groups" are present in those cartels, such as the CJNG (Knights Templar), the DEA labeled the Zetas as "the most technologically advanced, sophisticated, and violent."[7]

In 2006, the Zetas broke away from the Gulf Cartel to form their own DTO. A STRATFOR report indicates that Los Zetas is now the largest cartel in Mexico, operating in seventeen states, or more than half the country, while its rival and the second-largest cartel, Sinaloa, had operations in sixteen states.[8] Despite losing seventeen of its leaders in 2011, the Zetas remain a formidable, transnational force and are quickly gaining territory.

Zeta Tactics

Zetas should be viewed not as criminal enterprise but as a lethal, complex army. They have specialized training in navigating and operating in all terrains; they have river swimmers, divers, jungle experts, and training in urban warfare. Money from their drug trade and other nefarious activity enables Zetas to buy top-of-the-line equipment; they have tanks, surface-to-air missiles, RPGs, night vision equipment, boats, helicopters, and aircraft. They often operate in small-fire teams and use snipers and countersnipers.

Their executions are savage; they often set their targets on fire, decapitate them, and saturate their bodies with bullets. The violence is escalating in their ongoing battle with the Sinaloas; in May 2012, Lazcano gave orders for the massacre and dismemberment of forty-nine innocent civilians in the so-called Mother's Day massacre. They also engage law enforcement (LE) and the military, using ambush tactics and the element of surprise to kill officers before they can react. A new tactic in the States may be to monitor LE activity, looking for patterns or routines, and then ambush and kill. In southern Arizona, "spotters" are routinely used by drug cartels to locate and report back to drug and human traffickers the location of Border Patrol agents and other LE so they can avoid arrest. These spotters are heavily armed, stealthy, and capable of targeting LE. The killing of Border Patrol agent Brian Terry, who was shot with an AK-47 in Rio Rico, Arizona, was celebrated in the cartel world as a victory. The brazen shooting was a first and possibly opened a "new chapter" with regard to tactics and escalation of violence against LE, where they are not merely watching and monitoring but shooting.

CASE STUDY: LOS ZETAS HITS ON SENIOR MILITARY OFFICERS

When Gen. Mauro Enrique Tello Quinonez retired after decades of service with the Mexican Army, he still wanted to serve his country. He therefore willingly accepted a posting as a security advisor and senior counterdrug official in Cancún. Unfortunately, his first day on the job turned out to be his last: Tello was kidnapped, brutally tortured, and shot eleven times. In February 3, 2009, his body, along with the mutilated and bullet-ridden bodies of his driver and security officer, was found in a car alongside a road in Cancún. Tello was not the only high-ranking army officer killed in the city, which is best known for its lucrative tourist industry. In 2006, Lt. Col. Wilfrido Flores Saucedo and his aide were gunned down on a Cancún street; the assailants escaped and were never captured. Luckily, in Tello's case, the military had several leads and quickly moved in to assume control of the investigation. A corrupt Cancún police chief was removed from his position and put under house arrest. His detainment was quickly followed by the apprehension of seven men, all members of the Los Zetas. A Zeta leader, Octavio Almanza, was among those arrested for his direct involvement in the general's assassination. Almanza, who was a Mexican soldier himself from 1997 to 2004, was stockpiling an impressive cache of weapons when arrested; officials seized forty-three rifles and handguns, two grenade launchers, twenty-three grenades, a rocket launcher, and more than 12,000 rounds of ammunition. Almanza was sending a clear, unequivocal message to the Mexican government, one repeated both across Mexico and along the U.S. border: the Zetas are unafraid and battle ready.[9]

We should not underestimate the sophistication of this group; unde-tected, they plan and practice for operations, performing surveillance and patiently waiting for the right time to strike. The brazen daytime attack on a casino in Monterrey, Mexico, in August 2011 leaving at least fifty-two people dead is an example of the escalation and calculation of Zeta violence. Twelve gunmen entered the casino and started shooting into the crowd, with other attackers simultaneously dousing exits with gasoline and throwing grenades into the building to start multiple fires. Such attacks are less about the target (in this case, a casino) and more about the message.

The Zetas are also known for their *sicarios*, or assassins. Take the case of Rosalio Reta, a U.S. citizen born and raised in Laredo, Texas. At the age of the thirteen, Reta was kidnapped by Zeta members and taken to Mexico, where he became a Zetita, or "little Zeta," attending tactical training camps. His initiation came shortly thereafter, when he was directed to shoot a man in the head at a bar in Nuevo Laredo. He returned to live in Laredo at the age of fifteen, where he was used by the Zetas to kill several men and young boys throughout Texas. Reta's assassinations and apprehension are detailed in the 2012 book *The Executioner's Men* by George W. Grayson and Samuel Logan, the most comprehensive book available on the Zetas. However, Reta wasn't the only Zeta hit man in Texas; during the 2012 trial of Gerardo Castillo-Chavez, a Zeta on trial for racketeering and weapons charges, cartel members confirmed the presence and activity of several *sicario* cells in the United States. Castillo-Chavez and other Zetas were rolled up in Laredo during "Operation Prophecy," an investigation of the killing of Americans in vicinity of the border.[10]

Increasing Reach in the United States

In addition to *sicarios*, the Zetas have clearly been operating in the bor-der region for many years; in November 2008, for example, a Zeta leader named Jaime González Durán was arrested a stone's throw across the border from McAllen, Texas. However, the stunning 2011 arrest of fifteen Zetas in Chicago perfectly illustrated the reach of the group within our borders. The case detailed the movement of drugs from Nuevo Laredo, Mexico, through Texas and into Chicago, via a U.S. fugitive working for the Zetas. The street value of this cell was staggering: feds seized 12 million U.S. dollars in cash and 250 kilograms of cocaine.[11] According to the FBI, in addition to all of the border states, Zeta cells are believed to be present in Tennessee, Oklahoma, South Carolina, and Georgia.[12]

One Laredo detective said the Zetas are expanding their activities in the United States through legitimate businesses: "They own used car lots on both sides of the border, restaurants, discotheques, liquor stores."[13] These companies are likely used to launder drug money and invest in "clean" activities. One concerned politician in Nuevo

Laredo believes the Zetas may inject themselves in the political process there. "We could see them running for mayor, even governor, in the future."[14] Although the political aspirations of the group are unknown, Hezbollah provides a good model of how a dangerous, nefarious group can engage in the "care and feeding" business and build a relationship of goodwill toward citizens who will then harbor and protect their activities. Hezbollah was able to infiltrate the political process in Lebanon to the point where they legitimately had a seat at the table for several high level UN meetings. We can't rule out a Zeta move to take territory and entire towns and secure political positions through these subversive measures, in addition to their bloody campaign in Mexico. Certainly, as one door closes, they will seek other avenues to pursue their goals.

A battle is also raging for control of Interstate 35, a highly desired route for drug traffickers. I-35 begins at the border in Laredo and traverses major cities like Dallas, where, according to a Justice Department memo, Zetas have been active since 2003 as part of the Gulf Cartel. Following the shooting death of Dallas police officer Mark Nix, law enforcement agents have been looking for Maximo Garcia Carrillo, a suspected Zeta and the triggerman in the shooting who owned a house in the Oak Cliff suburb of the city. On the other side of Dallas, I-35 has intermittent empty stretches of highway but eventually passes through Oklahoma City, Kansas City, and Minneapolis. The interstate ends in Duluth, Minnesota, at the Canadian border. The importance of this corridor to the cartels is significant; as the former head of the DEA's El Paso Intelligence Center once stated, "Drug traffickers kill for I-35." More recently, the Zetas have also become involved in the human-smuggling business, charging a 10 percent commission for use of their border *plazas*, pipelines, and the Interstate 35 corridor. It seems incredible that the Zetas charge smugglers to operate on U.S. real estate, and it is even more egregious that they would buy property and live illegally in our cities, right under the nose of law enforcement.[15]

CASE STUDY: LOS ZETAS CARTEL AMBUSH IN HOUSTON

Houston is a major distribution hub for illegal drugs. Every advantage the city enjoys makes it a magnet for drug trafficking: major highways, access to waterways and ports, and strong international trade. Cartel activity in Houston has steadily increased over the last few years.

On the afternoon of November 21, 2011, confidential informant Lawrence Chapa was doing what he had done many times before:

drive a semi loaded with drugs for delivery to unsuspecting traffickers, under the watchful eyes of a joint counterdrug task force. Chapa was a fifty-three-year-old licensed big-rig driver with the "street cred" and mannerisms necessary to be a productive informant. He had an arrest record for cocaine possession, resisting arrest, and assault on a store clerk just a few months before, but he was a long-term asset, reportedly on the books for at least ten years. His family was unaware of his prior cooperation with the feds and shocked that he would risk his life for this operation, possibly done in the name of making a few bucks. On the day of the operation, Chapa rendezvoused with law enforcement in the morning at the U.S./Mexico border in the Rio Grande Valley. The vehicle used for the operation was a fuel truck, as is commonly employed by traffickers to avoid detection and limit searches to the external chassis if pulled over and challenged. This load was a mere 300 pounds of marijuana, nothing compared to the thousands usually delivered. Plainclothes officers trailed Chapa. When the truck arrived in the Houston area, the buyers informed Chapa of a change in the delivery destination. He made his way down Bourgeois Road (a suburban area of northwest Houston) in Harris County, an area with a quiet neighborhood, nice homes, and an elementary school.

As he headed up the dead-end road, toward an industrial park, several black, high-end SUVs converged at an intersection and opened fire. The truck cab was quickly sprayed with bullets. Two shooters ran to the truck, pulled opened the cab door, and fired on an unarmed Chapa, who put his hands in the air. A gunman pulled Chapa from the cab, throwing his lifeless body on the ground. Officers raced to the scene, running over one of the gunmen in an attempt to stop the shooting. A Harris County deputy in plainclothes was downed by friendly fire when he was misidentified. Fortunately, he will make a full recovery from a gunshot wound to the leg.

In the chaos, several vehicles fled the scene, leaving behind four shooters and a Lincoln Navigator. Police chased several gunmen on foot through the adjacent neighborhood with successful apprehensions. Fernando Tavera, just nineteen years old, is a U.S. citizen from Houston and confessed to killing Chapa, exclaiming to arresting officers, "I emptied my clip into that [expletive]." Tavera had a prior misdemeanor marijuana possession charge in Harris County. Ricardo Ramirez and Rolando Resendiz, Mexican citizens and two of the other shooters, in their mid-thirties, also had prior brushes with law enforcement in the Houston area. A fifth gunman who fled the scene, Alfredo Gomez, was arrested several weeks after the shooting. The five men were charged with capital murder and reportedly identified connections to the Los Zetas drug cartel in their separate confessions. Louis Guthrie, director of special crimes and narcotics for the Liberty County Sheriff's Department, stated, "This shootout is the latest example of cartel-related violence to hit the streets of Houston and Harris County."

Questions over the Houston attack persist, such as if the shooters knew Chapa was an informant, wouldn't they assume he was being followed by LE and *not* attack? Many close to the investigation believe this speaks to the culture of the Zetas to carry out planned attacks in city limits, during the daytime, and with disregard for the presence of LE. Based on Tavera's statement indicating Chapa was the target, the fact that the load was just 300 pounds and, the fact that the shooters were numerous, armed, and lying in wait (after calling in a venue change), all evidence suggests this was a hit on Chapa. Somehow, he was compromised and paid the ultimate price. The attack in Houston wasn't a failed mission for the Zetas: it was the successful elimination of an enemy.

The Zetas are employing guerilla warfare tactics, use the element of surprise, and learn from failures and adapt accordingly. This rogue special operations unit has announced their arrival in our country—are we prepared?[19]

Interaction with Dark Networks

In late 2011, after the Zetas tortured and killed three bloggers in Mexico for negative chat about the group in online forums, the hacker group "Anonymous" engaged, initiating "Operation Cartel" and vandalizing websites with anti-Zeta propaganda. The cartel retaliated by locating and kidnapping an "Anonymous Iberoamerica" member. When the hacker group threatened to release 25,000 personal e-mails exposing the identities of sixty Los Zetas members, the cartel released the victim. However, it was a victory for the Zetas: the victim had a note in his pocket saying that for every name Anonymous published, they would kill ten civilians, starting with the victim. Anonymous called a "truce" with the Zetas and backed away from their campaign.[17]

Nexus with Gangs

The Zetas are increasingly wielding control over such U.S. gangs such as MS-13, the Mexican Mafia, and the Texas Syndicate. The FBI's 2011 Gang Assessment, covered in the previous chapter, indicates a number of alarming trends including that street gangs in the United States are growing in size, operating at the border, and forming ties with DTOs.[18] The imitation of tactics typically indicates some type of liaison at the training or operational levels; gang members in our country are now engaging in nontraditional crimes such as human trafficking and alien smuggling. They are acquiring high-powered weaponry and showing new sophistication in terms of recruitment and communication. These attributes make them attractive to cartels to work their street-level issues, launder money, and move product.

Law enforcement believes the Zetas may have already have used MS-13 in several operations in the United States, providing training and weaponry. Information gleaned from secret jailhouse recordings in early 2012 unveiled a pact between MS-13 members deported from the United States back to Guatemala and stateside Zetas. Also, Guatemalan authorities believe the Zetas have trained a small group of Maras in at least one camp inside Mexico.[19] MS-13 has evolved beyond knives and machetes and now carry AR-15s, M-16s, and AK-47s, which may be been supplied by the Zetas. They are also employing new tactics, similar to Zeta "warnings" in Mexico, such as cutting off fingers and creating massacres at public locations. The Zetas have bragged about recruiting 5,000 MS-13 members in Guatemala, although this number has not been verified. Guatemala's Peten province, which borders Mexico and Belize, is now Zeta country, and they are expanding operations in the region through land grabs and the wanton killing of resisting farmers and villagers. With the acquisition of territory, the Zetas are now clearly a 3G2 gang.

Criminal Activity Expanding

It is estimated that only 50 percent of the Zetas' money is in the drug-trafficking business, and they have routinely shown the ability to expand into unexpected areas to launder and generate money. For example, in June 2012 horse-racing complexes owned by brothers in New Mexico and Oklahoma were the targets of a law enforcement investigation that uncovered a multimillion-dollar money-laundering scheme by the Zetas. Another source of Zeta revenue are the Pemex Corporation oil pipelines in Mexico; the company estimates that 5,000 siphons have been attached to their pipelines and three million barrels of oil were stolen in 2011 alone, for a loss of $475 million to the company.[20]

Savvy Propaganda Campaigns

The Zetas are known for sending "messages," including a recruiting banner in an area where the average daily wages are around five U.S. dollars. The sign calls out to any soldier or ex-soldier and says, "Why be poor? Come work for us" and "We're offering you a good salary, food

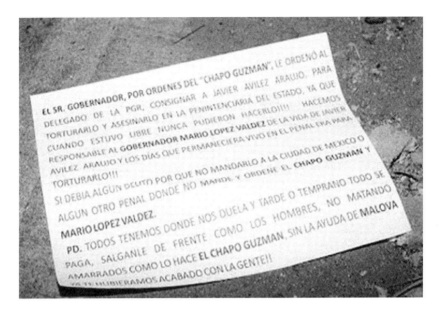

FIGURE 5.3   Zeta leaflet, unattributed photo taken by Mexican law enforcement.

and medical care for your families."[21] The Zetas have also targeted the *ni-ni*, young boys who go to neither school nor work, by offering them money and "prestige." In May 2012, the group employed a new propaganda tactic, one not previously seen in the cartel battles. Thousands of leaflets were dropped from aircraft during the early morning hours over the Sinaloa capital city as a warning to the governor of the region and Chapo Guzman, leader of the Sinaloas, to stop working together or face dire consequences (see Figure 5.3).

DTOS CROSS THE BORDER: CARTELS
IN THE HEARTLAND

According to a September 2011 report by General McCaffrey and Dr. Robert Scales, "drug cartels exploit porous borders using all the traditional elements of a military force, including command and control, logistics, intelligence, information operations and the application of increasingly deadly firepower."[22] Indeed, the DTOs have slipped past the border and into our heartland, and nearly every state in our country is experiencing Mexican DTO activity. The cartels are using multiple points of entry at the border via *plazas* or tunnels, leveraging contact with gangs inside the United States to move drugs, and recruiting. In 2008, DTOs were present in 230 cities in the United States; startlingly, this number rose to more than 1,000 U.S. cities by 2010, according to the U.S. Justice Department.[23] Figure 5.4 depicts cartel activity in the various regions of the United States.

Cartel violence is emerging in our cities; for instance, DTO-related home invasions in the Phoenix area are on the rise. In June 2008, several men wearing Phoenix Police Department uniforms forced their way into a Phoenix home, killing an occupant and spraying the home with fifty to one hundred bullets.[24] As violent crime in the nation fell 10 percent in 2010, it rose in Arizona, including an increase in murders, which tracks with DTO violence: the cartels don't send warnings like the Mafia or other organized crime syndicates—they kill outright.

In addition to violent home invasions, kidnappings in Phoenix are also prevalent; in fact, Phoenix is now the number 2 kidnapping capital of the world, behind Mexico City. DTOs, especially the Zetas, use kidnappings to obtain demands; however, even if demands are met, the kidnapping typically ends in murder. A new technique copied from one widely used in Mexico involves "victimless" kidnapping and ransom. A cell phone is stolen and loved ones called and told of its owner's kidnapping. The family is instructed to give credit card and bank account information to secure the return of the victim. Later, with their funds depleted, they find that their loved one was never in danger at all.

Our citizens have been killed by the cartels not only in Mexico but at border crossings and in our own country. The cartels routinely issue a "green light," authorizing the killing of police and military. According to the Department of Homeland Security, in 2010 the Barrio Azteca issued a "green light" authorizing the murder of law enforcement officers in El Paso.[25] The Barrio Azteca gang formed in Texas prisons in the 1980s and is affiliated with a Mexican gang, the Aztecas, who carry out hits for the Juárez Cartel's La Linea enforcers. Shortly after the "green light" was given, the Aztecas targeted and killed pregnant U.S. consulate employee Leslie Ann Enriquez Catton and her husband at the border in Ciudad Juárez. The husband of another consulate employee, Jorge Salcido, was also killed in the attack. Miraculously, the Catton's young child was unharmed, strapped in a car seat.[26] High-profile murders of U.S. law enforcement agents by DTOs include ICE special agent Jaime Zapata and Border Patrol agent Brian Terry.

LE Operations against DTOs in the United States

The following law enforcement operations illustrate the vast amount of cartel activity occurring in the United States.

DTO	Drugs Trafficked	U.S. Presence by Region
Sinaloa Cartel	Cocaine Heroin Marijuana MDMA Methamphetamine	Florida/Caribbean Great Lakes Mid-Atlantic New England New York/New Jersey Pacific Southeast Southwest West Central Great Lakes Southeast Southwest
Los Zetas	Cocaine Marijuana	Florida/Caribbean Great Lakes Southeast Southwest
Gulf Cartel	Cocaine Marijuana	Florida/Caribbean Mid-Atlantic New England New York/New Jersey Southeast Southwest
Juárez Cartel	Cocaine Marijuana	Great Lakes New York/New Jersey Pacific Southeast Southwest West Central
Beltran Leyva	Cocaine Heroin Marijuana	Southeast Southwest
La Familia Michoacana	Cocaine Heroin Marijuana Methamphetamine	Southeast Southwest
Tijuana/AFO Cartel	Cocaine Heroin Marijuana Methamphetamine	Great Lakes Pacific Southwest

FIGURE 5.4   Activities by Mexican-Based TCOs in the U.S. (2011).

Operation Dark Angel

In 2012, Operation Dark Angel targeted the DTO Armando Mendoza-Haro, named after its leader, to stop the flow of methamphetamines from Mexico into Colorado, Utah, and California. In addition to Mendoza-Haro, twenty other group members were arrested across the country. Dark Angel also uncovered a major money-laundering scheme moving millions of U.S. dollars cross-border through a bulk cash scheme leveraging unsuspecting drivers inside their benign vehicles, such as milk trucks. Drug sale proceeds were also moved via layered transactions back to Mexico, skillfully avoiding U.S. banking system reporting limits. The Dark Angel operations highlighted a growing problem regarding meth; after the United States imposed strict regulations on the components such as the drug pseudoephedrine to push meth production out of the country, super labs in Mexico have stepped up to supply users with the product. In 2012, the Mexican military made the largest single seizure of methamphetamine ever, fifteen tons, worth around 1 billion U.S dollars, outside of Guadalajara.[27]

NEXUS CASE STUDY: PSEUDOEPHEDRINE

In 2002, four Detroit men with ties to Jordan, Yemen, Lebanon, and other Middle Eastern countries smuggled pseudoephedrine from Canada to locations in the Midwest—primarily Detroit and Chicago. Pseudoephedrine, which is used in cold and allergy medications, is an essential ingredient in methamphetamine, a powerful and popular drug also known as ice or crystal meth. The stolen chemical was sold to Mexican-run methamphetamine operations in the western United States, with some of the proceeds of the resulting drug sales diverted to Middle East accounts linked to terrorist groups. The drug ring was broken up as part of a massive DEA investigation called Operation Mountain Express.[28] DEA agents told the author that although seizures of this amount are fairly routine, the connection to Mexican cartels and an international terrorist group was unexpected and extremely worrisome.

Project Delirium

Project Delirium was a two-year counternarcotics operation specifically targeting La Familia Michoacana (LFM) ending July 20, 2011. Delirium resulted in 2,000 arrests and seizure of twelve tons of drugs and sixty-two million U.S dollars in thirteen states. A key LFM leader was arrested in Mexico during the U.S. operation. Delirium was a follow-up to Project Coronado from 2009, which exposed LFM operations in four major U.S. cities.

Project Deliverance

A two-year counternarcotics operation, Deliverance ended on June 9, 2010, with a coordinated takedown of more than 2,200 drug traffickers in nineteen states by federal, state, and local law enforcement agencies. Officers also seized the following assets: $154 million; 2,600 pounds of heroin and methamphetamine; 71 tons of cocaine and marijuana; and more than 500 weapons and 500 vehicles.[29] This activity, related to LFM and other cartels, was present not only in border states but in unexpected areas such as Wisconsin, Montana, and Tennessee.

Project Xcellerator

Xcellerator was a two-year, multiagency operation targeting the Sinaloa Cartel's activity in the United States. Ending in February 2009, Xcellerator investigators pinpointed seventy drug distribution centers in twenty-six states with agents arresting 750 traffickers and confiscating twenty-three tons of cocaine (worth 364 million U.S. dollars). Notably, many of the Sinaloa's drug hubs were not in major metropolitan areas. For example, one distribution center was located in Stow, Ohio, a quiet community of 35,000. The Sinaloas were using the small community airport to move drugs between Stow and distribution hubs in California.[30]

Project Reckoning

In 2008, more than 175 Gulf Cartel operatives working in the United States were arrested as part of the DEA's Project Reckoning, which identified networks reaching from the Mexican border to Georgia, New York, North Carolina, and other states. In all, the DEA seized 60 million U.S. dollars in cash and over forty tons of illegal drugs belonging to the Gulf Cartel.[31]

A common thread was discovered through these operations: DTOs may be attempting to reduce their visibility. Some reports indicate that in the last few years, they have relocated operations out of major cities and now target small towns to serve as their distribution hubs and lab locations, similar to the Stow, Ohio, example. For example, super meth labs operated by traffickers associated with cartels have been discovered in suburban areas like Smyrna, Georgia, and Modesto, California. Additionally, several small towns in the United States are being overrun with DTO-related activity. Places like Casa Grande, Arizona, and the Vekol Valley, both outside of Phoenix and well inside of the border, bear watching and could be the first front in the war against DTOs in our country.

NEXUS AREA: TERRORISTS, SIAS, AND DTOS

In addition to the DTOs, terrorist factions and citizens from countries sponsoring terror are exploiting the chaos at the border. An investigative report prepared by the House Committee on Homeland Security entitled *Line in the Sand: Confronting the Threat at the Southwest Border* paints a worrisome picture regarding its porosity.[32] For example, in 2011 463,000 illegal aliens (IAs) were apprehended at the border; however, officials believe that just 10 to 30 percent of IAs crossing into the United States are detained, meaning at least 4 million may have successfully crossed. Illegal aliens known as "Other Than Mexicans" (OTMs) are also actively attempting to enter the United States through Mexico. U.S. Customs and Border Protection (CBP) reports that in 2010, they apprehended 59,017 OTMs at the border. The law dictates that illegal aliens be detained by Immigrations and Customs Enforcement (ICE) and given a hearing. However, the courts cannot handle the workload due to the sheer number of cases; therefore OTMs are returned to their country of origin with a future court date, if they wish to return and plead their case for citizenship. Most do not and simply disappear.

Of OTMs caught trying to illegally enter the United States, most are from Central and South American countries. The data are worrisome due to the presence of FARC, Hamas, Hezbollah, and al Qaeda in those regions. However, of even greater concern are the thousands of IAs attempting to cross the border from "countries of concern" or state sponsors of terror, special-interest aliens (SIAs). Each fiscal year, CBP is directed by law to compile an OTM list, including SIAs. The data are not releasable to the public but may be obtained through a Freedom of Information Act (FOIA) request to the Border Patrol. Figure 5.5 illustrates the number of SIAs apprehended at the Mexican/U.S. border FY 2007–2010. Certainly, many SIAs are smuggled by DTOs, and the opportunity for terrorists and DTOs to interface in this realm is extremely high.

Terrorists and others with nefarious intentions have already crossed into the United States at the Mexican border. ICE investigations revealed that many SIAs were moved from the Middle East to staging areas in Central and South America before being smuggled illegally into the United States. Hezbollah has been present and active in South and Central America for at least twenty years and now have a presence in Mexico. A study done by Georgetown University found that the number of immigrants from Lebanon and Syria living in Mexico exceeds 200,000, and according to the 2010 Mexican census, 1.1 million Mexicans consider themselves Arab. Hezbollah will likely infiltrate their communities to receive sympathy, funding, and safe harbor, similar to their activities in the tri-border region of South America. ICE officials have testified that members of Hezbollah have already entered the United States across the

Country of Interest	SIAs Apprehended in FY2007-2010
China	4,157
Russia	197
Pakistan	149
Somalia	79
Iraq	59
Iran	56
Yemen	33
Afghanistan	21
Syria	12
North Korea	5

FIGURE 5.5   SIA Data obtained by Judicial Watch and Atlanta TV station WSBTV through FOIA request. (*Source:* Judicial Watch, Judicial Watch Obtains New Border Patrol Apprehension Statistics for Illegal Alien Smugglers and "Special Interest Aliens," 2011.)

southwest border,[33] and in 2011, a former undercover law enforcement officer spoke out regarding his discovery of Hezbollah safe houses in Tijuana and Durango.[34] In September 2012, Rafic Mohammad Labbon Allaboun was arrested in Mexico and returned to the United States for violating probation. Allaboun was born in Beirut and came to the United States in 1986, becoming a dual citizen. He was arrested for credit card fraud and spent two years in jail; authorities suspected the fraud was linked to Hezbollah's money-laundering activities but could not prove the charge in court. Allaboun violated the terms of his probation and traveled to Yucatán, Mexico, where he was arrested by law enforcement; Allaboun was carrying a fake passport identifying him as a citizen of Belize at the time of arrest. Authorities suspect him of involvement with a branch of Hezbollah active in Central America and the Yucatán. Finally, Hamas is also believed to be operating in Tijuana and is likely liaising with Hezbollah or sympathizers/fund-raisers.

Al Qaeda may be also present in the border region. An example is Ahmed Muhammad Dhakane, who was born in Somalia and moved to Brazil in 2007 to set up a large human-smuggling operation. Dhakane was arrested at the border in 2011 and applied for political asylum in the United States. However, during the application process, he failed to mention his connections to al-Barakat and Al-Ittihad Al-Islami (AIAI), both Specially Designated Global Terrorists (SDGTs) by the State Department. In fact, AIAI was at one time Somalia's largest militant Islamic group and officially aligned itself with al Qaeda in the late 1990s. Dhakane

FIGURE 5.6 Extremist Patches Found in Texas. (*Source:* A Line in the Sand: Confronting the Threat at the Southwest Border.)

confessed in court that he had smuggled seven terrorist group members into the United States across the Mexican border along with numerous men from Somalia, Nigeria, and Middle Eastern countries at the behest of the groups.[35] He is serving a ten-year sentence for his activities. In 2010, Al Shabaab, also aligned with al Qaeda, recruited a U.S. citizen living in Kenya, Anthony Joseph Tracy, to assist with smuggling 271 Somali nationals across the border and into the United States. Several were captured; however, most remain at large.

A government report regarding the radical Islamist threat at the border includes apparent photographic proof of presence. A jacket found in Jim Hogg County, Texas, by the Border Patrol had Arabic military patches: one depicting an airplane flying over a building and heading toward a tower, and another showing an image of a lion's head with wings and a parachute emanating from the animal. The bottom of one patch read "martyr" and "way to eternal life"[36] (see Figure 5.6).

Finally, during a live television broadcast on February 2, 2009, Kuwaiti professor Abdallah Nafisi recommended that al Qaeda bring anthrax through Mexico to attack the United States. His suggested plan was that the attacker stand near the White House and drop four pounds of anthrax, spreading it like "confetti" and killing 330,000 (see Figure 5.7). Nafisi also encourages the white supremacists in the United States to follow through with bombing nuclear power plants, including one on Lake Michigan. His Internet video is easily accessible and rebroadcast on many radical Islamist websites. The comments attached to the bottom of the video on social networking websites are filled with radical Islamist ranting and encouragement for operatives to execute Nafisi's plan. In the video, he states:

FIGURE 5.7   Screenshot of Abdallah Nafisi explaining the effect of four pounds of anthrax smuggled across the U.S. border and released.

There is good reason for the Americans' fears, because al-Qaida used to have in the Herat region. ... It had laboratories in north Afghanistan. They have scientists, chemists, and nuclear physicists. They are nothing like they are portrayed by these mercenary journalists—backward Bedouins living in caves. No, no. By no means. This kind of talk can fool only naïve people. People who follow such things know that al-Qaida has laboratories, just like Hezbollah. Hezbollah has laboratories in Southern Lebanon in which it produces weapons and sells them. Hezbollah has laboratories in Southern Lebanon from which it sells weapons to Romania and Hungary. They call someone a terrorist, say "He's a friend of mine. They are the most honorable people in the world."

CORRUPTION AT THE BORDER: OPENING THE GATES

Corruption of government officials, law enforcement, and military officers in Mexico continues to plague this battle and give advantage to the DTOs. For instance, Mario Villanueva Madrid, former governor of the Mexican state of Quintana Roo, was charged with providing police protection to assist the Juárez Cartel with moving cocaine and laundering money through U.S. corporations. Others recently rounded up include a bodyguard of another governor, police involved in the shooting of an army general, and several police chiefs.

With their successful government infiltration in Mexico, DTOs have now brought this brand of corruption into the United States. They are actively attempting to compromise the CBP system by recruiting or planting operatives. Since 2004, more than one hundred CBP agents have been arrested or indicted for drug smuggling, money laundering, conspiracy, or human smuggling, succumbing to the lure of vast sums of money. Perhaps the most grievous case was that of Michael Gilliland, a retired Marine. His sixteen years of duty with CBP came to an unceremonious end with a federal conviction for helping hundreds of people enter the United States unchecked through the Otay Mesa crossing in San Diego where he was posted. He worked with two Mexican women who ran smuggling rings south of the border; Gilliland accepted bribes upwards of $100,000.[37] In 2009, Luis F. Alarid, a veteran of both the U.S. Army and Marines Corps who completed two tours of duty in Iraq, was arrested for allowing trucks from Mexico to pass through his checkpoint, carrying loads of marijuana and illegal immigrants. He was paid in cash and purchased a motorcycle, a flat-screen TV, and other high-priced electronics with his earnings. He told investigators that when weighing the offer to break the law, he considered the jail time he might get and that he could do it "standing on his head."[38] Finally, Oscar Ortiz-Martinez, who worked as a customs inspector in Calexico, and Lorne "Hammer" Jones, a canine handler at the San Ysidro and Otay Mesa border crossings, were arrested in September 2010 in separate investigations and will face trial in late 2012.[39] In 2006, Border Patrol agents and brothers Raul and Fidel Villarreal pocketed over 1 million U.S. dollars in just one year while assisting human-smuggling rings. Using official government vehicles to bring Mexicans and Brazilians across the border, the brothers were working with a corrupt Tijuana police chief to facilitate their smuggling activities. After being tipped off in 2008 about the undercover investigation, the brothers fled to Mexico, where they were arrested by authorities and returned to the United States. Raul Villarreal was long a public face of the Border Patrol who frequently appeared on television as an agency spokesman. One of the "clients" from Brazil said she paid $12,000 to be driven across the border in a police vehicle.[40] The brothers received a jail term of sixty years in prison.

Cartels also attempt to plant operatives within CBP. Margarita Crispin joined CBP in 2003 with the full intent of working with drug smugglers, and before her arrest, she allowed thousands of pounds of marijuana to pass through her inspection lane in El Paso. In 2008, Crispin was sentenced to twenty years in prison and ordered to forfeit $5 million in bribes she was paid while wearing the CBP uniform.

As the need for agents grows, the hiring pool is increasingly tainted. CBP officials have testified that of the 15 percent of applicants asked to take a polygraph, 60 percent of them fail and are unsuitable for duty. Twenty-two percent of the applicants who are not subjected to polygraph investigations fail the Single Scope Background check.[41] CBP would like to poly all applicants but lack the resources; one of the reasons may be the need to fund internal corruption probes. In the last four years, the number of internal affairs investigators leapt from just five in 2006 to over 200 in 2012. The FBI is also involved in the fight: it now fields six Border Corruption Task Forces with hundreds of agents solely working bribery and corruption issues along the 2,000-mile border between the United States and Mexico. The thought of who or what could cross into our country at these compromised border areas keeps many homeland security professionals awake at night.

DTOS: FOREIGN TERRORIST ORGANIZATIONS?

In a rebuttal to an editorial appearing in the *Dallas Morning News* in April 2011 entitled "Let's Call Mexico's Cartels What They Are: Terrorists,"[42] Arturo Sarukhan, Mexico's ambassador to the United States stated his opinion on the topic loud and clear. According to the ambassador:

> The editorial should be better headed "Let's Call Mexico's cartels what they are: very violent, well-financed transnational criminal organizations." These transnational criminal organizations, which operate in both our countries, are not terrorist organizations. They are very violent criminal groups that are well-structured and well-financed. They pursue a single goal. They want to maximize their profits and do what most businesses do: hostile takeovers and pursue mergers and acquisitions. They use violence to protect their business from other competitors as well as from our two governments' efforts to roll them back. There is no political motivation or agenda whatsoever beyond their attempt to defend their illegal business.
>
> Misunderstanding the challenge we face leads to wrong policies and bad policy making. If you label these organizations as terrorist, you will have to start calling drug consumers in the U.S. "financiers of terrorist organizations" and gun dealers "providers of material support to terrorists." Otherwise, you really sound as if you want to have your cake and eat it too. That's why I would underscore that the editorial page should be careful what it advocates for.[43]

Given the material covered in this chapter and the definitions of international and domestic terrorism given in previous chapters, consider your stance on the issue. At least one of our lawmakers takes a quite opposite stance; in March 2011, Republican representative Michael McCaul of Texas introduced H.R. 1270 to Congress, directing the secretary of state to declare the following Mexican drug cartels as Foreign Terrorist Organizations (FTOs):

1. The Tijuana/Arellano Feliz Organization
2. The Los Zetas Cartel
3. The Beltran Leyva Organization
4. La Familia Michoacana
5. The Sinaloa Cartel
6. The Gulf Cartel/New Federation

Arguably, these organizations pose more of a danger to our national security than several dormant groups residing on the FTO list, November 17 and Aum Shinriyko/Aleph, for example. Designation would allow federal law enforcement to more easily pursue and prosecute Americans who are complicit in providing material assistance to the cartels, whether money, housing, logistics, medical assistance, or weapons. The issues put forth by the ambassador in his letter to the editor regarding drug users and nefarious gun dealers being complicit as related to FTO designation and the laws are provocative, but both activities are illegal. Perhaps the added weight and ramification of dealing with a terrorist organization would finally dissuade these destructive activities in our country.

Designation would also harness and focus all the powers of the state, such as diplomatic and economic, against the DTOs. Our country could mount a broad, coordinated effort to attack DTO financing, logistics, and operations with the purpose of dismantling the groups. Lacking this legislation, our government will continue to see each DTO event as an individual crime and not leverage our federal fusion centers to connect dots. Factoring in the potential nexus with terror groups, this lack of strategic-level intelligence gathering, sharing, and synthesis is worrisome. Consider that it took the (thankfully) failed Times Square bomb attempt to get the Pakistani Taliban on the FTO list, when it was clear prior to the event that they threatened the United States and were recruiting American citizens to become operatives and terrorists within our country. Perhaps being more proactive with the DTOs is prudent.

FINAL THOUGHTS

Are the Mexican cartels a U.S national security risk, or have we overblown the threat? Is their activity in the United States terroristic or merely criminal in nature? After exploring the data in this chapter, you may now answer the question differently. Certainly, we should continue to monitor DTO activity south of the border, in anticipation of what we likely will see very soon on our own soil. We must also be careful not to neglect threats to the northern border where terrorists, money launderers, and DTOs have already penetrated or attempted to cross illegally into our country from Canada and back. The old saying is certainly true: a nation is only as strong as its borders.

American citizens are unprepared for the acts of extreme violence and the threads that will be pulled from the fabric of society by the DTOs as they advance their agenda in our communities. Constructing the legal foundation for dealing with the DTO threat is paramount, such as adding cartels to the list of designated terrorist organizations and revisiting Posse Comitatus to use military force against them on our soil as needed. Underestimating this enemy and its sophistication, determination, and vast resources puts our nation at extreme risk.

Not all terrorist and criminal groups have access to the immense funds generated in the narco-trafficking trade. Other groups must rely on traditional sources of funding or exploit the booming e-commerce industry to fund their illicit activities, as the next two chapters will explore.

REFERENCES

1. Mark Potter, "Mexican Drug War 'Alarming' U.S. Officials," June 25, 2008, http://worldblog.nbcnews.com/_news/2008/06/25/4376042-mexican-drug-war-alarming-us-officials?lite.
2. U.S. House Armed Services Committee, Confirmation Hearing, May 12, 2009.
3. U.S. Department of Justice, "National Drug Threat Assessment," National Drug Intelligence Center, 2011.
4. Robert R. Martin, "The National Park Service and Transnational Criminal Organizations—Is a Crisis Looming?" American Military University, 2012.
5. Olga R. Rodriguez, "Mexico Cartel Stitches Rival's Face on Soccer Ball," January 9, 2010.
6. William F. Jasper, "Escalating Chaos on Our Border," *The New American*, March 17, 2010.
7. DEA, "National Drug Assessment," 2008.
8. STRATFOR, "Mexico Security Memo: Guns, Money and Los Zetas Incursions in Sinaloa Territory," 2012.
9. Adapted from Jennifer L. Hesterman, "The Mexican Drug War Spills over the Border," *Counter Terrorist Magazine*, June/July 2009, 26–38.
10. U.S. Department of Justice, "Texas Jury Convicts Zeta Hitman 'Cachetes,'" (2012).

11. DEA, "Twenty Charged in Chicago with Various Drug Trafficking Offenses, Including Five Allegedly Tied to the Mexican 'Zetas' Cartel," 2012.

12. FBI, "Los Zetas Expanding Reach into Southeast and Midwest United States," 2008.

13. George W. Grayson and Samuel Logan, *The Executioner's Men* (Livingston, NJ: Transaction, 2012), 188.

14. Ibid.

15. Jennifer L. Hesterman, "The Mexican Drug War Spills over the Border."

16. Hesterman, "Los Zetas Cartel Ambush in Houston," *Counter Terrorist Magazine*, 2012.

17. Adam Clark Estes, "Anonymous and the Zetas Cartel Declare a Truce," *Atlantic Wire*, November 4, 2011.

18. U.S. Department of Justice, "National Gang Threat Assessment," 2011.

19. "Zetas and MS-13 Join Forces in Guatemala," Fox News Latino, April 7, 2012, http://latino.foxnews.com/latino/news/2012/04/07/zetas-and-ms-13-join-forces-in-guatemala/.

20. Patrick Corcoran, "Oil Theft Is Big Business for Mexican Gangs," *InSightCrime: Organized Crime in the Americas*. March 20, 2012, http://www.insightcrime.org/insight-latest-news/item/2373-oil-theft-is-big-business-for-mexican-gangs.

21. Manuel Roig-Franzia, "Mexican Drug Cartels Making Audacious Pitch for Recruits," *Washington Post*, May 7, 2008.

22. Barry R. McCaffrey and Robert H. Scales, *Texas Border Security: A Strategic Military Assessment* (Mico, TX: Colgen LP, 2011).

23. U.S. Department of Justice, "National Drug Threat Assessment."

24. Sylvia Longmire, *Cartel* (New York: Palgrave Macmillan, 2011).

25. U.S. Department of Homeland Security, "Officer Safety Alert," 2010.

26. http://www.justice.gov/opa/pr/2011/March/11-ag-299.html.

27. Ben West, *"Dark Angel" and the Mexican Meth Connection*. STRATFOR Global Intelligence, 2012.

28. Rodney Thrash, " Drug Ring Linked to Terror," *Detroit Free Press*, September 2, 2002.

29. FBI, "Project Deliverance," http://www.fbi.gov/news/pressrel/press-releases/201cproject-deliverance201d-results-in-more-than-2-200-arrests-during-22-month-operation-seizures-of-approximately-74-tons-of-drugs-and-154-million-in-u.s.-currency.

30. U.S. Department of Justice, "Operation Xcellerator Press Conference," http://www.justice.gov/dea/speeches/xcellerator.pdf.

31. DEA, "Project Reckoning," 2008.

32. U.S. House Committee on Homeland Security, Subcommittee on Investigations, *A Line in the Sand: Confronting the Threat at the Southwest Border*, 2006.
33. Ibid.
34. "Terrorist Group Setting Up Operations Near Border," ABC 10 News, May 4, 2011, http://www.10news.com/news/27780427/detail.html.
35. Investigative Project on Terrorism, "USA v. Ahmed Muhammed Dhakane," http://www.investigativeproject.org/case/370.
36. U.S. House Committee on Homeland Security, *A Line in the Sand*.
37. PBS Frontline, "The Corruption Case of Michael Gilliland," *Frontline*. PBS. 2008, http://www.pbs.org/frontlineworld/stories/mexico704/interview/reed.html.
38. Randal C. Archibold, "Hired by Customs, but Working for Mexican Cartels," *New York Times*, December 17, 2009.
39. California Watch, "Details Emerge as Ex-Border Patrol Brothers Fight Corruption Charges," *Sacramento Bee*, May 32, 2012.
40. Elliot Spagat, "Border Patrol Agents Set for Corruption Trial," *San Francisco Chronicle*, June 24, 2012, http://www.sfgate.com/news/article/Border-Patrol-agents-set-for-corruption-trial-3658857.php.
41. Senate Report 111-338, *Anti-Border Corruption Act of 2010*, 2010.
42. "Let's Call Mexico's Cartels What They Are: Terrorists," *Dallas Morning News*, Editorial, April 7, 2011, http://www.dallasnews.com/opinion/editorials/20110407-editorial-lets-call-mexicos-cartels-what-they-are-terrorists.ece.
43. Arturo Sarukhan, "Choose Labels Carefully," *Dallas Morning News*, Letter to the Editor, April 11, 2011.

CHAPTER 6

Traditional Terrorist and Criminal Financing Methods
Adapting for Success

> At 12:01 a.m. this morning, a major thrust of our war on terrorism began with the stroke of a pen. Today, we have launched a strike on the financial foundation of the global terror network. Money is the lifeblood of terrorist operations. Today, we're asking the world to stop payment.[1]
>
> —**President George Bush**
> *Introducing Executive Order 13224*
> September 24, 2001

Just thirteen days after the September 2001 attacks and the declaration of a national emergency, then-President Bush signed EO 13224, *Blocking Property and Prohibiting Transactions with Persons Who Commit, Threaten to Commit, or Support Terrorism*. Attached to the order was a list of easily recognizable terrorist groups but also more obscure financing actors such as charities, trusts, and export companies. Although the intelligence community always suspected that funding to terrorists was coming from these sources, the tragic events of 9/11 and the subsequent unraveling of the money trail officially brought the situation to the table.

Many countries joined the United States in an international campaign to tighten money-laundering and terrorist financing streams. The Financial Action Task Force (FATF) is the world's anti-money-laundering and counterterrorist financing standard-setting body established in 1989. In October 2001, FATF developed the "Eight Special Recommendations" to address terrorist financing, with a ninth added in 2005. They also amplified and updated the FATF "40 Recommendations on Money Laundering," which was originally adopted in 1990 and revised in 1996 and again in 2003. The cumulative effect of FATF's actions certainly led to greater financial transparency, more meticulous accounting practices, and stricter regulatory oversight around the world. FATF also brought countries of interest and regimes under scrutiny such as Russia and China.

However, terrorist financing often occurs licitly, as witnessed by the money transfers between countries to support the training, living expenses, and transportation needs of the 9/11 operatives. Even the expanded powers of the Uniting and Strengthening America by Providing Appropriate Tools Required to Intercept and Obstruct Terrorism Act (USA PATRIOT Act), which broadened anti-money-laundering requirements to a wider range of financial service companies and increased information sharing, likely would not have stopped the financing of the hijackers.

I was fortunate to attend a weeklong classified government course on terrorist and criminal financing, studying the 9/11 money trail and learning firsthand how actors are still exploiting old methods as well as seeking vulnerabilities in emergent banking and commerce sectors. This type of deliberate, methodical market penetration and the ability to morph tactics are hallmarks of modern groups, which act with sophistication and in parallel to legitimate economy.

FUNDING TERROR

Richard Clarke, former terrorism coordinator for the National Security Council, once testified: "When I first asked the CIA in 1995, in that era, to look into terrorist financing, they said: 'well, after all, you have to understand it doesn't take a lot of money to do a terrorist act.' What they failed to understand was that it took a lot of money to be a terrorist organization."[2] Much has been discussed in the media about the mere $450,000 needed to directly finance the 9/11 terrorist attacks and the $10,000 expended to cripple the USS *Cole* and kill U.S. servicemen. A false impression emerged in the public that the money trail is not sizeable, worrisome, or integral to a terrorist operation. In fact, prior to 9/11 and over a ten-year period, al Qaeda was estimated to receive between $300 million and $500 million in cash, averaging $30 to $50 million a year.[3] Approximately 10 percent of the group's spending was on terrorist operations and attacks, while 90 percent was used to maintain the infrastructure of the network, including payments to other groups for support or to increase al Qaeda's influence in these regions.[4] The al Qaeda model clearly shows that money spent on a terrorist attack may merely be the tip of the iceberg.

Terrorist organizations need money and resources not only to carry out an operation but perhaps most importantly to recruit, maintain safe havens, train, travel, take care of day-to-day expenses, and in some groups, provide for the families of dead martyrs. The assets required to fund such extensive, global operations synonymous with modern terrorist groups come from a variety of licit and illicit sources such as individuals, organizations, and the criminal enterprise.

One widely used estimate is that economic activity-related terrorist group activity accounts for a staggering $1.5 trillion, or 5 percent of annual global output.[5] Furthermore, the cost of doing business may be rising for terrorists, especially al Qaeda. Similar to a business expanding into franchises, splinter groups need resources to sustain themselves, driving the cost of doing business higher. Also, as terrorist plots increase in complexity or delve into the WMD realm, the cost of equipment, expertise, and keeping operations off law enforcement's radar will rise. These emergent needs will likely lead groups to previously untapped sources for money, manpower, and other support.

An old soldier's axiom provides excellent context to the importance of pursuing terrorist and criminal financing: "Amateurs study tactics; professionals study logistics." The money trail is perhaps the key to preventing future operations, more so than any other aspect of terrorism investigative work. A transaction can typically be broken down into a series of smaller steps, allowing investigators to further penetrate an operation. The identification of individual, illicit transactions, the behavior of the actors accomplishing licit transactions, and other information gathered from video surveillance, cell phone records, and computer Internet Protocol (IP) addresses can certainly unravel plots and destroy organizations. Therefore understanding the methodologies employed and keeping an eye on developing techniques are critical to successful investigatory penetration.

EARNING, MOVING, STORING

When the FBI transported Ramzi Yousef by helicopter over Manhattan following his capture in 1995 for the bombing of the World Trade Center's Twin Towers, an FBI agent pulled up Yousef's blindfold and pointed out the lights of the World Trade Center were still glowing. As the FBI agent stated, "They're still standing," Yousef is reported to have responded, "They wouldn't be if I had enough money and explosives."

Tactics

To frame the discussion of terrorist and criminal financing activities, it is important to first differentiate between traditional methods employed by groups and their members to earn, move, store, and/or launder their assets. This model is especially helpful when applied to transnational and virtual finance issues.

Earn

Nefarious groups earn money through a variety of activities. Donations from wealthy supporters and personal wealth of group members are two of the "cleanest" sources. Without bin Laden's personal wealth and infusion of cash into the group, al Qaeda may not have succeeded or be the vast enterprise it remains today. By nature, these funding streams are not business activities and are thus untraceable, impermeable ways to generate funds. International charities and use of "tithing" by religious believers is the next desirable activity, mixing illicit and licit funds to complicate the money trail. When necessary, the organization may move on to other activities such as involvement in commodity smuggling, intellectual property crime, organized retail theft, identity theft, "419" scams, and mortgage fraud. Narco-trafficking also yields great profit, as was covered in the previous chapter exploring Mexican cartels and their vast wealth accrued by feeding the appetite for illegal drugs around the world. Nearly all international terrorist groups are also involved in the drug trade; for example, the Abu Sayyaf Group exploits marijuana plantations in the Philippines; the Taliban leverages the poppy crop; and Hezbollah, FARC, and al Qaeda are all involved in the Latin America drug trade.

Move

Money is typically moved through nontransparent systems in which terrorists and criminals can hide transactions and the movement of funds across borders. Legitimate systems are sometimes used, although the means of movement will be illicit in nature. Informal value transfer systems (IVTSs) such as hawala are still being exploited, despite renewed regulation and scrutiny. Financial transactions through licit systems may be also layered, adding additional protection to the movement. The sophistication and international aspect of such laundering activities have long been underestimated; one expert believes that terrorist organizations have shown the same skills as any Wall Street investor in channeling assets into legal structures and businesses in pursuit of their broader goals.[6]

Store

Groups may store assets in commodities maintaining or increasing in value over time such as diamonds or gold. Precious metals and stones are regarded as currency in many parts of the world and are relatively easy to smuggle, untraceable, and able to escape detection by canine or X-ray. Bulk cash can also be considered a method of storage.

EARNING

Charities

The use of charities to raise funds for terrorist groups is a persistent concern in the counterterrorism community. Modern charities are global in nature, and many are the equivalent of large-scale corporations. The use of charities to raise funds is desirable primarily because of the ability to quickly comingle illicit funds with licit funds, making a direct link between the financier and terrorist act virtually impossible. Further, for contributors wishing to finance a terrorist group, their identities are protected due to lack of paper trail and the charity's ability to hide within and be protected by a large, overarching religious organization. For example, per the U.S. Treasury, despite the best efforts of the UN, United States, and others Hamas still raises tens of millions of dollars per year using charitable fund-raising as cover. Unfortunately, the Internet and virtual "nonbanks" have unintentionally kept illicit charities in business.

Designation

When the U.S. government receives information that a charity is the source of terrorist funding, the designation process begins. The legal authority for designation rests with the Department of Treasury's Office of Foreign Assets Control (OFAC), which designates a person or organization as a Specially Designated Global Terrorist (SDGT). Once designated, OFAC will freeze assets pending an investigation, in conjunction with EEO 13224, the Trading with the Enemy Act of 1917, and the USA PATRIOT Act.

The process of designation is complex and lengthy; the burden of proof is extensive and the diplomatic wrangling burdensome. Upon being designated, a group's tax-exempt status is revoked, meaning donors cannot deduct any contributions and the organization must pay federal income tax.[7] Despite these obstacles, spurred by the horrific events of 9/11, governments made swift and great progress to identify and close off charitable sources of terrorist financing. For instance, in the months after the attacks, more than $136 million in monetary assets were frozen and 1,400 accounts were blocked worldwide when it was determined that the parent charities were assisting al Qaeda or other terrorist groups.[8] However, before declaring victory in the designation process, we have to consider the nature of the beast. Since licit funds are intermingled with illicit funds, it is unknown how much money in the designation process is actually withheld from terrorists. Further, upon designation, all funds are frozen as it is impossible to separate the "good" money from the "bad," and incoming donations are stopped. Many argue that the designation results in the withholding of money from those who need it most, those living in third-world conditions or in war-torn Middle Eastern countries. For example, among the accounts blocked since 9/11 are twenty-three belonging to Islamic charities that collect and donate money for medical, educational, housing, and other needs for impoverished people. Therein lays the dichotomy of designation ... and why it remains an attractive source of funding for terrorist groups.

Reviewing case studies from past designations is extremely valuable to understanding how they were detected, designated, or stopped, or as in some cases, simply changed names and opened again for business.

CASE STUDIES: CHARITIES

- In 2003, the Treasury Department revoked the tax-exempt status of three Muslim charities accused of diverting contributions to help bankroll terrorist activities:
  - Benevolence International Foundation of Palos Hills, Illinois, had direct connections to bin Laden, and its leader, Enaam Arnaout, pled guilty to aiding Islamic fighters in Chechnya. The organization had branches in Bosnia, Chechnya, Pakistan, China, and Russia, allowing money launderers to easily move and hide assets.[9]
  - Global Relief Foundation of Bridgeview, Illinois, was a multimillion-dollar business, sending more than 90 percent of donations overseas to bin Laden and the Taliban. Organization leaders consistently lied to investigators about the scope and destination of these funds.[10]
  - Holy Land Foundation for Relief and Development of Richardson, Texas, had offices in three states and raised 13 million U.S. dollars in 2000 alone. It was the largest Muslim charity in the United States; although claiming donations went to aid Palestinians, it was singled out for support of Hamas, mainly to the families of suicide bombers.[11]
- The Al-Haramain Islamic Foundation was tied to al Qaeda and designated by Treasury. As a result, in 2003 the Saudi government ordered Al-Haramain to close all of its overseas branches. However, they continued to operate; the branch in Bosnia-Herzegovina simply renamed itself

"Vazir" and resumed the terror-funding business.[12] This example illustrates the ease of designated charities to reorganize, evade authorities, and continue fund-raising.

- The al Taqwa financial empire operated in the Middle East, Turkey, Europe, and the Bahamas. Al Taqwa, which means "Fear of God," funneled tens of millions of dollars to al Qaeda, Hamas, and other terrorist groups through charities and informal banking systems. The two central figures in al Taqwa, who live abroad, were placed on an international list of terrorist financiers, a designation that requires member nations to seize their assets and ban them from traveling internationally. However, the individuals continued to travel, operate a hotel, and own several pieces of real estate.[13] The case underscores the difficulty of disrupting the shadowy world of terrorist financing without strong international assistance.

In all, over fifty charities were designated after the 2001 Executive Order 13224; for a complete list and details, see "Protecting Charitable Organizations" at the U.S. Treasury website.[14]

The U.S. government may also target and designate individual "businessmen" for their charity-related dealings. Consider the case of Abdurahman Alamoudi, a very popular and charismatic Muslim imam, who pled guilty to several financing charges and is serving a twenty-three-year prison sentence. Alamoudi was born in Ethiopian-occupied Eritrea and immigrated to the United States in 1979, becoming a naturalized U.S. citizen in 1996. He held a Yemeni passport and was allied with the State Department-designated foreign terrorist organization (FTO) Muslim Brotherhood. While visiting in London in 2003, Alamoudi received $340,000 in cash from a Libyan and was detained a few days later at Heathrow Airport as he attempted to board a flight to Syria with the money on his person. During his detention with British authorities, Alamoudi specifically stated his intentions to launder the Libyan money back into his U.S. account in small sums, under the legal threshold, through Saudi banks. British authorities let Almoudi leave the country, and a few days later, he was arrested at Dulles International Airport, sans the money. Notably, Alamoudi lied on his U.S. customs form completed on the aircraft, omitting his recent travels to Libya, Lebanon, Yemen, and Egypt. He was charged and convicted of illegal transactions with a terrorist regime, passport fraud, conspiracy to fund terrorists directed against U.S. forces in Iraq, and providing material support for terrorists in the United States.

Alamoudi ran, directed, founded, or funded at least fifteen Muslim political-action and charitable groups representing the public voice of Islamic Americans. The FBI submitted evidence showing that Alamoudi's American Muslim Foundation (AMF), a charitable offshoot of his American Muslim Council (AMC), funded two suspected jihadist terrorists arrested in Oregon who wanted to detonate a bomb at a Christmas tree-lighting ceremony. Also worrisome was Alamoudi's involvement with the certification of Muslim chaplains for the Department of Defense. Notably, through AMC he spun off the American Muslim Armed Forces and Veterans Affairs Council, one of three Islamic organizations to certify chaplains for the military. Alamoudi also had political savvy; he and a group of Muslim leaders met with President Bush in Austin in July 2002. Alamoudi's case is disturbing, particularly when his power, connections, and possible motives are taken into account.

The last charity designation by U.S. Treasury was in 2009, indicating that this type of fund-raising stream may be on the decline. However, charities mixing licit and illicit funds haven't gone away; they've merely gone virtual. The rise of e-commerce and anonymous financial transactions outside of the regulated banking system, as discussed in the next chapter, provides effective workarounds.

Zakat

Zakat-al-Mal is another fund-raising mechanism receiving far less attention than charities but possibly with greater significance. In a little known report prepared for the UN by terrorist-financing expert, Jean-Charles Brisard, Zakat is singled out as the most important source of terrorism funding, and most of the funds are moved through the legal banking system.[15]

The literal meaning of the word *Zakat* is cleansing and growth. Zakat is charitable giving, part of every devout Muslim's obligations, and typically peaks during the season of Ramadan and is paid on or before Eid. An individual who possesses wealth equal to or above a set minimum amount (called Nasab) is obliged to give Zakat. The Qur'an specifies eight purposes for which the money from Zakat can be used[16]:

1. The poor
2. The needy
3. Those employed to administer the collection, distribution, and administration of Zakat as compensation
4. Individuals who have been recently reconciled to the "Truth" (Mu'allafat-al-Qulub) including new Muslims, or those who are willing to support the Muslim state but need to be compensated
5. Freeing of those in bondage or slavery

6. Those in debt
7. In the cause of Allah: those who are going out or working in the cause of Allah (including the task of conveying the message of Islam) or in a battle declared by an Islamic state for just cause
8. The wayfarer; a traveler who is in need of help during his travel

Certainly, the interpretation of these Zakat destinations could be varied, with donors believing their intentions are pure but with money funding illegal or terrorist activities.

According to Brisard's estimate, Saudis contribute approximately 10 billion U.S. dollars per year in Zakat donations, which then usually take the form of bank transfers to approximately 240 charities. He estimates that between $300 and $500 million gathered through Zakat were given to al Qaeda in the years leading up to 9/11.[17] The lack of bookkeeping for Zakat makes it difficult to identify contributors or beneficiaries. Also, countries are extremely sensitive about the monitoring of religious giving. In response to intense scrutiny of the Zakat system following the attacks and international pressure, Saudi authorities removed Zakat "collection boxes" from outside of their mosques and businesses, but the amount of money collected in those boxes represented only $60,000 a year.[18] Although plenty of funds collected through Zakat reach the intended recipients, much of it goes to questionable sources and activities. In Pakistan, for example, scholars note that Zakat recipients have included "orphans" with living parents, "impoverished women" decorated in gold jewelry, and "old people" who long since died.[19] The anonymity and mixing of funds collected through Zakat makes this method extremely vulnerable to terrorist fund-raising activities.

Commodities Smuggling and Organized Retail Crime

The exploitation of high-use products within the United States is an increasingly popular fund-raising tool for criminal and terrorist groups. In commodity-smuggling schemes, high-demand products such as cigarettes are purchased in one state and sold in another with a higher tax rate. This not only reaps a profit for the criminal group, it causes loss for the victimized state, as would-be buyers leave the traditional marketplace to make black-market purchases. In organized retail crime (ORC), products aren't purchased but stolen and then resold by a criminal enterprise to reap the profit. Products are shoplifted, acquired through cargo theft, or purchased with stolen credit cards. Individuals known as "boosters" then convert the product on the street for profit. ORC organizations are very sophisticated and compartmentalized and operate similarly to criminal entities involved in drug trafficking or human smuggling. Stolen products range from perfume to the latest ORC hot product, Tide laundry detergent.

CASE STUDIES: COMMODITIES SMUGGLING AND ORC

- A multimillion-dollar interstate cigarette-smuggling ring contributed its proceeds to Hezbollah. Twelve people were indicted in this scheme for purchasing low-tax cigarettes in North Carolina (5-cent tax per pack) and reselling them in Michigan (75-cent tax per pack). Not only did this scheme raise millions for Hezbollah, but it exacted a $2 million tax loss for the state of Michigan between 1997 and 1999 as buyers purchased black-market cigarettes. The leader of this cell stated that some of the proceeds were for the "orphans of martyrs" program to benefit the families of those killed in the group's operations or by Hezbollah's enemies.[20]
- Operation Milk Money was a federal investigation of an ORC ring involved in the theft and interstate transportation of stolen baby formula. The primary targets were Honduran nationals who stole and resold thousands of cans of powdered baby formula on a monthly basis, with an estimated annual loss to the retail industry in excess of $1 million dollars. Financial transactions were accomplished to conceal the nature, source, ownership, and control of the illicit proceeds. One target structured approximately $208,744 in cash by making deposits in amounts less than $10,000 in an attempt to avoid FinCEN's (Financial Crime Enforcement Network) reporting requirements. Operation Milk Money resulted in twenty-one arrests.[21]
- In 2010, the largest cargo theft case in U.S. history took place at an unmarked Eli Lilly warehouse in Connecticut. In this sophisticated operation, thieves stole over $75 million of antidepressants and other prescription drugs. The actors cut a hole in the roof, rappelled inside, disabled the security system, loaded pallets into their tractor trailer, and simply drove away. Operation Southern Hospitality, a joint law enforcement operation, later arrested eleven members of the ring, which not only executed the Eli Lilly burglary but also were involved in the theft of $20 million in other goods, including thousands of bottles of formula, thousands of cases of cigarettes from an Illinois warehouse, sixty-four cell phones, and 200 inflatable boats. Before their arrest, the men were able to collect $20 million in sales of the stolen drugs.[22]

These cases illustrate the market savvy exhibited by criminal and terrorist groups: focus on the greatest possible profit margin and move a product with high, consistent demand. U.S. Immigration and Customs Enforcement (ICE) is the lead agency battling ORC, through its Homeland Security Investigation (HSI) arm. In July 2009, HSI initiated an ORC pilot program and the follow-on SEARCH initiative (Seizing Earnings and Assets from Retail Crime Heists) to help combat the transnational organized crime networks involved in this illicit activity. The interstate and international shipment of stolen goods and corresponding movement of illicit proceeds from their sale make charges related to Title 18 United States Code 1956, laundering of monetary instruments, possible. SEARCH pulls together the efforts of federal, state, and local law enforcement, prosecutors, and the financial and retail community to provide a multifaceted approach to deterrence and prosecution.

Profits generated from commodity smuggling and ORC are laundered through the U.S. financial sector. Therefore any vulnerability in banking or money services business (MSB) systems, whether technological, human, or other, will be exploited by actors to move or store their illicit proceeds. FinCEN is heavily involved in disseminating information regarding red flags and typologies to MSBs and financial institutions. All types of money-laundering techniques and exploitation of e-commerce have been detected as related to commodities smuggling and ORC. Since 2009, ICE has initiated more than 120 criminal investigations, with sixty-three arrests and over $6 million in property seized.[23]

Intellectual Property Crime (IPC)

IPC is occurring throughout the world and generates an unbelievable amount of profit. In fact, counterfeit-goods trade is estimated at $450 billion annually, representing 5 to 7 percent of global trade value. In the United States alone, losses to counterfeiting are staggering, estimated by the FBI at $200 to $250 billion annually.[24]

Intellectual property refers to the legal rights corresponding to intellectual activity in the industrial, scientific, and artistic fields. These legal rights, most commonly in the form of patents, trademarks, and copyright, protect not only the moral and economic entitlement of the creators but also the creativity and dissemination of their work. Based on this understanding, IPC refers to counterfeited and pirated goods, manufactured and sold for profit without the consent of the patent or trademark holder. IPC is a black-market activity operating parallel to the formal economy and includes the manufacturing, transporting, storing, and sale of counterfeit or pirated goods. Examples of pirated goods are CDs, DVDs, cigarettes, clothes, shoes, designer purses, and computer software. Any hot commodity is ripe for exploitation; for example, when Rosetta Stone rose in popularity, it became a favorite for counterfeiters who then sold their products on Craig's List or eBay and laundered money through PayPal. No product line is safe from counterfeiters, and even inexpensive items such as condoms or NFL pennants have been replicated.

The 2011 IPC seizure report by Customs and Border Protection indicates a 24 percent rise in the counterfeit goods seized over the previous year.[25] Also, China remains the primary source for counterfeit and pirated goods, representing 62 percent of all seizures with footwear, pharmaceuticals, perfume, electronics, purses, designer clothes, and watches leading the way. India and Pakistan are now on the top ten IPC country list due to their increasing activity in counterfeit pharmaceuticals.[26] China has entered a new market and is now heavily involved in the counterfeit cigarette trade; according to the Center for Public Integrity, the country now produces 400 billion counterfeit cigarettes each year, which would provide two packs for every person on earth. Some reports estimate that a full 8 percent of China's GDP comes from the sale of counterfeit goods.[27]

CASE STUDIES: INTELLECTUAL PROPERTY THEFT AND TERRORISM

- Hezbollah: Hezbollah funding comes from as far away as South America. In February 2000 an individual was arrested in the tri-border region of South America selling pirated music and game CDs and using the profits to fund a Hezbollah-related organization in Lebanon. In a true example of exploitation of the global market, the goods were produced in Europe and sent to a free-trade zone in South America by Hezbollah sympathizers, further identified as Lebanese criminals. Smuggling the goods to a third country in South America avoided import duties and taxes, and sales were provided through a network of Middle East militants and sympathizers. In 2010, $3.5 million was funneled to Hezbollah from DVD pirating in South America, and funneled through a shell in Miami.
- Ethnic-Albanian extremists: Large portions of consumer goods for sale in Kosovo are counterfeit. The sales openly occur and there is limited enforcement of existing laws. In Kosovo, there is a long-standing relationship between criminal organizations and ethnic-Albanian extremist

groups mentioned earlier; it is suspected that funds generated from IPC benefit both criminal organizations and these extremist groups.

- Chechen separatists: In 2000, a joint operation between Russian law enforcement agencies and private industry resulted in the breakup of a CD-manufacturing plant run by an organized crime group, which was remitting funds through unregistered MSBs to Chechen separatist rebels.
- Radical North African terrorists: These groups launder profits from IPC through charitable giving or Zakat via mosques, imams, or nonprofit organizations in Europe sympathetic to radical fundamentalist causes. In this example, terrorists do not engage in the actual IPC but just reap the profits, making this even a less risky venture.
- Al Qaeda: In late 2000, a container of counterfeit perfume, creams, cologne, and shampoos was shipped by a member of al Qaeda from Dubai and intercepted by Danish Customs in Copenhagen. Further investigation showed that al Qaeda sought to profit from the sales of these counterfeit items.

Source: Interpol Files.[28]

IPC is a lucrative criminal activity with low initial investment and high financial returns, possibly even higher than drug trafficking. For instance, an Xbox game costing 40¢ to duplicate can be sold on the black market for $20, realizing unbelievable profit. The link between organized crime groups and counterfeit goods is well established. IPC is a global criminal activity on the rise and quickly becoming a lucrative method of funding for a number of terrorist groups.

Why might IPC become an increasingly important source of illicit financing for terrorist groups? One reason is that local law enforcement finds it difficult to treat IPC as a high-priority crime, typically due to their lack of manpower resources or technical investigative knowledge. In a large heist such as the Eli Lilly theft, federal law enforcement naturally must engage. However, when it comes to duplicating Rosetta Stone DVDs in a small operation and selling them at flea markets or on eBay, the investigation and prosecution costs may seem greater than the value of stopping the operation. If IPC is pursued in smaller cases, the result is often seizure of goods or halting of production but no further investigation of the money trail, which is often complex and robust, with untraceable cash-based transactions.

Trafficking in counterfeit goods is a relatively easy criminal activity. A terrorist could make profit solely from the sale of counterfeit or pirated goods and does not need to be involved in the actual production or fabrication. Thus there are relatively low entry costs, and the illicit profit margins are high. The profit/risk ratio is attractive not only to criminals but also to loosely networked terrorist groups who do not have the capacity to generate funds through sophisticated criminal activity.

Demand for "knockoff" products is widespread due to public perception that purchasing these goods is not a criminal offense and general lack of understanding regarding underlying criminal activity. Think of the numerous vendor stands found in big cities, hawking "designer" purses, scarves, and sunglasses bearing the same logos and identifiable as fakes only by the trained eye. Counterfeit goods are now part of mainstream America, which has an insatiable desire for luxury goods with most lacking the resources to purchase them.

The relationship between legitimate and counterfeit sales is not fully clear and may contribute to IPC challenges. A complicating issue is ambiguity, acceptance, or even enthusiasm on behalf of the targeted corporations. For example, in 2007 an operation in New York City seized 291,699 pairs of fake Nikes from two warehouses, with a street value of $31 million, if authentic. The counterfeiting ring was operating in China, New York, and at least six other American states. A Nike executive speaking to the *New York Times* on the condition of anonymity said counterfeit Nike trade in China, which produces one pair of counterfeit shoes for every two pair legitimately produced by Nike, probably doesn't cut into their profits. He considered the activity "a form of flattery."[29] Should funds used in a terror attack be traced back to illicit Nike profits, this executive may have a different viewpoint.

Thanks to technology, standing on a cold street corner is unnecessary for the savvy criminal. Simply visit an online auction site and you can find thousands of ads for counterfeit goods. With both the lack of oversight on auction sites and the "nonbanks" allowing for obscure fund transfers, this type of selling is particularly attractive to criminals. Some experts estimate that the cost to U.S. business is rising due to IPC and could eventually top $600 billion annually unless stronger action is taken. Within the Office of Management and Budget, the Office of the U.S. Intellectual Property Enforcement Coordinator handles IPC issues. In response to rising concerns, the office issued a strategy signed by the White House in 2010 addressing the issue. As a result, a fifty-person team of federal agents was formed to focus solely on IPC.[30] This low-risk/high-return activity and others like it bear watching as we close down other sources of terrorist funding.

As the manufacturing hub for luxury leather goods and accessories, Italy is attempting to strictly enforce IPC laws. I witnessed the carabinieri actively pursuing and closing down knock-off leather-purse vendors in both Florence and Venice. The vendors don't actually have stands, instead keeping their wares in large duffel bags. Usually tipped off by phone calls from fellow vendors or an elaborate whistling system, they will quickly pack the purses into their large bags and run. Signs are prominently displayed throughout Italy, educating the public that IPC is a crime (see Figure 6.1).

The United States must similarly crack down on IPC. Educating the public would go a long way toward this goal; I would bet most women carrying counterfeit bags have no idea what illicit activity they have inadvertently funded.

EMERGENT THREAT: COUNTERFEIT PRESCRIPTION DRUGS

The counterfeit-drug market is worth a staggering $55 billion per year, and the sale of high-demand knockoff drugs such as Viagra is on the rise with many criminal and terrorist groups entering the arena. Not only do counterfeit drugs impact the bottom line for corporations, they present serious health risks due to adulteration or "cutting" of ingredients using harmful chemicals and while in transport and storage. Introducing different varieties of drugs to the market also alters the virus in a way that makes it harder to eradicate and treat. In fact, one estimate suggests that about 700,000 deaths are linked to counterfeit antimalaria and antituberculosis drugs.[31]

Identity Theft

The sophisticated white-collar crimes of identity theft and credit card fraud are no longer just a consumer issue. When federal investigators unraveled the 9/11 money trail, it suddenly became clear that identity theft was an issue related to global terrorism and national security. The hijackers used phony identification, Social Security numbers, and birth dates to establish bank accounts and create their lives in the United States. Landlords, flight schools, banks, and other institutions were victims and unwitting contributors to the terrorist operation. Seven of the hijackers obtained identification cards through the Virginia Department of Motor Vehicles (DMV) even though none lived in the state. They took advantage of rules allowing individuals to meet residency requirements with a simple notarized letter, a system fraught with fraud and long

FIGURE 6.1   Photo taken by author in Florence, Italy in 2010.

abused by immigrants, immigration lawyers, and local notaries. Despite previous warnings from the FBI and DMV investigators, the department maintained the rudimentary identification system.[32]

Identity fraud and related crimes in the financial sector are often the source of terrorist fund-raising. According to identity theft expert Judith Collins of Michigan State University's Identity Theft Crime and Research Lab, "all acts of terrorism enacted against the United States have been facilitated with the use of a fake or stolen identity."[33] Terrorists need to blend in when working the logistical aspects of the operation, such as obtaining clothing and components of weapons and, most importantly, fulfilling transportation needs such as rental vehicles and airline tickets. Most Americans don't use cash for these purchases, and the terrorists would bring unwanted attention if they were to do so, thus the need for credit cards. Passports are also extensively used by terrorists moving between countries of interest and the target; the use of stolen identities and fake passports has been documented in many terrorism cases in the last ten years. The 9/11 Commission Report stated accurately on page 384 that "travel documents are as important as weapons."

In its simplest form, a stolen credit card enables the criminal to purchase goods or withdraw money, at least until the theft is detected and the owner cancels the card. Credit applications abound, and it is simple for criminals to open multiple accounts in the name of other individuals or using an alias and then simply disappear before being caught. In more complex schemes, bogus credit cards are manufactured then distributed for nefarious use. More attractive because of its transparency and ability to access the subject's credit for a longer period is an emergent criminal act called "skimming." Skimming was first detected as a criminal tactic when master counterfeiter and terrorist supporter Youssef Hmimssa was arrested just days after 9/11 when he was caught providing fake visas and other identification documents to a suspected terrorist cell in Detroit. His apartment yielded documents including a day planner that the government says contained sketches of a U.S. air base in Turkey and a videotape of potential future terrorist targets in Los Angeles, New York, and other locations. He confessed his crimes and has gone public to explain how easy identity theft and fraud is to perpetrate. In 2003, Hmimssa was called to testify to the Senate Finance Committee to enlighten lawmakers, and his testimony was both riveting and troubling. In support of his efforts, Hmimssa recruited a fellow Moroccan, both a taxi driver and waiter at a north suburban restaurant, to steal customers' credit card numbers. He provided his codefendant with a pocketsize device resembling a pager. With a single swipe, the skimming device copied encoded information on the card's magnetic strip. The driver/waiter would swipe customer credit cards through the device and then give the skimmer to Hmimssa, who downloaded the information using a laptop computer. In all, the pair skimmed about 250 credit card account numbers and bilked customers of over $100,000. In the last few years, criminals have become savvier and have started putting skimmers on gas pumps and ATM machines. With wireless technology, the card data is immediately transferred.

Identity theft and related crimes have been detected in many terrorist cells in the last five years. Ahmed Ressam, a member of the Armed Islamic Group (with ties to bin Laden), was caught in December 1999 at the U.S.-Canadian border with one hundred pounds of explosives stashed in the wheel bed of the trunk of his rental car. He had assumed the name Benni Norris, which he used to obtain a passport, false birth certificate, and student ID as well as to open bank accounts. He told authorities he relied on welfare and petty crime, including credit card fraud and trafficking in identity documents, for support. He was linked to a theft ring suspected stealing more than 5,000 items, including computers, cellular phones, passports, and credit cards, with the goal of financing Muslim extremist groups.[34] In his so-called millennium plot, Ressam planned to detonate a large explosive device at the Los Angeles International Airport. Others involved with the operation told FBI agents they supported themselves through credit card fraud and used proceeds from the scam and others to finance their mission. They used countless stolen and fraudulent identities, including thirteen stolen from the membership computer of a Bally's fitness club in Boston. They also had plans to buy a gas station and use the business as an avenue to secretly obtain credit card numbers, placing a camera in a location where it would be possible to watch people punching in their PIN numbers.

Al Qaeda uses credit card scams and identity theft extensively. The 9/11 hijackers had a scheme in Spain to raise money for the attacks, and according to authorities, "the pattern was very clear within the North African contingent of al Qaeda members operating in Europe. Every time you arrest one of them he has twenty different identities and twenty different credit cards."[35] Other suspected terrorist cells operating in the United States, Canada, and Europe have employed a variety of scams to steal millions of dollars from credit card companies. At a Senate hearing, the former deputy assistant director of the Secret Service gave senators a glimpse of two groups of Middle Easterners with ties to terrorist organizations who allegedly were involved in massive credit card fraud in the United States, bilking financial institutions of $21 million. Dennis Lormel, chief of the FBI's Financial Crimes Section, told the House Financial Services Committee, "The ease with which these individuals can obtain false identification or assume the identity of someone else, and then open bank accounts and obtain credit cards, make these attractive ways to generate funds."[36]

According to federal agents, an emerging area of concern related to credit cards is often referred to by law enforcement as a "bust-out" scam, involving the use of credit card "courtesy checks." Typically, several checks are attached to the monthly credit card statement, or for those paying online the checks come through the mail separately, and can be used by the consumer in any fashion with charges going against the credit card. The checks are widely accepted, so with just one extra piece of fabricated identification, the criminal can use all of the checks in short order, even exceeding the consumer's line of credit. A bust-out scam was first uncovered in 2001 when two groups of Middle Easterners with extensive affiliations to known Islamic terrorist organizations were arrested for various identity theft and fraud crimes.[37] A quick survey of colleagues found they simply throw the checks in the trash, unaware there is personal account information contained on the check that could be used by a counterfeit ring.

The link between terrorists and sophisticated white-collar crimes such as identity theft and related fraud is irrefutable. Technological advances have only made this crime easier to commit, and it remains a lucrative means of raising funds for terrorist groups.

Other Fund-Raising Methods

U.S. officials believe that "a substantial portion" of the estimated millions of dollars raised by Middle Eastern terrorist groups comes from the $20 to $30 million annually brought in by the illicit scam industry in America.[38] These scams, covered in Chapter 2 as related to Nigerian transnational crime, include advance-fee schemes conducted through e-mail such as "you've won the lottery," inheritance notifications, or correspondence appearing to be from a family member who is traveling and needs emergency funds. Unfortunately, U.S. citizens, typically the elderly, fall for these schemes to the amount of $1 to $2 billion each year, and elder financial exploitation is a new area of focus for FinCEN. This criminal activity typically originates in Nigeria and is known as "419 fraud," referring to Section 419 of the Nigerian penal code addressing such crimes. Proceeds from 419 fraud have now been linked to the lethal al Qaeda affiliate terrorist group Boko Haram.[39]

In some instances, alert front-line personnel at wire service companies or banks are able to intervene to stop a fraudulent 419 transaction completion. However, criminals are changing tactics to avoid detection, giving explicit instructions to customers on how to structure payments. For example, one victim was identified after sending a total of $75,000 to the same individual in a series of more than one hundred wire transfer transactions at a money transmittal service in the United States.

Mortgage Fraud: Emergent Earning Method

As we closed formal funding streams, terrorists and criminal enterprises simply find other avenues of exploitation. For instance, mortgage loan fraud is the fastest-growing white-collar crime in the United States, climbing dramatically from 4,500 cases in 2001 to almost 30,000 cases in 2011. The housing boom fed fraudulent activities, with billions of dollars changing hands and expedited loan processes requiring minimal paperwork. The FinCEN Suspicious Activity Report (SAR) summaries contain a plethora of information regarding money laundering and terrorist financing activities.

By asking financial and other reporting institutions to indicate not only the primary reporting identifier (in this case, mortgage fraud) but secondary activities as well, data emerge regarding other embedded criminal activities (see Figure 6.2).

Secondary Activities in Mortgage Loan Fraud SARs: January–June 2009

Secondary Activity Indicated	SARs	Percentage of Mortgage Loan Fraud SARs (rounded)
False statement	9,017	28%
Identity theft	980	3%
Consumer loan fraud	296	1%
Misuse of position or self-dealing	186	1%
BSA/Structuring/Money Laundering	168	1%
Commercial loan fraud	93	<1%
Wire transfer fraud	84	<1%
Check fraud	69	<1%
Defalcation/embezzlement	41	<1%
Counterfeit instrument (other)	28	<1%
Counterfeit check	22	<1%
Credit card fraud	17	<1%
Bribery/gratuity	13	<1%
Mysterious disappearance	10	<1%
Check kiting	10	<1%
Computer intrusion	7	<1%
Counterfeit credit/debit card	3	<1%
Debit card fraud	1	<1%
Terrorist financing	0	0

FIGURE 6.2 FINCEN: Secondary activities in mortgage loan fraud. (*Source:* FinCEN, "The SAR Activity Review Trends Tips & Issues," 2009.)

Since the mortgage market has slowed, criminals are now engaging in "rescue fraud": loan modification, debt elimination/consolidation, and foreclosure rescue scams preying upon innocent home owners who are desperate to save their homes. As foreign entities and continuing criminal enterprises engaged in home loan-related fraud, it is easy to see that the country's economic crisis was also a national security crisis, something many fail to recognize.

CASE STUDIES: TERRORIST FINANCING THROUGH MORTGAGE FRAUD

- Al Qaeda: a mortgage fraud ring in Salt Lake City was tied to the late Abu Musab al-Zarqawi, AQ leader in Iraq. At least $40,000 was transferred from Sharif Omar in Salt Lake City to an account in Jordan. From there, the money went to his brother in Iraq, Shawqi Omar, who was an associate of al-Zarqawi.[40]
- Al Qaeda: Tarik Hamdi was charged with mortgage-loan fraud by U.S. investigators investigating an Islamic charity, the International Institute for Islamic Thought of Herndon, Virginia. Hamdi worked for the charity and was also investigated for ties to terrorist financing. He delivered a satellite phone battery to al-Qaeda operatives for bin Laden's personal phone, which he used to coordinate the 1998 U.S. embassy bombings in Kenya and Tanzania.[41]
- Hezbollah: Nemr Ali Rahal of Dearborn, Michigan, pled guilty to mortgage fraud in a terrorism-related case. He had obtained more than $500,000 by falsifying mortgage applications. His home contained an assortment of Hezbollah-related recruitment material including a videotape of Rahal at a 2002 Hezbollah rally in Lebanon. Interestingly, Customs officials had also stopped Rahal and his son the previous year for having military-grade explosive residue on their passports as they reentered the United States from Canada.[42]
- Hezbollah: In another Dearborn case, Mohammed Krayem and Mahmoud Youssef Kourani transferred more than $200,000 obtained through real estate fraud and cigarette smuggling to Kourani's brother, Haider Kourani, the Hezbollah chief of military security for southern Lebanon, to fund a scheme to purchase military equipment from the United Nations Protection Force for an attack on Israel.[43]

- Hamas: Again in Dearborn, Ahmad and Musa Jebril, were convicted of mortgage fraud charges after defrauding six banks for $250,000 and dozens of people of up to $400,000. The Jebrils were active supporters of Hamas, were training a cell of local men to wage jihad against the United States, and had been dismissed from their local mosque, where Musa was an imam, for their radical activities.[44]

MOVING

A Paper Chase in a Paperless World: Informal Value Transfer Systems

FinCEN defines informal value transfer systems (IVTSs) as any system, mechanism, or network of people receiving money for the purpose of making the funds or an equivalent value payable to a third party in another geographic location, whether or not in the same form.[45] Transactions generally take place outside the conventional banking system, leaving only handwritten records, if anything, in their wake. Expatriates and immigrants often use IVTSs as a trusted and ancient process to send funds to friends and family in their home countries.

Companies conducting business in countries without a formal financial system also use IVTSs. Due to their versatility, anonymity, and location outside of the regulated U.S. banking system, IVTSs are extremely vulnerable for exploitation, and terrorists and criminals routinely use the method to launder proceeds from illicit activities. After a 2010 FinCEN advisory regarding the continued illegal or suspicious use of IVTSs to move money, specifically detailing how criminals were working around current laws, financial institution SAR filings increased by 559 percent over the next year. The massive filings indicated that despite attempts to "regulate" IVTSs, illicit transfer activity business is booming.

Before the FinCEN IVTS advisory, SAR filers primarily described suspicious activity as occurring between the United States and Latin American countries. However, after the advisory, filers reported not only exchanges with Latin America but also many suspicious Middle Eastern transactions, most involving the United Arab Emirates (UAE), Yemen, and Iran. Other trends related to the new IVTS filings included:

- Reference to unregistered and/or unlicensed money services business (MSB)-related activity in 30 percent of all relevant SARs
- "Bank Secrecy Act/Structuring/Money Laundering" characterization of suspicious activity in 91 percent of SARs when describing IVTS/MSB-related activities

- Suspicious activities conducted by 2,481 subjects: 51 percent with domestic addresses, 41 percent with foreign addresses, and 8 percent not associated with any addresses. Almost 40 percent of foreign addresses were located in Venezuela, while the majority of domestic subjects had addresses in New York and California.
- A change in terminology: a SAR filer stated international customers began calling IVTS transfers "loans" after learning that suspicious transactions could precipitate account closures. Overall, filers reported references to "loan repayments" or "loans" in 15 percent of SARs.

Figure 6.3 shows the type of suspicious activity in 2010 SAR filings.

FinCEN continues to address the problem of licensed MSBs in the United States doing business with unlicensed entities abroad. For countries lacking a formal banking system and wishing to do business in traditional, unlicensed manners, IVTS remains vulnerable to money laundering and criminal/terrorist financing activity. For some foreigners living in our country, IVTS is the only way to send money home (see Figure 6.3).

Suspicious Activity Characterizations Reported in Depository Institution SARS

Characterization of Suspicious Activity – Part III, Field 35	Number of Occurrences	Percentage
Bank Secrecy Act/Structuring/Money Laundering	1,103	91.84%
Bribery/Gratuity	10	.83%
Check Fraud	2	.17%
Commercial Loan Fraud	2	.17%
Computer Intrusion	1	.08%
Counterfeit Instrument (other)	1	.08%
Credit Card Fraud	4	.33%
Defalcation/Embezzlement	7	.58%
False Statement	10	.83%
Misuse of Position or Self Dealing	7	.59%
Mortgage Loan Fraud	3	.25%
Wire Transfer Fraud	14	1.17%
Other	197	16.40%
Terrorist Financing	7	.58%
Identity Theft	1	.08%
Characterization left blank	4	.33%

FIGURE 6.3 SAR filings from financial institutions related to illicit money transfers. (*Source:* "The SAR Activity Review Trends Tips & Issues," 2011.)

Hawala

Much has been written about the use of an IVTS system called "hawala" by terrorists to move money. Attention was focused on the hawala method when it was discovered that the al Barakaat informal banking system was used multiple times to move funds for al Qaeda. The group used hawala to help finance the American embassy bombings in Kenya and Tanzania in 1998 and again in 2001 to move massive funds out of Afghanistan in advance of U.S. military operations. Most assume that improved hawala filing requirements and increased scrutiny of cross-border financial transactions closed the door IVTSs; however, the increase of SAR filings and data released by FinCEN is worrisome. U.S. Treasury officials admit that hawala transfer is still posing challenges for those trying to shut down methods of illicit transfer. The language in the USA PATRIOT Act regarding hawalas is found in Subtitle C, which makes it a crime to run an unlicensed money-transmitting business, punishable by five years in prison. Regardless, thousands of hawalas operate in the United States in mom-and-pop types of operations, and it is estimated that over $30 billion leaves our country annually through this money transfer method.[46] The sheer number of hawala operations in the country makes this law almost unenforceable unless nefarious activity is detected through some other activity.

Informal banking systems are ancient and known by many names reflecting cultural origins. Hawala and hundi are terms commonly referred to when describing Indian, Pakistani, and Middle Eastern IVTS systems. Hawala is a system in which money does not physically cross international borders. The transfer is quick (can send money internationally in the time it takes to place a phone call), easy, and based on trust. The money is not physically moved across any borders; for instance, the sender gives the cash to an agent in the States, who calls an agent at the forward location and has the sum immediately delivered to the recipient. Receipts are typically not given on either end of the transaction, and no log is kept regarding the identities of the sender and receiver. The amount of money transferred is the only concern, thus a paper trail is nonexistent. The agents work out the monetary issues between themselves to balance their books, usually by transferring goods, paying off other debts, etc. The system is unregulated and undocumented and provides the obscurity desirable to terrorists.

Governments have taken action to regulate this informal, nontraditional transfer system. In the "Abu Dhabi declaration" on hawala, some Arab states agreed to implement a reporting system. In the UAE, business applications are now required and hawaladars are certified. However, as we attempt to inject standards internationally, the cultural significance of this ancient system cannot be overlooked. Islamic banking traditions appeal to Islamic people—they are familiar and trustworthy. For instance, remitters know their money is not being investing in pork, used for gambling, or used in other ways contrary to their faith, concerns that keep them from using the U.S. banking system. Also, many of the areas where relatives of expatriates live are inaccessible by other means, such as Western Union. Also, money transmittal companies charge steep fees, whereas hawalas run concurrent with another business, typically offering transactions at no cost to the customer.

CASE STUDY: HAWALA

A recent investigation into an unregistered hawala business in the United States sheds light on this ongoing problem and how cross-border activity can be prolific. A hawala owner operating in behalf of U.S. citizens wanted to send money to OFAC-sanctioned countries outside the legitimate banking system. A third party in one of the nonsanctioned countries facilitated wire transfers back to the United States into the owner's personal bank account. The hawala operators profited on both ends by manipulating the exchange rates to their benefit and charging a fee. The defendant used the millions of dollars he received for providing this service to purchase real estate and securities. Information gathered through Bank Security Act provisions was instrumental in identifying the various accounts, wires, deposits, and patterns of activity, leading to the unraveling of the scheme.[47]

The bottom line is that the hawala system of informal monetary transfer cross-border persists, especially in countries with OFAC sanctions.

STORING, EARNING, AND MOVING

Precious Metals and Diamonds

According to the GAO, the commodities terrorists tend to exploit are of high value, easy to conceal, and hold their value over time.[48] The 2003 Money Laundering Strategy further warns that "while maintaining our vigilance over traditional means of value transfer, we must also focus on alternative means—trading in commodities such as gold, gems and precious stones and metals."[49] The precious-stone and -metal market is certainly an area susceptible for exploitation. For example, gold's shape can be altered into any form through smelting, a desirable attribute to smugglers. Six al Qaeda operatives arrested in Berlin for plotting attacks in 2003 were financing their operation with gold smuggled from Dubai in an elaborate two-year scheme that included melting, adding extra materials, then reshaping into benign-looking objects and selling at a profit at $7.5 million. Gold smuggling in India is prevalent, with couriers doing everything from hiding the metal in their bodies to disguising it as food. The terrorist group that attacked Mumbai in 2003 and 2008, al Qaeda affiliate Lashkar-e-Taiba, was financed partially by a notorious gold smuggler, Dawood Ibrahim, the "Don of Mumbai." Although gold smuggling remains prevalent in certain areas of the world, however, diamonds probably serve as the best example of a traded, global commodity that could be exploited by terrorists to earn, move, and store their assets.

Douglas Farah, a former *Washington Post* correspondent and author of the book *Blood from Stones*, broke a story garnering worldwide attention in December 2002 regarding purported links between al Qaeda and the diamond market. This connection was widely reported in the press and caused upheaval and concern among those in the diamond industry. Federal law enforcement agencies have extensively investigated his claims but will neither officially confirm nor deny that his sources exist, his information is reliable, or there is an al Qaeda connection to the diamond industry. However, it is an established fact that al Qaeda was involved in diamond-mining and diamond-trading organizations in the 1990s, and although these operations did not come to fruition, it certainly speaks to their interest in and prior knowledge of the industry.[50] Hezbollah has long been known to be in the diamond-smuggling business between Lebanon and the west coast of Africa, especially cash-strapped Sierra Leone.

Diamonds are especially easy to smuggle because of their low weight. According to the Congressional Research Service in 2002, one pound of uncut diamonds is worth approximately worth $225,000.[51] If the diamonds are cut and polished, there are 2,200 carats in a pound, meaning the street worth could be in the tens of millions of dollars. This is compared to a pound of cash ($45,000) and a pound of gold at 2012 prices ($25,000). Diamonds are untraceable, making them more attractive than serial-numbered bills. Stones are odorless and thus can be smuggling past working dogs and equipment designed to identify smuggled drugs and money; they can also be swallowed or hidden in other objects such as stuffed animals and clothing. Diamonds are often unmarked and untraceable and can easily be used in lieu of cash in business transactions.

Diamond mines are located in remote, poor, and often lawless areas of Africa. The area of possible al Qaeda activity, according to Farah, were the diamond markets of Sierra Leone and Liberia, which, although representing less than 2 percent of the $7 billion global diamond market, have some of the best stones in the world. Mr. Farah's investigation into al Qaeda financing reported that they started pursuing the diamond market after assets were frozen by the United States following the embassy bombings in 1998.[52] If factual, this supports the theory that as we close traditional funding sources, al Qaeda may move into nontraditional areas to earn, move, and store assets.

Looking at the antithesis always helps when developing countermeasures in the finance realm. Therefore we should explore the factors that might preclude criminal and terrorist groups from delving into the diamond world. For example, significant expertise in gemology is an absolute necessity; diamonds exported from Africa are uncut and to the untrained eye simply appear to be dirty glass. Also, diamonds are not as easily launderable as cash or even gold; they have a targeted market and resources are expended in purchasing, movement, and selling activities. Even though paper trails are mostly nonexistent in black-market trade, multiple transactions create witnesses, something very undesirable to terrorist organizations. Finally, there may be significant cultural issues to overcome for the terrorists involved. For instance, the Antwerp diamond market is dominated by those of the Jewish faith, thus business activities associated with unloading the diamonds for cash might be a very significant hurdle for a traditional Muslim terrorist group. Strengthening all of these areas in the industry could keep bad actors from penetrating.

At the very least, diamonds are traded on the black market and used by African warlords to fund some of their violent activity, giving advent to the terms "blood diamonds" or "conflict diamonds." In 2002, forty-five nations (including the United States) met in Switzerland to discuss illicit diamond sales and use of profit to pay for weapons in African wars. The State Department appointed an official as special negotiator for issues regarding these "conflict diamonds," and the group developed new regulations for governments of diamond-producing nations, now known as the Kimberley Process Certification Scheme. Participating governments must not only license diamond miners but also develop "tamper-proof" ways to ship and move rough diamonds across borders. On the buying end, cutting centers (such as those in Antwerp) must ascertain and certify the origin of the rough diamonds.[53] These cutters are the terrorist's last "wicket," since cut-and-polished diamonds are practically untraceable. Unfortunately, certain aspects of the Kimberley Process are voluntary and unenforceable, with some African nation-states refusing to participate. These aspects make the diamond market ripe for exploitation for criminals and terrorists.

SPECIAL FOCUS: WHY DIAMOND
TRADE IN ZIMBABWE MATTERS

Issues that seemingly do not affect our national security typically
do, upon closer inspection. For instance, in 2011 Zimbabwe president Robert Mugabe threatened to quit the Kimberley Process,
the body that ensures diamonds do not fund conflicts. He boldly
stated, "We can sell our diamonds our own way." Zimbabwe is a
nation in steep decline. Throughout the last decade, the life expectancy has fallen from age sixty to age thirty-seven for men, and
is down to just age thirty-four for women. The country is riddled
with poverty and conflict. It is ranked close to last in almost every
category: GDP, health, peace/stability, and human rights. The
main currency officially sanctioned by the government is surprising: the U.S. dollar.

The diamond trade provides the best export commodity and
source of cash flow for the country. However, with a corrupt,
unstable government and weak rule of law, there is rampant smuggling and trade of illegally mined diamonds to countries such as
Israel, Belgium, and South Africa. Although the stones coming out
of Zimbabwe constitute less than one-half of 1 percent of the world
diamond trade, some are of very high quality and can command
up to $1,000 per carat for an uncut stone. The World Diamond
Council has continually highlighted Zimbabwe's lack of adherence
to international standards in the last few years and voiced their
concern about diamonds fueling conflict and illegal activities in the
region. Zimbabwe is one of the few African nations not infiltrated
by al Qaeda or narco-traffickers. Keeping them in the Kimberley
Process is good not only for the diamond trade but also for international security.

Money Laundering

After funds are secured by criminals and terrorists through licit or illicit
activity, they typically seek to "launder" the proceeds. Money laundering is the practice of engaging in financial transactions in order to conceal the identities, sources, and destinations of the money in question.
Traditional money laundering makes "dirty" money "clean" after the
crime has been committed. Think of traditional criminal money laundering as simply putting a dirty one-dollar bill into a vending machine,
hitting the "change return" button, and receiving four clean quar-
ters. Now think on a larger scale. For example, casinos are extremely

	Criminal	Terrorist
Motivation	Greed	Ideology
How money is obtained	Illicit activities such as IPC, ORC, narco-trade	Licit activities such as charities, cash donations, hawala
Purpose	Money is already "dirty," crime has occurred, attempting to make clean	Money is clean, then used for terrorist ops
Cash Amount	Large amounts, many transactions	Small, less frequent transactions
Business	Fronts and Shells	Mostly fronts, some shells
Scope	Global; able to fund ops from afar	Global; able to fund ops from afar
Complexity	Hard to tie to operations	Hard to tie to operations

FIGURE 6.4 Differences/similarities between criminal and terrorist money laundering. (*Source:* Jennifer Hesterman, *Transnational Crime and the Criminal-Terrorist Nexus: Synergies and Corporate Trends*, ed. Air University Press, 2005.)

vulnerable to money laundering; the patrons exchange the dirty money for chips and then cash out. Or they hold the chips and cash out when ready. Alternatively, laundering can be as complex as washing money through an international corporation or a chain of businesses. The crime has been committed, and the resulting money must be dealt with.

However, terrorist-related money laundering is a far different activity. The crime (terrorist operation) has not yet occurred. The money is clean, such as donations from charities or through Zakat, and will be put to use to fuel the terror operation in some manner. Therefore the laundering operations are slightly different in scope and activity, although no less complex and hard to detect. Based on discussions with financial forensic experts, I developed the chart in Figure 6.4 to compare traditional criminal and terrorist money laundering.

Appendix A of the 9/11 Commission Report details the 9/11 money trail, with data regarding the numerous money transfers between al Qaeda abroad and the hijackers in the United States.[54] I found it shocking how easily the hijackers changed tactics when challenged by bank employees and others, simply forging paperwork, changing transfer amounts, or visiting different employees until the answer was "yes." They had a goal and were undeterred. Most of the money moved forward to the operational cell came from charitable contributions or Zakat, transferred in small amounts and deposited into licit bank accounts. A very telling fact: the terrorists deeply respected the source of their money and meticulously returned the unused money back to handlers in the UAE in the days preceding the attacks. I was told by federal agents who prepared the money trail information for the 9/11 Commission that the transactions to return the money were detected only when store employees came forward with information after recognizing the terrorists when images were broadcast on television. Agents used the last monetary transactions by the hijackers then backtracked, unraveling the entire 9/11 money trail to identify handlers and, in some cases, donors.

The scope of money laundering in countries bordering the United States is extremely worrisome. Following 9/11, Canada began to take a hard look at money laundering within its country's borders. The fledging financial transactions and reports analysis center of Canada (FINTRAC) quickly uncovered $500 million in suspected dirty money stashed away in mutual funds, Canadian banks, and other financial institutions. The Canadian government now estimates that $17 billion of criminal proceeds are laundered there each year and that organized crime costs their taxpayers over $100 billion annually.[55] Figure 6.5 illustrates money laundering offenses in Canada in 2009.

The U.S. government is working to identify and halt terrorist money-laundering efforts. According to a Federal Reserve anti-money-laundering examiner, due to the PATRIOT Act there has been unprecedented cooperation between the domestic and international financial community, law enforcement, and regulators. In the United States, this cooperation has resulted in a rapid exchange of vital financial information between law enforcement and banks. On an international scale, this information sharing has severely damaged laundering havens and resulted in significant forfeiture and freezing of terrorist assets.[56]

Multiagency task forces are very effective in countering the money-laundering threat. ICE's Operation Cornerstone is a multiagency task force of law enforcement agents with financial expertise assembled in 2002 to "identify and assess the means and methods used by criminals to exploit financial systems in order to transfer, launder and otherwise mask the true source of criminal proceeds." This continued focus on money laundering should yield more information regarding similar ongoing terrorist laundering activities and at the very least serve as a deterrent (see Figure 6.5).

Fronts, Shells, and Offshores

Fronts, shells, and offshores are corporate methods used by organized crime and terrorists to launder money. Front operations are legitimate businesses whose books are used to wash the money. Often, another operation is going on out the back door such as drug trafficking or

Commonly Observed Money Laundering (ML) Designated Offense Types	Proportion of Cases of This Type Involving Transactions at MSBs in Canada (%)
Substantive offense (not specifically identified)	30%
Drug Offenses	25%
Fraud	20%
Terrorist Financing (TF)	12%
ML (and/or TF) plus tax evasion	4%
Human trafficking	2%

FIGURE 6.5   Money laundering at Money Service Businesses (MSB) in Canada involving other criminal offenses. (*Source:* FINTRAC, "Money Laundering and Terrorist Financing (ML/TF) Typologies and Trends for Canadian Money Services Businesses (MSBs)" 2010.)

prostitution, and the dirty money is pushed back through the front, the legitimate business. Consider the case of European and Caribbean-based al Qaeda supporters, Youssef Nada and Ahmed Idris Nasreddi, who ran the Bank al Taqwa, a designated financier of the 9/11 operation. They also operated multiple businesses including Nasco, which makes cereal and baked goods and sponsors soccer tournaments in Nigeria. All of these activities were complicated fronts and fund-raisers for their money-laundering business, and the intertwining of licit and illicit fund made the case extremely difficult for terrorist financing officials to prove. Bin Laden himself knew the value of fronts and made extensive use of a "honey house" and bakery businesses in Yemen to store and move his clean money prior to 9/11.[57] An example of how a U.S. company could possibly be used in this manner is the Boston software firm PTECH Inc. In late 2003, employees alerted the FBI that a key investor was Yasin al-Qadi, who was on the U.S. Treasury Department's list of Specially Designated Global Terrorists. Mr. al-Qadi is a Saudi businessman suspected of diverting millions of dollars to al Qaeda and Hamas while at the helm of the State Department terrorist-designated charity Blessed Relief Foundation. Al-Qadi's investment in PTECH was a way to conceal money that could later be used for terrorist operations.[58] As our country continues to experience economic turmoil, businesses, universities, and other enterprises seeking investors must be ever vigilant that they don't become a conduit for money laundering or worse.

A "shell" is a slightly more complicated business venture; simply put, it is a company that doesn't exist. The minimalist forms of a shell would be a hotel room with a phone and answering service, an empty office space with a fax machine, or even a post office box at a local mail services store. Criminals will pay cash for the rented space, set up a toll free phone number, run ads in newspapers and online, and then collect money through mailed checks or credit card numbers for a nonexistent service or product. They quickly close the business, staying a step ahead of authorities.

In the most complicated form, a shell could also be an "offshore" venture or investment racket; in the global environment, with communications technology, this is certainly an easy way to raise funds without risk of detection. I recently spoke with the compliance officer for a major international bank who stated that offshores are an area of ongoing concern in terms of terrorist money making and laundering.

CASE STUDY: SHELLS, CASINOS, AND MULTIPLE MONEY-LAUNDERING TECHNIQUES

Casinos have historically been used as a place to launder money. For instance, a man with a compulsive gambling addiction embezzled millions of dollars from a public utility and lived the life of a "high roller" for several years before being caught. The defendant admitted to a scheme in which he created dummy companies with corresponding bank accounts and falsified documents for the companies' sales to the county of bogus water well capacity rights. The stolen money was from a water utility fund comprising payments received from thousands of ratepayers and developers.

The case began when an alert bank noticed several unusual transactions, including cash payments made to two credit card accounts of approximately $8,000 each, but the balances on the cards were less than $200.[59] The man used this scheme to hide the embezzled money.

Bulk Cash Smuggling

A less sophisticated way of moving cash is though smuggling. According to the Treasury Department, bulk cash smuggling refers to moving currency, traveler's checks, or similar instruments across borders by means of a courier rather than through a formal financial system.[60] Although risky since the mission will fail if detected, bulk cash smuggling is still attractive to terrorists; it is easy to move large quantities of money at once, there is no paper trail or third parties involved (other than the courier), and the group maintains total control over movement. Also, in the Arab culture it is not uncommon for individuals to carry a large amount of currency on their person, so bulk cash may not draw attention. Bulk cash smuggling is the preferred method for drug dealers to move money cross-border.[61]

When bulk cash is smuggled in support of the narco-trade or terrorist financing, the amounts moved are staggering. For instance, in December 2003 at least six men believed to have links to al Qaeda and carrying what some intelligence reports estimated was $23.5 million were apprehended in Syria as they attempted to leave the country.[62] Treasury officials believe al Qaeda may be relying more on couriers because of the crackdown on the traditional banking sector.[63] While U.S. authorities have also spotted couriers with bulk cash leaving Saudi Arabia and Kuwait, they have not been able to stop them since U.S. officials have no jurisdiction.[64]

Operation Firewall is an ICE law enforcement project targeting criminal organizations involved in the smuggling of large quantities of U.S. currency. The operation's role is not only to actively investigate bulk cash smuggling cases but also to train Mexico, Canada, and other countries on how to recognize and mitigate the problem. Internationally, finance ministers and central bank presidents from G-7/8 countries recently discussed ways to deal with the emerging bulk cash-smuggling problem. One possible option under review is for countries to consider adopting some type of $10,000 reporting requirement similar to the United States. Of course, our laws did not stop potential terrorist Zacarias Moussaoui; on February 23, 2001, upon landing in Chicago on a flight originating in London, he simply declared his $35,000 in cash that he had on his person and exited the airport.[65]

E-gambling and E-gaming: Emergent Money-Laundering Concerns

The e-gambling and e-gaming industries have exploded in the last five years and are a hotbed of illegal activity. From child predators preying through interactive Xbox games, to drug sales and using the benign virtual gaming platform as an anonymous, untraceable communication tool, what started as a fun and exciting industry is now heavily scrutinized for illegal activity. These platforms are also ripe for money-laundering activity, as once value is assigned to something, whether real or virtual, it becomes usable to launderers and vulnerable for exploitation.

E-gambling
Casinos have always been an attractive way to launder money since cash can be exchanged for chips, which are then held, transferred to another actor, or simply cashed out at a later time. E-gambling provides a new venue for money laundering, adding anonymity and the ability to transfer funds cross-border outside the traditional banking system. The U.S. government was initially unsure how to proceed with e-gambling and was very cautious in terms of companies within our borders. Companies in

Europe capitalized on the void and the insatiable appetite of potential customers, and Europe is now the world's biggest online gambling market, accounting for an estimated $12 billion of that sector's almost $30 billion revenue for 2010. Overseas, governments have not shied away from e-gambling despite inherent risks, largely due to the enormous profitability. The government of Denmark, for instance, takes 20 percent of the gross earnings from companies hosted in their country. Countries like Gibraltar, Malta, and Montenegro also seized the opportunity to establish online gambling venues and have ongoing disputes with the United States as our country attempts to halt proliferation of online betting. Many U.S. citizens patronize e-gambling companies on foreign soil; in fact, Antigua is thought to hold 25 percent of the U.S. e-gambling market.

Prior to the rise of the Internet, money-laundering activities in the gambling and gaming world came with a trail of paper, surveillance video, and witnesses, making it somewhat easy for law enforcement to investigate. However, many laws do not pertain to e-gambling enterprises and apply only to on-the-ground casino operations. Compounding the problem is the simultaneous boom in nonbanks and the prepaid-card industry. These factors are contributing to a worrisome "perfect storm" scenario. Since it has more experience with the sector, the best vulnerability assessments regarding e-gaming and e-gambling are coming out of the European Union. According to the Levi Report,[66] the most comprehensive review of e-gambling to date, the following are areas of risk regarding e-gambling:

1. Online gaming firms can credit winnings or unused funds back to an account other than the one on which the original bet was made.
2. Virtual fronts and shells can be established, providing a way to anonymously run gaming transactions and move money.
3. It is now possible to play "peer-to-peer" games, where value transfers can occur between human players. An example of exploitation is if two players are complicit in money-laundering activity or want to transfer funds off the radar, one will deliberately lose the game, and the other will send him or her funds. "Dirty" money can be easily moved this way.
4. Payment can be made in (and out) of the game via anonymous use of nonbanks or prepaid cards. We will cover both of these funding methods in the next chapter.

E-gaming

Bitcoins are an experimental digital cash commodity, typically earned, stored, and moved through e-games or auction sites or by providing services online. Accounts can be set up anonymously, and Bitcoins are a peer-to-peer commodity, meaning money can be moved between player accounts without third-party involvement. They are also acceptable for payment at many stores and even some restaurants and hotels. Bitcoins can also be cashed out through anonymous prepaid cards or through nonbanks such as PayPal. Hackers have been able to steal Bitcoins from player accounts and the gaming hosting companies themselves, with some heists topping $300,000. In an April 2012 criminal and cyber assessment report, the FBI expressed concern regarding the money-laundering potential within the Bitcoin industry.[67] The FBI estimates that the Bitcoin economy is worth $35 to $43 million. One dealer, Mr. Gox, moved over $8 million in one month, with coin value fluctuating wildly from $4 to $30 in a six-month period. Linden Dollars, the virtual digital currency used in the Second Life virtual platform, are also vulnerable and have been similarly exploited.

Online gambling companies do collect a significant amount of data on the IP addresses, gaming, and gaming finance patterns of their customers, which are used to construct profiles against which to assess the risks posed by particular customers. Gaming sites are not as fastidious about recognizing and reporting customer trends and patterns. Also, since there are no regulations regarding registration, third-party Bitcoin dealers have emerged on the Internet, further obscuring transactions and increasing the money-laundering risk. Other actors have designed computer programs creating Bitcoins; they anonymously cash out and simply disappear.

Unfortunately, lacking guidance or regulation, e-gambling companies vary on customer spending limits or ceilings. Typical of traditional casinos, the company will engage only if the betting ceiling somehow threatens the livelihood of the business. Naturally, gambling sites with the highest spending and betting ceilings are more at risk for money laundering and other nefarious activity. A stronger legal construction could provide a better framework for e-gambling and e-gaming companies to lessen the vulnerability and money-laundering risk.

CASE STUDIES: E-GAMBLING AND E-GAMING

- In 2011, the FBI charged owners of three e-gambling companies with bank fraud, wire fraud, money laundering, and illegal-gambling offenses. The "Full Tilt Poker Scandal" indictment explains how owners created phony virtual offshores and companies to launder billions of dollars collected from online players.[68]

The following cases are from the FBI's 2012 Bitcoin Report[69]:

- A cyber criminal selling a computer virus advised that he accepted payment only through Bitcoin and other similar digital currencies. The hacker group LulzSec was accepting donations from supporters with Bitcoins and used it to purchase Botnet programs.
- The online marketplace SilkRoad was accepting Bitcoins for narcotics and also provided a way for buyer and seller to anonymously interact. Customers could also leave feedback concerning the transaction.
- Unknown users opened 3,000 Bitcoin accounts to support a suspected money-laundering operation involving purchase of e-gold.

THE WAY FORWARD

Despite our best efforts, terrorist and criminal groups continue to exploit tried-and-true methods of earning, moving, and storing funds such as charities, zakat, and the counterfeiting, smuggling, and theft of commercial goods. As the case studies illustrated, groups will adapt for success and pursue avenues with the least resistance and greatest vulnerability.

We will next explore how e-commerce is providing a new frontier for those engaged in financing illicit activities. Fueled by globalization and the proliferation of the uncontrolled Internet, it seems that going outside of the formal network to earn, move, store, and launder money may be easier than ever.

REFERENCES

1. Executive Order on Terrorist Financing: Blocking Property and Prohibiting Transactions With Persons Who Commit, Threaten to Commit, or Support Terrorism, (September 24, 2001).
2. U.S. Senate Committeee on Banking, Housing and Urban Affairs, Richard Clarke's Statement, "The Financing of Terror Organizations," 2003.
3. Ronald K. Noble, "The Links between Intellectual Property Crime and Terrorist Financing," U.S. House Committee on International Relations, 2003.

4. Jean-Charles Brisard, "Report to the UN: Terrorism Financing: Roots and Trends of Saudi Terrorism Financing," 2002.

5. Alan Cowell, "Terrorism's Cost in a Global Economy," *New York Times*, November 9, 2003.

6. Ibid.

7. "Treasury Revokes Tax-Exempt Status of 3 Muslim Charities," Associated Press, November 14, 2003.

8. Gregory Vistica, "Frozen Assets Going to Legal Bills; U.S. Has Linked Confiscated Funds To Financing Terror," *Washington Post*, November 2, 2003.

9. U.S. District Court, Northern District of Illinois, *U.S. v. Enaam Arnaout*, April 2002.

10. *Global Relief Foundation, Inc. v. Paul H. O'Neill, Colin L. Powell, John Ashcroft, R. Richard Newcomb, and Robert S. Mueller, III,* June 11, 2002.

11. GAO, "Terrorist Financing: U.S. Agencies Should Systematically Assess Terrorists' Use of Alternative Financing Mechanisms," November 2003.

12. "U.S. Saudi Arabia Target Four Branches of Al-Haramain in Fight against Terrorist," January 22, 2004.

13. Ken Dilanian, "U.N. Report Finds 2 Terror Financiers Living, Doing Business Freely," Knight-Ridder News Service, December 5, 2003.

14. U.S. Treasury, "Protecting Charitable Organizations," http://www.treasury.gov/resource-center/terrorist-illicit-finance/Pages/protecting-charities_execorder_13224-a.aspx.

15. Brisard, "Report to the UN."

16. Ibid.

17. Ibid.

18. CSIS, "Transnational Threats Initiative, September Update," 2003.

19. U.S. House Committee on Financial Services, *Anti-Money Laundering: Blocking Terrorist Financing and Its Impact on Lawful Charities*, May 10, 2010.

20. CSIS, "Transnational Threats Initiative."

21. Jessica Hopper, "Formula for Theft Success: Steal Food for a Baby," ABC World News, April 13, 2011, http://abcnews.go.com/US/baby-formula-targeted-organized-retail-theft-rings/story?id=13293485#.UFnUWa6ur31.

22. U.S. Attorney's Office, "Eleven Indicted in Pharmaceutical Thefts," May 3, 2012.

23. Joseph Larocca, "ICE Announces Expansion of ORC Pilot Program," February 14, 2011, http://blog.nrf.com/2011/02/14/ice-announces-expansion-of-orc-pilot-program/.

24. FBI, "Intellectual Property Crime Rights Coordination Center," http://www.iprcenter.gov/.

25. U.S. Customs and Border Protection, "IPR Center Fiscal Year 2011 Seizure Report," 2012.

26. Ibid.

27. Te-Ping Chen, "China's Marlboro Country," Center for Public Integrity, 2009, http://www.publicintegrity.org/investigations/tobacco/articles/entry/1437/.

28. Noble, "The Links between Intellectual Property Crime and Terrorist Financing."

29. Nicholas Schmidle, "Inside the Knockoff-Tennis-Shoe Factory," *New York Times*, August 19, 2010.

30. The White House, *2010 Joint Strategic Plan on Intellectual Property Enforcement*, 2010.

31. Julian Harris, Philip Stevens, and Julian Morris, "Keeping It Real: Combating the Spread of Fake Drugs in Poor Countries," International Policy Network, London, 2009.

32. Robert O'Harrow, "Identity Crisis: Meet Michael Berry," *Washington Post*, August 10, 2003.

33. Frank Perri, "The Fraud-Terror Link: Terrorists Are Committing Fraud to Fund Their Activities," *Fraud Magazine* 12, no. 4 (July–August 2010), http://www.fraud-magazine.com/article.aspx?id=4294967888.

34. O'Harrow, "Identity Crisis."

35. Ibid.

36. "Fraud, ID Theft Finance Terror," *Chicago Tribune*, November 4, 2001.

37. Ibid.

38. U.S. Senate Committee on Homeland Security and Governmental Affairs, *Hezbollah: Financing Terror through Criminal Enterprise*, 2005.

39. Ultrascan, "Ultrascan HUMINT: Boko Haram," http://www.ultrascan.nl/Ultrascan_Humint_Boko_Haram_GSI_from_Inside_-Alert.pdf.

40. Patrick Poole, "Mortgage Fraud Funding Jihad?," *FrontPage Magazine*, April 11, 2007.

41. Mary Beth Sheridan, "Man Suspected of Bin Laden Link Accused of Fraud," *Washington Post*, August 8, 2005, http://www.washingtonpost.com/wp-dyn/content/article/2005/08/08/AR2005080801492.html.

42. Investigative Project on Terrorism, "Case 140: Nemr Ali Rahal," 2005.

43. Investigative Project on Terrorism, "Case 146: Mahmoud Youssef Kourani," 2005.

44. Poole, "Mortgage Fraud Funding Jihad?"

45. FinCEN, "Informal Value Transfer Systems," *Advisory* 33 (2003).

46. Claude d'Estree and Luke Andrew Busby, "U.S. Response To the Events of September 11, 2001: The USA PATRIOT Act, Title III," *Law in the War on International Terrorism*, 2001.
47. FinCEN, "The SAR Activity Review: Trends, Tips & Issues," 2010.
48. GAO, "Federal Agencies Face Continuing Challenges in Addressing Terrorist Financing and Money Laundering," March 4, 2004.
49. U.S. Departments of the Treasury and Justice, "National Money Laundering Strategy," 2003.
50. GAO, "Terrorist Financing."
51. Ibid.
52. Douglas Farah, "Report Says Africans Harbored Al Qaeda; Terror Assets Hidden In Gem-Buying Spree," *Washington Post*, December 29, 2002.
53. The Kimberley Process, www.kimberleyprocess.com.
54. National Commission on Terrorist Attacks upon the United States, "Appendix A: The Financing of the 9/11 Plot."
55. "Canadian Agency Finds Dirty Money," CSIS TNT September Update, September 2003.
56. "Federal Reserve Examiner Spreads Knowledge to Global Audience," Alert Global Media, November 2003.
57. U.S. Senate Subcommittee on Terrorism, Technology and Homeland Security, *Terrorism: Growing Wahhabi Influence in the United States*, June 26, 2003.
58. Jerry Seper, "U.S. Agents Raid Software Firm, Seeking Al Qaeda Money Link," *Washington Times*, December 7, 2002, 2.
59. FinCEN, "Trends, Tips and Issues: Foreign Corruption," 2011.
60. GAO, "Federal Agencies Face Continuing Challenges in Addressing Terrorist Financing and Money Laundering," March 4, 2004.
61. ICE, Operation Cornerstone, http://www.ice.gov/cornerstone/.
62. Douglas Farah, "Syria Seizes Six Arab Couriers, $23 Million," *Washington Post*, December 20, 2003.
63. Jeannine Aversa, "Nations to Discuss Ways to Cut Off Terrorists' Financing," Associated Press, February 4, 2004.
64. Farah, "Syria Seizes Six Arab Couriers."
65. Indictment: *US versus Zacarias Moussaoui*, December 11, 2001.
66. Michael Levi, Money Laundering Risks and E-gaming: A European Overview and Assessment (Wales, UK: Cardiff University, 2009).
67. FBI, "Bitcoin Virtual Currency: Intelligence Unique Features Present Distinct Challenges for Deterring Illicit Activity," 2012.
68. *U.S. v. Scheinberg et al.*, 2011.
69. Ibid.
70. FBI, "Bitcoin Virtual Currency."

CHAPTER 7

Terrorists and Criminal Exploitation of E-commerce
Following the Money Just Got Tougher

As witnessed in the previous chapter regarding money-laundering methodology, we routinely underestimate the sophistication of criminals and terrorists. The things we use, they use. They also have the right people on the payroll to interpret and find work-arounds to the law. Often, they will investigate and exploit vulnerabilities in software and devices. Whether driven by a radical ideology or the lure of money and drugs, criminals and terrorists are persistent and will change tactics and evolve until their goal is achieved. They are also working in the same "space," either together or through parallel activities.

Take a look in your wallet. I would guess in addition to a debit card and at least one credit card, you may have a preloaded card for your favorite coffee haunt, a gift card, a subway or rail card, and possibly a card to top up your cell phone or wireless modem. You probably have a smartphone and possibly an app allowing you to scan it at the coffee store or at the toll booth on the highway. It may surprise you to learn these now-commonplace financial instruments are also used by criminals and terrorists to store, move, and launder vast amounts of money. Considering that the first web-enabled smartphone debuted in 2000 and the iPod was introduced in late 2001, technology has advanced at an extremely rapid pace—and along with it, the e-commerce enterprise.

All good investigators know the value of the money trail to an investigation. Whether tracing a petty fund in a continuing criminal enterprise or millions of dollars moved by an international terrorist group, the origin, path, and destination of the money tell a unique story about the operation. This story often yields evidence allowing infiltration of the group, identification of its key players, and ultimately the eradication of the organization or one of its cells. The last chapter covered the financing activities related to the 9/11 hijackers and how they were challenged by bank personnel and others when opening bank accounts, moving money, and obtaining identification. Unfortunately, technology has provided new opportunities to avoid human interaction and the related challenges as encountered by the hijackers. Offering volume and speed, electronic funds transmissions are exciting and useful to all of us yet enable those with nefarious intentions to also move at lightning speed. When customer registration is necessary, a limited amount of information is required, and the lack of personal interaction between company and customer means the system is ripe for fraud and exploitation. New payment methods also include many layers eventually making transactions anonymous and even harder to detect and infiltrate. These inherent vulnerabilities can enable the transfer of money between members of a terrorist organization or the storage, movement, and "cleansing" of dirty money by criminals. As we close down other funding sources, terrorists and criminals will find easier avenues to exploit since money is the lifeblood of their operations.

One downside to technological advances: terrorists and criminals are users, just like law-abiding citizens. Unfortunately, with corporations rushing cutting-edge products to market, technology is often fielded without complimentary safeguards to prevent exploitation by those engaged in illegal activities. The emerging nexus between telecommunications technology, as related to illicit financial transactions, is one such area of concern.

NEW PAYMENT METHODS DEFINED

The Financial Action Task Force (FATF) is an intergovernmental body working internationally to combat money laundering (ML) and terrorist financing (TF). FATF was established in 1989 by the G-7 Summit, whose members were alarmed by the rising tide of money laundering, exacerbated by technological and communication advances. FATF studies money-laundering techniques and trends and serves as an international policy-making body advocating legislative reform.

In 2006, concerned with the increasing use of technology for banking and commerce and recognizing related vulnerabilities, FATF issued a study entitled *Report on New Payment Methods* (NPMs), sounding the alarm.[1] NPMs allow customers to transfer money directly through technical devices such as personal computers, mobile phones, or data storage cards. These alternatives to the traditional banking system partially arose from customer demand for convenience and speed and from tracking with rapid technological advances such as Wi-Fi Internet and smartphones. Also, the banking community sought NPMs to provide access to those who are excluded from traditional financial services such as individuals with poor credit ratings, minors, and residents of under-banked regions. Governments embraced this new type of banking, with the EU enthusiastically stating in 1998, "It is vital that development is allowed to take place unimpaired by strict technological rules which will hamper innovation and restrict competition."[2] Our government also liberally leverages NPM technology as a work-around for citizens who do not want to use the formal, regulated banking system.

NPMs are also referred to as "e-money," "digital cash," or "e-cash." These methods allow electronic, cross-border transfer of value between individuals and organizations. It is important to note that e-cash was intended to be analogous to physical cash by design: it offers unconditional anonymity and prevents the ability to trace transactions since payments are not linked to a particular customer account. Other features are rapid transactions and the ability to accumulate value on devices and through smart cards. Everything making this system attractive to law-abiding citizens makes it equally as appealing to criminals and terrorists.

Typologies and Concerns

In their 2010 report, a follow-up to the 2006 warning, FATF defined typologies and trends regarding NPM exploitation. Several concerns are persistent across NPMs and facilitate criminal financial transactions such as the use of a third party to hide transactions, person-to-person (P2P) transactions occurring outside of a formal system, and the lack of human oversight with regard to confirming personal identification or identifying suspicious activity.

Use of a Third Party

The use of third parties in transactions has further complicated the process of identification, prevention, mitigation, and prosecution. Whereas "merchant" was formerly a term used in conjunction with a commercial entity, anyone who can access the Internet is now legally a merchant and in business. Of particular concern is third-party funding, which includes fake or stolen identities. Money launderers can also use strawmen or nominees as an added step to layer and obscure the transaction process and provide themselves another line of defense against being identified by law enforcement. A strawman is a front person used as a cover for some questionable activity, perhaps a legitimate Internet business owner who is helping launder dirty money through his operation. A nominee holds the funds in lieu of the actual owner, adding more layers to an already opaque system. The strawman or nominees are both complicit in the illegal activity.

Unwitting sellers and buyers can easily become involved in criminal operations. The use of a third party such as a remittance business (Western Union, for example) to instantly move money is of great concern. This is especially true when customer due diligence (CDD) measures are not undertaken. According to FATF, the following CDD measures must be accomplished by all businesses transmitting money:

a) Identifying the customer and verifying customer's identity using reliable, independent source documents, data or information.
b) Positively identifying the beneficial owner, if a stand-in for the customer is used in the transaction, and taking reasonable measures to verify the identity of the beneficial owner.
c) Obtaining information on the purpose and intended nature of the business relationship between institution and customer.
d) Conducting ongoing due diligence by constant scrutiny of transactions undertaken throughout the course of the relationship. This due diligence will ensure transactions are consistent with the institution's knowledge of the customer, their business and risk profile, including, where necessary, the source of funds. Any transactions falling outside of the known business activity of the individual would thus become suspicious and possibly reportable.

Naturally, since many money transactions at remittance businesses are onetime occurrences, many of these procedures are not followed or are ignored. Alternatively, as employees get to know their customers, they may be less diligent or even become complicit in the illegal activity, as evidenced by several criminal cases in the last year.

Person-to-person (P2P) Transactions

NPMs often allow the direct transactions between parties, possible with the host company acting only as a facilitator, incurring no liability. Examples of P2P transactions include the ability to send money between smartphones, grant loans through e-banks, or trade gold and other digital assets on the Internet.

Lack of Human Interaction and Oversight

Regarding other NPM methods, FATF is also concerned about the exploitation of the non-face-to-face nature of these accounts. The Bank

Secrecy Act (BSA) of 1970 requires banks and remittance agencies to take part in a process called "Know Your Customer" (KYC). KYC refers to both of the following:

- Customer due diligence that financial institutions and other regulated companies must perform to identify their clients and ascertain relevant information pertinent to conducting financial business.
- Knowledge of bank regulations which governs those activities.

KYC is a policy and process meeting the intents of the customer identification program (CIP) mandated under the BSA and USA PATRIOT Act. KYC policies are extremely important in preventing identity theft, financial fraud, money laundering, and terrorist financing. Controls typically include:

- Collection and analysis of basic identity information
- Name matching against lists of known criminals or those on watch lists
- Determination of the customer's risk in terms of propensity to commit money laundering or identity theft
- Creation of an expectation of a customer's transactional behavior
- Monitoring of a customer's transactions against their expected behavior and recorded profile
- The customer does not present themselves in person, risk of deception increases

Positively validating identity is not possible since documents forwarded online could easily be fraudulent, manufactured, or stolen. Human intelligence collection and observation for behavioral red flags cannot be accomplished virtually, and challenging the customer is impossible.

NPMs provide convenient work-arounds for criminals and terrorists to CIP, KYC, and many other anti-money-laundering regulations and requirements for the financial sectors. Interestingly, FATF reports that the number of suspicious bank wire transfers in previously heavy markets is down, attributed by some to the increase in use of NPMs by criminals.

NPM FINANCING

The amount of money moved nefariously through NPMs varies considerably by source and amount. As we will study in this chapter, cases show that laundering activity can be a few hundred to a few million dollars. NPMs can be funded in several ways such as cash, money orders, or funds transferred from other anonymous NPM products. Customers of small businesses such as phone shops and local, nonfranchised stores mostly use cash to purchase prepaid cards, cash vouchers, and mobile top-up cards. Naturally, cash funding increases ML/TF risk, especially through unlicensed merchants and those with insufficient training in anti-money-laundering (AML) and counterfinancing of terrorism (CFT) compliance. Of greater concern to law enforcement are anonymous-to-anonymous funding methods using NPMs since there is an insufficient paper trail regarding how the transaction was funded or the origin or destination of the funds.

Admittedly, NPMs have an overarching positive effect on national and global economic development due to the efficiency of transactions and access to financial services by the nonbanked population. In fact, the FDIC has indicated that as many as 20 percent of the population of the United States is either unbanked or underbanked.[3] However, legal and regulatory requirements did not keep pace with the e-commerce explosion. As found in other vast enterprises such as the transportation industry, no one exploits statutory voids better than criminals and terrorists.

For purposes of this discussion, the exploitation of nonbanks, prepaid cards, stored-value cards, and devices with stored value and digital precious metals is explored. Each method has a special ML/TF risk and has documented cases of exploitation by criminals and terrorists. Many of the cases presented in this book have been culled out of studies and reports issued by the government and independent task forces, as well as court records. After reading this chapter, you will have a firm understanding of NPMs and how their inherent vulnerabilities make them attractive to criminals and terrorists. You will also view gift card kiosks, auction sites, and smartphones differently, thinking about parallel users with nefarious intentions.

Nonbanks

A money/value transfer system (MVT) is a method for moving funds *or* value, whether through traditional or nontraditional means. The rise of Internet payment services and potential for ML/TF exploitation is a serious concern. Through privately held companies labeled by FATF as "nonbanks," Internet payment services allow customers to pay bills online, make purchases at participating websites, buy and sell items from auction sites, and even contribute to charities. Setting up an account is simple and requires little personal data, most of which can easily be fabricated. Users may also accumulate money in the account; when the owner is ready, he or she can liquidate several ways, including untraceable debit cards used to withdraw cash from ATMs worldwide.

Some Internet payment service providers apply a risk-based approach when identifying customers. If the risk profile of the customer and transaction is high, additional verification methods may be applied through simplified CDD versus enhanced CDD that would be found at a traditional banking institution. However, in the online environment the use of third parties to open accounts is possible, whether through identity theft or fictitious information. All that is typically needed to open accounts is an e-mail address, a phone number, and possibly a date of birth. Also, the sheer volume of users and transactions makes early identification of criminal behavior unlikely.

Internet-Based Nonbanks

Internet nonbanks and global e-commerce businesses have grown with the rise of online shopping, auction sites, and bulletin boards. PayPal, the most widely recognized, emerged as the result of a merger between two forward-thinking companies, Confinity and XCom. Confinity was originally developed to enable mobile payments from the Palm Pilot smartphone, and XCom was one of the original Internet financial service providers. EBay purchased PayPal for $1.5 billion in 2002, and the nonbank now operates in 190 markets with over 232 million accounts. PayPal allows customers to send, receive, and hold funds in twenty-five currencies worldwide and has annual revenue of $4.5 billion. The rise of PayPal certainly outpaced federal regulations, and due to fraud issues, the company has been forced to spend hundreds of millions of dollars fighting illicit activity. In fact, in 2008 the company purchased an Israeli security analysis company to assist, Fraud Sciences Limited, for $170 million. The vast operating space of this financial services corporation across platforms and borders is staggering. There are multiple red flags that will trigger investigation by PayPal; however, if the criminal stays under certain thresholds with multiple accounts and/or small transactions, it might still be possible to skirt the system. WebMoney is another international digital currency provider, headquartered in Russia, and falling even further outside of the regulations and control of the banking system. For instance, WebMoney's Credit Service permits anyone to loan money to anyone else using the WebMoney purse. The loaner sets the terms and conditions of the loan and then sends funds directly to another user. WebMoney accounts can be funded anonymously, using cash, via cards purchased at retailers around the world.

The registration process for an Internet payment service account typically involves the presentation of identifying and contact information by potential customers. For example, an e-mail address, telephone number, street address, and user ID and password will get the customer through the door of the company. By law, the information collected must be verified using a variety of methods, ranging from the examination of paper copies of identity documentation to the use of online identity verification solutions provided by third parties. Naturally, a seasoned money launderer will know how to avoid detection by using addresses that are fronts, stolen information, or even legitimate information from third-party actors such as nominees or strawmen. In order to use the Internet payment system, the account must be funded by the customer. Some companies allow a range of options for funding transactions, and the customer is not limited to using a major bank credit card, checking account, or savings account. A quick assessment of online payment service companies (internationally) reveals that most nonbank Internet accounts may be funded through:

- Credit or debit cards
- Prepaid cards (can be anonymous)
- Wire transfers
- Prepaid gift cards or gift checks (anonymous and transferable)
- Checks
- Postal orders and money orders
- Cash vouchers

Third-party collection methods through nonbanks are called cashier as a service (CAAS). Criminals have found vulnerabilities in software allowing them to check out without transferring funds between buyer and seller. CAAS does generate an electronic record, but recall that buyer and seller can be anonymous or hidden in false personas. Certainly, any type of software is susceptible to hacking or defeat by a determined actor. For more information regarding CAAS vulnerabilities, see Microsoft's 2011 report entitled *How to Shop for Free Online—Security Analysis of Cashier-as-a-Service Based Web Store*.[4]

Positive customer identification, tracking withdrawals and expenditures, and striving for transparency in the online nonbank system is difficult, at best. In terms of auction sites, the online nonbank system is much easier to circumnavigate if you are a seller than buyer. Most auction sites continue to change rule sets to favor buyers, thus leaving their "left flank" open for those who wish to exploit the selling aspects of the Internet marketplace. Later in the chapter, we will explore multimillion-dollar schemes where a seller "layers" transactions with multiple online personas, and funds raised on the Internet are pushed back through the nonbank and into multiple personal bank accounts.

The MSB

As touched on in the previous chapter, money services businesses (MSBs) are nonbank entities that provide transfer and exchange mechanisms. According to the Financial Crimes Enforcement Network (FinCEN), there are now 45,000 MSBs in the United States. People generally use MSBs to exchange or transfer value or to purchase or redeem negotiable instruments. This category includes: a currency dealer or exchanger; a check casher; an issuer, seller, or redeemer of traveler's checks or money orders; and money transmitters. MSBs operate almost exclusively on a "per transaction" basis, meaning there is no standing account or business relationship between the MSB and the customer.

Methods of Using MSBs to Move Money

Structuring Criminal activities regarding MSBs include structuring, in which a single transaction is broken down into multiple sequential transactions below the reporting threshold. Those thresholds would include mandatory reporting by the agent or additional record keeping. Occasionally, the money transmitter will simply ask that transactions not be recorded, trying to avoid detection. However, the MSB is obligated to report suspicious behavior via SAR. Therefore the money-laundering technique of choice for seasoned criminals is to structure their transmittals. The use of structuring can be found in most major cases involving the movement of money for nefarious purposes, starting with the 9/11 hijackers and funds moved back and forth between provider and user.

Structured transactions routinely involving the use of nominees or other proxies (or stand-ins for the actual perpetrator or owner) are prevalent in MSB fraud cases. A structured transaction is a series of related transactions that could have been conducted as one transaction. The actor purposely breaks down the transaction into separate activities to circumvent the reporting requirements of the BSA. Structured transactions can be accomplished simultaneously by operators at different locations or serially by the same customer and a complicit MSB employee. These extra steps are taken to conceal the beneficial ownership of the funds. In the money-laundering business, structured transactions are also known as "smurfing."

CASE STUDY: SMURFING

In a suspected drug trafficking-related case in Canada, members of an organized crime group used several individuals to send funds through an MSB to the same individual in the United States. The first smurf was followed twenty minutes later by a second smurf (a different individual) at the same MSB, who proceeded to send funds to the same beneficiary.[5]

Exploiting Negotiable Instruments A negotiable instrument is a transferable, signed document such as a check, bill of exchange, or promissory note. The instrument promises to pay the bearer a certain amount of money on a future date or on demand. Purchasing negotiable instruments and putting the proceeds of criminal activity into the formal system is a way of moving or storing money. Obtaining multiple instruments, breaking down the total amount being laundered into smaller sums, is another way of structuring or layering transactions. Securing a variety of instruments will create gaps in the transaction audit trail. The types of negotiable instruments involved in ML/TF activity in the MSB sector include the issuance of checks by the MSB (in lieu of cash), the issuance of bank drafts made payable to another MSB, and money orders.

CASE STUDIES: NEGOTIABLE INSTRUMENTS

- In a suspected terrorist financing case, FINTRAC observed transactions by an individual using an MSB to exchange thousands of Canadian dollars for U.S. dollars and obtaining anonymous checks from the MSB.[6]
- In a suspected drug case, an MSB filed Suspicious Transaction Reports regarding an individual who purchased multiple, nonsequential money orders (payable to himself or herself) in a possible attempt to obscure the customer's connection to a suspected drug trafficker.[7]

Refining Refining refers to the conversion of small-denomination bills to large-denomination bills. Commonly used by drug traffickers, this ML technique is used since large quantities of cash, especially in small-denomination banknotes, can be difficult to conceal or transport. Money launderers will therefore seek to convert or "refine" small-denomination banknotes ($5, $10, and $20 bills) into larger-denomination bank notes (such as $50 and $100 bills).

CASE STUDIES: REFINING

- In a suspected human-smuggling case, an individual with suspected ties to Eastern European organized crime simultaneously refined and exchanged foreign-denominated cash at an MSB.[8]
- In one case involving suspicions of laundering drug proceeds, the disclosure subject exchanged a total of $8,000 in $20 bills. This individual used the MSB in a regular pattern of activity, including transactions on consecutive days, refining the $20 bills.[9]

Digital Currency Exchange Systems

Another option for the illicit transfer of money is use of online currency exchange systems. These systems allow the transfer of funds from a variety of sources and currency types into another user's account. The source can be a nonbank like PayPal, bank wire (recall wire amounts less than $10,000 are not reportable in the United States), or other webmoney accounts. The receiver of the funds can "cash out" by moving funds to his or her bank credit card or ATM card, through wire transfer using an MSB. At one currency exchange site hosted by an IP address from Russia, it is possible to move money through Russian rubles, Vietnamese dongs, and gold certificates. (See Figure 7.1.)

To further blur the money trail, some online currency exchange sites allow the user to send funds to a variety of companies, to pay for Internet services, and even donate to charities. The possibilities for moving and hiding money are endless. (See Figure 7.2.)

Finally, it is possible to conduct anonymous banking through offshores and incorporating in other countries. Often, establishment of offshores through this method is accomplished through nonbanks and anonymous prepaid cards. As we studied in the previous chapter, an offshore nonbank offers greater anonymity to the customer and fewer restrictions on transaction limits. Figure 7.3 shows a screenshot of an online dealer offering anonymous offshore accounts and banking products.

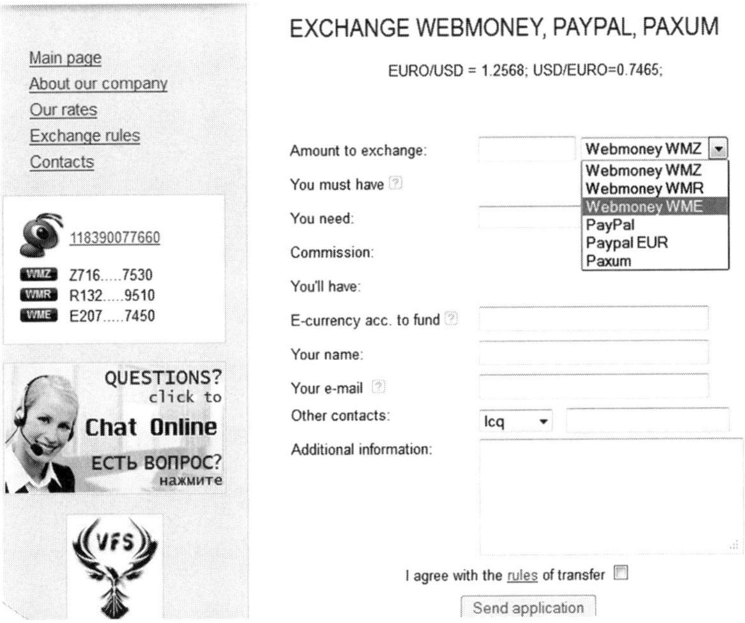

FIGURE 7.1   Anonymous online currency exchange system.

Internet
Internet Access (284)
Hosting & Domains (209)
Software (108)
Freelancers (10)
Network Security (23)
File, photo and video-hosting (41)
Postal Services (5)

Design & Advertising
Websites Creation and Design (23)
Banners and media networks (14)
Promotion & Optimization (24)
Content (texts, photos, video) (18)
Printing & Design (6)
Contextual Advertising (14)
Active Advertising Systems (5)

Business & Finance
P2P Loans and Lending Services (2)
Online E-Currencies Exchange (36)
Buy & Sell E-Currencies (67)
Referral & Affiliate Programs (11)

Digital Goods
Music (46)
CD, DVD &Video (42)
E-Books (40)
Mobile Content (19)
Help Desks & Forums (54)
Newspapers & Magazines (27)

Shopping
Sales&Deals (5)
Tech & Housewares (57)
Auctions (10)
Gifts &. Flowers (42)
Sport, Health & Beauty (20)
Clothing & Accessories (49)
Home & Office (11)
Food & Household (12)
Auto/Motor, spare parts (14)
Toys, Goods for Children (4)
Pets & Plants (2)
Medical Services (1)

Entertainment, Games & Gifts
Art, Crafts & Hobbies (13)
Online Games (90)
Online Gambling (116)

Pay Online
Mobile Communications (290)
Prepaid Services (32)
Telephony & VOIP (212)
Pay-TV (129)
Public Utilities (37)

Education & Social Life
Social systems & Community (12)
Educational Aids & Training Materials (8)
Translation Services (9)
Education & Literature (21)
Charity (8)
Bulletin Boards (14)

Travel
Taxi (1)
Travel Agencies (29)
Hotels &. Tickets (44)
Fuel (2)

FIGURE 7.2   Anonymous ways to spend and transfer WebMoney.

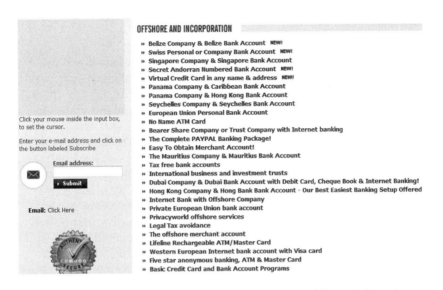

FIGURE 7.3   Anonymous offshore, incorporation, and financial products.

CASE STUDIES: DIGITAL CURRENCY EXCHANGE AND MONEY LAUNDERING

WESTERN EXPRESS INTERNATIONAL CURRENCY EXCHANGE COMPANY

On February 22, 2006, Vadim Vassilenko, Yelena Barysheva, and Alexey Baryshev were indicted for operating an illegal check-cashing and money transmittal business from 2002 through 2005. Their company, Western Express International, knowingly exchanging criminal proceeds for digital currencies. Through its websites, Western Express actively solicited overseas clients in Eastern Europe, Russia, and the Ukraine to operate illegally in the United States. Clients using fictitious, often multiple identities committed a variety of cyber crimes, such as reshipping, phishing, spoofing, and spamming. Items purchased with stolen credit card numbers were resold for digital gold, which was further laundered through Western Express. A total of $25 million flowed through the company's bank accounts over the four-year period.

GOLDAGE CURRENCY EXCHANGE COMPANY

On July 27, 2006, Arthur Budovsky and Vladimir Kats were indicted on charges of operating an illegal digital currency exchange and money transmittal business, GoldAge Inc., from their Brooklyn, New York, apartments. The defendants transmitted at least $30 million to digital currency accounts worldwide since beginning operations in 2002, with more than $4 million as part of a money-laundering scheme. Customers opened online GoldAge accounts with limited documentation of identity, and then GoldAge purchased digital gold currency, with fees sometimes exceeding $100,000. Customers could choose their method of payment to GoldAge: wire remittances, cash deposits, postal money orders, or checks. Finally, the customers could withdraw the money by requesting wire transfers to accounts anywhere in the world or by having checks sent to any identified individual.

Source: U.S. Department of Justice, 2008.

EMERGENT DIGITAL CASH CONCERN: LOOM

Loom is an anonymous digital online asset-trading system or method in which users can develop their own digital currency and stock shares, make interest-bearing loans, raise capital, and set up a gambling or lottery system. Users can sell, trade, and store cash-equivalent credits in their e-wallets. A Loom system operates outside of the formal banking or tax system. Porcloom is a niche system developed by "liberty activists" in New Hampshire with specific methodology to use multiple servers and encryption keys to frustrate any attempts by law enforcement to detect or intervene. I first discovered the Loom scheme on an anarchist site proposing it as a method to accomplish anonymous, free banking outside the purview of the government.

Finally, another excellent source regarding nonbanks and MSBs can be found in FinCEN's *SAR Activity Review—Trends, Tips & Issues*, which is published in May and October of every year with a summary of SARs and analysis of trends and emergent issues.[10]

Prepaid Access Cards

Law enforcement experts believe prepaid cards are an attractive alternative to bulk cash smuggling.[11] Several criminal and terrorist cases in the last few years illustrate the vulnerability and exploitation of this NPM. Cards are not subjected to the same rules as cash such as the Currency and Monetary Instrument Report (CMIR) seizure rules if they exceed the $10K threshold and are not declared. They can easily be smuggled without detection onboard a commercial aircraft, train, bus, or ship. High-value cards are lighter in weight and more compact than a bundle of equivalent-value paper bills. These physical properties along with easy, anonymous acquisition and lack of regulatory guidance make cards the ideal smuggling mechanism.

Interestingly, the launch of the first stored-value/prepaid product traces back to the magnetic stripe-bearing gift cards introduced by now-bankrupt Blockbuster Video in 1995 to replace their paper gift certificates. The trend caught on quickly, as gift cards were an attractive product to consumers and could be loaded with any value and used at any outlet. Gift cards were thought to be safer than paper certificates, since they provided security features against alteration. Following Blockbuster's introduction of the prepaid plastic gift card, there was a rapid rise in the industry. In 2000, Visa Inc. introduced its Buxx card, marketed to parents with children in college as a way to quickly and safely provide funds. MasterCard Inc. launched a competitor card for college students, iGen, in 2001, and American Express answered by marketing the first general-purpose use prepaid card in October 2002. The product quickly morphed from single-purpose, limited use to multipurpose, unlimited use with the ability to reload the card with additional funds, transfer funds between users, and withdraw cash from an ATM.

As the prepaid card market thrived, the Blackhawk Network company introduced kiosks at grocery and drug stores in 2001. The kiosks meant purchasers could avoid trips to specific retailers to buy gift cards and could quickly amass cards and value. There are now over 700 providers of prepaid access cards (host companies) and hundreds of thousands of retailers distributing their product. According to the Federal Reserve in 2007, of electronic purchases, prepaid card payments alone comprised over half of noncash payments to retailers and other outlets.[12] The Reserve also reports that prepaid cards are the fastest-growing major payment type, and there were over a billion dollars' worth in circulation in 2009. [13]

Cards are being used in ways previously not considered. Many contractors are using prepaid cards to compensate day laborers, who in turn can use them to send their money cross-border to relatives back home. Prepaid debit cards are also given to customers seeking "payday loans" or advances. The U.S. government is leveraging prepaid-card technology, using Electronic Benefits Transfer (EBT) systems. For instance, over 4 million people who receive Social Security benefits lack bank accounts; since many were cashing their checks through nonbanks, raising concerns about the security of their funds, the government decided to disburse benefits through EBT prepaid access cards.[14] Funds are also similarly distributed to natural-disaster victims through FEMA debit or American Red Cross cash assistance cards. Supplemental Nutrition Assistance Benefits (formerly known as food stamps) are now given to recipients on a prepaid card. Therefore, instead of forcing customers to use our highly regulated and monitored banking system, we have provided convenient work-arounds that unfortunately can be exploited. In July 2011, FinCEN released a document entitled "Prepaid Access Final Rule Balancing the Needs of Law Enforcement and Industry" amending Bank Secrecy Act (BSA) regulations to "provide a balance to empower law enforcement with the information needed to attack money laundering, terrorist financing, and other illicit transactions through the financial system while preserving innovation and the many legitimate uses and societal benefits offered by prepaid access."[15] The first order of business was to rename "stored-value cards" to "prepaid access cards." Prepaid access cards contain a magnetic stripe, and the funds are not actually stored on the card but in an account elsewhere that can be accessed or tapped by the user. This popular NPM includes phone, retail, and credit cards purchased with cash at many grocery and drug stores.

There are two types of prepaid access cards, limited-purpose or closed-loop cards and multipurpose, open-loop cards.

Limited-Purpose/Closed-Loop Cards

Limited-purpose or closed-loop cards are merchant-issued gift cards, calling cards, and subscriber identity module (SIM) cards. They can be used only for specific purposes, may have an expiration date, and usually cannot be reloaded. However, an unlimited number if these cards can be purchased anonymously with cash and then in turn can be sold through online auction sites, with the value transferred to a nonbank for subsequent liquidation through an untraceable ATM card. In the United States alone, the total funds loaded onto prepaid cards in 2009 exceeded $120.2 billion, according to research commissioned by MasterCard Inc. and conducted by the Boston Consulting Group.[16] The study predicted that the United States will account for 53 percent of the global prepaid-card market in 2017.

Law changes regarding gift cards typically favor users. Just prior to the 2010 holiday shopping season, the U.S. Federal Reserve worked to implement legislation aimed at limiting fees and expiration dates associated with retail gift cards.[17] This change was in response to an outcry by the public regarding monthly fees for nonuse of the card and cards expiring within a time period with a remaining balance reverting back to the card issuer. Under the new law, funds linked to cards must be usable for at least five years after a card is issued or last funded. Unfortunately, these lenient rules favor not only customers but those in the money-laundering business who are accumulating and hiding their dirty money.

Multipurpose/Open-Loop Cards

Of much greater ML/TF risk are these stored-value cards, which bear the name of a major credit card company and may also be purchased with cash in unlimited quantities. Value can be added online through a non-bank or with cash at a participating retailer, and most cards can be used internationally. When the card holder is ready to cash out, money may be withdrawn from most ATMs or the cards can also be sold online at auction or through an online gift card dealer. As long as the amount doesn't exceed the $10,000 ceiling by federal regulations, transactions occur off the radar screen. This opens the door to the "smurfing" activity discussed earlier in the chapter, where criminals spread a great deal of cash across many sources, neatly concealed from regulators and law enforcement. Open-loop cards are big business; the National Drug Intelligence Center's (NDIC) Threat Assessment indicates there are more than 7 million MasterCard and Visa prepaid debit cards in circulation.[18] The NDIC is concerned about drug traffickers who use prepaid cards to store, transfer, or hide their proceeds. Another concern: it is possible to use these cards not only to purchase goods but also to charge an amount above the sale price in order to get "cash back" as a way of laundering money.

Twin or partner cards are also a growing concern. Card companies are now issuing "twin" or "partner" cards to one customer; he or she keeps one card and passes the other to remittance receivers anywhere in the world. Each holder of these cards can access the original account and add or withdraw funds through the global ATM network. Money can be quickly loaded into the account at one location and withdrawn at an ATM thousands of miles away.

Obtaining an anonymous ATM card is quite easy. The following website shows customers how to receive a high-value anonymous ATM card and fund it through NPMs such as nonbank remittance agencies, money orders, or wire transfers (see Figure 7.4).

These anonymous cards can be used on Internet auction sites. They also can be sold online, and sellers don't need the physical card to move money, only the card number, expiration date, and three-digit security code. At one website of an overseas card dealer, there is no credit check, and the customer can set up his or her anonymous card for direct deposit of paychecks and federal tax refund. The anonymity of these cards makes the money trail extraordinarily difficult to follow.

US$30,000 monthly limit, Cash ATM Card!

Our banking source has been instructed to issue an extremely limited number of these highly valuable and hard to obtain $30,000 monthly ($1,000 daily) limit ATM Cards. The best news of all, this card never expires! It operates anywhere you see ATM logos/networks with more than 900,000 ATM machines available worldwide. **No name appears on the card, nor is any ID required to purchase it.**

This ATM Card is issued from a financial institution that is well known for its friendly handling of its customers. These hard to obtain cards are available in United States of America Dollars (USD). Your card can be used anywhere in the world to buy goods and withdraw cash from ATMs in the local currency.

The Basics

Money kept on this card is untouchable to all but the bearer of the card and its secret pin code.

You will receive no statements and no mail related to your transactions. In a world of increasing intervention, it is good to know that there are still places where you can have a nest-egg.

Your PIN number comes sealed and is delivered along with your card and full loading instructions upon receipt of a fully paid order.

You can check and verify your funds online. A special Internet access account is included with your order. [Sign up required.]

Funding your card with funds

Money can be paid in by Western Union, cheques, bankers draft, money orders or via a Swift or IBan wire transfer.

There is a US$30,000 limit concerning withdrawing funds per month. Max. Load: US$30,000 per month.

Deposits and correspondence should be sent to the source address given when you receive your card. Loading by e-currency is available, but there is a small surcharge to load. Full particulars comes with paid orders.

Here's how you get started:

Remit your payment of USD 660.00 to Privacy World, by Liberty Reserve, Western Union, MoneyGram or a bank wire. Sorry credit cards are NOT accepted for any of our banking products. We require a name or address and any picture ID is okay plus a current utility bill. All that is required for this exciting offer is your e-mail address, courier street address with contact telephone number (for courier purposes only,) and your payment.

Once we receive payment for your order, within a few working days we'll send you your 30k no name no ID ATM card and email you the courier tracking details.

FIGURE 7.4   Anonymous ATM cards.

E-purse or Stored-Value Cards (SVCs)

Unlike the previously mentioned cards, which have magnetic strips, the e-purse stores value directly on the card itself using a microchip. The SVC is like having money in your pocket, and no pin is needed to use the card—therefore value can be immediately drained. SVCs may be purchased in bulk with cash, held for an unlimited amount of time, and sold on an auction site. The most popular version of the e-purse is a smart card used for public transportation, toll booths, parking garages, and vending machines.

Emerging smart-card technology will allow users to leave their cards in pockets, wallets, or purses. A contactless smart card is one where there the card communicates with the reader through radio field induction technology. Another type of technology, near field communication (NFC), also relieves the customer from any manual input to the device or interaction with a person to enact payment. NFC is new technology that uses ultrasound to automatically pass payment information to the register. Vendors, or criminals with the right equipment, could easily overcharge cards or quickly drain accounts without the customer's knowledge. Some terrorist attacks are simply meant as power plays and to paralyze, such as through hacking activities; if commuters all turn to these cards, virtually "hijacking" highway toll booths or subway systems could leave rush hour traffic paralyzed.

CASE STUDIES: PREPAID CARDS

- Indonesian police reported that radical Islamic terrorists were observed selling phone cards, raising revenue upwards of $500 per day to fund operations.[19]
- A Mexican criminal caught at the border was using stolen credit cards to transfer value to prepaid cards.[20]
- In 2007, two defendants were prosecuted for purchasing closed-loop prepaid gift cards with stolen credit card account information. They used the gift cards to purchase merchandise, which they then returned to the store in exchange for new gift cards. Because the new prepaid cards were not linked to the stolen credit card account numbers, they were not affected when the theft of the credit card information was discovered. The defendants were convicted and ordered to pay $82,000 in restitution. Both were convicted of fraud and money laundering and served jail time.[21]

- Cards may be used as a form of payment for illicit activity. A joint ICE/IRS investigation uncovered a criminal organization in the United States with a coconspirator in Mexico who was creating phony credit cards. The coconspirator was paid for his assistance with retail gift cards. He then sold the gift cards, using the cash to buy U.S. phone cards, which were then smuggled into Mexico in a separate operation.[22]
- The DEA uncovered an operation where drug dealers were loading cash onto prepaid cards then sending them to suppliers outside of the country, who in turn liquidated funds using ATM machines.[23]
- In 1998, a phone card scam resulted in a $34 million loss for Deutsche Telekom. A crime syndicate was able to create the technology needed to recharge expired cards and resold them. The company had $38 billion in revenue in 1998; therefore the losses were not quickly identified. Reloaded cards were unaltered, meaning paying customers and merchants were unaware of the tampering.[24]

As the preceding cases illustrate, cards are extremely vulnerable to exploitation by money launderers. First of all, there is no limit to how many cards you can buy. You can buy them with cash or other prepaid cards. You can sell them on an online auction site, transfer the value to a "nonbank," and liquidate it via an anonymous ATM card that can be resold or used to quickly pull out funds. Unfortunately, these financial products were fielded without security measures baked in, and the convenience of users is priority number one. Putting rigor into the law retrospectively will likely result in an outcry from customers and merchants alike. Law enforcement and retailers must work around the system to identify criminal or terrorist use of these funding methods.

DEVICES WITH STORED VALUE

New technology embedding a debit or credit card into a SIM card is transforming the smartphone into an e-purse. The user can simply tap the phone against a terminal to complete a sales transaction, with funds automatically withdrawn from the account.[25] This emergent category of e-financing is labeled "mobile money services," and value is actually stored on a mobile phone with no external account. Subscribers can accumulate and store funds on the device in a mobile account known as an e-wallet.

Users can move money P2P, sending it directly to another device. They can use the funds to top up their airtime. All of these financial transactions can occur on throwaway phones, purchased anonymously with cash or prepaid cards. The throwaway phones, loaded with value, can also be sold on auction sites or bulletin boards. SIM cards loaded with value can be removed from phones and stockpiled and used later, or with the right technology, cloned. Mobile money systems certainly offer versatility for customers but typically operate with no regulation or oversight, making them extremely attractive to criminals and terrorists.

Although the P2P transmission of funds using a cell phone may be a foreign concept in the United States, we must remember that these NPMs are already fulfilling the needs of the unbanked across the world. In fact, experts at the World Bank predict that over 1 billion people will use cell phones to remit money domestically and across borders by 2015.[26] Mobile phone transaction services have grown 68 percent the last three years, with FATF forecasting $250 billion in financial transactions in 2012.[27] The United States is actually behind the curve when it comes to fielding this technology.

Let's stop for a second and discuss the evolution of throwaway devices. A throwaway device can be easily and anonymously purchased with cash at a convenience, drug, electronics, or grocery store. For phones and modems, the user does not need to subscribe to a provider to call, text, or enable Wi-Fi; he or she simply calls an automated service for activation. The phone or modem device phone number can be from any area code designated by the user and the balance topped up with prepaid phone cards. Once the user is finished with the devices, they can simply be thrown away. Originally, throwaway phones were inexpensive, rudimentary devices that could simply make phone calls and send text messages. The prepaid-cell market evolved, and soon it was possible to access the Internet on devices, with extra funds deducted from the account balance. Now, thanks to the increasingly expensive plans accompanying data-enabled smartphones, the industry has launched a line of throwaway smartphones such as BlackBerry and Droids. Users do not need to pay exorbitant monthly costs; they pay only when they use the device. Smartphones enable users to download applications, or apps, which can facilitate online banking, access Internet auction sites, and accomplish the same tasks as a laptop computer. The evolution of throwaway phones and modems has further complicated money-laundering detection and prosecution. Transfer of funds through mobile devices is accomplished either by Short Message Service (SMS) text message or an Interactive Voice Response (IVR) system. Both can be done anonymously and there is no human interaction, exploiting two of the primary money-laundering concerns regarding NPMs.

The U.S. government leveraged mobile-payment technology during recent operations in Afghanistan. In 2004, the UN established the Law and Order Trust Fund for Afghanistan (LOTFA) to pay the salaries of Afghan police. LOTFA funds were used to open more than 62,000 bank accounts in behalf of the police officers, requiring little identification or face-to-face interaction, and salary payments were made through direct deposit. This system was already ripe for exploitation by the Taliban. However, police were often on patrol or out in the field for weeks at a time and unable to access their funds at local banks or ATMs. Therefore, in 2008, the Roshan mobile company launched a new system called "M-paisa" in collaboration with First Micro Finance Bank, to bypass the formal banking system. M-paisa makes salary payments to police through mobile cell phones. The phones themselves then hold the value, and funds can be transferred to other parties through the use of pin codes. P2P transfers, loan disbursements, cell phone airtime purchases, merchant payments, and salaries' receipts and disbursement are all possible on a cell phone using M-paisa. Prior to its use in Afghanistan, the only other country in the world using M-paisa was Kenya, and it was still in the developmental stages. As with all NPMs, this method brought financial services to the unbanked population; however, it was extremely vulnerable, especially due to ongoing combat operations within the country. Having a phone holding value is akin to having a wallet stuffed with bills, putting individuals at risk for theft or, in some parts of the world, murder.

Mobile payments, also known as "m-payments," "proximity payments," or "micropayments," are point-of-sale cash transactions made through a mobile device. The sender takes the cash to a remittance center, which charges a modest service fee. The center then "sends" the amount to the recipient's e-wallet. The recipient gets a text message on the mobile device indicating the sum has been placed in the account, along with a pin number. The cash can then be collected at any participating remittance center, retail store, or, if business evolves as predicted, fast-food outlet. The entire transaction takes mere minutes, although the addition of human interaction may serve as a slight deterrent to launderers or those moving money for nefarious purposes. Of course fast-food and other retailers will not be held to the same Know-Your-Customer laws as the traditional banking industry.

The recent intersection of two popular NPMs has led to emerging ML/TF concerns. A partnership between a major Internet payment service and a global cellular phone company now allows instantaneous transfer of funds directly between nonbank accounts. These accounts can be loaded and drained in a matter of minutes, with the throwaway devices and anonymous ATM cards. As you can see, the use of multiple NPMs further obscures the money trail and pushes financial transactions out of regulatory channels.

Finally, we now have smartphone applications or "apps" that load value for a variety of retailers and mass transit directly on the smartphone. Major coffee chains and other routinely visited outlets pushed technology to develop a quick and efficient way for customers to check out. Once the customer loads money on the mobile device, he or she simply holds the screen with the bar code up to the register scanner and value is deducted from the account. In the tech-savvy customer's eyes, having multiple apps is seen as too fragmented and confusing. The insatiable desire for speed and efficiency will likely drive a change in service where values will be "bundled," meaning greater ability and tendency to amass value on device. For instance, perhaps one e-wallet account will hold funds for coffee, gas, and fast food. There is no limit as to how much value a user can put on a smartphone.

Further obscuring financial activity, MSBs are now offering prepaid cards and Internet payment services. They will also allow customers to transfer and receive funds to and from mobile-payment accounts. The combination of these methods will allow international funds transfers to occur off the radar of the traditional banking system. In addition to making our lives easier, these new advances in mobile payment technology will likely help criminals and terrorists move, store, transmit, and launder money in new ways. We can also expect smartphone theft to rise along with their intrinsic value, and if the owner did not password protect the device, loss of funds will be instantaneous as the criminal transfers the money by an SMS text message or voice. Passwords will likely be cracked or bypassed by savvier criminals. In short, we can expect technology to again outpace the legal system, and it is unlikely we will add protections after the fact.

EMERGENT AREAS OF CONCERN: REMOTE DEPOSIT CAPTURE (RDC)

RDC services allow customers to remotely deposit electronic check images to their accounts, creating a new channel for traditional deposit collection activities. You have likely used this service at an ATM; you feed the check into the machine, it scans it and verifies the amount, and then automatically puts the value into an account or disburses cash. Anything can be fed into the machine: personal checks, traveler's checks, or money orders. There are several areas of concern regarding RDC including structuring and money-laundering schemes, check fraud, check kiting (writing checks with insufficient funds in the account), or passing counterfeit checks.

AUCTION AND BULLETIN BOARD WEBSITES

With NPM money in hand, whether through a nonbank, stored-value credit cards, or a device loaded with value, the criminal or terrorist can use the funds to make illegal buys and/or launder money. The auction site business is booming, fed by nonbanks and the rising tide of Internet shopping; at any given time, there are at least 5 million items for auction or for sale on the Internet. Auction fraud accounts for roughly 48 percent of online fraud reports to the Federal Trade Commission (FTC), with almost 500 reports per week. These are only the reported cases; much is happening off the radar with nefarious sellers and buyers alike exploiting the rules for their own intents. It is important to note that on several auction sites, the seller can also (or only) offer a "buy it now" price, meaning an expedited transaction and the ability to advertise, complete the sale, close the ad, and simply disappear. Regarding bulletin boards like Craigslist, there have been several high-profile criminal cases involving these types of sites in the last few years, including murder and other violent crimes.

Why are auction sites and Internet bulletin boards so easily exploited?

- Users can access websites from any location in the world. They can *anonymously* access the Internet in several ways: through a throwaway modem purchased with cash at an electronics store; through a throwaway IP address purchased anonymously on the Internet; or from the Internet connection of a third party such as cyber cafes or business access points not registered to the customer.
- A customer can register in one country and connect from another country.
- Registration is very easy and very rapid.
- Registration is not face-to-face.
- A limited amount of information is required to register.
- There are no procedures to verify customer identification in certain cases.
- Anonymous e-mail addresses may be used as customer contact information and for the linked nonbank account.
- Transactions are rapid: quickly in and out.
- Layering is easy. There is no rule set regarding number of accounts. One can set up multiple personas and sell en masse, avoid detection, and rapidly accumulate funds.
- One can send the balance of a nonbank account immediately to someone else; just an e-mail address is needed.
- Customers have access to a wide range of items (from small-value items to high-value items) on sale on a wide range of commercial websites located all over the world.

- There is ambiguity: Goods can be sold for either a fixed or variable price. No authenticity check is performed by the hosting site and no check to ensure fair market value is achieved. A $10,000 diamond can be sold for $5 without raising a red flag, and a $5 starting bid for a used magazine can balloon to $10,000, also without raising a red flag.

AUCTION SITES

A simple search of the Internet yields auctions for everything from used household goods to fine jewelry, cars, boats, and aircraft. A buyer can also procure weapons, military uniforms, and even ambulances and police vehicles. It would be quite easy to outfit a group with clothing, weapons, and a mode of transportation within a short period of time.

In the haste to unload items on the Internet, some sellers have not thought through the process and the vulnerabilities related to buyers. For instance, in 2004 the following eBay auction item alarmed customers and led to several law enforcement advisories regarding the selling of service items online:

> EBAY ITEM # 3920661075: Warehouse Full of Police/Security Gear Uniforms More! "We are selling our Entire Inventory of State Police Uniforms and Gear! We have 14 Pallet Size Boxes filled with uniforms. This includes Short/Long Sleeve Uniform Tops, Uniform Pants, Patrol Jackets/Coats, Patrol Hats, Belts, holsters, Belt Pieces, Riot Gear and Much Much More."

Ambulances are routinely auctioned online, typically by small communities trying to move old stock (see Figure 7.5).

It is important to remember that there have been several cases of terrorists impersonating first responders in order to carry out their

Description	Make/Brand	Model	Year
2004 Sterling Acterra ID: 12	Sterling	Acterra	2004
1999 Freightliner FL60 Lifeline Highliner Ambulance #2 ID: 49 New Listing!	Freightliner	FL60	1999
1995 Ford Econoline E350 ID: R014	Ford	Econoline	1995
1996 International 4700 Rescue Squad ID: 4	International	4700	1996

FIGURE 7.5   Screen shot of an online ambulance auction.

attacks on hospitals, at checkpoints, and against government facilities. Sellers must understand that buyers can use NPMs to disguise their true identity and purchase items of any value online. The use of third parties might mean a seemingly "legitimate" buyer shows up to collect the goods or vehicle; however, they are just a front for the group with nefarious intentions. In these cases, it is better to contact law enforcement to ask for advice regarding the disposal or sale of first-responder equipment or property.

Auction Site Intellectual Property Theft (IPT)

As covered in the previous chapter, IPT is a rising concern in terms of criminal and terrorist funding. A quick visit to large auction sites reveals many high-priced items having been cheaply duplicated, wrapped in seemingly authentic covers, and then sold for low prices but at high volume. Criminals will exploit high-demand items, such as Rosetta Stone. I took the screen shot in Figure 7.6 from a popular U.S. Internet auction site.

As we all know, Rosetta Stone retails for hundreds of dollars; therefore the starting bid on this item is an immediate red flag that it is not authentic. Note that the seller has no previous sales and therefore probably has multiple identities and accounts on the site and is selling in bulk. Also, the seller is from another country; why would he or she pay to ship a low-priced item internationally for free, as indicated in the ad? Why sell this product to only U.S. customers? Ads like the one in Figure 7.6 are prolific on auction sites. With millions of sellers and buyers online at any given time, it is virtually impossible for the company to develop red flags to cover every possible fraudulent situation. The first line of defense is the consumer, who is unfortunately looking for a good, fast deal and falls prey to those with illicit intentions.

These case studies of actual and potential auction house exploitation highlight vulnerabilities.

FIGURE 7.6   Counterfeit Rosetta Stone language software on auction site.

CASE STUDIES: AUCTION SITE FRAUD

THE CASE OF NILTON ROSSONI

Nilton Rossoni, fifty-two years old, served time in a federal peniten-tiary for an extensive fraudulent scheme conducted on eBay between 2003 and 2008. During this period, he conducted over 5,500 fraudu-lent auctions on the site through 260 bogus accounts, 59 mail drops, six names, four bogus passports, and three banks. During his five-year operation, he collected $717,000 in the scheme. EBay, PayPal, and other entities used by Rossoni in his operation were unaware, and the fraud was actually detected by the U.S. Postal Inspection Service. According to prosecutors, Rossoni registered and estab-lished hundreds of eBay accounts and used various names, e-mail addresses, phone numbers, and mailing addresses on those accounts to post items for auction. He then purchased inexpensive items from himself and posted positive feedback on the transaction. Confident Rossoni was an honest broker because of his positive feedback, buy-ers lined up to buy a variety of products such as textbooks, computer flash drives, rotisserie grills, airline tickets, and designer luggage. Winning bidders were notified via e-mail to send a check or money order payable to one of number of aliases created by Rossoni and mail the payments to one of his mail drops. The checks were depos-ited into one of his three bank accounts. No items were shipped.

THE CASE OF JOHN P. LEARY (ALIAS RUSSELL DANA SMITH)

In 2003, John P. Leary opened his "Liquidation Universe" store in a strip mall in Utah. His store was empty; the business was solely on eBay, where he sold laptop computers for $1,000 each. However, computers were never shipped to paying customers. In just six months, Smith collected over $1 million from customers, laundering it through his credit union account. Upon receiving multiple com-plaints from buyers, eBay closed the account and notified the FBI. Smith was sentenced to four years in prison for his fraudulent activity.

POTENTIAL CASE STUDIES: AUCTION SITES
Money Laundering through Self-Purchase

Did you ever see a product on an auction site listed for an extraor-dinarily high amount? A recent search of a popular site yielded the following items:

- $24,000 postcard from 1911, with no unique characteristics and could be purchased in any antique store for a few dollars
- $50,000 pair of used name-brand tennis shoes probably worth $20
- Nondescript stuffed animals for thousands of dollars

Money launderers will often sell goods at an overrated price to the buyer—themselves. These items will not be offered for auction, only for sale. They can be purchased through a fictitious nonbank account or prepaid card. The money from the transaction then goes into their nonbank account and is withdrawn through cashier's check or ATM card.

FRAUD

In this case, the actor sets up an account through a nonbank using fraudulent information such as throwaway cell phone numbers and e-mail addresses. Small goods are listed for sale. The actor purchases several items from themselves, rating the transaction as outstanding and building their online profile. Once they have reached a certain seller status where customer confidence is likely, they commit the fraudulent act such as selling a "Rolex," obtaining the funds from the customer and never delivering the product or sending them an item of lesser value (legally completing the transaction). The actor then simply deletes their nonbank and auction site accounts and disappears.

Transactions such as those covered in the potential case studies provide additional security for the launderers by creating a record trail of actual delivered goods, requiring law enforcement to prove that the value of the sale is grossly out of proportion with the actual market value of the goods. Many online businesses, particularly auction sites, sell goods lacking a readily available market price. Also, overbidding is not unusual and could reflect legitimate transactions; therefore illicit transactions will be buried among the millions of items for sale on the site. There are red flags in the online auction system but multiple work-arounds for a hardworking criminal who is concealed among millions of reputable customers.

P2P WEBSITES

P2P transactions are growing in popularity, whether the buying and selling occurs through a site responsible only for the posting of ads and possibly assisting in the facilitation of the money transfer. For example, mediated customer-to-customer sites enable two people to transact outside of any regulated banking system and without electronic receipt or paper trail. These sites usually have some if not all of the following characteristics:

- Commercial websites such as Sell.com will facilitate the financial settlement between seller and buyer through PayPal, or the buyer can pay for the item through the mail directly to the seller via personal check or cashier's check.
- Often, the only indication of nondelivery of goods will be if the buyer complains.
- Most bulletin board "want ad"-style sites make customers sign agreements relieving the host of any responsibility regarding buyer or seller fraud.
- Only an e-mail address is needed for buyer and seller registration.
- Similar to auction sites, criminals can layer transactions by listing several ads, collecting the money and closing all related accounts.
- Rapid transactions are made through Internet nonbanks—quick payment and avoiding detection.
- Lack of human interaction leaves the space open for exploitation.

Craigslist and other similar bulletin board sites do not facilitate the monetary transaction between buyer and seller, and the only requirement to list or respond to an ad is an e-mail address. In the last ten years, there have been several widely publicized cases regarding murders, sexual assaults, and armed robbery occurring between unsuspecting buyers and sellers and those with criminal intentions. However, illicit financial transactions have also occurred on these websites, with sellers and buyers asking for wire transfers and using nonbanks to send payment for items prior to receipt or face-to-face meetings.

CASE STUDY: EXPLOITATION OF P2P SITES

The following are actual ads placed on Craigslist in which fraudulent sellers collected funds or bank account information through phishing from well-intended buyers (spelling and grammatical errors retained from original posts).[28] See http://www.craigslist.org/about/scams for other examples of actual scams.

- Hi. I am selling this car because my platoon has been sent back to Afghanistan and don't want it get old in my backyard. The price is low because I need to sell it before November 16th. It has no damage, no scratches or dents, no hidden defects. It is in immaculate condition, meticulously maintained and hasn't been involved in any accident...I do have the title, clear, under my name. The Denali has 35,000 miles VIN# 1GKEK63U16J138428. It is still available for sale if interested, price as stated in the ad $4,300. The car is in Baltimore, MD, in case it gets sold I will take care of shipping. Let me know if you are interested, email back. Regards!!!

- First of all I want to thank you for your interest for my car. I sell it at this price ($2,980.00) because I have been divorced recently. Now the car is in my property and as a woman i don't need it. This car is in excellent working conditions, no scratches, flaws or any kind of damage, slightly used in 100% working and looking conditions and comes with a clear title. From the beginning you have to know that for the payment I request only secure pay, I prefer the payment to be done using eBay services. We will use a safe payment method because I am affiliated at eBay and I have a purchase protection account for $20,000.00. The final price that I want for this car is $2,980.00 including shipping and handling. If you are interested in buying it please provide me your full name and address so I can initiate the deal through eBay. I will wait your answer very soon.

- Hello, I am looking for caring and honest person to watch my three years old daughter while I work, during our stay in the state and a friend introduced craiglist.com to me, I was searching on Childcare Babysitter, when your Ad post pumped up as a Childcare and Babysitter, am interested in your service as my babysitter/Childcare.. My Little daughter is (Mellina), I would like you to watch over her while i am at work in your Location, I reside in United Kingdom,I will be coming to the States in about two weeks time, Cos I just got a contract with Boss Perfume fashion industry down there, I work as a model and the contract will last for a month, the duration of our service wil be from 10am to 5pm, monday thru friday, I would like to know if she will be taken care of in your childcare centre/Home, or the hotel room where i would be lodging... how much u charge per week. she is just three years old as i have said earlier and i will be glad to update you and make the payment in advance to show you how serious i am. So please get back to me as soon as you can if you will be able to handle her and take very good care of her for me. Email me back. Your's faithfully

These ploys are crafted to obtained bank account information from unsuspecting merchants or service providers.

The FTC is heavily engaged in customer awareness of auction site and bulletin board fraud, but it is too late to put rigor or accountability back into a system that is now used by tens of millions of buyers. The host company is usually labeled as a "victim" as well in these cases and will escape culpability. Unfortunately, once the transaction occurs on a P2P site, the targets of the fraud rarely recover their funds and the perpetrator remains at large.

DIGITAL PRECIOUS METALS

Worthy of watching is the emerging commodity of digital precious metals as a way to store and move large amounts of cash. When the world economy collapsed, citizens lost their homes, vehicles, and more through foreclosure, and overall trust in the banking system waned. Along with this distrust and the desire to diversify portfolios, the demand for precious metals as an investment opportunity has grown. Companies prey on the fears of consumers, making statements such as "buying physical gold in your own name and storing it outside the banking system is the best way to protect your money."[29] Through this MVT system, buyers exchange options or rights to buy precious metals such as gold, silver, or platinum at the current price of the metal on the world commodity exchange. These derivatives can be exchanged between account holders, similar to other commodity or security derivatives. Also known as "paper gold" or exchange-traded funds (ETFs), they can also be used to purchase goods or services or liquidated through a variety of methods.

Through this service, users create an account and then secure cash deposits against gold, silver, and platinum held in "off shores" via the Internet. The reputable major companies engaging in this NPM actually hold vaulted precious metal in the name of the investor, employing major companies such as Brinks for security. Gold is the most popular product on the market, and GoldMoney is leading the way with over $2 billion in holdings, which is more precious metal than owned by several world economies. Many U.S. citizens are distrustful of the government's view on gold ownership in light of the gold confiscation in 1933 and the subsequent prohibition of gold ownership until 1974 and therefore ask companies to hold the gold for them, asking only for paper certificates as proof of ownership. Brokers typically store precious metals in vaults in London, Zurich, and Hong Kong. However, some companies will ship the gold to buyers on demand. As stated in the previous chapter, when laundering money physical gold is a great vehicle since it retains its value, can't be traced, is much less conspicuous than bulk cash, and can be melted, transformed, and resold. It is important to remember that paper gold is a financial asset, and physical gold is a tangible asset.

Everything that makes digital precious-metal investing attractive to law-abiding customers also makes it attractive to money launderers. For example, there is instant "transaction and clearing." When gold certificates are sold back to the company or otherwise transferred, payments are instant and the funds are available to be withdrawn globally or used in other transactions just moments after the sale. Unlike cashing in savings bonds or other monetary instruments, there are no lengthy bank settlement processes and transactions may occur 24/7. On many sites, the sale can be initiated and completed without human interface. Finding a buyer for physical gold is not as easy and requires physical contact between seller and buyer, something criminals and terrorists prefer to avoid. Therefore ETFs are perfect for those wishing to store, move, or transfer value quickly. FATF also reports that some companies in this international business allow investors to remain anonymous,[30] and a quick Internet query shows that several also allow the purchase of metals using a nonbank company or the aforementioned untraceable stored-value credit card purchased at any convenience store.

The digital precious-metals industry is not restricted in terms of the amount of assets held, size of individual accounts, or number of transactions that can be made in a certain period of time. For example, the now-defunct E-gold Ltd. Corporation did over $1 billion of gold business in 2006 alone, often facilitating more than $5 million in fund transfers per day. E-gold was also very controversial, since it also interfaced with emergent e-gambling business, mixing EFTs and gaming. The owners were ultimately convicted of various crimes, with investors' assets frozen until recent liquidation in 2012. The following case studies illustrate the vulnerability of digital precious metals for money laundering and other illegal activity.

CASE STUDIES: E-GOLD

E-GOLD LTD.

E-Gold Ltd. was an offshore incorporated in Bermuda but operating in Melbourne, Florida. At its peak, E-Gold maintained over 8 million accounts, with assets of $85 million in cash and physical gold reserves exceeding two-and-one-half tons (88,000 ounces). However, on April 27, 2007, after a three-year investigation, a federal grand jury indicted the company's owners on one count each of conspiracy to launder monetary instruments, conspiracy to operate an unlicensed money-transmitting business, and operating an unlicensed money-transmitting business under federal law, and one count of money transmission without a license. According to the indictment, persons seeking to use the alternative payment system E-Gold were required to provide only a valid e-mail address to open an account and no other contact information was required or verified. According to lawyers, "the defendants operated sophisticated and widespread international money remitting business, unsupervised and unregulated by any entity in the world, which allowed for anonymous transfers of value at a click of a mouse. Not surprisingly, criminals of every stripe gravitated to E-Gold as a place to move their money with impunity."[31] An analysis in January 2008 of the sixty-five most valuable E-Gold accounts showed that more than 70 percent were involved in criminal activity, according to the Justice Department. The company and its three directors pled guilty to conspiracy to engage in money laundering.

ShadowCrew was a cyber crime message board/forum operating under the domain name ShadowCrew.com from August 2002 to October 2004. The group consisted of 4,000 members and was an international crime syndicate, involved in massive identity theft and fraud. The e-gold system provided a quick, easy, and efficient way to launder their proceeds. Omar Dhanani, a ShadowCrew operative, was an E-Gold Ltd. customer and reportedly moved amounts ranging from $40,000 to $100,000 a week from proceeds of crime through e-gold.[32]

E-DINAR

The Islamic e-gold and e-silver trade is a niche industry, catering to those wishing buy and sell the dinar, coin currency unofficially used in several Middle Eastern countries. E-dinar is the largest broker online of the unique gold coins. The parent company of e-dinar has been in business since 1992, minting their own Islamic gold dinar to provide their customers the proper weight and standards in line with religious specifications found in the Qur'an. This digital gold company was established in Malaysia as an offshore in 2000 and acquired by the aforementioned E-Gold Ltd. in 2003. However, in 2004 the company broke away from E-Gold due to the latter's interface with the online gambling industry and reestablished itself as a sole proprietor of e-dinar. The dinar retains a unique fungibility and can be used to pay zakat and dowry as required by Islamic law.

E-dinar's parent company is located in Dubai, which has strict laws regarding e-banking and commerce and KYC procedures. An applicant must send a certified copy of a passport or photo ID to the company either by fax (accounts of less than $1,000) or through the mail (accounts over $1,000). However, certifiers of personal identification can be accountants, lawyers, members of the banking community, police officers, or "any individual that is qualified to undertake certification services in your country of residence."[34] To fund the e-dinar account, customers may not use a wire service such as Western Union; however, they can use checks and money orders obtained from an MSB. Paper gold may be exchanged for any international currency, and although third-party (outside-party) exchanges are not permitted, account holders can act P2P and transfer gold to any other e-dinar member. The e-dinar provides instant settlement; the moment the certificates are liquidated, the funds transfer to the specified account. E-dinar does not publish information regarding the amount of gold held or traded; however, in 2008 their president stated in a rare interview that e-dinar had 9,000 customer accounts in total.

On the e-dinar website (see Figure 7.7), we also see some subtle undertones of the perceived future of one currency on earth: "Abu Bakr

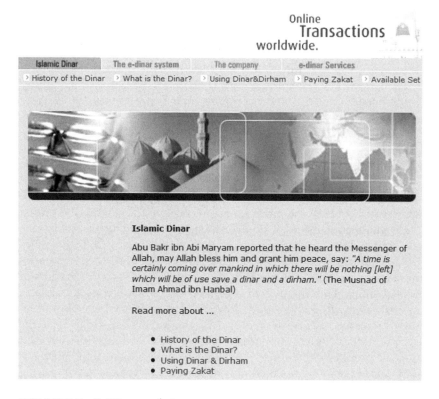

FIGURE 7.7   E-Dinar website.

ibn Abi Maryam reported he heard the messenger of Allah, may Allah bless him and grant him peace, say: A time is certainly coming over mankind in which there will be nothing [left] which will be of use save a dinar and a dirham." The e-dinar industry clearly believes it is preparing its clients for a future collapse in the global market.

THE BATTLE AHEAD

Financing is the lifeblood of a criminal or terrorist enterprise. Traditional criminal money laundering makes "dirty" money "clean" after the crime was committed; terrorists launder "clean" money by moving and storing it for the purposes of financing training and future operations. The use of NPMs makes both illicit activities possible, and the generation of additional funds during the laundering process is a bonus and made easier thanks to technology. Both groups also stand to benefit from the liaison between telecommunications, nonbanks, and Internet commerce. Money is no longer specifically handled by banks and credit unions but also by gas stations, drug stores, and retailers. The roles and participants in the process are not easily defined nor are their specific or legal responsibilities. Should merchants worry about how a stack of prepaid cards, phones, modems, or computers will be used? Should sellers of merchandise on the Internet worry about customer intent? Do these parties get involved or trust that another safety net is out there?

The lack of physical evidence in mobile transactions, compounded by the ease of moving and storing money through various NPMs, should be of great concern to policy makers and the law enforcement community alike. The NPM case studies explored in this chapter demonstrated the following worrisome typologies:

- Third-party funding (including strawmen and nominees)
- Exploitation of the non-face-to-face nature of many NPM accounts
- The speed of transactions and ability to layer activities and quickly amass money
- Complicit NPM providers or their employees; those who are recruited and "flipped" to support illegal activity, or those well placed by the criminal enterprise

Anonymity is easy with today's technology and work-arounds; however, companies engaged in development activities could significantly help law enforcement by increasing transparency of payments, enacting improved customer identification procedures, increasing awareness by customers of system vulnerabilities, encouraging robust suspicious-transaction reporting, and limiting transactions in terms of monetary amount and/ or frequency.

Technology changes at a rapid pace, and lawmaking is a lengthy process; therefore, government intervention is usually too late once NPM technology is fielded and has tens of millions of faithful users. Also, to be sound, rule making must be technologically neutral, meaning it can't be developed for each device or each type of business activity. However, the government can increase compliance monitoring and impose greater sanctions on companies who do not have sufficient safeguards in place to prevent illicit activities or at least generate a red flag for further reporting to law enforcement. In light of the rapidly changing and robust NPM industry, a new type of proactive financial forensics is clearly needed to follow the money trail before an operation occurs.

FATF, FinCEN, and FINTRAC are all heavily involved in monitoring and reporting e-commerce exploitation, but until technology is delivered to market with secure features "baked in," those with nefarious intentions will stay a step ahead. Interestingly, FinCEN tried to reduce vulnerabilities by once proposing that retailers keep customer information on everyone buying a prepaid access card. Can you imagine the outrage if our government enacted this regulation now? However, when prepaid cards appeared on the scene, had we started with this type of reporting requirement, it would simply be an expectation at checkout. Now, due to the proliferation of NPMs and nonbanks, new laws such as limiting purchase of prepaid cards to $1,000 worth of prepaid cards per day, per retailer won't work. In a metropolitan area, the customer can just walk down the block to the next prepaid-card retailer. Certainly, had we started down this path allowing only major, heavily regulated banking systems such as Visa and MasterCard to issue and control prepaid cards, the resulting foundation and structure would have prevented the proliferation and eventual abuse of cards. The e-commerce "genie" is now out of the bottle.

Once criminals and terrorists have funding, they require manpower and an anonymous way to form, train, and motivate the group. The Internet provides the perfect platform to fulfill these needs, as the next chapter will explore.

REFERENCES

1. FATF, *Report on New Payment Methods*, 2006.
2. FATF, "Money Laundering Using New Payment Methods," 2010.
3. Federal Deposit Insurance Corporation, *FDIC National Survey of Unbanked and Underbanked Households*, 2010.

4. Rui Wang et al., *How to Shop for Free Online—Security Analysis of Cashier-as-a-Service Based Web Stores*, May 2011, http://research. microsoft.com/apps/pubs/?id=145858.
5. FINTRAC, "Money Laundering and Terrorist Financing (ML/TF) Typologies and Trends for Canadian Money Services Businesses (MSBs)," 2010.
6. Ibid.
7. Ibid.
8. Ibid.
9. Ibid.
10. FinCEN, "SAR Activity Review—by the Numbers," http://www.fin-cen.gov/news_room/rp/sar_by_number.html.
11. http://www.usdoj.gov/ndic/pubs11/20777/20777p.pdf.
12. Federal Reserve, "Non-cash Payment Trends in the United States: 2003–2006," 2007 Federal Reserve Payments Study, December 2007.
13. Federal Reserve, "2010 Federal Reserve Payments Study," 2010.
14. FATF, "Money Laundering Using New Payment Methods," 2010.
15. FinCEN, "The SAR Activity Review Trends Tips & Issues," 2011.
16. Payment News, "MasterCard Releases Prepaid Market Sizing Report," *Payment News*, July 12, 2010, http://www.paymentsnews. com/2010/07/mastercard-releases-prepaid-market-sizing-report. html.
17. Meena Thiruvengadam, "Fed Targets Gift Card Fees," *Wall Street Journal*, November 17, 2009, http://online.wsj.com/article/ SB125838564151550609.html?mod=WSJ_hpp_sections_news.
18. http://www.usdoj.gov/ndic/pubs11/20777/20777p.pdf.
19. http://www.asiamedia.ucla.edu/article-southeastasia.asp?parentid= 34173.
20. http://www.businessweek.com/magazine/content/05_50/b3963115. htm.
21. FATF, "Money Laundering Using New Payment Methods," 2010.
22. http://www.ice.gov/doclib/pi/cornerstone/pdf/CS1206.pdf.
23. http://www.ice.gov/doclib/pi/cornerstone/pdf/CS1206.pdf.
24. James Glave, "Pirates Cash In on Weak Chips," May 22, 1998, http://www.wired.com/science/discoveries/news/1998/05/12459.
25. http://in.rediff.com/money/2003/dec/22betterlife.htm?zcc=ar.
26. Michael Klein, World Bank, 2008.
27. FATF, "Money Laundering Using New Payment Methods."
28. Craig's List, "About Scams," http://www.craigslist.org/about/scams.
29. GoldBroker.com, https://www.goldbroker.com/buy-physical-gold. html.
30. http://www.fatf-gafi.org/dataoecd/30/47/37627240.pdf.

31. U.S. Department of Justice, "Money Laundering in Digital Curren-
    cies," http://www.justice.gov/ndic/pubs28/28675/sub.htm.
32. http://www.businessweek.com/magazine/content/06_02/b3966094.
    htm.
33. U.S. Department of Justice, "Money Laundering in Digital Currencies."
34. E-dinar, "Customer Identification and Acceptance Policy,"
    https://www.e-dinar.com/html/4_7.html.

CHAPTER 8

Exploitation of Social Networking and the Internet

Facebook and Twitter abetted if not enabled the historic region-wide uprisings of early 2011.

—Arab social media report regarding the Arab Spring uprisings[1]

Most would agree that globalization, fed by technological advances in the information system and telecommunications realms, has overwhelmingly been a "good thing." Our world is connected like never before, and those formerly isolated are now part of the landscape, able to access critical medical information, tap educational resources, and answer almost any question in two clicks.

Unfortunately, terrorists and criminals are similarly thrilled with globalization. They, too, can answer any question in two clicks such as how to build bombs, find addresses and personal information about targets, and secure blueprints for federal buildings. They can communicate in real time and disappear before law enforcement can connect dots. With the lack of international laws and enforcement, as well as a universal definition of "terroristic speech," some bad actors are even hiding in plain sight. Terrorist groups are now leveraging the Internet to recruit, train, and spread propaganda, especially "global brands" such as al-Qaeda, Hezbollah, and Hamas. In the last year, social networking sites such as Facebook, Twitter, and MySpace were used as vehicles for international and domestic terrorist communication. Loosely affiliated cyber criminal groups such as "Anonymous" have aptly demonstrated electronic theft and sabotage capabilities against major corporations. Exploring how we arrived at this dangerous juncture gives insight into current and future exploitation of the Internet, although it is quite impossible to "unring" this bell.

THE INTERNET:
A TWENTY-FIRST-CENTURY BLACK SWAN

The Black Swan theory is a metaphor describing a surprising event with major impact thought to be impossible but then rationalized by observers in hindsight. The combination of low predictability and large impact of Black Swan events as related to nefarious groups is central to this book's narrative concerning asymmetric tactics and fifth-generation warfare.

In the first century CE, a Roman poet, Juvenal, called something presumed not to exist or deemed impossible a "Black Swan." Interestingly, Dutch explorer Willem de Vlamingh spotted a black swan in Australia in the 1600s while traveling through the area. The discovery of this creature, thought to be nonexistent, was deemed the "Black Swan Problem" and introduced the concept of "falsifiability" to the scientific world. Scientists soon realized that which they thought was unequivocally true might be proven otherwise.

Modern Black Swan events were characterized by Nassim Nicholas Taleb in his 2010 book *The Black Swan: The Impact of the Highly Improbable*. Taleb regards almost all exceptional scientific discoveries, historical events, and artistic accomplishments as Black Swans, or undirected and unpredicted events. The rise of Adolf Hitler, the personal computer, the Internet, and the September 11 attacks are Taleb's examples of Black Swans. Taleb's comments in a *New York Times* article are important to frame our discussion regarding the social networking phenomena:

> What we call here a Black Swan (and capitalize it) is an event with the following three attributes. First, it is an outlier, as it lies outside the realm of regular expectations, because nothing in the past can convincingly point to its possibility. Second, it carries an extreme impact. Third, in spite of its outlier status, human nature makes us concoct explanations for its occurrence after the fact, making it explainable and predictable.
>
> I stop and summarize the triplet: rarity, extreme impact, and retrospective (though not prospective) predictability. A small number of Black Swans explains almost everything in our world, from the success of ideas and religions, to the dynamics of historical events, to elements of our own personal lives.[2]

Major axioms of the Black Swan theory include:

1. The disproportionate role of high-impact, hard-to-predict, and rare events beyond the realm of normal expectations in history, science, finance, and technology

2. The noncomputability of the probability of the consequential rare events using scientific methods (owing to the very nature of small probabilities)
3. The psychological biases making people individually and collectively blind to uncertainty and unaware of the massive role of the rare event in historical affairs

The theory refers only to unexpected events of large magnitude and consequence and their dominant role in history. Such events, considered extreme outliers, collectively play vastly larger roles than regular, predictable occurrences. In short, these are game-changing events, such as the rise of modern terrorist groups, cartels, and transnational organized crime groups.

Black Swan logic makes *what you don't know* far more relevant than what you do know. Therefore, in the counterterrorism business, we should be exploring "anti-knowledge" or what we don't know and what we don't expect from the enemy. In the security realm, we typically use specific data to make strategic decisions instead of stepping back and viewing the entire issue with all of its complexities and changing environmental factors. We expect groups to engage in a similar manner as in the past, and we harden facilities and screen people accordingly. Unfortunately, we expend an inordinate amount of resources to prevent history from repeating itself, while the groups work to hit us from an unexpected or asymmetric angle. As discussed in Chapter 3, this resource drain and diversion of manpower is exactly what the enemy hopes to elicit, and we often play right into their hands. The story of the Maginot Line shows how we are conditioned in this manner. After World War I, the French built a wall along the previous German invasion route to prevent reinvasion. However, Hitler simply went around the wall and marched into France. Overrelying on past events as a predictor of future action, underestimating the creativity of the enemy, and the inability to think outside of the box clearly leave us vulnerable.

Similarly, with the Black Swans of rapid technological and communication advances, we were wholly unprepared for how social networking would change our society, the definition of "community," and the manner in which people communicate.

RISE OF SOCIAL NETWORKING: ARE WE USERS ... OR TARGETS?

The early view of computers was that they worked in isolation, perhaps supporting a work area or a student at a library. Visionaries saw beyond this construct, working to find ways to connect computers,

Major Social Networking Sites

Site Name	Year Fielded	Unique Monthly Visitors in 2012
Friendster	2002	5 million
LinkedIn	2003	110 million
Second Life	2004	1 million
MySpace	2006	70 million
Facebook	2007	750 million (175 million log in daily)
Twitter	2008	250 million
Pinterest	2012	10 million and rapidly climbing

FIGURE 8.1   Major social networking sites, history, and usage. (*Source:* "Top 15 Most Popular Social Networking Sites, July 2012," http://www.ebizmba.com/.)

and ultimately, their users. The first person-to-person online communication forum was developed in the 1980s, with the Bulletin Board System (BBS). Bulletin boards were independent online meeting places, produced by code and allowing users to communicate within a central system. Eventually, users could also share and download files or games. I remember accessing BBS on my brother's rudimentary Radio Shack Tandy computer using an extremely slow dial-up connection that tied up our home phone line and charged per minute. We were amazed while communicating with strangers around the country, one sentence at a time, connecting with people our age and who shared our interests.

America Online was first to market the Internet, selling subscriptions for access and leading the "e-mail-for-the-masses" revolution in 1993. The next Internet revolution occurred in the early 2000s, when we witnessed the rapid rise of social networking sites, which are now part of daily life for many. Evaluating the sheer number of accounts is not valid, since many are inactive; tracking by unique monthly visits gives a much clearer picture of users (see Figure 8.1).

Consider this: what the business world sees as users and potential buyers of the myriad goods advertised on these sites, the enemy sees as targets. Every time you connect with a stranger on the Internet, you have potentially exposed yourself to someone with nefarious intentions. Every piece of information posted on the Internet, whether "locked," deleted, or otherwise protected, can be gathered by those with the right skills and software. Advertising companies are also able to gather information from your profile and online activity to place targeted advertisements on your webpages and even send e-mails with tailored content. Therefore we should expect that any lawless group or individual with the right tools and skills can accomplish the same goal.

THE MIND AS A BATTLEFIELD:
THE WAR OF IDEOLOGY

The Internet is a virtual world where people can be compelled (even unconsciously) to change their opinions, join movements, and even take up arms for a new, compelling cause. These new members are not forced to join; they are volunteers—which always make the best recruits, in both licit and illicit groups. The social sciences provide an outstanding framework for understanding how groups can easily strike deeply into the psyche of our nation and citizens by leveraging the power of the Internet.

Shifting the Cognitive Center of Gravity

In military doctrine and strategy, much emphasis is placed on the center of gravity (COG); typically, the COG is perceived as the organization's leadership, logistics trail (finances and supply), infrastructure (training camps and headquarters), and the operational or armed division of the organization. Prussian strategist Carl von Clausewitz stated: "Out of these characteristics a certain center of gravity develops, the hub of all power and movement, on which everything depends. That is the point against which all our energies should be directed." History is replete with examples where attacking the COG worked.

Unfortunately, postmodern history is also replete with examples of how attacking COGs did not lead to success, either because the enemy was underestimated as in Vietnam or due to the characteristic of the new brand of warfare, which is fought not only with iron on a physical battlefield. Leaders of al Qaeda have been killed or jailed; however, others have stepped up in the myriad successful splinter groups around the globe. Their base of operations in Afghanistan was destroyed; however, they merely scattered and now claim territory with training camps in at least five other countries. Policy makers, strategic planners, and operators must consider the unique COGs of postmodern terrorist groups, cartels, and transnational criminal organizations. What is their specific "hub of all power and movement, on which everything depends"? For radical Islamist terrorist groups, the hub is ideology, as discussed in Chapter 3. The new threat is not confined to nation-state borders, easily contained or mitigated. The ideology is the enemy, and the Internet is the perfect platform for its propagation.

It seems that rather than engage in cyber warfare by deliberately targeting and destroying our information and communication systems to deny service, terrorists appear to instead be using our networks to wage societal warfare to affect our cognitive center of gravity (CCOG).

CCOG shifts occur over a long period of time, as the opposition subtly changes and moves our core values and beliefs. This type of attack is not overt or anticipated and can be accomplished subtly by implanting thoughts, ideas, and counterideologies into our daily life. The "attack" may be through the introduction of false flags and information or flooding the system with "chatter" to divert analysts from the actual mission and target. Consider al Qaeda's new campaign to expose fractures in our populace and how the Internet could be used as a means to divide popular opinion on hot-button issues such as profiling, immigration, or military operations abroad resulting in civilian casualties. When citizens begin to doubt their government's goals and ability to take care of them, they are vulnerable to other messages and courses of action, resulting in a shift in the CCOG away from our core toward their goals. Naturally, the Internet provides a perfect platform for all of these activities.

Preying on Maslow's Needs: Affiliation

Today's youth want to belong to movements and to contribute to something important. They are very idealistic and want to have a greater say on every topic, including decisions made by our government. The April 2012 grassroots effort to engage private citizens in a national campaign regarding Lord's Resistance Army warlord Joseph Kony was a perfect illustration of their passion and, in some cases, naïveté. Many were amazed how a short, engaging video went "viral" so quickly, with 100 million viewers within days; data showed that the video was heavily viewed from mobile phones and was most popular with thirteen- to seventeen-year-old females and eighteen- to twenty-four-year-old males. Although the effort fizzled in execution in terms of blanketing towns with stickers and propaganda, it forced the U.S. government and others to account for their efforts to engage and stop Kony and resulted in the addition of thousands of extra troops from Uganda, Sudan, and others on the ground in Africa. The Kony event proves the Internet can be a powerful tool to capture the hearts and minds of millions in a short period of time, this time in a positive, constructive manner; hopefully, the next viral video won't have the opposite effect.

Regarding the radical jihadist realm, there aren't just lone videos but entire "channels" with recruiting propaganda. For example, the "Jihadi Fan Club" channel on YouTube has 200 plus videos and over 300 subscribers, each with their own stations filled with jihadi videos and sentiments. Read the comment section on these video sites and it becomes alarmingly clear there is a large group of Americans who are radicalized and pro-jihad. The leader of the Jihadi Fan Club proclaims:

> This Channel is dedicated to the Muslim youth! Don't waste the best years of your life (your youth) watching movies, playing video games and shopping. Use the strength that you have in your youth to push for change by fighting in the way of Allah (swt) against the evils of oppression and disbelief! Don't be foolish by waiting until you are too old to fight in the way of Allah (swt) because it may be too late.

Many of the videos are compelling and aimed specifically at youth, gently nudging the "off" switch to "on."

Social Cognitive Theory at Play

With cognitive theory, consequences or costs are not factors, and future beliefs and expectations will drive today's actions. In social cognitive theory, people observe others to see what they are or are not doing and then follow suit, consciously or subconsciously. We are exposed to this daily, with mass media the vehicle for delivering the "message." Sometimes the message is positive, such as with government public health and education campaigns, and the careful selection of those portrayed in the advertisements and proper wording and vernacular to connect with the target group. Advertising companies are also experts at cognitive campaigns; for example, ads for diet drinks show the before-and-after pictures of an actress convincing potential buyers they will have the same success. People then spend large amounts of money and even sacrifice their health to look like her, even after reading the fine print that "results aren't typical." The hook worked. There are many of these "hooks" in jihadist propaganda, and they are much more compelling than what may be found in our "democratization campaigns."

A dangerous form of cognitive theory involves social engineering, a form of psychological manipulation with activities such as desensitizing and then shifting perspective. For instance, if a person believes it is inevitable that a certain belief will spread or movement will grow, they may be compelled to join a group, even one they loathe. Nazi Germany is a perfect example, where the "pitch" from Hitler before marching into a country was "join us now and make it easier for all of us." History is replete with examples of social reengineering from the 1920s, when the government replaced Tsarist Russia with a new Soviet culture, to create the "New Soviet man." The Soviets were masters at social engineering, using mass media and popular culture to infuse the new message and mass relocations to obtain the demographic "mix" sought in the new society. China also used mass relocations in their "Great Leap Forward" and "Cultural Revolution" program in 1958, in which they successfully shifted an entire culture in three years. Terrorist groups, cartels, and gangs all unwittingly use cognitive theory to take control of territory and infrastructure. With communication technology and social networking, any future mass cultural shifts initiated by small groups or lone actors will likely take far less time, with governments likely lagging with their response and engagement.

Marketing Ideology and Fear

As covered briefly in Chapter 3, at its very core terrorism is nothing but an elaborate marketing campaign. The main product is fear; however, by-products include recruitment, empathy seeking, and fund-raising. Like all marketing operations, terrorism is meant to shift the public center of gravity through use of symbolism or themes, and these techniques can be overt or covert. We must also remember that for many groups, this is a long marketing campaign; the enemy is patient and thinks in terms of millennia, not years. Our children's children may indeed be struggling with the same terrorism and transnational crime issues we are today, and a quick fix is simply not possible.

Every day I scan numerous websites in an open-source intelligence collection activity supporting research, lecture, and writing efforts. In the spirit of "know thy enemy," an axiom of the great war strategist Sun Tzu, I also access current web caches of various jihadi sites and the pages of domestic and ethno-separatist terror groups. Often it is just the same day-to-day rhetoric; however, I have sensed a shift from outright violent threats to a more subtle, understated threat. For instance, seemingly benign, friendly organizations are using webcasts to facilitate understanding and discussion of the Muslim religion. Facebook pages appearing friendly and inviting will pull in the curious and then redirect them elsewhere for further discussion on topics. Of course many groups don't sugarcoat the message or their hate for the United States and also use the open forums to spread false information and propaganda. With the Internet, they are literally "hiding in plain sight": why should groups go underground when their Internet activities are perfectly legal?

Hizb-ut-Tahrir (HuT)

HuT is an international pan-Islamic political organization. Although HuT is not a U.S. State Department designated terror group, it is considered a terrorist group in other countries and has played a role in the Islamist radicalization and recruitment process by inducing a politically charged atmosphere. A key tenet of the group is to pursue a caliphate, or Islamic state to benefit Muslims and non-Muslims; however, under their established rule set, non-Muslims would be unable to vote for leaders or hold any office in the caliphate. Formed in 1953, HuT attempted coup attempts in Jordan, Syria, and Egypt in the late 1960s and early 1970s. The group currently has over 1 million members in forty countries, and international intelligence agencies established ties to Khalid Sheikh Muhammed, Abu Musab al-Zarqawi, and al Qaeda. HuT is banned in several countries such as England, Russia, and Turkey.

Enter HTA (Hizb-ut-Tahir America), comprised of American citizens and based in Chicago, where it holds regular Khilafah (caliphate) conferences in large suburban hotels.[3] For those who cannot attend, the event is broadcast live as a webcast. Having run the wickets of registering and answering laborious questions, I have joined telecasts anonymously and find the sessions educational but somewhat frightening in tone. The rhetoric during the conferences can reach a fevered pitch, with audience members angrily shouting. During the 2011 conference, I captured the following statements: "The Army is pulling together and the Caliphate will be restored. The Ummah will live under Islam"; "The United States will be ruled by the law of Allah"; and finally, "The military will be under the control of Islam when the Caliphate is restored." Should you join one of these sessions, after protecting your computer's IP address and using a free public Wi-Fi site, or a throwaway modem purchased with cash, be sure to participate in the chat forum with other attendees who are mostly U.S. citizens. I think you will find the discussions a startling eye-opener. Attendance of HTA conferences through webinar is a must for all counterterrorism analysts, as it is live and raw, without the forthcoming edits and mitigating commentary.

Past issues of HTA's e-newsletter, *The Shield* (www.theshield-newsletter.com), are widely distributed on the Internet and have asked Muslims to rethink their identity as Americans, proposing that the United States is not their constituency; theirs is the Muslim world. Past newsletters, now deleted from the web, hinted that Jews and Christians are the enemies of Muslims. Part of the problem is an overarching lack of agreed upon definitions; for instance, what is a terrorist website? What are the language differences between informing and inciting citizens to uprising and action? Consider the Internet advertisement for the 2012 HTA conference shown in Figure 8.2. The venue on the advertisement backed out just few days before the event due to hate mail, phone calls, and threats, but the HTA was able to find another location nearby.

The September 2012 uprising in the Muslim world, in reaction to a video made by a California man defaming the Prophet Mohammed, is

FIGURE 8.2   Screenshot of Hizb-ut-Tahir America's 2012 conference advertisement.

the perfect example of how the Internet has become a lightning rod for intense protest and revolt. With countries around the world calling for the United States to prosecute the video's creator and block access to it on the Internet, the balance between freedom of speech and national security has never been more delicate or contested.

Exploitation by Other Groups

Hamas and Hezbollah are masters at using the web to achieve social objectives and goals for their communities. As previously discussed in the financing chapters, they use foundations, with ever-changing names and websites, to raise funds for widows and those orphaned by their operations, and also seek donations to build schools and hospitals. Naturally, this community-building activity creates goodwill (and safe harbor) and furthers recruiting goals. Many citizens have donated money without realizing it is funding activities of internationally designated terrorist groups.

Al Qaeda's "glossy" Internet magazine, *Inspire*, was produced by American Samir Khan, who was killed along with Anwar Alwaki in 2011 by a missile fired by a Predator in Yemen. Many analysts originally thought *Inspire* was too sophisticated and well produced to be from a terrorist group and labeled it a hoax. However, it was soon apparent that *Inspire* was the product of AQAP, and Khan infused the magazine with articles such as his work entitled "I Am Proud to Be a Traitor to America" and articles on bomb building, the assembly and cleaning of semiautomatic weapons, and inspiring and educating terrorists. Most alarming was the call for individual jihad, inciting lone wolves to action. Naturally, the death of Khan did not mean the end of the magazine or other slick products from the al Qaeda publishing house. Finally, the Taliban, who many Americans assume reside in tents and caves, are outstanding Internet users. Their primary website, translated into English at http://www.shahamat-english.com/, is filled with jihadist propaganda and transmits daily (false) reports boasting of "successful" battles with the coalition (see Figure 8.3). Other nefarious groups, tired of being the target of hackers, attempt to hide by crafting a page that looks like a generic site with ads, even using banners for legitimate U.S. businesses. Clicking on the correct area will give passageway to the real website.

There are hundreds of public websites for domestic religious and racial hate groups such as white supremacists, neo-Nazis, the Ku Klux Klan, and Christian Identity. MS-13 and the Los Zetas Cartel also use the Internet to communicate and coordinate operations. The anarchists have a current news site with chat rooms and blogs. There is something for everyone on the Internet, and it is literally just two clicks away. Once landing on the page, the casual reader is now the target of a well-constructed marketing campaign and can be pulled further into the discussion, the recruitment, and the education process. In addition to serving as a recruiting and indoctrination platform, the Internet has also become an outstanding operational and logistics platform. As we have clamped down on the ability of criminals and terrorists to travel freely and communicate via satellite phones, groups can use the Internet for logistics and planning. They can remain anonymous and fire at will.

FIGURE 8.3   Taliban website, captured September 20, 2012.

LOOKING THROUGH A NEW LENS
AT SOCIAL NETWORKING

Second Life

In Chapter 6, we discussed how Second Life can be used to raise, store, and launder money through the use of virtual currency, the Linden. However, much more is happening in this virtual environment of 1 million unique users than just illicit monetary activity. While teaching homeland security for a major university, I took a two-week course on how to use Second Life to supplement the college classroom. Once I familiarized myself with the environment, I ventured far beyond the classroom and found an incredible underground world filled with anonymous strangers who want to communicate, interact, as well as buy and sell products.

For those who haven't ventured into Second Life, I strongly encourage you to visit this parallel world. The first step is to anonymously create an avatar and select what locations to "fly" to, typically an island, city, or buildings, many crafted after actual locations. Once there, you can visit nightclubs, concert venues, restaurants, shops, hotels, museums, universities, movie theaters, and bookstores. Some islands are protected by a fence prohibiting the avatars from flying in if they are not "recognized" or do not use the correct password. The user may also create a building or island and password protect it, allowing select avatars to access the area. Inside the building, it is possible to post videos, pictures, or billboards. Users can start their own church and hold open or closed services. Communicating with other avatars is accomplished by typing in text, voice, blinking, or hand signals. If clandestine communication is desired, it could be done by arranging books on a shelf in a certain way where the letters spell words, communicating completely off the radar. The myriad ways terrorists, cartels, gangs, and criminals can interact in this environment is extremely worrisome.

Law enforcement is engaged in Second Life. I spoke with a former Second Life task force member who relayed that authorities have detected radical recruitment, drug deals, and even discussions about hits in the platform. In this virtual world, avatars can also physically assault, rape, and "kill" each other. Users have sued the company, claiming corporate negligence and their own psychological injury from these events, but lacking precedence, courts typically dismiss the cases without settlement. Of course law enforcement doesn't have the resources to constantly or deeply monitor platforms such as Second Life, and the lack of regulatory due diligence in behalf of site hosts means the activity will likely continue. Figure 8.4 is a screenshot of my avatar visiting an al Jazeera password-protected conference center.

Every international terrorist group now uses Twitter to communicate including al Qaeda, Hamas, and Hezbollah. Almost all of the major U.S. hate groups and many militia groups also use Twitter to connect and spread their messages and ideology. Since the advent of Twitter in 2008, the Taliban uses their account to tweet updates from the battlefield through @alemarahweb messages with false information about their victories against the coalition with the intent to motivate their troops and swaying opinion with the citizens of Afghanistan (see Figure 8.5).

The anarchists use Twitter as an operational tool, to inform their protestors where to take the march, literally giving directions such as "avoid the park, too many cops" or "turn left at the street ahead, not right." Up-to-the-minute instructions regarding protest sites and police activity are also sent out to cell phones via mass text messages. These real-time adjustments by groups have surprised and, at times, overwhelmed law enforcement during anarchist protests in the United States and Canada in recent years. Two anarchists were arrested for using Twitter during the 2009 G20 summit in Pittsburgh to transmit police locations and activity; they were arrested in their hotel room, which was turned into a communication command center. They were initially charged with hindering prosecution, criminal use of a communication facility, and possessing criminal instruments; however, the charges were eventually dropped. Naturally, the anarchists use Twitter at every event

FIGURE 8.4   Password protected, invitation only lecture in Second Life.

now, creating a fresh account for every day of the protest. I monitored their chatter during the 2011 International Monetary Fund conference in Washington, DC, and took the screen shot shown in Figure 8.6.

LinkedIn

This professional social networking site made news when a Russian spy ring was cracked by law enforcement in 2010, and it was discovered they were using LinkedIn as a way to establish credibility, communicate, and connect with potential contacts. The case was a wake-up call for many site users, as many of the spies' contacts were reputable professionals and even government workers, who provided endorsements for the spies, having worked or attended school together. Many of the Russians are still on LinkedIn with updated profiles indicating their return to Moscow.

FIGURE 8.5   Taliban Twitter, captured September 20, 2012.

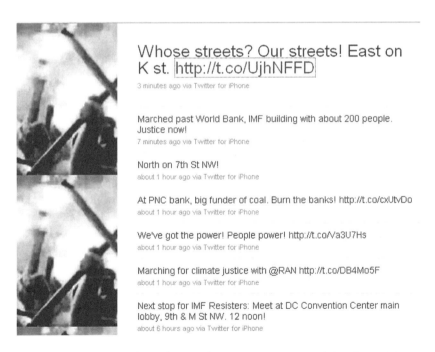

FIGURE 8.6   Screenshot of Anarchist Twitter captured April 16, 2011.

Obviously, there are many trustworthy people on the site; however, there are numerous phony profiles made by individuals with a variety of intentions from benign to nefarious. Some job seekers will create multiple fake LinkedIn personas, and then endorse their profile, adding to their credibility. For others, after targeting and connecting to the right people, they will attempt to penetrate intelligence and law enforcement groups to access and engage members. With LinkedIn members listing every piece of data regarding their personal and professional lives, including security clearances and credentials, they are extremely easy targets. There are also thousands of special-interest groups, and screening is left up to a volunteer group member; the company does not engage in the process. It would be quite possible for a member to use a fictitious profile to set up a group and control the membership, as a platform for communication, recruiting, or even operational planning.

Facebook

With 175 million people using Facebook daily, it is by far the most popular social networking site in the world. Naturally, bad actors are also drawn to the site to connect, recruit, and spread their ideology. The use of Facebook by terrorist groups to recruit came into focus in 2008 when al-Shabaab targeted young men from the United States, and twenty Somali-Americas between the ages of seventeen and twenty-seven vanished from their homes in Minneapolis with no explanation. After one of the men, Shirwa Ahmed, committed a suicide bombing in Somalia on October 29th, the dots were connected; the men were recruited by al-Shabaab to leave their homes and join the war in Somalia. Many of the men knew each other and studied at the Abubakar As-Saddique Islamic Center or the more radical Imam Shafi Mosque in Minneapolis. The youngest recruit was a high school senior with college aspirations, outstanding in calculus and chemistry. All recruits had been in the States since they were young children and were, from all accounts, happy and well adjusted.

After they were incentivized and motivated to leave their homes for Somalia, they executed a sophisticated plan devised by their handlers. Passage was provided for—airline tickets, passports, and a complete travel itinerary from Minneapolis to Somalia. They traveled separately and made connections in different U.S. and foreign cities. The tickets were paid for with cash through a local travel agency. All preparations were accomplished without family members knowing, and the men simply disappeared at the prearranged time, without saying goodbye. Figure 8.7 shows a screen shot of the Facebook page of Bashir Maxamed Caydid, a cover name used by Mohamoud Hassan, a

FIGURE 8.7   Facebook page of Mohamoud Hassan.

twenty-three-year-old engineering major at the University of Minnesota. Hassan was one of the initial al Shabaab recruits who then reached back to his group of friends to persuade them to join him in Somalia. Farther down on this page, he pressed his friends by saying: "Why are you sitting around in America, doing nothing for our people?" Hassan successfully enticed four friends to leave their homes and join him; two later died in suicide attacks and the others were never heard from again. Hassan was killed while walking on the street in Mogadishu with other al Shabaab members. Relatives of these men have testified at congressional hearings about their sons and how they were recruited, groomed, and lured from their homes via the Internet to become terrorists. Other young men have gone missing from the Somali communities around the country.

In 2010, a German national al Qaeda sympathizer, Arid Uka, attacked U.S. troops as they were boarding a bus at the Frankfurt International Airport. Uka was actively connected to radical Islamists on Facebook and through web chat rooms, where he was encouraged to kill Westerners in the name of jihad. The day of the shooting, Uka watched a YouTube video of the abuse of a Muslim woman by U.S. soldiers. Although the clip was actually taken from a movie, he believed it was authentic, became enraged, grabbed his loaded weapon, and went to Frankfurt Airport seeking American soldiers. Facebook was also used extensively during the "Arab Spring" uprisings as citizens from countries connected in a new and powerful way to almost simultaneously revolt against their governments.

Facebook provides a wealth of information for those targeting individuals, such as pictures, names of children, addresses, and other personal identifying information that could be used in a kidnapping or

assassination plot. If not properly safeguarded, this information is available to the public through a simple Google search. The newest version is
Muslimbook, http://muslimbook.co.za/, which is hosted in South Africa
and now hosts a variety of extremist pages and discussion.

YouTube

In my research several years ago, I found a jihadist video produced
by American "most wanted" terrorist, Abu Mansoor al-Amriki (formerly Omar Hammami), who used hypnotic, rap-styled music to entice
Americans to join al Shabaab in Somalia. Hammami left the United
States for Somalia in 2006 and quickly rose through the ranks and now
leads al Shabaab. Growing in size and strength, Shabaab now controls
a large part of Somalia and is possibly exacting proceeds from pirating
in the Horn of Africa. As previously discussed, Shabaab has expertly
reached back into the U.S. Somali community to recruit soldiers for the
front line.

"First Stop Addis" has disappeared and reappeared many times on
YouTube, and a simple keyword search will pull up the latest version.
The music is almost mesmerizing and the message clear and compelling. Hammami himself sings the lyrics. As we continue to study how
the radicalizing switch gets turned from "off" to "on" in the human
brain, these videos provide insight into how the enemy is tapping into
certain messages and themes to persuade and encode, then distribute
through the Internet. Clearly, the use of rap in this video is a marketing
tool to target demographically. Other videos posted on this "channel"
include jihad songs with English translation, and a video of children
being trained in martial arts and firearms in an al Qaeda camp. It is also
interesting to read the comments of viewers posted below this genre;
some are obviously Americans and pro-Jihad. (See Figure 8.8.)

Hidden Messages on the Web

The ancient art of steganography (Greek for "covered writing") has
been used throughout history to hide and pass messages. The butterfly
drawing in Figure 8.9 is from a 1901 book by Sir Robert Baden Powell,
founder of the Boy Scouts, who was previously in the British military
as a Secret Service reconnaissance scout in the Mediterranean. In *My
Adventures as a Spy*, Powell reveals how he went on recon missions in
Dalmatia as a "butterfly collector." A good artist with solid understanding of nature, his cover as a butterfly collector allowed access to fields
and roads near military posts. Throughout his travels, he constructed a

FIGURE 8.8   Screenshot of "First Stop Addis" taken September 20, 2012.

portfolio of butterfly drawings that in reality was a field manual depicting military installations and the locations of batteries and fortifications.

Modern-day steganography includes the art of hiding information in the pixels of photographs. The computer assigns every pixel three numeric values corresponding to the amount of red, green, or blue in the color the pixel displays. By changing those values ever so slightly, it is possible to hide code in the pixel numbers, without changing the picture's overall appearance. The seemingly benign photograph of Washington, DC, in Figure 8.10 actually contains the blueprints of a major international airport.

Analysts believed for many years that steganography was being used by bad actors via the Internet. Their suspicions were confirmed with the arrest of the Russian spy ring in 2010. According to the Justice Department criminal complaint, several of the spies communicated with handlers in Russia through steganography, transmitting messages through at least 100 seemingly benign images on public Internet pages.[4] Naturally, with the vast World Wide Web, it is nearly impossible to detect these types of activity without some type of suspicion or scrutiny. Now consider the ability to post pictures and hide them behind multiple password-protected "walls," such as those found in virtual worlds like Second Life. In this case, steganography could easily be used to transmit

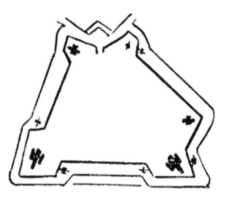

FIGURE 8.9   Steganography by Robert Baden Powell (1901).

information and communicate outside the watchful eyes of law enforcement. However, it isn't inconceivable that software programs could be developed to scan the Internet, perhaps entire Google image pages, to look for this type of pixel alteration.

ENTER HACKERS AND CYBER VIGILANTES

> Soon, every interstate conflict, however minor, may be accompanied by some form of hacker war that is beyond the control of ruling governments.
>
> —Dr. Dorothy Denning[5]

Dr. Denning has studied cryptography and data and system security for almost thirty years. Her 2008 comment regarding nonstate actors

FIGURE 8.10   Night picture of Washington, DC containing an airport map, FBI. (*Source:* Gary Kessler, "An Overview of Steganography for the Computer Forensics Examiner," http://www.fbi.gov/about-us/lab/forensic-science-communications/fsc/july2004/research/2004_03_research01.htm/).

engaging in battle was very prescient, almost predicting the rise of shadowy groups such as Anonymous, an international "hacktivist" organization. Hacktivists are a group of politically motivated hackers who act out of protest and to force change in government policies or laws. Anonymous originated in 2003 and started its hacking activity in 2008, first defacing corporate websites and them moving to system attacks. The group's social issues range from fighting Internet censorship and surveillance, to bringing down child pornography sites and outing their users for arrest. Over time and after arrests of several members, the group has grown to a loose, leaderless worldwide coalition of members who use Internet sites such as 4Chan to meet and plan operations. Anonymous became widely known for their targeting of Visa, MasterCard, and Paypal as related to their companies freezing accounts related to the Wikileaks site. The group is fearless and has taken on the Justice Department, the FBI, the Pentagon, the Vatican, the Church of Scientology, and Amazon with website defacement or denial of service attacks. *Time* magazine gave Anonymous gravitas when naming the group as one of the "100 Most Influential People in the World" in 2012. Anonymous is clearly a force to be reckoned with, one of those Black Swans not predicted but now fully explainable.

Democratic nations believing in freedom of speech and expression may monitor the web through their law enforcement and intelligence agencies or gather data related to an investigation, but do not actively disable sites perceived to be threats. An exception would be if the hosting company of a website of a designated FTO is located in the United States; the company will be compelled to remove the page and can face legal action for supporting a terrorist organization. However, in murkier areas such as YouTube and Facebook, the agencies are hamstrung by the lack of overarching international and national laws regarding the Internet. Websites are even more difficult to "police"; savvy groups may pay for domains from Russia or China to sidestep U.S. laws regarding nefarious activity. Compounding the problem are the vast, "faceless" social networking enterprises themselves; citizens reporting suspicious activity on YouTube, Facebook, or LinkedIn typically find that no action is taken by the company. If action is taken, the actors merely reappear under a new identity and profile, or rename their videos; since the only "credential" needed to establish an account is an e-mail address, they are impossible to trace or block,

However, a new genre of hackers rose since the 9/11 attacks, moving into the space where our government won't or can't venture. Frustrated citizens have stepped in where others have not, and are taking up "arms" themselves as patriot hackers or cyber vigilantes. As this book clearly illustrates, postmodern warfare and criminal activities engage private citizens and put them directly in the crosshairs. Terrorists, cartels, and criminals with their eye on the prize, whether to spread ideology or put drugs in the hands of paying customers, view citizens as collateral damage in their battles or use them as pawns in their deadly games. The question then begs: do private citizens have a new, unique right to "self-defense" by hacking or defacing jihadist and TCO websites? Does this self-defense include baiting the targets into incriminating discussions or even meeting them with the guise of collecting information to later give to law enforcement? Many legal questions have yet to be answered in this realm, but one thing is known: several of these campaigns have met with success, although merely putting a dent into a much larger and vexing problem.

th3j35t3r and th3raptor

> If the law can do nothing, we must take the risk ourselves. I am not the law but I represent justice.
>
> —Sherlock Holmes[6]

I was given rare insight into the world of cyber vigilantes when contacted by "Jester," or *th3j35t3r* in 3l33t or l33t language after he read my blog regarding his activity to temporarily take down jihadist and Taliban Internet pages. Jester says he is prior military, Special Forces, although he is careful not to identify in which country's military he served. He reportedly spent time in Afghanistan and watched friends die on the battlefield. Although there have been many attempts by rivals to identify him by name, the Jester is somehow able to stay anonymous; therefore, verifying any parts of his story is impossible. However, it became evident through our conversation that unlike other vigilantes, his fight is very personal. I found him patriotic, well intentioned, and thoughtful. He often struggles with whether his activities are judicious in light of the possible ramifications, from legal and safety perspectives. The Jester has targeted jihadists, the office of the president of Iran, Wikileaks founder Julius Assange, and Anonymous, receiving death threats. He does not make complaints about the threats to law enforcement, since it will expose his identity and may also open him to legal action for his hacking activity.

Cyber experts agree that Jester is very skilled and employs techniques not seen before and not easily duplicated. Fortunately, as his XerXeS program used to target jihadist sites could bring down most any website in the world instantly, he is on our side of the fight. Jester's goal isn't to permanently bring down a website; instead, it is to randomly disrupt and take the site off line or replace the page with his own text and graphics, typically for thirty minutes. The site then returns to normal, with no damage done, other than to the psyche of the owner and users. Interestingly, Jester's disruption of jihadists' sites has publicly invoked their anger and frustration. Perhaps this is due to our counterterrorism measures to clamp them down, and the Internet is their last line of clandestine electronic communication and virtual lifeline to the world.

In 2012, a new patriot hacker entered the scene, known as th3raptor. th3raptor is a self-proclaimed grandfather, ex-military member, and father of a current military member who singlehandedly took down al Qaeda's Shamukh chat forum and Ansar al-Mujahideen website, a meeting place for jihadists. Both sites were dark for two weeks. His blog statement regarding the event is telling: "Anything I can do to disrupt and demoralize the enemy is worthwhile and on the table."[7] It is hard to tell if th3j35t3r and th3raptor are men, women, young, old, or even the same person. Such is the anonymity offered by the Internet.

Other Notable Vigilantes

Although perhaps more interesting, Jester is not the first cyber vigilante. Shannen Rossmiller is a lawyer and mother of three from Montana who taught herself Arabic and began engaging in chat rooms on jihad websites in 2003. She spent years creating her personas and the persistence paid off: posing as an al-Qaeda sympathizer, she ensnared several radicalized Americans. One would-be terrorist was convicted and is spending thirty years in jail for offering to use explosives on U.S. pipelines. Rossmiller's most notable case is that of an Army National Guard specialist she met in an online Jihadist forum, volunteering to help the mujahedeen after he deployed downrange to Afghanistan. He was arrested just prior to his deployment and is serving a life sentence for treason.[8]

In 2008 Bill Warner, a private investigator and self-proclaimed cyber crusader, gathered information leading to a government shutdown of three extremist websites hosted by a Tampa, Florida, Internet service provider. One website contained graphic images and video of attacks on U.S. troops in Iraq and Afghanistan, along with propaganda such as inflated casualty counts. Prior to being pulled, the site had 19 million hits in ten months.[9]

Video vigilantes such as those with "YouTube Smackdown" patrol popular websites for jihadist postings, flag them, and work with site owners through established procedures to have the videos pulled. YouTube claims to have had more than 15,000 videos removed, as well as several dedicated "channels" maintained by groups such as the Taliban. Usually, the service provider is happy to comply with the removal requests because providing services to known terrorists or designated terror groups violates existing laws. However, the perpetrators typically create new user names and channels, uploading the same video over and over.

Aaron Wiseburd is not a vigilante but the creative force behind "Internet Haganah," a repository of extremist site information. Wiseburd gathers and stores intelligence on the site (accessible to all), and states he has dismantled thousands of extremist sites on his own. The quote on his webpage serves as his mantra: "Asymmetric warfare: It's not just for the other guys."[10]

Finally, a new army of "scam mail vigilantes" numbers 1,000 and is growing. Their target: scam communication, the Nigerian "419 advance-fee fraud" covered in previous chapters. Scams relay the good news of an inheritance or a lottery win, tell a tragic story about a child, or inform of a hot, new investment scheme and ask for bank account information and wiring instructions. Sadly, many people fall for this ploy, and there is 5 percent growth each year in the amount of loss to the public, according to UltraScan, a Netherlands-based research organization studying 419 scams. In their final publicized study on the subject, UltraScan reported that global revenues to groups perpetrating this fraud exceeded $9 billion in 2009, with a total of $49 billion lost to date.[11] We can expect that this number has climbed in recent years as the tactic morphs with the times. These scams are a rising concern in the counterterrorism realm with respect to fund-raising. A recent UltraScan report stated, "Between

2003 and 2008, there was evidence of a terrorist connection in the slip-stream of 419 fraud networks, supporting attacks. In 2008 and 2009, there was evidence directly linking 419 to (attempted) attacks."[12] The group receiving these funds is now known as Boko Haram, the al Qaeda franchise that executed the synchronous, well-planned attacks in 2012 killing hundreds in major Nigerian cities.

The vigilantes participate in "scam baiting," which targets these illicit e-mail fund-raising schemes by sending bogus replies, tracking IP addresses of the sender, and reporting them to authorities. Scam bait-ers have also defaced websites and embarked on campaigns to persuade e-mail providers to do more to combat this crime.

CASE STUDY: CYBER VIGILANTES AND PATRIOT HACKERS: HELPING OR HURTING?

Depending on whom you ask, private citizens engaging the enemy on the Internet either helps or hinders the fight against terror. This is an important question since patriot hacker and vigilante activity not only persists but is growing, and the actors are increasingly savvy and effective.

I informally surveyed a group of industry and counterterror experts and found that the arguments for cyber vigilantes are equally as compelling as those against. Consider the following questions and corresponding thoughts:

1. Does the hacking interfere with intelligence collection? Government agents likely know about the sites and are actively monitoring and possibly engaging. Cyber vigilan-tes may unwittingly interfere with clandestine information gathering or psyops activities.
2. On the other hand, how much actionable intelligence can really be gleaned from these sites, most often meant for recruitment, propaganda, and insurrection?
3. Hacking jihadist sites may cause owners to simply move them or worse, go further underground with their infor-mation, which results in more work and resource expen-diture for intelligence collectors. We are in a manhunt for terrorists, and their use of the Internet can often yield valu-able data about their location, communication patterns, and contacts. The hackers may see only a piece of what is perhaps a much larger puzzle or picture being constructed by intelligence analysts.

4. However, if taking down a site stops recruitment and pros-
   elytizing, and if this prevents even small numbers of U.S.
   citizens or others from taking up arms against our country, is it worth it?

5. Taking down the site hurts the morale of the enemy and
   undermines their confidence now. There is more to gain
   from this effort than watching the same rhetoric for years
   gathering little intelligence.

6. Bringing down the sites means less access to open-source
   information by those supporting the broader counterterror effort. Analysts, theologians, social scientists, psy-
   chologists, and professors visit extremist sites to glean
   information on shifting ideology, social trends, and subtle
   changes in behavior. Perhaps "know thy enemy" has never
   been more applicable than it is in this fight, and removing
   websites may diminish valuable insight.

7. The more people involved with threat reduction and national
   security, the better. Resources are finite and the vigilantes are
   force multipliers. They may accomplish work others can't or
   won't do. We are at war; they are engaging asymmetrically,
   and so should we.

8. Our citizens are the targets in this war. They have the
   right to "take up arms" and defend themselves and their
   children from what is being transmitted into their homes
   through the Internet.

Perhaps cyber vigilantes are no different from child predator vigilantes on the Internet who enter chat rooms and post ads in the
hopes of identifying a predator for law enforcement. This is community policing for the twenty-first century.

Something to consider: while preparing to fight cyber war on a large
scale, we might recognize that the most influential changes in this battle
for the mind are actually happening at the micro level, page by page,
e-mail by e-mail. Individual actors in this realm hold the same power
and large groups, and in the words of Jester, lone wolves work faster, eat
more, and are harder to track and capture.

THE WAY AHEAD

The ways people connect on the Internet are growing exponentially;
in 2012, sites such as Pinterest and Instagram seemed to come out of

nowhere and instantly had millions of users who were virtually sharing pictures and information with total strangers. Clandestine "burn e-mail" sites can now send an e-mail anonymously, and once opened by the user, the note simply disappears within seconds. The price of hardware such as e-readers is so low they are virtual throwaways now and can be paid for with cash or gift cards, used to communicate by sending PDF and Word files, and simply thrown away. With chalkboard chatting, multiple users interact with each other in real time, erasing words and pictures.

Naturally, everything can be found in cyberspace *after* a terrorist is arrested, a plot is unraveled, or a successful attack occurs. But the key to approaching this new kind of threat is to proactively prevent the Black Swans from arising. How can intelligence agencies and law enforcement possibly keep up on a daily basis with these ever-evolving communication platforms and detect the key conversations that will help them connect the dots? At what expense, in terms of both time and energy?

We've unwittingly created an environment conducive for infiltration by nefarious groups who are sophisticated, have vast resources, and are patient. As such, with our current construct, the following assumptions must be made:

1. New web applications will likely be exploited.
2. Technological solutions will likely be defeated.
3. Social networking site companies do not have a culture of due diligence and they do not strive to know their customers, unlike other industries, such as banking and commerce.
4. Therefore users of the Internet are extremely vulnerable, and targets for recruitment, fund-raising, or worse by terrorists and criminals.

As we inch closer to a national policy on cyber warfare, lawmakers continue to propose language that would make computer attacks to deny terrorists the use of the Internet to communicate and plan attacks as a "clandestine" and "traditional military" activity. House Armed Services Committee vice chairman Mac Thornberry (R-Tex.), who drafted the language as part of the House-adopted 2012 defense authorization bill, said he was motivated by hearing from commanders in Iraq and Afghanistan frustrated by an inability to protect their forces against attacks they thought were enabled by adversaries spreading information online. "I have had colonels come back to me and talk about how they thought they could do a better job of protecting their troops if they could deal with a particular website," he said. "Yet because it was cyber, it was all new unexplored territory that got into lots of lawyers from lots of agencies being involved."[13] Unfortunately, this language was struck from the final bill.

The discussion regarding nefarious use of the Internet and lack of oversight and controls can be very disheartening—or very enlightening. Just understanding the enemy's intentions will go a long way toward protecting our infrastructure. During my military career, I observed how we never developed a product or fielded a new piece of equipment without the "enemy" in mind. From initial brainstorming sessions to every stage of development, we "baked in" countermeasures. And similar to for-profit companies, we were also in a rush to field technology since our soldiers' lives and our nation's defense were at stake. If a similar posture was accepted by corporations, acknowledging the existence of an enemy, and keeping that enemy in mind in every step of the development and fielding process, we may prevent technology and products from being used for destructive outcomes.

Once criminals and terrorists have funding through traditional or e-commerce-exploited sources, and manpower recruiting through the Internet, they will move to the planning stage. The sharing of tactics between these dark networks, whether through bomb building, training, or operational approach, is the next emergent area of concern.

REFERENCES

1. Arab Social Media Report, http://www.arabsocialmediareport.com/home/index.aspx.
2. Nassim Nicholas Taleb, *The Black Swan: The Impact of the Highly Improbable*, 2nd ed. (New York: Random House, 2010).
3. "Hizb ut-Tahrir," http://www.hizb-america.org/.
4. U.S. Department of Justice, "Criminal Complaint," U.S. District Court for the Southern District of New York, 2010.
5. Dorothy Denning, "The Web Ushers In New Weapons of War and Terrorism," in *Scientific American*, August 18, 2008.
6. Sir A. Conan Doyle, *His Last Bow: Some Reminiscences of Sherlock Holmes* (New York: Oxford University Press, 1917).
7. th3raptor, "Defending the Cyber Landscape for God and Country," http://th3raptor.wordpress.com/.
8. Shannen Rossmiller, "My Cyber Counter-Jihad," *Middle East Quarterly* 14, no. Number 3 (2007):43–48.
9. Carmen Gentile, "Cyber Vigilantes Track Extremist Web Sites, Intelligence Experts Balk at Effort," March 22, 2008, Fox News, http://www.foxnews.com/story/0,2933,340613,00.html.
10. "Internet Haganah," 2012.

11. Ultrascan, http://www.ultrascan-agi.com/public_html/html/pdf_files/419_Advance_Fee_Fraud_Statistics_2009.pdf.
12. Ultrascan, "Ultrascan Humint: Boko Haram," http://www.ultrascan.nl/Ultrascan_Humint_Boko_Haram_GSI_from_Inside_-Alert.pdf.
13. Ellen Nakashima, "List of Cyber-Weapons Developed by Pentagon to Streamline Computer Warfare," *Washington Post*, May 31, 2011.

CHAPTER 9

Sharing Tactics

Choose a friend. He will help you. Alas, he deserts you. Choose an enemy. He will fight against you. Lo, he corrects and perfects you.

—Sri Chinmoy

In the world of terrorism and crime, a "failed" operation is nonexistent. As the press covers every detail of weapon failures and the investigatory process leading to discovery and mitigation, the enemy watches and learns, perfecting their technique for the next event. As Chapter 3 illustrated, postmodern, mature groups will naturally gravitate toward a working relationship with others to leverage skills and resources. Nefarious groups not only copy successful recruiting, morale boosting, and fund-raising methodologies but also duplicate tactics working for other organizations and study failed operations to learn how to perfect their own. Groups will work together to share tactics and techniques, especially those with "niche" capabilities, who gladly sell or trade expertise. Ideology is no concern when the shared enemy is "the state," which seeks to limit influence, power, and money. When a group or lone wolf successfully attacks, the Internet comes alive with praise from factions not even remotely connected to the attacker. A victory for one is truly seen as a victory for all.

The following is a short overview of one theory regarding how warfare has progressed along with the industrial age and advances in communications and logistics technology.

FIRST-GENERATION WARFARE (1GW)

1GW Is defined by such terms as "formation warfare" or "line and column" warfare. The most influential characteristics of 1GW are:

1. Wars or battles are conducted by organized military units of nation-states.
2. Military technologies are limited to individual weapon systems such as a sword and shield; bows and arrows; spears; and eventually the musket. Cannons and artillery pieces were introduced during the later stage of 1GW.

This era of warfare existed up until the era of the American Civil War.

SECOND-GENERATION WARFARE (2GW)

2GW is defined by such terms as "trench warfare" or "linear fire and movement" warfare. The most influential characteristics of 2GW are:

1. Wars or battles are conducted by organized military units of nation-states.
2. There is more reliance on fire and maneuver, in conjunction with coordinated indirect-fire operations to support advancing line formations, as well as cavalry maneuver elements.

The 2GW era of warfare existed up through World War I.

THIRD-GENERATION WARFARE (3GW)

3GW is defined by such terms as "maneuver warfare." The most influential characteristics of 3GW are:

1. Wars or battles are conducted by organized military units of nation-states.
2. There is increasingly sophisticated maneuver warfare over sea, land, and air with the new technological capability of ships, tanks, jeeps, and aircraft.
3. Doctrine also evolves in 3GW such as attacking an opponent's rear by "bypassing" the front lines.

The 3GW era existed through World War II.

FOURTH-GENERATION WARFARE (4GW)

4GW is defined by such terms as "insurgent warfare," "asymmetrical warfare," or even "unconventional warfare." 4GW characteristics introduce:

1. The first instance where the opponents are not necessarily comprised of an organized military or a state-sponsored military.
2. Asymmetric tactics, techniques, and procedures over long periods of time to mitigate the superiority and strength of its enemy, which it cannot defeat in traditional or conventional battle style.
3. Focus on the political will to fight, concentrating on tearing down the opponent's fortitude to stay engaged in battle.

Some subscribers to the generational warfare theorem contend that 4GW has defeated a superpower twice—the Americans during the Vietnam War and the Soviets during the Soviet-Afghan War. Concepts and theory of 4GW theory can actually be traced back to the early 1900s with Mao Tse-Tung defeating the nationalist armies of China in the Chinese Revolution.

FIFTH-GENERATION WARFARE (5GW)

Fifth-generation warfare theory is still being studied, not yet having a clear definition. 5GW is typically described as "unrestricted warfare" and it may include cyber war, "financial jihad" to attack world financial markets, and attacks against the power grid. The Chinese are the world's leading 5GW thinkers; a book by two former Chinese colonels, Qiao Liang and Wang Xiangsui, *Unrestricted Warfare: China's Master Plan to Destroy America*, provides a current definition: "Unrestricted warfare is warfare that uses all means whatsoever; means that involve force or arms and means that do not involve force or arms; means that involve military power and means that do not involve military power; means that entail casualties and means that do not entail casualties; all to force an enemy to serve one's own interest."[1]

For purposes of the study of terrorism, crime, and cartels, a working definition might be: use of both conventional and unconventional military tactics and weapons; incorporation of political, religious, and social causes; incorporating global strategic information operations campaigns and leveraging the Internet and media; can be conducted by organized or unorganized groups; may be nation-state led or non-nation-state led; with a purpose to disrupt and defeat superior opponents in order to achieve their will.[2] We are clearly moving toward this type of warfare, which is difficult to mitigate or defend.

DRUG-TRAFFICKING ORGANIZATIONS AND TERRORIST GROUP INTERFACE

As discussed in previous chapters, Hezbollah has a strong presence in Latin America and has been detected at the Mexican border. Although they are likely in the region merely to profit from lucrative drug trafficking, we are now seeing their "footprint" in various cartel activities.

Tunnels

The tunnels built by the cartels to clandestinely cross from Mexico into the United States have grown increasingly sophisticated. Authorities have discovered more than 150 tunnels since 1990, most crude and incomplete but a few operational with tracks to move carts loaded with drugs across the border. In July 2012, DEA and ICE agents discovered a 240-yard, $1.5 million tunnel under a strip mall in San Luis, Arizona, expertly constructed with six-foot ceilings and wood walls, and equipped with ventilation, lighting, hydraulic systems, and other high-tech components. Not the standard dirt tunnel through the sewer, DEA agents believed it was the work of experienced engineers.[3] A former U.S. law enforcement agent with extensive experience working undercover in Mexico believes the expertise and construction features seen in the latest cartel tunneling efforts point to Hezbollah's involvement.[4] Hezbollah has constructed a network of tunnels in Lebanon used to secure themselves from Israeli airstrikes. The tunnels have medical facilities, dormitories, lighting, and heating and cooling systems. Recent reports from Beirut indicate that with the help of Iran, Hezbollah has tunneled mountains in the Beqaa region and into Syria.[5] Tunnels in the Middle East are nothing new; consider the vast network discovered by coalition forces in Iraq in Operation Iraqi Freedom, including high-tech underground corridors from Saddam Hussein's palace to the airport. Also, Hamas has constructed a network of 400 main and 1,000 feeder tunnels between the Gaza Strip and Egypt, many of which can accommodate vehicles. The tunnels are used to smuggle medicine, construction material, fuel, and other goods embargoed due to the ongoing Israel-Palestinian conflict.[6] The bottom line is that if the cartels want better tunnels, they will turn to the Middle Eastern experts.

Bombs

A new weapon in the cartel's battle for control debuted in July 2010 with the successful detonation of a VBIED in the border city of Ciudad Juárez. The Juárez Cartel deliberately targeted first responders by placing a bound, wounded man in a police uniform at the scene, luring law enforcement and medical personnel to the area. A nearby vehicle, inconspicuously laden with twenty-two pounds of Tovex, exploded moments later killing three people and wounding twenty. Tovex is a water gel explosive widely used as a substitute for dynamite for industrial and mining purposes. Theft of Tovex in Mexico is a common occurrence; in February 2009, masked gunmen stole 900 cartridges of the substance from a U.S. firm in Durango, Mexico.[7] In July and August 2012, a wave of car bombings in northeast Mexico targeting a city hall and the homes of security officials were detonated by the Zeta and Gulf cartels as part of their campaign to influence local elections. VBIEDs are widely used by insurgents in Iraq and Afghanistan and terrorist groups such as Hezbollah and al Qaeda. However, the cartels' use of these new tactics was a game changer in Mexico's battle and calls for increased vigilance on the U.S. side of the border as the violence pushes north.

The number of Hezbollah operatives operating in Mexico has increased in recent years. In 2009, former Syrian military officer Jamal Yousef was arrested New York City on narco-terror charges for his involvement in a weapons-for-cocaine scheme between Hezbollah and FARC, using Mexico as a safe haven. According to the indictment, a weapons cache of 100 M-16 assault rifles, 100 AR-15 rifles, 2,500 hand grenades, C4 explosives, and antitank munitions was stolen from Iraq by Yousef's cousin, a member of Hezbollah, and moved to the home of family members in Mexico, also affiliated with the terrorist group. Yousef planned to deliver the weapons to FARC in Colombia, in return for 2,000 pounds of cocaine, but the DEA intervened; he pled guilty and faces fifteen years in prison.[8] Although Yousef appears to have been a lone operator, Jameel Nasr was an international Hezbollah operative, taking direction from Lebanon to establish a Hezbollah network in Mexico and throughout South America. Nasr traveled regularly between Lebanon, Venezuela, and Tijuana and was arrested in 2010 by Mexican authorities upon his return from one of the trips. Mexican authorities said Nasr had been "entrusted with forming a base in South America and the United States to carry out operations against Israeli and Western targets."[9]

In late 2011, prosecutors in Virginia charged a Lebanese man, Ayman Joumaa, with smuggling at least "tens of thousands of kilos" of Colombian cocaine in the United States with 85,000 kilos sold to the Los Zetas Cartel. Joumaa and his associates laundered over $250 million in proceeds through Spain, West Africa, Lebanon, Venezuela, and Colombia.[10] According to the U.S. Treasury Department, Hezbollah derived financial support from the criminal activities of Joumaa's network through the sanctioned Lebanese Canadian National Bank of Beirut.[11] In 2011, a former undercover law enforcement officer discussed Hezbollah interface with DTOs, saying the group receives cartel cash and protection in exchange for giving their expertise from "money laundering to firearms training and explosives training." He also discussed his discovery of Hezbollah safe houses in Tijuana and Durango.[12]

Finally, the shocking case of the Iranian plot to kill Saudi Arabia's ambassador to Washington, DC, revealed how the cartels may be used to carry out attacks for rogue regimes or nation-states. In October 2011, authorities arrested Mansour J. Arbabsiar, an Iranian-American car salesman in Texas, in connection with the plot. According to his indictment, Arbabsiar's cousin in Iraq, somehow affiliated with Iran's Revolutionary Guard Corps (IRGC) Quds Force, reached out to him to set up the assassination using a Mexican cartel. The plot entailed the bombing of a Washington, DC, restaurant while the ambassador was having lunch. Arbabsiar traveled back and forth to Mexico to meet with representatives of Los Zetas Cartel to arrange the hit and provided a $100,000 down payment from Iran as a sign of good faith, a small portion of the $1.5 million that would be paid for the entire operation. Confidential informants alerted U.S. law enforcement, who then monitored all the bank transactions, telephone calls from Iran, and Arbabsiar's conversations with what he thought were cartel members.[13]

IRA INC.

Unfortunately, with countries hyperfocusing on al Qaeda and its splinter groups, some terrorist factions like the IRA have regrouped, recruited, and grown in strength under the radar. Two splinter factions of the IRA are still active: the State Department-designated Real IRA (RIRA) and the less powerful Continuity IRA (CIRA). The IRA has long been recognized for their mastery of bomb building. The group pioneered the use of mobile phones to trigger bombs, a technique successfully used in the tragic 2004 al Qaeda train bombings in Madrid. IRA pipe bombs have been imitated by many groups, leaving a unique and traceable fingerprint pointing to cooperation and training. Following a relative period of calm in the mid-2000s, the world was reminded that the Irish Republican Army is still a terrorist group with an agenda and the resources to attack. In the March 7, 2009, Massereene Barracks shooting, RIRA dissidents brazenly ambushed and killed two British soldiers and wounded four other people during the attack at an army base. The shooting set off a string of bombings throughout the next two years, damaging courthouses and police stations as well as private homes and vehicles of law enforcement officials. A large-scale attack occurred on February 17, 2010, when police in Newry, Northern Ireland, received a coded message from IRA bombers. They were able to clear the area around the courthouse just minutes before a 250-pound car bomb exploded. The Newry event was the first large car bomb attack in Ireland since the deadly Omagh attack in 1998 and the bombing of a police station in 2000. Officials in Ireland know that due to the sophistication of the bomb and other data not released to the public that the CIRA and RIRA are now sharing tactics and have "cross-fertilized." The police were informed that the bomb was set to go off in thirty minutes; however, the actual explosion was seventeen minutes after the call. Whether this was an attempt by the attackers to also target first responders is unknown but worthy of noting.

On May 16, 2011, authorities in London received a coded bomb message from the IRA, the first such message received in ten years. Although no bombs exploded, old fears were renewed in the city as the Tube and airports were evacuated as a precaution. Other smaller attacks are taking place across Northern Ireland, including live mortars left outside police stations and a car bomb killing a police officer. The attacks are widespread and persistent, and aimed specifically at law enforcement, the government, and financial institutions. Many attacks have also been foiled in Ireland in the last few years, including a second bomb in Newry, set to go off in a major shopping district.

The IRA has worked with several terrorist groups in the last twenty years to help them perfect their bomb-making skills. For instance, the IRA and FARC have a relationship dating back to the late 1990s when they shared bomb-building techniques. In August 2001, the "Colombia 3" case exposed the relationship when three IRA members were arrested when attempting to leave the Bogotá airport, traveling on false passports with traces of explosives on their clothing. The three were convicted but escaped and returned to Ireland, which has no extradition treaty with Colombia. Also in 2001, the House of Representatives Committee on International Relations published the findings of its investigation into IRA activities in Colombia, detailing the connection with FARC, identifying fifteen more IRA terrorists who had traveled to and from the country, and estimating the IRA had received at least $2 million in drug proceeds for the training. FARC has carried out several large car bomb attacks in Colombia in the last ten years, including a 2003 attack at a nightclub with a car laden with 200 kilograms of explosives.

Interestingly, the IRA-FARC relationship was facilitated by the Spanish Basque Separatist group, ETA, which has worked with FARC for several decades exchanging technology and material. For example, a remote-controlled VBIED technique used in the first Gulf War was copied by the IRA and taught to ETA. The groups have also exchanged bomb-building material, such as the transfer of Semtex and C-4 between the groups in 2002.[14]

The IRA-Palestinian relationship is well documented and extends back to the 1970s when the groups shared bomb-building techniques in Libya and Lebanon's Bekka Valley.[15] Ireland has been vocal about their support of the Palestinian cause, even sending flagged ships to participate in the "Gaza Freedom Flotillas." Following Operation Defensive Shield in which Israel engaged in a military campaign in Gaza, a British explosives expert working with the Palestinian Red Crescent discovered 200 "exact replicas" of IRA-issue pipe bombs in Jenin.[16] Separatist groups tend to affiliate with each other, understanding the political ideology and fight against the ruling government; therefore, it seems only natural that the IRA would align with groups such as ETA and Hamas.

Since at least 2000, the IRA has had a relationship with violent factions in the Balkans, receiving arms and sharing tactics. This association came to light with the seizure of a shipment of arms, including rocket launchers, leaving the Balkans for Ireland in July 2000. The two groups continue to liaise, as evidenced by an assassination plot revealed in 2010, when an RIRA leader was arrested for attempting to hire a hit man from the Balkans to murder a British military general officer. RIRA members have also been arrested in Lithuania and Slovenia while attempting to procure arms.

There has also been anecdotal evidence of IRA-al Qaeda interaction, including the transfer of material between Irish dissidents and a Muslim extremist tied to al Qaeda in Ireland in 2008. Lacking official acknowledgment of the incident, we can only speculate that the two groups might work together for material or training purposes. Al Qaeda is active in the United Kingdom as evidenced by their successful and thwarted attacks, and Interpol was hunting two al Qaeda terrorists in Ireland in 2008.

HEZBOLLAH AND HAMAS: PARTNERING FOR SUCCESS

Hezbollah and Hamas, also known as the Islamic Resistance Movement, operate in the same "space" in terms of benefactors such as Iran and Syria and financing activities in the tri-border area of South America. Although the ideologies differ, the two groups are forming an increasingly strong partnership in the Middle East. For instance, during the December 2008 to January 2009 Gaza War, Hamas and Hezbollah maintained continuous communication in all phases of the conflict. During the battle, Hezbollah's influence on Hamas's tactics was apparent with the group relying more on rocket attacks and less on suicide operations. Iranian sources report that Hezbollah trained Hamas in military tactics used to attack Merkava tanks, the main battle tank employed by the Israeli Defense Forces (IDF). A Hezbollah parliamentary official confirmed the tactical exchange.[17]

IEDS, FERTILIZER, AND STICKY BOMBS

If a tactic is successful, it will be duplicated. In the last ten years, insurgents successfully attacked coalition forces with crude devices and devastating impact. However, the use of IEDs is not contained in war zones; in 2011, there were 4,744 global IED incidents, 6,278 deaths, and 17,040 wounds around the world.[18] IEDs are being used by drug-trafficking organizations, separatist groups, and antigovernment activists. Understanding the threat and how it could move to the homeland courtesy of domestic actors or radicalized lone wolves is critical to mitigate the danger.

IEDs

Military operations in Afghanistan and Iraq were greatly affected by the insurgents' use of improvised explosive devices, or IEDs. IEDs are homemade, low-tech devices routinely using pressure plates and radio-controlled triggers to destroy vehicles passing on roadways or attack soldiers on foot patrols. IEDs were responsible for 1,316 of the 3,171 U.S. and coalition casualties in Afghanistan since 2001, with the bulk of the deaths occurring since 2008. Many other soldiers who survived an IED blast lost one or more limbs. Insurgents will likely spread their IED knowledge gleaned from recent operation, as did Waad Ramadan Alwan, an Iraqi citizen who moved to Kentucky in 2009 after winning a visa as a political refugee. Unbeknownst to government officials, Alwan was an Iraqi insurgent who planted IEDs on roads traveled by U.S. troops between 2003 and 2006. Soon after his arrival in the United States, Alwan began working with another Iraqi refugee, Mohanad Shareef Hammadi, to secure weapons to send to Iraq to aid al Qaeda in Iraq in operations against coalition forces. A confidential source who worked for the FBI repeatedly met with Alwan, who detailed his use of IEDs in Iraq to kill Americans and made elaborate IED diagrams. Using his particular "signatures," the military was able to determine that Alwan's fingerprints were on an unexploded IED in Iraq the military had kept for evidence. Both men were arrested while they secured a shipment of stinger missiles and weapons they thought were destined for Iraq.[19]

Recognizing this persistent and grave threat to the troops, the Pentagon established the Joint Improvised Explosive Device Defeat Organization (JIEDDO). The JIEDDO leadership recently testified about the possible use of IEDs at home, stating "the domestic IED threat from both homegrown extremists and global threat networks is real and presents a significant security challenge for the United States and our international partners."[20] Data supports this assertion; according to JIEDDO, since 2007 there are 500 attempted IED detonations per month outside of Iraq and Afghanistan. As explained in one of their *Inspire* magazine issues, one of al Qaeda's new tactics is the call to individual jihad, motivating lone wolves into action. The summer 2010 edition also encourages lower-tech attacks through homemade bombs, giving detailed instructions on how to construct a pipe bomb and devices with timers. The Taliban continues to adapt in Afghanistan even as we wind down the mission; two recent trends are less use of metal in devices, lowering detection capability, and more targeting of foot patrols to raise the level of fear among the troops.

Fertilizer

Urea nitrate fertilizer is used in the farming industry, and although it is rarely used in bombs due to its quick decomposition rate, under the right circumstances it can be deadly. For example, the compound was successfully used the 1993 attack on the World Trade Center, with terrorists using approximately 1,500 pounds to construct the weapon. Theft of urea nitrate is common in the Middle East; for instance, in February 2010 over 5,600 tons (11 million pounds) of urea nitrate were stolen and never recovered. Another compound, ammonium nitrate fertilizer, is a powerful agent when used in bombs. Ammonium nitrate was used by Timothy McVeigh in the Oklahoma City bombing and in the 2002 nightclub bombings by Jemaah Islamiyah in Bali in which 202 people died. The agent is extensively used in IEDs and was thus banned in Afghanistan as a resource for farmers; ISAF soldiers began seizing ammonium nitrate from Afghani farmers, paying them cash and destroying their supply.

Many security experts are concerned about the potential use of ammonium nitrate in the United States. A hearing titled *Securing Ammonium Nitrate: Using Lessons Learned in Afghanistan to Protect the Homeland from IEDs* explored tighter restrictions on the selling of fertilizer and methods for tracking sales. Rep. Dan Lungren, a California Republican and chairman of the subcommittee, expressed his concern for the threat, stating, "Is there any question that those who are dedicated to killing Americans would not exploit vulnerabilities in the United States to use IEDs here?"[21] In response to domestic concerns and those of our allies, ICE initiated Program Global Shield, an international law enforcement effort fighting the illicit trafficking of precursor chemicals used in nitrate explosives by monitoring their cross-border movements.

Sticky Bombs

Although variations of this device have been used in warfare since World War I, the modern version was detected in Iraq in 2004 when insurgents sporadically used a magnetic strip to stealthily attach IEDs to vehicles. Known as "Obwah Lasica" in Arabic, the magnetic bomb is a simple, homemade device turning a vehicle into a moving VBIED. In Iraq, the campaign accelerated as attackers met with success and learned from mistakes. Bombers increased the volatility of the devices, using C4 and accelerants to increase the scope of the explosions, and began specifically using the weapon as an assassination tool against

Iraqi officials. Between 2008 and 2009, there were at least 400 vehicle explosions involving sticky bombs, and other groups around the world began to copy the tactics. In January 2012, an Iranian university professor working at a key nuclear facility was killed when two assassins on a motorcycle affixed a magnetic bomb to his vehicle in Tehran. The next month, the exact same operation took place in Delhi; this time the target was an Israeli embassy vehicle in what was labeled a revenge killing. In July 2012, an Afghan women's affairs official was killed and her husband and daughter critically wounded when a magnetic bomb exploded, destroying her vehicle. The same month, a convoy of twenty-two NATO trucks were destroyed when one magnetic bomb exploded, causing the other vehicles to ignite. In August, Syrian rebels used the tactic to kill two judges in Damascus.

A quick look online and the instructions for building and using a sticky bomb are readily accessible. One site encourages their use on the hulls of ships. There is no limit to the imagination of would-be attackers, and the proliferation of this weapon should be of great concern domestically.

FIRST RESPONSE AND THE THREAT OF SECONDARY DEVICES

It's what people like us do: without concern for our personal safety, we race to the scene of an attack to assist survivors. We are hardwired to respond this way, and our response is instinctive. Unfortunately, in modern terror and crime events, the instinct to run toward the fight, not away from it, could be deadly. My military colleagues often tell stories about the use of secondary and tertiary devices in Iraq and Afghanistan. The insurgents set off the first IED, wait until other soldiers rush in, and then set off a second device, and sometimes a third.

International terrorist and rebel groups have successfully employed the "double-bomb" tactic to target first responders. For instance, secondaries targeting responders in other notable attacks include the Jemmah Islamiyah bombing in Bali in 2002, an anti-American attack by Hezbollah at the McDonald's in Lebanon in 2003, and the 2004 police station bombing in Athens by the Revolutionary Struggle group. In March 2010, in Dagestan, a Chechen suicide bomber dressed in a police uniform approached investigators and residents who had gathered at the scene of a car bomb explosion near a school and detonated his explosive vest. In April 2010, the primary al Qaeda bombing in Algeria was followed by a secondary one, detonated one hour later and killing a soldier. The same month, Chechen rebels bombed a train in Dagestan and remotely detonated a secondary device to target first responders.

Domestic terrorists also use this technique. Almost every attack perpetrated by Eric Rudolph included a secondary device, specifically targeted toward emergency personnel. For example, prior to the Atlanta abortion clinic bombing in 1997, Rudolph called in the bomb threat and watched as office members evacuated and gathered in certain areas of the parking lot. He planned this into his operation months later; after he bombed the clinic, a second device went off an hour and a half after the first, injuring seven first responders. The Hutaree Christian Militia was planning to kill a law enforcement officer and then ambush the funeral procession. If this plot had gone as planned, the secondary attack would have been a surprise and may have killed and/or injured hundreds.

First responders must train to this tactic, understanding that they very likely may be the target. Louis R. Mizell, a terrorism expert and former U.S. intelligence agent for the State Department, has compiled a database of 300 double-bomb attacks by more than fifty terrorist groups in the world over the last ten years. His advice: "The reality of today's double-bomb tactic dictates that first responders have three primary jobs at a site: attending to the wounded, dispersing the crowd, and finding a second bomb." Mizell's recommendations to first responders—what he calls "double-bomb protocol"[22]—are:

- Teams searching for a bomb should work in concentric circles outward from the wounded.
- If manpower allows, another team should concurrently identify likely high-threat second-bomb containers outside these circles, such as lone parked cars, suspicious individuals, and trash cans.
- The wounded and attending first responders should be protected by portable barriers that have been determined bomb free, such as police cars and ambulances if possible.
- Be aware: terrorists have studied evacuation procedures and exploited them in the past.

Law enforcement is keenly aware of the threat, and at least once a year the FBI issues a bulletin concerning the use of secondary devices and stressing caution when arriving at the scene of an attack. The NYPD and LAPD have trained for such an event, especially in light of the catastrophic loss of life to first responders on 9/11. Certainly, training for secondary devices is the key. Similar to other counterintuitive procedures, like recovering a vehicle sliding on an icy road by steering into the spin, training will override instinct and save lives.

A worrisome tactic from Afghanistan is worthy of watching; extremists will patiently train alongside coalition forces for days, weeks, or even months at a time, earning their trust. At some point, they will detonate a suicide bomb vest or draw a weapon and kill their trainers.

Again, this speaks to the patience of the enemy, and our culture, which is very trusting in nature. The combination can be fatal, as was also seen in the killing of CIA agents at the Khost post by an informant, who gained their trust and was able to skip security checks and walk right into their midst and detonate his device.

USE OF HUMAN SHIELDS BY TERROR GROUPS ON THE RISE

Law enforcement personnel should prepare for the possible use of children, women, and the elderly as human shields by terrorists (international or domestic) on our soil. Human shields tactics are the deliberate placement of civilians around targets or combatants to prevent the enemy from firing. The use of human shields is prohibited by the Fourth Geneva Convention, Protection of Civilian Persons in Time of War, which was passed in 1949 as a result of atrocities perpetrated by the Nazis during World War II. Specifically, the article states, "The presence or movements of the civilian population or individual civilians shall not be used to render certain points or areas immune from military operations, in particular in attempts to shield military objectives from attacks or to shield, favour or impede military operations."[23] The tactic is actively used by terrorist groups worldwide who don't adhere to Geneva conventions or worry about worldwide condemnation of their activities.

Hamas

Independent reports give detailed evidence that Hamas used hospitals, school, homes, and mosques to hide weapons and soldiers during the Gaza War, an Israeli military initiative from December 2008 through January 2009. At twenty-five miles long and six miles wide, with a population of 1.5 million, Gaza is the sixth most densely populated place on earth, providing a very complex battleground situation. The UN report on the war mentions the possible use of children, women, and the elderly as human shields by Hamas; however, Malam, an Israeli intelligence think tank, produced a report using declassified material such as videotapes, maps, and operational plans recovered on the ground by IDF troops. The information indicates that Hamas hid IEDs in and around civilian homes and hospitals, and a screen shot from a video taken from a helicopter appears to show the use of children and the elderly as human shields for soldiers engaged in operations. Of the 1,444 Palestinians killed in the offensive, approximately 340 were children.

LTTE

The Liberation Tigers of Tamil Eelam (LTTE) were defeated by the Sri Lankan government in May 2009 in a final, violent offensive on a northern beach in the Vanni region. During the months leading up to the conflict, the United States used satellites to monitor the situation, releasing photos to the public to show how LTTE herded hundreds of thousands of citizens on the beach for use as human shields in their final standoff with government forces (see Figure 9.1). Many died of starvation, execution, or due to government shelling, and some escaped only to be captured and put into government internment camps. The remaining civilians, approximately 130,000, were forced to stay in one square mile of beach and be part of the battle in May. Though there has been no final accounting of civilians killed in the final offensive, the UN estimated at least 40,000.[24] A BBC film entitled "Sri Lankan's Killing Fields" documents the atrocities performed by the government and the rebels in "no fire" and "safety zones," as well as hospitals, schools, villages, and convoys of refugees deliberately pulled into the conflict.[25] In 2012, a Sri Lankan general admitted to war crimes, including the extrajudicial killing of civilians.

Although it seems inconceivable to us that a terrorist group, cartel, or lone wolf would use human shields, we must remember the power of ideology, especially radical religious dogma, which empowers believers with a sense of justification for their illegal and immoral activities. We must mentally prepare and train to engage in even the most horrific of scenarios, including the exploitation of innocent civilians to further goals.

ASYMMETRIC THREATS

Terrorists have always employed asymmetric tactics to achieve their goals; they often strike in unanticipated ways to maximize results. Never has asymmetric warfare been more prevalent than in the last decade, from the use of civilian airliners as missiles on 9/11 in the United States, to the seaborne staged attack on eleven targets in Mumbai in 2008. From an engagement perspective, these unexpected events can catch us unprepared and morally conflicted. For instance, on September 10, 2001, military pilots never considered they might be ordered to shoot down a civilian airliner in our airspace, and we didn't train for this possibility. However on 9/11, a new page was added to the tactics book when the enemy used airplanes and hostages as missiles. Modern terrorist groups don't follow the Geneva Convention. Schools, hospitals, churches, shelters: everything is on the table; everything and everyone is a target. The last decade is replete with examples; for instance, the Chechens have

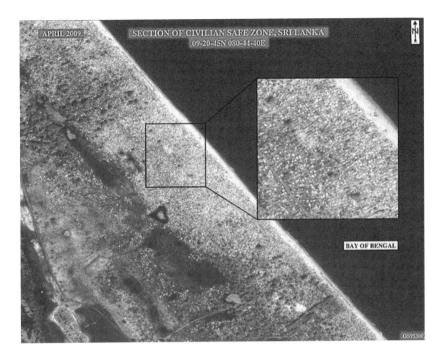

FIGURE 9.1 U.S. National Photographic Interpretation Center satellite photograph of human shields used by LTTE during Sri Lanka's final offensive. Intelligence officers estimated this shows 25,000 tents in an 8-mile-square radius.

successfully used asymmetric warfare against the Russians. The Muslim minority group rose up following the collapse of communism as a violent separatist group, dragging Russia into two wars in the 1990s and leading to the deaths of tens of thousands of fighters on both sides of the conflict. The Chechens moved to an insurgency model and became master bombers and hostage takers, using the element of surprise in target selection and timing. In the 2002 hostage taking at Moscow's Dubrovka theater, at least forty attackers pulled up to the front door of the theater during the second act and entered en masse. The element of surprise was also used in the Chechen's 2004 attack on the Beslan school in North Ossetia, in which they struck on the first day of school when parents were attending an assembly and rolled up to the building in police and military vehicles. In both cases, the sieges lasted for days, and unprepared responders and military officials made poor decisions and tactical mistakes contributing to the deaths of hundreds of hostages.

The Chechen "Black Widows," or *shahidkas*, are women who seek retribution for the deaths of their soldier husbands and volunteer for suicide bombing missions. The use of women, children, and the disabled is another proven asymmetric tactic shared among groups. In 2008, two disabled women were unwillingly used by al Qaeda in Iraq to attack an open market in Baghdad; the devices were strapped to their wheelchairs and remotely detonated. Also in Iraq, a female suicide bomber attacked a group of women and children at a play-group gathering, killing fifty-four. Months later, in Pakistan, terrorists bombed a hospital, specifically targeting those they wounded in an earlier attack. In 2011, a man dressed as a cleric and a small boy were walking toward a government building in Karachi; alert police approached the pair and found that they were both wearing bomb vests. In 2012, a fourteen-year-old suicide bomber walked into a group of his friends playing outside the NATO building in Kabul, Afghanistan, killing six. Of the 140 terrorist attacks I have tracked worldwide from January to June 2012, 47 suicide bombings were accomplished either with a vest or a vehicle. In addition to IEDs, this is a popular weapon for attackers.

Although we routinely harden targets such as headquarters buildings, communications, and utilities infrastructure, we have numerous vulnerabilities with soft targets. We also have biases preventing us from identifying a suicide bomber, and profiling simply may not be the 100 percent solution. As with those who wish to do us harm, we must dissect every terrorist event, learning and adapting.

WMD

According to the FBI, weapons of mass destruction (WMD) are defined in U.S. law (18 USC §2332a) as: "(A) any destructive device as defined in section 921 of this title [i.e., explosive device]; (B) any weapon that is designed or intended to cause death or serious bodily injury through the release, dissemination, or impact of toxic or poisonous chemicals, or their precursors; (C) any weapon involving a biological agent, toxin, or vector ... ; or (D) any weapon designed to release radiation or radioactivity at a level dangerous to human life." WMD is often referred to by the collection of modalities that make up the set of weapons: chemical, biological, radiological, nuclear, and explosive (CBRNE). These are weapons that have a relatively large-scale impact on people, property, and/or infrastructure.[26]

The use of WMD is on the table for all groups: terrorists, criminals, and even cartels. As covered in Chapter 4, in the name of political ideology Bhagwan Shree Rajneesh (now known as Osho) contaminated salad bars at ten restaurants in 1984 with salmonella, sickening 751 people. The religious cult Aum Shinryko (now known as Aleph) used Sarin in coordinated attack against five trains in Tokyo in 1995, killing 13 and affecting upwards of 5,000 others. Although the dispersion methods

were not perfected, the element of surprise led to many first responders racing to the scene without protective gear, becoming casualties
themselves. Large-scale bombs such at the one detonated by Timothy
McVeigh in Oklahoma City are considered weapons of mass destruction
due to the high destruction and casualty rate.

Nuclear-smuggling activities are on the rise, and with "loose nukes,"
or at the very least unsecured material in the former Soviet republics, the
concern is high that the building blocks for a radioactive device could fall
into the wrong hands. Certainly we know that in 1998, al Qaeda operative Mamdough Mamud Salim attempted to purchase highly enriched
uranium in Western Europe to use as a building block for a nuclear
weapon. In 2002, a twenty-five-page document with information about
nuclear weapons design was found in an al Qaeda safe house in Pakistan.
Al Qaeda also attempted to purchase spent nuclear fuel, perhaps hoping
to use it in a dirty bomb. In the chemical and biological realm, recall
that the ten-volume *Encyclopedia of Afghanistan Resistance* found in
Jalalabad contained formulas for manufacturing toxins, botulinum, and
ricin and provided methods for dissemination. At Tarnak Farms, the former Afghan training camp near Kandahar, Afghanistan, al Qaeda not
only provided firearms training but also experimented with biological
warfare in a special laboratory. Ahmed Ressam, the Algerian al Qaeda
member who was caught at the Canadian border before he could execute
the 2000 "millennium attack" of the Los Angeles airport, testified that
al Qaeda taught him to poison people by putting toxins on doorknobs,
and he engaged in experiments in which dogs were injected with a mixture containing cyanide and sulfuric acid. Finally, al Qaeda members
were seeking to fly crop dusters that analysts believe may have been used
to disseminate anthrax and chemical or biological agents.[27]

Regarding biological warfare, in 2009 Algerian newspaper *Anahar
al-Jadeed* reported that forty AQIM terrorists died at a training camp in
Algeria from their infection with bubonic plague.[28] Speculation abounded:
was it a dead rat causing the deaths, or an experiment gone bad? We'll
never know; however, *Inspire* magazine has encouraged its readers to
manufacture ricin, botulism, and sarin in their homes, even encouraging
them to get a Muslim microbiologist to assist, if needed. Domestic terrorists may also use the al Qaeda guides as a template for constructing
their own weapons; in 2008, the FBI arrested Roger Bergendorff, who
had ricin, a schematic for an injection pen, weapon silencers, and the
Anarchist Cookbook in his Las Vegas hotel room. After recovering from
ricin poisoning, he was sentenced to three-and-one-half years in prison.
Bergendorff never gave an exact motive behind his activities, but clearly
it is dangerous to have private citizens tinkering with toxic biological and
chemical compounds. We need to continue to work to get materials off of
the Internet and out of the hands of would-be attackers.

Perhaps the mostly accessible WMD is chlorine, an easily obtained chemical that could sicken or kill hundreds of people, under the right conditions. AQI used chlorine in several VBEID attacks against coalition forces in Iraq in 2006; although more casualties arose from the bomb blasts, the terrorists kept trying different methodologies to perfect their technique and used it thirteen more times in the war. Chlorine can be a silent killer; in 2005, two trains collided in Graniteville, South Carolina, in the middle of the night, releasing sixty tons of chlorine gas. Unsuspecting residents who heard the collision drove through the cloud, stayed in their homes, or kept working their outdoor night-shift jobs. In all, 9 people died and over 250 were sickened by the gas, which causes nausea, dizziness, and vomiting. Certainly, chlorine is easily obtained; therefore, we have to educate suppliers on how and what to report in terms of suspicious buys or patterns.

Do al Qaeda or other foreign or domestic terrorist groups have WMD? Those of us who live in the "open-source world" don't have the definitive answer to the question; however, we can turn to government reports and congressional testimony to provide an accurate barometer. For instance, take the December 2008 report entitled *The World at Risk*, issued by the Graham/Talent Commission, a bipartisan group that spent six months examining the WMD issue. When Senator Graham briefed Congress he ominously stated, "Terrorists could mount nuclear or biological attack within five years." Statements from the report are also very telling: "The Commission believes that unless the world community acts decisively and with great urgency, it is more likely than not that a weapon of mass destruction will be used in a terrorist attack somewhere in the world by the end of 2013. The Commission further believes that terrorists are more likely to be able to obtain and use a biological weapon than a nuclear weapon."[29] Synthetic manufacturing is causing increased concerns, as chemically synthesized DNA can replicate those found in agents occurring in nature, and more worrisome, enhance their effects. According to Vahid Majidi, the assistant director of the FBI's Weapons of Mass Destruction Directorate, the agency is working to keep this emergent technology from falling into the wrong hands.[30] Working to prevent access to materials and instructive manuals is critical. Our response agencies must also continue to train to the threat, anticipating the absolute worst; failure is not an option in the WMD realm.

Perhaps instead of studying why groups would use WMD to further their goals, it is much more productive to question why they wouldn't use the tactic. In historic examples of nefarious use of chemical and biological weapons, they were vastly ineffective in causing the anticipated mass casualties. Reasons for not selecting this type of attack include the high probability of deadly contamination during the manufacturing process, as well as selecting the proper delivery technique that will avoid detection, cause the element of surprise, and inflict mass casualties. The "group of guys" plan is certainly easier to execute. Consider the Lashkir el-Toyba attacks on Mumbai that killed 170 people and brought the world to a standstill; although the perpetrators had conducted extensive surveillance and used satellite phones and commandeered boats for the operation, it was basically low tech and highly effective.

FINAL THOUGHTS

The sharing and copying of tactics between groups is extremely worrisome, as they continue to learn and perfect techniques. Law enforcement and international authorities must continue to monitor travel patterns of suspected go-betweens and couriers, engaging aggressively if needed to stop training and resource pipelines. The proliferation of information on the Internet contributes to this realm, and an international body with a set of governing laws would go a long way in preventing publications such as al Qaeda's *Inspire* and the *Anarchist Cookbook* from showing up in the homes of would-be killers. We can expect that tactics used by insurgents downrange might be copied by other groups, or their operatives living in other countries.

REFERENCES

1. Qiao Liang and Wang Xiangsui, *Unrestricted Warfare: China's Master Plan to Destroy America* (Los Angeles, CA: Pan American, 2002).
2. 5th Generation Warfare Educational Institute, http://www.5gwinstitute.com/.
3. Elliot Spagat and Jacques Billeaud, "Drug Tunnels Discovered between U.S.-Mexico Border Contained Railcar System, Tons Of Pot," July 13, 2012. http://www.huffingtonpost.com/2012/07/14/drug-tunnels_n_1673317.html.
4. "Terrorist Group Setting Up Operations Near Border," ABC 10 News, May 4, 2011, http://www.10news.com/news/27780427/detail.html.
5. Sobhi Monzer Yaghi, "Israel Is Preparing for War Tunnels and Hezbollah Elements in the Southern Syrian Border," July 2, 2012, http://www.aljoumhouria.com/news/index/15409.
6. Kifah Zaboun, "Gaza Tunnel Trade: Matter of Life and Death for Hamas," August 31, 2012, http://www.asharq-e.com/news.asp?section=1&id=30885.

7. Alicia A. Caldwell, "Car Bomb in Mexico Drug War Changes the Ground Rules," *Guardian*, July 17, 2010, http://www.guardian.co.uk/world/feedarticle/9178042.

8. U.S. District Court, Southern District of New York, "Sealed Indictment: Jamal Yousef," http://www.fas.org/programs/ssp/asmp/externalresources/2009/Yousef,Jamaletal.S3Indictment.pdf.

9. Investigative Project on Terrorism, "Mexican Arrest Indicates Hizballah Seeking Foothold," July 7, 2010.

10. U.S. District Court for the Eastern District of Virginia, "Sealed Indictment: Ayman Joumaa," http://www.investigativeproject.org/documents/case_docs/1856.pdf.

11. Sebastian Rotella, "Government Says Hezbollah Profits from U.S. Cocaine Market Via Link to Mexican Cartel," ProPublica, December 13, 2011.

12. "Terrorist Group Setting Up Operations Near Border."

13. U.S. District Court, Southern District of New York.

14. Andy Oppenheimer, "How Terrorists Acquire Technology and Training: Lessons from the IRA " *The Detonator*, September/October 2009.

15. Rachel Ehrenfeld, "IRA + PLO =Terror," *National Review*, August 21, 2002.

16. "The Irish-Palestinian Connection," CrethiPlethi, 2010.

17. Benedetta Berti, "Assessing the Role of Hezbollah in the Gaza War and Its Regional Impact," *Terrorism Monitor* 7, no. 4, March 3, 2009, http://www.jamestown.org/single/?no_cache=1&tx_ttnews%5Btt_news%5D=34575.

18. U.S. House Committee on Homeland Security, *Securing Ammonium Nitrate: Using Lessons Learned in Afghanistan to Protect the Homeland from IEDs*, July 12, 2012.

19. U.S. District Court, Western District of Kentucky, "Criminal Complaint: Waad Ramadan Alwan," Investigative Project on Terrorism, http://www.investigativeproject.org/documents/case_docs/1568.pdf.

20. U.S. House Committee on Homeland Security, *Improvised Explosive Device Threats*, July 12, 2012.

21. U.S. House Committee on Homeland Security, *Securing Ammonium Nitrate*.

22. Michael A. Gips, "Secondary Devices a Primary Concern," *Security Management* 47, no. 7 (2003).

23. "International Humanitarian Law—Treaties & Documents," http://www.icrc.org/ihl.nsf/WebART/470-750065?OpenDocument.

24. United Nations, *Report of the Secretary-General's Panel of Experts on Accountability in Sri Lanka*, 2011.

25. Jon Snow, "Sri Lanka's Killing Fields," BBC, United Kingdom, 2011.

26. FBI, "Weapons of Mass Destruction," 2012.
27. Jack Boureston, "Assessing Al Qaeda's WMD Capabilities," *Strategic Insights, Naval Postgraduate School* 1, no. 7 (September 2002).
28. "Black Death Kills 40 al-Qaeda Fighters in Algeria," *Al Arabiya News*, January 20, 2009, http://www.alarabiya.net/articles/2009/01/20/64603.html.
29. Commission on the Prevention of WMD Proliferation and Terrorism, *World at Risk: Report of the Commission on the Prevention of WMD Proliferation and Terrorism*, 2008.
30. U.S. Senate Committee on Homeland Security and Governmental Affairs, *Ten Years after 9/11 and the Anthrax Attacks: Protecting against Biological Threats*, October 18, 2011 2011.

CHAPTER **10**

Conclusions about the Nexus and Thoughts on Resiliency and the Way Forward

> There is another type of warfare—new in its intensity, ancient in its origin—war by guerillas, subversivism insurgents, assassins; war by ambush instead of by combat; by infiltration instead of aggression, seeking victory by eroding and exhausting the enemy instead of engaging him.
>
> **President John Fitzgerald Kennedy**
> *Address to Graduating Class*
> *U.S. Naval Academy*
> June 6, 1962

Fifty-one years later, President Kennedy's words still ring true; the players may have changed, but transnational criminals and terrorists still seek to erode and exhaust those who stand in the way of their success. The synergy between groups, sharing resources and tactics, will further their collective agenda to gain power and erode security; induce fractures, internal strife or apathy in society; and wait patiently for the opportunity to move in and take control.

Commonalities shared by these dark networks make their liaison increasingly likely. Leadership is decentralized; therefore, decimation, or killing the first string, will not mean the end of the organization. Modern groups are transnational and loosely organized with cells operating like business franchises, with their own funding and training. Whether driven by vast sums of money, loyalty, power, or religion, the ideology is powerful glue holding the organization together. They are flexible, can change tactics and morph to avoid attention, and will expertly leverage technology for recruiting, morale boosting, and secure communication. Although these organizations have "curb appeal" to the disaffected, poor, and those seeking affiliation, members are increasingly educated, middle-class, and well adjusted, possibly just angry at "the system." When pursuing operational objectives, they will resort to excessive violence, have a basic lack of respect for human life/dignity, and have disregard or contempt for the law and its enforcement agents. Finally, members make a conscious, voluntary decision to join the organization but feel tremendous pressure to stay; leaving could mean death.

The so-called drug war has been in progress since 1982; yet after billions of dollars to counter their efforts and strengthen borders, the cartels are stronger than ever and now operating in our country. Almost twelve years have passed since the attacks of 9/11, yet we are still at war with al Qaeda. The mafia and other transnational criminal organizations are permanent fixtures on the criminal scene, and we have shifted from an eradication strategy to merely coping. We are learning that asymmetric approaches and use of "soft" instruments of power are essential in this battle, *interweaved* with military and law enforcement engagement, if needed. Perhaps the use of containment and deterrence, strategies policy makers typically do not find appealing, are necessary as we try to marginalize the threat and condense the playing field. Negotiation, often viewed as a tool used from a position of weakness, is a form of communication, information gathering, and relationship building that should not be overlooked.

This book presented a compelling and fresh view of the nexus of groups with dissimilar goals and ideologies. The following thirteen conclusions about the nexus and its actors are presented as a departure for further study and discussion.

THIRTEEN CONCLUSIONS
ABOUT THE NEXUS AND ITS ACTORS

1. We routinely underestimate the sophistication of adversaries, which gives us a dangerous blind spot and them the asymmetric advantage. For example, criminals and terrorists use the same technology we use, sometimes more effectively. They have scientists, engineers, doctors, and lawyers either on the payroll or participating freely due to a shared ideology. They are not afraid to pursue emergent funding methods or tactics.
2. No operation is a failed operation. Modern criminal and terrorist groups are always learning from their mistakes, improving techniques, and morphing in structure and

methodology. They may learn more from failure, since every detail of why and how their mission was unsuccessful is often available in the press. When we freely discuss an unraveled plot, an unexploded bomb, or the discovery of illicit financing schemes, the enemy is watching and perfecting.

3. We have a short-term memory; as a nation, we prefer to move on quickly from violent events and often experience "security fatigue" and even complacency with the passing of time. Conversely, we have very patient enemies who will wait until we are most vulnerable, then strike for maximum effect. This paradox reveals what may be our biggest vulnerability.

4. Fear is a goal of modern terrorist groups, just as much as loss of life. The mere insinuation of a capability drives us down a path that the enemy hopes we travel, exhausting ourselves financially and mentally to put our national psyche at ease. Before spending billions of dollars and precious lives to counter a threat, we need to corroborate and obtain "proof that our proof is true."

5. Our world is connected like never before thanks to advances in technology. This connectivity bleeds over into the crime and terror realm; events happening in other countries directly impact ours. Successful tactics, whether in the funding, logistics, or operational realm, will be copied or shared, and we should expect to see them in the homeland and train our first responders and law enforcement accordingly.

6. The shift to human capital for terror groups is now critical. As recruiting efforts continue, liaison with organized crime is likely tap expertise and manpower.

7. Understanding how the switch is flipped from "off" to "on" in the mind of a newly radicalized American is critical to our operations to intercede in jihadist recruiting efforts on the Internet and in our communities.

8. Understanding how to turn that switch back "off" before releasing convicted jihadists into society after prison is equally as important.

9. After reading this book, you will likely never look at new communications or e-technology the same way. In the haste to get products to market, technology is fielded without thought given to the 1 percent of the population who

will exploit it for their nefarious purposes. The "genie is out of the bottle" on social networking sites, e-banking, and smartphones; all are used extensively in the criminal and terrorist realm.

10. We can do much to combat the threat, but there are forces we can't change such as globalization, technological progress, and human nature. As in war, there are powers at work like fog and friction that will take a perfectly good plan or a thorough investigation and unravel it within seconds. We need to get comfortable with the "inescapable unknowables" in the counterterrorism world and put more value on intuition and creative thinking.

11. We are part of the environment and, thus, part of the problem; our actions (or nonaction) impact criminal and terrorist groups and could be a contributing factor to their success. Humility and introspection are powerful tools in this fight.

12. Two of our nation's biggest enemies continue to be sunk cost and groupthink; if something isn't working, we must cut our losses and move on quickly. We cannot afford to be surrounded with "yes men." The nature of the asymmetric realm means those outside of the traditional skill set and competencies may have the best ideas and insight; harnessing all expertise will yield a superior solution. We must keep working to break down the silos and build trust cross-agency.

13. Groups can strategically partner without having a relationship, which is why we find unexpected partnerings such as al Qaeda and the Mafia. Expect the unexpected to enhance the investigatory process.

RESILIENCY AS A WEAPON

Regarding terrorism, perhaps we should take a more pragmatic approach, viewing the situation scientifically, removing fear and emotion from the equation and replacing it with data. The United States has a very small number of terrorist attacks and people killed per capita in comparison to many other countries. Obviously, any loss of life is tragic, and the stunning events of 9/11 altered the course of history. However, no matter how extensive our resources and efforts, it is very likely that some attacks will be successful. The ability of groups and lone wolves to communicate clandestinely, plan off the grid, and work together to share resources shifts the odds to their favor.

We are now working to build reliance in our population so that when we are next attacked, our citizens can deal with the trauma appropriately. They will have confidence in their survival, and collectively, our country can quickly recover psychologically and move onward. Perhaps what is needed is a culture shift of *living with terrorism*, instead of *dying from it*—dying in the sense of resource-draining activities, internal political debates about security that fracture our united front against threats, and the "death from a thousand cuts" proposed by bin Laden. The resiliency approach is similar to England's coping with incessant IRA attacks and fear campaigns, or Russia's handling of Chechen attacks. I was once riding the Tube in London in the mid-1990s when coded threats were still being called in by the IRA. An announcement was made to immediately evacuate the station and people listened; they calmly yet quickly exited the station. When riding the Washington, DC, metro, in a city that has been attacked with several other significant plots thwarted, I often wonder if such an announcement was made, how would people react? Would they feel inconvenienced because they were missing their train and ignore the announcement? Or would there be panic and a stampede to get out of the station? With most commuters now using headphones and fully immersed in their virtual worlds, would they even hear the announcement?

Most experts agree that another coordinated mass-casualty event such as 9/11 is unlikely, but the threat of WMD, particularly a bio event or a dirty bomb, will have a shock factor associated with it and our citizens must be prepared. They must be educated on the threat and become force multipliers. There is a general hesitation to share this type of information, perhaps because we don't want to cause panic; however, education is the best way to lower fear, as people will feel they can protect themselves and their loved ones. As witnessed in several natural disaster events in our country since 9/11, citizens are generally overreliant on the government, lacking supplies at home as simple as flashlights, radios, batteries, and water. Yet first responders and relief agencies are resource constrained and will not be there to answer every call in times of disaster or uncertainty. Our citizens do not understand what it means to "shelter in place" or any of the other orders that may be given during a national emergency. The combination of lack of education about the threat, overreliance on the government for help, and lack of response resources is potentially disastrous for our country. The pragmatic approach of baking resilience into our culture would counter the current atmosphere of infallibility.

Although this book has painted a grim picture of the crime and terror threats in our world, in our corner we have the most competent, professional law enforcement, first responders, military personnel, and government civilians in the world. They are clearly the greatest weapon and deterrent in the eternal fight against crime and terror.

Glossary

1GW: First-generation warfare. 1GW is defined by such terms as "formation warfare" or "line and column" warfare. This era of warfare existed through the era of the American Civil War.

2GW: Second-generation warfare. 2GW is defined by such terms as "trench warfare" or "linear fire and movement" warfare. The 2GW era of warfare existed up through World War I.

3GW: Third-generation warfare. 3GW is defined by such terms as "maneuver warfare"; doctrine also evolves in 3GW such as attacking an opponent's rear by "bypassing" the front lines. The 3GW era existed through World War II.

4GW: Fourth-generation warfare. 4GW is defined by such terms as "insurgent warfare," "asymmetrical warfare," or even "unconventional warfare." Used in Vietnam to defeat U.S. forces and in Afghanistan to defeat the former Soviet Union.

5GW: Fifth-generation warfare. 5GW is an emergent school of thought regarding the future of warfare. 5GW is typically described as "unrestricted warfare." May include cyber war, "financial jihad" to attack world financial markets, and attacks against the power grid. Use of both conventional and unconventional military tactics and weapons; incorporation of political, religious, and social causes; incorporating global strategic information operations campaigns and leveraging the Internet and media; can be conducted by organized or unorganized groups; and may be nation-state led or non-nation-state led. 5GW is conducted by lesser powers with a purpose to disrupt and defeat superior opponents in order to achieve their will, be it religious, political, or money and power driven in nature.

1G2: First-generation gangs. 1G2 are traditional street gangs with a turf orientation. When they engage in criminal enterprise, it is largely opportunistic and local in scope. 1G2 are limited in political scope and sophistication.

2G2: Second-generation gangs. 2G2 are engaged in business. They are entrepreneurial and drug centered. They protect their markets and use violence to control their competition. Their operations sometimes involve multistate and even international areas.

3G2: Third-generation gangs. 3G2 have evolved political aims. They operate or aspire to operate at the global end of the spectrum, using their sophistication to garner power, aid financial acquisition, and engage in mercenary-type activities.

AFO: Tijuana/Arellano Felix Organization. A Mexican drug-trafficking cartel.

Agent: A person or business that acts on behalf of a principal entity in providing payment services. FATF defines the term "agent" as any person who provides money or value transfer service under the direction of or by contract with a legally registered or licensed remitter (for example, licensees, franchisees, concessionaires).

AGOCC: Attorney General's Organized Crime Council.

ALF: Animal Liberation Front.

AML: Anti-money laundering.

AQ: al Qaeda.

AQAP: al Qaeda or Ansar al-Sharia in the Arabian Peninsula.

AQI: al Qaeda in Iraq.

AQIM: al Qaeda in the Lands of the Islamic Maghreb.

ASG: Abu Sayyaf Group. A radical Islamist terrorist group headquartered in the Philippines.

Asymmetric warfare: Warfare in which belligerents are mismatched in their military capabilities or their accustomed methods of engagement. In such a situation, the militarily disadvantaged power must press its special advantages or effectively exploit its enemy's particular weaknesses if the disadvantaged power is to have any hope of prevailing. Alternatively, using an adversary's strength against him, while exploiting his weaknesses.

ATS: Amphetamine-type stimulants.

Beneficial owner: A "beneficial owner" is someone on whose behalf a company is run, whether or not they are listed on documents as the nominal owner.

Bitcoin: A virtual commodity used in e-gaming to buy, store, and sell value.

BLO: Beltran Leyva Organization. A Mexican drug-trafficking cartel.

BOC: Balkan organized crime.

Brick-and-mortar exchanger: An exchanger that conducts all business on a face-to-face basis, such as a traditional bank.

BSA: Bank Secrecy Act. The BSA was originally passed by Congress in 1970 and was amended several times, including provisions in Title III of the USA PATRIOT Act. (See 31 USC 5311-5330 and 31 CFR Chapter X.) The BSA is sometimes referred to as an "anti-money-laundering" law ("AML") or jointly as "BSA/AML."

Cash vouchers: A prepaid product that can be purchased at several retailers and used for person-to-person (P2P) transactions on the Internet.

Cash-back: Merchant points of sale (POS) used to withdraw cash by overpaying for purchased merchandise and receiving the overpaid amount in cash.

CBP: U.S. Customs and Border Protection. CBP was created in 2003 by combining the U.S. Customs Service, Immigration Inspection Service, Animal Plant and Health Inspection Service, and U.S. Border Patrol into one border agency.

CCEs: Continuing criminal enterprises. A group of individuals with an identified hierarchy, or comparable structure, engaged in significant criminal activity.

CDD: Customer due diligence. Critical to the AML/CTF process, CDD requires institutions participating in financial services to know their customers, gather information for positive identification, and record their activities.

CFT: Combating the Financing of Terrorism Activities to stop the financing of terrorism through e-commerce and other channels.

CIP: Customer Identification Program. CIP requires banks and other financial institutions to adopt written procedures to ensure proper identification of new *customers*.

CIRA: Continuity Irish Army.

CMIR: Currency or monetary instruments.

COG: Center of gravity.

CCOG: Cognitive center of gravity.

CTR: Currency Transaction Report. The CTR is filed to report cash transactions in excess of $10,000 during the same business day. The amount over $10,000 can be in either one transaction or a combination of cash transactions. It is filed with the Internal Revenue Service.

DCP: Digital currency provider. DCPs keep and administer accounts for their customers, but typically do not directly issue "digital currency" to their customers/account holders. Instead, customers purchase their digital currency from exchangers, who will then transfer the purchased amount of digital currency into the customer's DCP account. Funds kept in DCP accounts may be denominated in fictitious currencies or in real currencies.

Digital currency exchanger: (See "digital currency provider.")

Digital precious metals: The digital currency provider denominates the funds in units of precious metal through the Internet and supposedly invests funds received in that respective precious metal as a means of deposit protection.

DHS: U.S. Department of Homeland Security.

DOD: U.S. Department of Defense.

DOJ: U.S. Department of Justice.

DTO: Drug-trafficking organization.

EBT: Electronics benefit transfer. Social Security, food assistance, and other state benefits paid to recipients on prepaid cards, as opposed to through the formal banking system.

(E)POS: (Electronic) point of sale. Merchant or shop that accepts a certain payment method as a means of payment. A POS usually requires certain technical devices or terminals in order to be able to make use of the payment method like a card terminal to swipe the prepaid card, or special device software.

Electronic money ("e-money"): Electronically, including magnetically, stored monetary value for the purpose of making payment transactions.

Electronic purse: An electronic purse, or e-purse (also referred to as a "stored-value card" as the value is stored on the card), is value stored electronically in a device such as a card with an integrated circuit chip (called a smart card or chip card).

ELF: Earth Liberation Front.

EO: Executive order.

EOC: Eurasian organized crime.

ETA: Basque Fatherland and Liberty. A Basque separatist terrorist group in Spain.

FARC: Revolutionary Armed Forces of Colombia.

FATF: Financial Action Task Force. The Financial Action Task Force is an international policy-making and standard-setting body dedicated to combating money laundering and terrorist financing.

FBI: Federal Bureau of Investigation.

FDA: Federal Drug Administration.

FEMA: Federal Emergency Management Agency.

FinCEN: Financial Crimes Enforcement Network. FinCEN is a bureau of the U.S. Department of the Treasury. The director of FinCEN is appointed by the secretary of the treasury and reports to the undersecretary of the treasury for terrorism and financial intelligence. FinCEN's mission is to enhance the integrity of financial systems by facilitating the detection and deterrence of financial crime.

FINTRAC: Financial Transactions Reports Analysis Centre of Canada. FINTRAC is Canada's financial intelligence unit, created in 2000. It is an independent agency, reporting to the minister of finance, who is accountable to Parliament for the activities of the center. It was established and operates within the ambit of the Proceeds of Crime (Money Laundering) and Terrorist Financing Act (PCMLTFA) and its regulations.

FOIA: Freedom of Information Act.

FTO: Foreign terrorist organization.

GRECO: Group of States Against Corruption. A body of thirty-seven European countries and the United States; a forum to discuss and evaluate anticorruption efforts of member states.

HA: The Hells Angels outlaw motorcycle organization.

Hawala: An ancient and informal banking system in which money does not physically cross international borders.

Hegemon: A nation-state or other group that exercises hegemony. A hegemon acquires some degree of consent from the subordinate, as opposed to dominance purely by force.

Hegemony: Hegemony is derived from the Greek word *hēgemōn*, meaning leader. However, the concept of hegemony has evolved through the years into one of domination and is now widely accepted and used to explain the dominance of one social group over another. Hegemony is an indirect form of government of imperial dominance in which the hegemon (leader state) rules geopolitically subordinate states by the implied means of power rather than by direct force.

Homeland Security: A concerted national effort to prevent terrorist attacks within the United States, to reduce America's vulnerability to terrorism, and minimize the damage and recovery from attacks that do occur. (National Strategy for Homeland Security, 2002.)

HSI: Homeland Security Investigation. The branch of ICE that investigates ORC.

HUMINT: Human intelligence.

HTA: Hizb-ut-Tahir America. The American affiliate of HuT.

HuT: Hizb-ut-Tahrir. An international pan-Islamic political organization, banned in several countries.

ICE: Immigration and Customs Enforcement; falls under DHS.

Ideology: Ideology is visionary theorizing; a systematic body of concepts especially about human life or culture; the manner or the content of thinking characteristic of an individual, group, or culture; and the integrated assertions, theories, and aims that constitute a sociopolitical program.

IED: Improvised explosive device.

ILEA: International Law Enforcement Academies. ILEA advance the common fight against international crime and promote the rule of law; directed by the U.S. Department of Justice.

INL: Bureau of International Narcotics and Law Enforcement Affairs. INL is a U.S. State Department activity.

Intellectual property crime (IPC) or intellectual property theft (IPT): The counterfeiting or pirating of goods for sale where the rights holder has not given consent.

International terrorism: Terrorism involving citizens or the territory of more than one country (as per 22 USCS 2656f).

Internet payment services: Internet payment services are payment services operating exclusively on the Internet that are not or are only indirectly associated with a bank account and may also be provided by nonbanks.

IOC: Italian organized crime.

IPC: Intellectual property crime. Counterfeited and pirated goods, manufactured and sold for profit without the consent of the patent or trademark holder.

IRGC: Iran's Revolutionary Guard Corps.

IVTS: Informal value transfer system. A system, mechanism, or network of people that receives money for the purpose of making the funds or an equivalent value payable to a third party in another geographic location, whether or not in the same form.

JDL: Jewish Defense League.

JI: Jemaah Islamiyah. A radical Islamist terrorist group affiliated with al Qaeda and headquartered in Indonesia.

JIEDDO: Joint Improvised Explosive Device Defeat Organization. A Department of Defense organization to defeat the improvised explosive device (IED) through counter-IED (C-IED) efforts.

Kleptocrat: A government official who steals funds earmarked for public amenities, such as schools, hospitals, or roads.

KYC: Know-your-customer. The activities of customer due diligence companies providing financial service must perform to identify their clients and ascertain relevant information pertinent to doing business.

LCN: La Cosa Nostra. Italian Mafia group.

LE: Law enforcement.

LFM: La Familia Michoacana. A Mexican drug-trafficking cartel.

Linden: Virtual currency used in Second Life virtual world on the Internet. Can be bought, traded, and sold with real money.

LTTE: Liberation Tigers of Tamil Eelam. A terrorist group mostly defeated in Sri Lanka in 2009.

MDPV: Methylenedioxypyrovalerone. MDPV is a psychoactive drug with stimulant properties, also known as bath salts or plant food.

Merchant: A business or individual that sells goods or services to consumers and maintains an arrangement with an acquirer to process transactions.

MIL: Monetary Instrument Log. The MIL must indicate cash purchases of monetary instruments, such as money orders, cashier's checks, and traveler's checks, in value totaling $3,000 to $10,000, inclusive. This form is required to be kept on record at the financial institution and produced at the request of examiners or auditors to verify compliance. A financial institution must maintain a Monetary Instrument Log for five years.

MLAT: Mutual Legal Assistance Treaties. MLATs leverage our ability to fight transnational crime. The MLAT allows U.S. authorities to obtain evidence and other types of law enforcement assistance from other countries, and foreign governments may use the treaty to request assistance from the United States.

ML/TF: Money laundering and terrorist financing.

MNC: Multinational corporation.

Mobile banking: Users can access traditional banking services through their mobile telephone. This is different from mobile payments in the sense that the regulated entity is a bank providing traditional banking services.

Mobile money services: A subtype of mobile payment service, where subscribers are able to store actual value on their mobile phone (similar to e-purses). They may use phone credits or airtime as tender for payment.

Mobile payment services: Allows nonbank and nonsecurities account holders to make payments with mobile phones.

Money remittance: A term commonly used to describe international money or value transfers by economic migrants to their home nation.

MSB: Money service business. Per FINCEN, a business is an MSB if it offers one or more of the following services: money orders, traveler's checks, check cashing, currency dealing, or exchange of stored value; and if it conducts more than $1,000 in money services business activity with the same person (in one type of activity) on the same day; or if the business provides money transfer services in any amount.

MVT: Money or value transfer service. Money or value transfer service refers to a financial service that accepts cash, checks, other monetary instruments, or other stores of value in one location and pays a corresponding sum in cash or other form to a beneficiary in another location by means of a communication, message, or transfer or through a clearing network to which the money/value transfer service belongs. Transactions performed by such services can involve one or more intermediaries and a third-party final payment.

NCCT: Non-Cooperative Countries or Territories. A "black list" designation used to identify countries not cooperating with FATF recommendations for combating money laundering.

NCTC: National Counterterrorism Center.

NDIC: National Drug Intelligence Center. A U.S. Department of Justice organization.

Negotiability: The level of acceptance across retailers for different payment methods. Some payment methods may have high negotiability because they are widely accepted, but others may be very limited.

NFC: Near field communication. New technology that uses ultrasound to pass payment information from a mobile device to the register.

NPM: New payment methods. For the purposes of this book, the term "new payment methods" encompasses prepaid cards, mobile payment services, and Internet payment services.

NPS: National Park Service.

Nominee: A person who holds monetary instruments such as cards, money orders, checks, etc., in behalf of the actual owner.

OCC: Organized Crime Council.

OFAC: Office of Foreign Assets Control. Works in the U.S. Treasury Department to administer and enforce U.S. economic and trade sanctions against targeted foreign countries.

OLC: Organizational life cycles.

OMG: Outlaw motorcycle gang.

OPDAT: Office of Overseas Prosecutorial Development, Assistance and Training. Falls under the Department of Justice.

Open-loop prepaid card: A prepaid card that can be used at a wide range of terminals (vs. closed-loop prepaid cards with limited negotiability).

ORC: Organized retail crime. An activity where goods are stolen through shoplifting, cargo theft, or rings, then resold by a criminal enterprise to reap the profit.

P2B: Person-to-business transaction.

P2P: Person-to-person transaction.

PFLP: Popular Front for the Liberation of Palestine. A forty-five-year-old terrorist group whose goal is the establishment of a Palestinian state.

Phishing: Phishing is a criminal technique used to illegally obtain valuable information. For example, consumers will be sent fake e-mails from addresses that mimic those of banks. These e-mails will then dupe consumers into entering their account details.

POS: Points of sale.

Prepaid card: A payment card preloaded with funds. The card can then be used at businesses where the card type is accepted, including on the Internet and abroad.

Prepaid card issuer: A bank or other financial institution that issues prepaid cards. The term "issuer" is also used in connection with other types of NPM "value," e.g., issuer of electronic money or of digital currencies. The issuer is the entity that the customer has a contract with, and from whom the customer can demand redemption or withdrawal of funds.

Prepaid Internet payment products: Products offered by firms that allow customers to send or receive funds through a virtual prepaid account. In some jurisdictions, these firms may not fall within the definition of a "credit institution."

Processor: A company that processes transactions on behalf of an acquirer or merchant.

Red flags: Indicators of suspicious activity where a product's actual use deviates from its expected usage. Red flags should therefore be tailored to the product's characteristics.

Remittance agencies: Nonbanks that transfer money through wire services or checks.

RICO: Racketeer Influenced and Corrupt Organization.

RIRA: Real IRA.

RLG: G8 Roma-Lyon Group. The RLG is an international body that fights transnational crime.

SAR: Suspicious Activities Report. Filed by banks, MSBs, or other entities to report suspicious financing activities to the U.S. government.

SDGT: Specially Designated Global Terrorist. A designation authorized under U.S. Executive Order 13224 administered and enforced by the Office of Foreign Assets Control (OFAC) of the U.S. Treasury Department. SDGTs are entities and individuals who OFAC finds have committed or pose a significant risk of committing acts of terrorism, or provide support to terrorists and terrorist organizations.

SEARCH initiative: Seizing Earnings and Assets from Retail Crime Heists. An initiative by ICE/HIS to combat ORC.

Shelter in place: To stay where one is in the event of an emergency. Requires that people stay inside a building away from windows. All windows and air intake systems should be closed. Wet towels or tape may be used to seal cracks. If there is a danger of explosion, windows should be covered.

SIA (special-interest alien): Designation of an illegal alien from a country of interest or state sponsors of terror who attempts to cross the border and enter the United States.

Smart cards: Cards featuring an electronic chip that stores value on the card.

Smurfing: A specific type of structuring involving the coordinated use of nominees for the purposes of breaking down what would be a large-value transaction into several "below threshold" amounts.

SPLC: Southern Poverty Law Center. A nonprofit organization that tracks hate groups and crimes.

STR: Suspicious Transaction Report. Where there are reasonable grounds to suspect that a transaction or an attempted transaction is related to a money-laundering or terrorist financing activity, a report must be submitted to FINTRAC within thirty days.

SVC: Stored-value card. A prepaid card with a microchip that stores value on the card.

Strawman: A real or fictitious individual used by others as a front for illegal activities such as money laundering and fraud.

Terrorism: Premeditated, politically motivated violence perpetrated against noncombatant targets by subnational groups or clandestine agents (as per 22 USCS 2656f). The unlawful use of force or violence against persons or property to intimidate or coerce a government, the civilian population, or any segment thereof, in furtherance of political or social objectives. Domestic terrorism involves groups or individuals who are based and operate entirely within the United States and U.S. territories without foreign direction and whose acts are directed at elements of the U.S. government or population (FBI).

TFC: Threat focus cells. FBI subgroups convening to focus on specific threats.

Throwaway: Any electronic device that can be purchased anonymously with cash, used in money laundering or fraud, and then simply discarded. Throwaways used in illicit activity include smartphones, computer modems, computers, printers, and electronic reading devices with Internet connectivity.

TICOT: Top International Criminal Organizations Target List. Issued by the AGOCC annually.

TIPR: Trafficking in Persons Report. Issued annually by the U.S. State Department.

TOC: Transnational organized crime.

TTP: Tehrik-e Taliban Pakistan.

TVPA: Trafficking Victims Protection Act. A U.S. resolution to protect victims of human trafficking.

UNIFIL: UN Interim Force in Lebanon.

UNODC: United Nations Office on Drugs and Crime.

USA PATRIOT Act: Uniting and Strengthening America by Providing Appropriate Tools Required to Intercept and Obstruct Terrorism Act.

VBIED: Vehicle-based improvised explosive device.

WMD: Weapons of mass destruction. Any explosive, incendiary, or poison gas; bomb, grenade, or rocket having a propellant charge of more than four ounces; missile having an explosive incendiary charge of more than one-quarter ounce; mine or device similar to the preceding; weapon involving a disease organism; or weapon that is designed to release radiation or radioactivity at a level dangerous to human life (source: 18 USC 2332a as referenced in 18 USC 921).

Zakat-al-Mal: Zakat is charitable giving that is part of every devout Muslim's obligations and typically peaks during the season of Ramadan and is paid on or before Eid.

Appendix: List of Foreign Terrorist Organizations

United States Department of State
Bureau of Counterterrorism
September 21, 2012

Foreign Terrorist Organizations (FTOs) are foreign organizations that are designated by the secretary of state in accordance with section 219 of the Immigration and Nationality Act (INA), as amended. FTO designations play a critical role in our fight against terrorism and are an effective means of curtailing support for terrorist activities and pressuring groups to get out of the terrorism business.

CURRENT LIST OF DESIGNATED FOREIGN TERRORIST ORGANIZATIONS

1. Abdallah Azzam Brigades (AAB)
2. Abu Nidal Organization (ANO)
3. Abu Sayyaf Group (ASG)
4. Al-Aqsa Martyrs Brigade (AAMS)
5. Al-Shabaab
6. Ansar al-Islam (AAI)
7. Asbat al-Ansar
8. Aum Shinrikyo (AUM)
9. Basque Fatherland and Liberty (ETA)
10. Communist Party of the Philippines/New People's Army (CPP/NPA)
11. Continuity Irish Republican Army (CIRA)
12. Gama'a al-Islamiyya (Islamic Group)
13. Hamas (Islamic Resistance Movement)
14. Haqqani Network
15. Harakat ul-Jihad-i-Islami/Bangladesh (HUJI-B)
16. Harakat ul-Mujahidin (HUM)
17. Hizballah (Party of God)
18. Islamic Jihad Union (IJU)

19. Islamic Movement of Uzbekistan (IMU)
20. Jaish-e-Mohammed (JEM) (Army of Mohammed)
21. Jemaah Islamiya organization (JI)
22. Jemmah Anshorut Tauhid (JAT)
23. Kahane Chai (Kach)
24. Kata'ib Hizballah (KH)
25. Kongra-Gel (KGK, formerly Kurdistan Workers' Party, PKK, KADEK)
26. Lashkar-e Tayyiba (LT) (Army of the Righteous)
27. Lashkar i Jhangvi (LJ)
28. Liberation Tigers of Tamil Eelam (LTTE)
29. Libyan Islamic Fighting Group (LIFG)
30. Moroccan Islamic Combatant Group (GICM)
31. Mujahedin-e Khalq Organization (MEK)
32. National Liberation Army (ELN)
33. Palestine Liberation Front (PLF)
34. Palestinian Islamic Jihad (PIJ)
35. Popular Front for the Liberation of Palestine (PFLP)
36. PFLP-General Command (PFLP-GC)
37. al-Qaida in Iraq (AQI)
38. al-Qa'ida (AQ)
39. al-Qa'ida in the Arabian Peninsula (AQAP) or Ansar al-Sharia
40. al-Qaida in the Islamic Maghreb (formerly GSPC)
41. Real IRA (RIRA)
42. Revolutionary Armed Forces of Colombia (FARC)
43. Revolutionary Organization 17 November (17N)
44. Revolutionary People's Liberation Party/Front (DHKP/C)
45. Revolutionary Struggle (RS)
46. Shining Path (Sendero Luminoso, SL)
47. United Self-Defense Forces of Colombia (AUC)
48. Harakat-ul Jihad Islami (HUJI)
49. Tehrik-e Taliban Pakistan (TTP)
50. Jundallah
51. Army of Islam (AOI)
52. Indian Mujahideen (IM)

IDENTIFICATION

The Bureau of Counterterrorism in the State Department (S/CT) continually monitors the activities of terrorist groups active around the world to identify potential targets for designation. When reviewing potential targets, S/CT looks not only at the actual terrorist attacks that a group has carried out but also at whether the group has engaged in planning and preparations for possible future acts of terrorism or retains the capability and intent to carry out such acts.

DESIGNATION

Once a target is identified, S/CT prepares a detailed "administrative record," which is a compilation of information, typically including both classified and open-sources information, demonstrating that the statutory criteria for designation have been satisfied. If the secretary of state, in consultation with the attorney general and the secretary of the treasury, decides to make the designation, Congress is notified of the secretary's intent to designate the organization and given seven days to review the designation, as the INA requires. Upon the expiration of the seven-day waiting period and in the absence of congressional action to block the designation, notice of the designation is published in the *Federal Register*, at which point the designation takes effect. By law, an organization designated as an FTO may seek judicial review of the designation in the U.S. Court of Appeals for the District of Columbia Circuit not later than thirty days after the designation is published in the *Federal Register*.

Until recently, the INA provided that FTOs must be redesignated every two years or the designation would lapse. Under the Intelligence Reform and Terrorism Prevention Act of 2004 (IRTPA), however, the redesignation requirement was replaced by certain review and revocation procedures. IRTPA provides that an FTO may file a petition for revocation two years after its designation date (or in the case of redesignated FTOs, its most recent redesignation date) or two years after the determination date on its most recent petition for revocation. In order to provide a basis for revocation, the petitioning FTO must provide evidence that the circumstances forming the basis for the designation are sufficiently different as to warrant revocation. If no such review has been conducted during a five-year period with respect to a designation, then the secretary of state is required to review the designation to determine whether revocation would be appropriate. In addition, the secretary of state may at any time revoke a designation upon a finding that the circumstances forming the basis for the designation have changed in such a manner as to warrant revocation, or that the national security of the United States warrants a revocation. The same procedural requirements apply to revocations made by the secretary of state as apply to designations. A designation may be revoked by an Act of Congress or set aside by a court order.

LEGAL CRITERIA FOR DESIGNATION UNDER SECTION 219 OF THE INA AS AMENDED

1. It must be a foreign organization.
2. The organization must *engage in terrorist activity*, as defined in section 212 (a)(3)(B) of the INA (8 U.S.C. § 1182(a)(3)(B)),* or *terrorism*, as defined in section 140(d)(2) of the Foreign Relations Authorization Act, Fiscal Years 1988 and 1989 (22 U.S.C. § 2656f(d)(2)),** *or retain the capability and intent to engage in terrorist activity or terrorism.*
3. The organization's terrorist activity or terrorism must threaten the security of U.S. nationals *or* the national security (national defense, foreign relations, *or* the economic interests) of the United States.

LEGAL RAMIFICATIONS OF DESIGNATION

1. It is unlawful for a person in the United States or subject to the jurisdiction of the United States to knowingly provide "material support or resources" to a designated FTO. (The term "material support or resources" is defined in 18 U.S.C. § 2339A(b)(1) as "any property, tangible or intangible, or service, including currency or monetary instruments or financial securities, financial services, lodging, training, expert advice or assistance, safe houses, false documentation or identification, communications equipment, facilities, weapons, lethal substances, explosives, personnel (one or more individuals who maybe or include oneself), and transportation, except medicine or religious materials." 18 U.S.C. § 2339A(b)(2) provides that for these purposes "the term 'training' means instruction or teaching designed to impart a specific skill, as opposed to general knowledge." 18 U.S.C. § 2339A(b)(3) further provides that for these purposes the term 'expert advice or assistance' means advice or assistance derived from scientific, technical or other specialized knowledge.
2. Representatives and members of a designated FTO, if they are aliens, are inadmissible to and, in certain circumstances, removable from the United States (see 8 U.S.C. §§ 1182 (a)(3)(B)(i)(IV)-(V), 1227 (a)(1)(A)).
3. Any U.S. financial institution that becomes aware that it has possession of or control over funds in which a designated FTO or its agent has an interest must retain possession of or control over the funds and report the funds to the Office of Foreign Assets Control of the U.S. Department of the Treasury.

OTHER EFFECTS OF DESIGNATION

1. Supports our efforts to curb terrorism financing and to encourage other nations to do the same
2. Stigmatizes and isolates designated terrorist organizations internationally
3. Deters donations or contributions to and economic transactions with named organizations
4. Heightens public awareness and knowledge of terrorist organizations
5. Signals to other governments our concern about named organizations

Index

9/11. *See* September 11th attacks

A

Abu Haf al-Masri Brigades, 19–20
Abu Sayyaf Group (ASG), 19–20
Achille, David, 126
Afghanistan
  al Qaeda in, 2
  narcotics trafficking, 12
African organized crime, 20, 22
  al Qaeda, cooperation with, 73
  drug trade in, 21, 22
  FBI initiatives, 31
  unrest, 21–22
AFRICOM, 21
Agroterrorism, 111–112
Akbar, M. J., 116
Al Qaeda, 1, 45, 55
  Afghanistan, in, 2
  Africa, in, 2
  African attacks, 73
  al Qaeda in Iraq (AQI), 70–71
  al Qaeda in the Arabian Peninsula
    (AQAP), 69–70
  al Shabaab; *see* Al Shabaab
  charities fronting for; *see under*
    Funding terrorism
  credit card scams/identity theft
    committed by, 182
  criminal nexus, work with, 73, 74
  funding for, 166
  goals, 73
  ideology, 67–68
  intellectual property crimes
    committed by, 177
  leaderlessness, 58, 67
  Middle East, in, 2

  mortgage fraud as route to
    funding, 185
  motivation of members, 61
  offshoots, 67, 70–72
  persistence of threat of, 66
  publishing house arm, 253
  rise of, 68–69
  South and Central American
    activity, 155
  Tehrik-e-Taliban Pakistan (TTP),
    71
Al Shabaab, 71, 72
Al-Awlaki, Anwar, 70
Al-Haramain Islamic Foundation,
  170–171
Alamoudi, Abdurahman, 171, 172
Aleph. *See* Aum Shinryko/Aleph
America Online, 246
American Muslim Foundation, 172
Anarchism, 96, 106–107, 108–109,
  253
Anarchist Cookbook, 291
Animal Liberation Front (ALF), 110,
  112–113
Anonymous, 147, 243
Anthrax letters, 121
Anti-Semitism, 95, 103
Arab Spring, 13, 259
Aryan Nations, 95
Ashley, Grant D., 8
Asian transnational crime
  characteristics, 18
  groups, 18
  Macau, in, 19
  Malaysian straits, 18–20
  origins in the U.S., 18